'Helen Duncan
The Mystery Show Trial'

Robert Hartley

H Pr (Publishing)

This paperback edition published in 2007
by H Pr (Publishing)
157 Squires Lane
London N3 2AA

A catalogue record for this book is available from the British Library.

ISBN 978 – 0 – 9553420 – 8 - 0

Front Cover designed by Jim Keary

Robert Hartley is a documentary film director who has made films for television. He trained at the National Film & Television School and he won the British Film Institute Award as Outstanding Newcomer to British Film & Television and other international film awards. Prior to becoming a film director he worked as a research child psychologist with children from London's East End and he has a doctorate in psychology from London University. He has published research as a child psychologist and he has also taught documentary film production at London Metropolitan University. In the course of researching films on the subject he has developed an interest in the spiritual nature of our lives, spirit phenomena and healing.

Contents

List of Illustrations

Integrated illustrations

Picture Section

Acknowledgements

I need to thank a number of people Mr. & Mrs. Reginald Burrell, Mrs. Joan Wellington, Katherine Anderson, Deborah Molera, Miranda Miller, Susan Wilson, Mrs. Kathleen Newton, Mrs. Madeleine Pierson, Denis & Dolores Callender, Colin Roberts, Nora Harris, Sheena Callender, Mr. Eric Spencer, Mary Scroby, Professor Tim Drever, Mr. Ken Reeves, Carl and Di Moore, Mrs. Ann Bradstock, Mr. Russell England, Malcolm Gaskill, Donald West, Mrs. Mary Martin, Mr. Martin Sherrington, Mrs. Mary Parsons, Mrs. Kashevski, Mr. & Mrs. Surman, Roberta Butland who were kind enough to offer what they knew about the events in question. Others who deserve my sincere thanks for their help in the research are Alan Law, James Dawson, Jack Horsford, Valerie Lundquist and Alan Crossley, who has since passed away.

I need to thank the late Professor Arthur Ellison who was happy to advise me and offer his time, however unexpected a request might come. I need to thank Helen Dunne for the information she gave me, which led me to the path I took. She undertook to campaign for Helen Duncan when few people were interested in the cause and she undertook her task as one of service and in so doing she is an example to us all.

I wish to thank the staff of the many libraries and archives who provided information. These include the The British Library, The British Newspaper Library, The Island Archive at Guernsey, the SPR Library and its Archive at Cambridge University Library, The Guildhall Library London, Portsmouth City Library, Dundee University Archive, the Family Records Centre, the Probate Office Holborn, The British Film Institute Library, The National Archives, The National Film Archive, The East Anglain Film Archive, The Theatre Museum, the Birkdale & Ainsdale Historical Society, the Portsmouth Museum and Record Office, Westminster Reference Library, the BBC Written Archives and the National Maritime Museum.

I am also grateful to The News Group, The News of the World, Guardian News & Media Ltd. 1998, The Daily Mail, Express Newspapers, The Yorkshire Post, The Evening Times, The Leicester Mercury, The Evening Standard, Associated Newspapers, The New Statesman for giving permission to quote from their publications, The BBC for giving permission to quote from The Listener

Acknowledgements

and the BBC Radio 4 programme 'The Last Witchcraft Trial', The News, Portsmouth for allowing me to quote from the Evening News and the Hampshire Telegraph, John Pearson for granting permission to quote from his book 'The Life of Ian Fleming', Buz White for granting permission to quote from Charles Loseby's papers, David Highams Associates for giving permission to quote C. E. Bechhofer Roberts, Portsmouth City Council for quoting from a council document, The Society of Psychical Research for giving permission to quote from their Proceedings, Sheena Callender for using the photograph of William and Bessie Lock, Weidenfeld and Nicolson, Orion Publishing Group for allowing me to reproduce the photograph of Ian Fleming from 'Ian Fleming' by Andrew Lycett, the Senate House Library, University of London, Harry Price Library of Magical Literature for using photographs HPG/1/4/3 (xiii), HPG/1/4/3 (vii) & HPG/1/4/2 (xi).

I also need to thank Mrs. Catherine Kirby of Newquay for sending me Gena Brealey's manuscript of her book about her mother Helen Duncan and Jim Keary for helping design some of the illustrations. I must also thank Martin Murphy, John Hensman, Janice Lake and Joy Dansette for their help in the preparation of the book.

INTRODUCTION

A Mystery Tour

It all started several years ago. I was working as a freelance film director making documentary films for Channel Four. I had come out of film school and was early in my career working in television. I was idealistic and wanted the freedom to make important films where I had some control over them. At the time I plumped for Channel Four rather than the BBC because I thought they offered me the greater freedom I desired. I had trained at the National Film & Television School so like others before me I saw myself as someone who got involved and rolled up my sleeves in whatever situation I found myself. We had been trained to deal with any eventuality because if you are filming in a remote area and something goes wrong the buck stops with you. Like most film directors we all believed in Murphy's Law and knew it applied to every project or film we embarked on. If things can go wrong, they will go wrong. Knowing this law accompanied the film making process, it prepared you to face every eventuality.

Years earlier I had trained as a psychologist doing research with poor working class children in schools in London's East End. I had had a similar education to those I was researching, having had a history of school failure. Through an unusual set of circumstances and some struggle I eventually got to university and obtained a doctorate in Psychology. My research examined the strategies disadvantaged children use when they try and solve problems but that's another story. I had changed track to become a film-maker because I felt an urge in my heart and from the experience I had with the children that I worked with, it could not be done justice to, in an academic arena. I had wanted to be a film maker for many years and once I had my got my doctorate, I immediately went off to train as a director. I thought I could have more chance of changing the world if I could communicate with millions of people through film.

If you have aspirations to be an independent film maker then you are competing with larger companies with staff and resources dedicated to originate ideas, develop and research them and then propose them to Commissioning Editors at the Broadcasters. As they are larger outfits they carry far more weight than a lowly freelancer such as I. As I had had some international success with a number of the films I had directed and I believed in my ability, I worked hard to come up with ideas and research them as well as I could. Then I would write a proposal and send it to Commissioning Editors to see whether there was any interest.

It is against this background of having to generate original ideas that I spent time researching and then writing them up as film proposals. It was at this time that that I happened across the world of mediums and spirits.

My father had died and left a degree of confusion in the family with conflicting accounts of his intentions. By chance, I bumped into an old Liverpudlian friend who told me how she thought she was going crazy because, when in a girlfriend's kitchen she saw an old lady cooking some food, whom no one else could see. These types of visions recurred and they increasingly disturbed her until she disclosed what she had seen, to her friend. She was reassured that she wasn't going mad but that she had seen her friend's dead grandmother who apparently was often around her kitchen. My friend explained she had had a clairvoyant vision and that following her relief that her sanity was intact she had explored this new ability and attended classes. She asked me whether I thought she was mad and what I thought of it. I said I knew nothing about the subject but that I was open to life and certainly, I take seriously what people describe of their experiences. What sensible psychologist or film director wouldn't?

As I was about to depart I remembered my own circumstances and said well, if its true that people survive their death then my Dad must still be alive and it might be useful if I spoke to him. My friend recommended a medium in East Barnet, London and so I made an appointment. My interest in the field was ignited by that encounter. The medium, Peggy Goodwin, brought my grandmother, mother and father through; she was accurate in terms of identifying them, the nature of our relationship, the distinctive words and expressions they used and the information that was reported.

It was a shock but then my 'film maker's' mind thought there might be a good film in this subject. The next few months saw me reading everything I could find about mediums and spirits, contacting leading mediums in the country, the President of the SNU Gordon Higginson, going to numerous demonstrations and joining the Noah's Ark Society, which specialised in physical mediumship. Physical mediumship refers to those mediums who can do physical things. This might be to materialise objects or people, produce voices out of the air or through levitating cylinders called 'trumpets', which can whiz around a room at high speed; or transfiguration mediums whose face changes into the features of the deceased, so that people can recognise them. These are the developed forms of physical mediumship. The more primitive forms are table turning, where wooden tables can stand on one of two legs and move around a room when people touch it lightly and respond to questions, or table tapping when taps emanate from the table in simple code to convey messages .

I sat in on many courses and demonstrations at the Arthur Findlay College. Later I became familiar with trance mediumship, some forms of physical mediumship and I witnessed numerous clairvoyant communications.   The college was extremely welcoming and I am very grateful for the generous assistance they gave me.

I saw myself both as a scientist and a film director, but how could one make sense of the visions and information mediums reported?   I found it very convincing when I received communications and information about my family that I had no prior knowledge of, only to discover later that it was true. Certainly the mediums appeared not to be drawing information from my mind by telepathy because I had no knowledge of the information they were giving until older family members and independent investigation verified it.

I had to think about this field clearly, so I recruited an advisor who was extremely knowledgeable in the area, Eileen Roberts. Eileen was an elderly experienced medium, an authority on mediumship and highly respected throughout the Spiritualist community. She ran the Institute of Spiritualist Mediums. I also made contact with the Brazilian Spiritists in London who follow Allan Kardec's work. Kardec was a barrister and French educator, who tested mediumship communication by asking the 'spirits' a series of progressive questions about human life and published the answers in 'The Spiritis Book'. Spiritism is a branch of Spiritualism but one that emphasises spirituality as opposed to phenomena and accepts reincarnation. Spiritists have written hundreds of books on a range of subjects, many by automatic writing mediums, direct from the purported 'spirit world'. Many professionals take an active interest in it and there are seven million Spiritists in Brazil.   Spiritism concentrates more scientifically on mediumship and phenomena and encourages serious study of the subject. When an issue arose that needed clarification I phoned Eileen and discussed it with the Spiritists. Between the two I managed to get a sound perspective on what may be occurring.

Incidentally, I also explored the realm of psychic/spiritual surgery, which seemed to represent good evidence for scientific exploration. I also developed an interest in researching and using spiritual healing with people suffering from emotional and psychological problems, which appealed to my background as a psychologist.

As a filmmaker my tools are a tape recorder and a camera, so I needed sound to record and an image to film. My research and my logic led me to conclude that clairvoyant messages from a medium while personally evidential, may mean little to those who don't know the recipient or the person who is purportedly communicating from the spirit world. Physical phenomena offered the good way forward because I would perhaps have something to film that was independent of the medium. The voices created are not produced by the medium. Flying objects or materialised forms naturally offer wonderful images and evidence, if filmed in a way that shows they are not part of some elaborate illusion. Whilst some people may hallucinate, there was no evidence that documentary film or video cameras hallucinate. I had reached the same conclusion that other scientists had, that the only real proof rested with filming physical mediumship, using different cameras recording the scene from different angles. But as a film director my working method was a little different from that of a scientist.

In order to make good documentary films you need to spend time and gain the trust and the permission of the people you wish to film. If you are going to make a good film and communicate it to millions of people you must research the subject thoroughly because films can do as much harm as good. But, who did I need to gain the permission and trust of? Naturally the mediums, but the Spiritualist mediums I spoke to told me that they weren't doing anything, it was the spirits working with them who were producing the phenomena. Many of the messages from these mediums referred to 'trusting the spirits'.

I thought long and hard about this issue. I concluded that I must approach this film in the same way I approach all my films. I must be honest, seek the trust of those involved to show that I am someone trustworthy enough to portray them to the public. It seemed to me that my customary working method applied equally to the living and the 'spirits' if they existed.

One afternoon at Stansted Hall, when discussing my ideas with Gordon Higginson, the President of the SNU I raised this issue. How can I get the mediums to co-operate, I asked? He replied 'I'll tell them to'. 'How can I get the spirits to agree?' He replied 'Go and ask them'. 'Go and ask them? How do I do that?' He told me that a medium Ivy Northage was coming to Stansted and he suggested when she goes into trance and her guide named Chan is talking, he will ask for questions, 'Then you can ask him your question'.

A week later as I was driving to Stansted from London, I thought I must be mad. I am going to Stansted to ask a spirit about my film idea and what the spirits thought about it. In my film career I had interviewed members of the Russian Mafia, corrupt policeman, disturbed psychiatric patients, politicians, nervous business managers, troublesome adolescents, the unemployed, five year old children and I had even contacted the KGB but I had never asked a spirit whether I could film them!

I found myself seated in a large panelled room along with 25 other people, where a small thin, frail lady in her 80s was standing on a small platform speaking in the voice of a Chinaman. When question time arrived, I asked my question; 'I am a film director interested in making a film about the phenomena mediums produce. What is the spirit world's view of such a project? Would they wish to co-operate?'

Chan replied 'Why do you want to make the film?' I said I thought it was important. He asked again 'Why do you want to make the film?' I replied 'I thought it is important for people to know whether they survive after death or not. He repeated the question whatever answer I gave. Eventually I thought yes it would do me some good as well but that applies to any issue one addresses in this way.

I started to feel a little hot and uncomfortable as if he were aware of my thoughts but I thought as I am a sincere person who does try to help others and if the spirit world think I'm not and don't wish for me to make a film then that's OK with me. I'll do something else. He then stopped repeating the question and I felt a cold breeze come from nowhere and I cooled and sat down. He went on to say that of course the spirit world would like films to be made as long as they were done for the right reasons. I had my answer.

As we are referring to spiritual matters and film-making, I should declare that I prayed before starting each film I made in the hope it would make a contribution to the world and that I would do the subject justice. Coming from a background where I had had very limited opportunities for many years I saw the opportunity of making films as something beyond my wildest dreams. It was very special to me. I should also declare that I had been brought up going to Sunday school, I attended my local church into my teens and was in the church choir, but as I got into science and adopted a more 'critical' view of the world, my faith had diminished. Nevertheless where I held responsibility for the welfare of other people as a psychologist and film director, I prayed for help.

Believing I wanted to make the film for the right reasons and as I hadn't been turned down when I asked my question to a 'spirit', I decided I would go ahead. I would take the Spiritualists and the 'spirits' at their word and try and gain the 'spirits' trust even though I can't see them. I reasoned that if they 'aren't there' then nothing will occur and that would be similar to many other film projects that failed to develop. But if the spirits 'are there' then I reasoned I should get an answer from them eventually. I will have to wait and see.

It seemed to me that the field in which I was entering could not be approached in the usual scientific way. Having worked as a research child psychologist for many years I was familiar with adopting inventive research methods. Most psychological research is based upon studies being carried out with naïve subjects or participants. The predictability of the findings often rested on the fact that the subjects were not informed of the purpose of the experiment. If subjects knew what the researcher was seeking to discover then naturally they could take a position towards it and change their response.

In the research area I was entering into it seemed clear that if the phenomena was authentic, then there was an 'intelligence' which knew the purpose of the study and that they had the choice to co-operate or not, or to decide how they might respond. This changed the dynamics of the research encounter dramatically. Surely if a breakthrough was going to be made in this field then this issue needed to be addressed. If there was an 'intelligence' who knew the intentions of the researcher and who determined what results I might get then I needed to communicate with it.

My plan was to work hard, analyse the field, present my proposal in the normal way to those from whom I was seeking access, the 'spirits', just as I would to an institution that I was seeking to make a film about. After my initial research and when my ideas were formulated I sat down and wrote two proposals.

My first proposal was a scientific one, outlining the current position of the research field, how in my view it was in 'their' best interests to support my project to allow themselves to be filmed and how I would film them. For over a hundred years many eminent scientists have studied mediums and the phenomena they produce yet unlike other scientific fields once the research is written up, it is seldom built upon. When another scientist reads it they don't quite know what to do apart from point out possible flaws or alternative explanations. Frequently they go away, do some research of their own which leads to a paper or books being published and because no one can quite believe what is being described actually took place, if phenomena did occur, the same process recurs. The only way to move the field on, to my mind, are for people not present at the actual séance to be able to see and judge for themselves what took place. A record has to be made which demonstrates that the medium or others were not acting fraudulently. This was the basis of my scientific proposal.

My film proposal was a little different. It was clear to me from my experiences in séances, studying and analysing the communications that took place, that something profound and dramatic was occurring for many of the people involved. Hearing someone apparently from the other side of life, talk to the person seated near me and have a conversation was very moving. Many tears were shed. The love and joy of the reunion was very dramatic. Words of love, reassurance and evidential messages from family members were very common. On occasion, spirits seemed pleased that they know that the one left behind wishes to join them, but they are told not to think of such things, as they must try to carry on. Afterwards, I sought the people out and asked them about their discussion. They assured me it was the same voice as their husband or wife who had died a short time before and all the information was accurate. No film director could ignore the drama inherent in the situation of two people communicating across the two sides of life in a loving way.

This characterised the vast majority of the experiences I witnessed at seances and demonstrations. There seemed to be loving contact and communication across two worlds. Given the nature of the situation I wished to film, I proposed to film it scientifically in such a way that excluded the possibility of fraud, by approaching the filming in a structured way, so I could assert that it was authentic. But I also wished to capture the personal drama and stories that were being experienced. I could then present a wealth of footage to write up as a scientist, for other scientists to analyse and discuss while for the public to use this as a foundation to present and capture the personal experience of the encounter. Boldly I ended my proposal, saying that unless the spirit world agree to allow 'spirits' to be filmed then the situation will remain the same as in the last hundred years, that no real progress will be made and understandably, a sceptical public and scientific community will remain. People were right to be sceptical and I reasoned one should do everything humanly possible to answer the questions that arise. This was my analysis, so if they did not want to allow themselves to be filmed then they should either let me know or I should abandon the proposal.

I informed them that my role was to try and present the filming in an honest, clear and powerful way but what was said or communicated was their responsibility. I will work to demonstrate that the phenomenon was authentic, as my goal was to convey the truth. I will work with them in order to reach the point when we are both confident filming is ready. I will not broadcast the 'failures' from this preparatory phase. These will undoubtedly occur because I realise that preparing for filming would be an experiment for both of us and adjustments will probably need to be made. I proposed that we collaborate on the project. I finished typing my proposals in the same way I would if I was sending a film proposal off to a commissioning editor at a broadcast company. However, instead of posting the envelope, I informed the spirit world in my thoughts that here are my proposals, which I am submitting for their consideration and I await your answer.

In support of my proposal, I argued that having a film-maker and psychologist conducting the filming it would relieve the pressure on their mediums. What customarily occurred was, a medium reports that a particular form of physical phenomena has occurred and certain people from the 'spirit' world have identified themselves, made communications and been recognised. Once this is reported in the press, scientists and sceptics write to the newspaper pointing out the reasons why this report might be unfounded.

Naturally there are always factors that could interfere with any observation, which haven't been taken into account in any particular demonstration. Once the sceptics or debunkers direct their attention to particular claims then frequently the medium feels let down and a little fearful. As a result they tend to withdraw from public announcements of their work, preferring to work quietly or with contacts in the Spiritualist community around the country. Having a film-maker who knows how to organise the scientific aspects of the mediumship protects the medium, because the medium is not making the claims. I proposed that I would be making the claims, presenting the evidence and conducting the discussion with interested and critical parties, hopefully along with other collaborators. In the past the medium has tried to take control of this feature of their work, and they have become upset when trying to discuss the sorts of scientific issues that arise. Naturally the personal experience of producing the phenomena is completely different from the nature of the considerations that take place for scientists studying it, who look at possible alternative explanations. By taking this responsibility away from them, the medium is able to concentrate upon their job with their guides, which is to be a medium, pure and simple, to sit in a dedicated way and demonstrate their phenomena for a spiritual purpose. They are responsible for their mediumship. It is unreasonable to expect ordinary men and women who produce the phenomena to be familiar with the media and scientific issues involved in their work.

I put this point forward as a further reason why my approach might be adopted. It avoids all the sorts of problems of mediums trying to present their evidence to debunkers and then defend themselves in the frequently hostile media and getting caught up with the types of difficulties other mediums had encountered in the past. Accusations of fraud would start and stop with me, not the medium. I would be the one working with the medium and their controls and presenting the evidence, so any problems came down to my research not the medium. We could then conduct further studies to test the points raised from any discussion of the results and so hopefully build up a body of evidence without the usual mishaps.

I had also come to the conclusion that I could not really understand what the mediums and recipients were experiencing unless I was prepared to get involved and participate myself. This is something many film directors do when researching films but scientists tend not to. Repeatedly I was left wondering what was actually going on when witnessing communications from mediums. Being detached and objective left me detached. How can you study something if you aren't prepared to get involved? There certainly have been fraudulent mediums just as they are fraudulent people in every walk of life including the film world, scientists, doctors and policeman. I wasn't interested in fraudulent mediums. I was interested in investigating the possibility of there being a spirit world, so my starting point was to find the very best mediums with the best reputations.

During this early phase of my exploration I noticed strange phenomena around me! I noticed tapping coming from the walls and ceiling in my flat. Sometimes the raps were like very loud cracks or bangs. Sometimes they occurred when other people were present who also heard them. I did not think much of it at first, but as it continued I found that it seemed to coincide with particular thoughts I was having. As I formulated my ideas and I considered the implications of the different experiences I was witnessing during my research, if I came to a constructive conclusion, at that precise moment I'd hear I loud crack on the wall near me or on the ceiling. Taps might also appear to come from furniture or objects in the room. The tapping occurred over many months and I noticed that it seemed to occur at precise moments. These taps seemed to me to be indicating that the thought I'd had had been approved of or confirmed in some way. I found myself even thanking 'them' as if they were leading my thoughts in a particular direction. On investigation I found that this type of tapping around one's home is not uncommon for people who attend Spiritualist circles, although sometimes it can be disturbing. The tapping I experienced was always positive and even enjoyable.

The literature also referred to many similar instances of raps occurring from the very beginning of Spiritualism in America with the Fox sisters. Peter Chadwick, the psychologist describes a similar experience, but in his case the rapping was disturbing and reinforced negative associations. It occurred while he was suffering from schizophrenia and the rapping answered him in a way similar to the séance room or the Fox sisters experience, one rap for Yes, two raps for No. His difficulties receded when he started to read aloud from the New Testament. I had a friend who was also plagued by such rapping around her home that also seemed malevolent and which disturbed her greatly. They started when she was trying to go to sleep or when she was entertaining her close fiends and wanted quiet. She eventually managed to get rid of the disturbance through prayer and asking loving spirits to come and protect her but she needed to be strong to cope with the fear that the rapping induced. Rappings seem intent on gaining your attention. Once they have done so, then the recipient needs to find out what they wish to communicate. It is spiritual or malevolent? If it is the latter then get rid of them and do so in a loving way, so you are not disturbed or made fearful, which is their intent.

On one occasion when I went to see a medium give a clairvoyant demonstration as part of the research, the medium came to me and said that my mother wanted me to buy some flowers for her on Mother's Day. The day came and I bought some flowers and lit a candle above the fireplace. I sat and sent my thoughts to her. When it was bedtime, at about 11.30pm I said aloud that now I was going to bed and that it was a shame she could not make her presence felt this evening. After completing the sentence as if by reply I heard tapping coming from the tiles in the fireplace. They were made at a regular beat that went on for about 30 seconds. The tapping was quite loud. I was surprised to say the least and I said 'thank you'. Needless to say, like most people I had never experienced the tiles around my fireplace emit any sound let alone loud tapping. After this experience the tapping seemed to be an accepted part of life until it gradually ceased about eighteen months later.

Other strange physical events started to occur. When going along to a demonstration of clairvoyance, as part of my research, the medium came to me and said that there was a person I knew in the spirit world named Jack, who wanted to give me a message. I said I couldn't remember anyone by that name. The medium said 'Don't worry, he (the spirit) says he'll show you who he is over the next few days'. I was intrigued, but forgot about this unusual message until a few days later as I was entering my flat. As I opened the door I noticed something was wedged under it from the inside. I carefully opened it and pulled out a piece of A5 card. It was a photograph of an under 14 year old Sunday football team I used to play for in the Regents Park League, called Mildmay. The photo looked familiar as I had had it in a box of photos somewhere in the flat, although I had no idea where it was. I was puzzled. What was this photograph doing under my door? How could it have got there? I looked at all the players and saw at the end of the back row, the manager of the team, a man we called Jack Knife. He had been my manager for several years for various teams I played for. I now remembered someone named Jack and the only explanation I can give for this photograph apparently moving to a position where I would notice it was the message I had received a few days earlier. When I looked for the box of photographs, the photo was not there. It was another case of a correspondence between what I had been told by a medium purportedly passing on a message from the 'spirit world' and something occurring, which had no other apparent logical explanation.

On another occasion, early one evening, after spending sometime considering my research into the subject, as I stood up to walk across the room I felt something on my hair and startled I used my hand to brush it away, thinking it was a fly. I then felt something touch my face and as I stepped back I saw a small piece of paper float to the floor in front of me. As I picked it up I noticed it was a very small torn off corner of a newspaper with a medium's name written on it in my handwriting. I remembered that some weeks before I had written the name on a newspaper to remind myself to contact her but had completely forgot about it. I wondered how on earth it had become torn and appear to float onto my face while standing in the middle of my room. It was unexplained and it still baffles me but there I had been reminded of a contact that I had needed to make.

Other more down to earth strange experiences occurred! When I reported what I had experienced to my friends, when, for example after returning from watching a medium or describing what had occurred at a séance I attended, my friends started to look at me very strangely. Although I was accurately and objectively reporting what I saw and I explained I had not come to any definite conclusion about it, I found I was being thought of as possibly a little unbalanced. Friends started to worry about me or some even became angry and agitated. This seemed very strange I thought. Why should they get so upset and my integrity and 'sanity' be questioned because I was reporting something unusual?

I found that if one reports unusual phenomenon then the reporter may well be seen as a discreditable source. I soon realised the dilemma scientists are faced with when they discuss ideas and experiences which are alien or at variance to the mainstream view. I reasoned that once a scientist stops reporting their observations for fear of ridicule or incredulity then it was time to stop being one notwithstanding that science as an enterprise ceases. Even though I continued my discussions with my two hats on, as a scientist and film-maker, the question that was important to me was the approach one would need to adopt in order to achieve a valid demonstration and test of the phenomena. It is clear why many scientists are a little apprehensive to enter the field because there is some fear and prejudice against it.

During my research I also found that some scientists got extremely angry and emotionally affected about any efforts to discuss the scientific issues that would need to be addressed for a valid demonstration. They seemed to be debunkers rather than scientists, wanting to show that it was all a fraud and very emotionally attached to this viewpoint. It was as if they were fearful that it might be demonstrated to be true. For some, endeavouring to come to an agreement about a valid scientific study which might demonstrate whether it was authentic seemed to contradict either strongly held religious or materialist beliefs. One I contacted felt betrayed, that I, a fellow scientist wanted to devise a legitimate test, and appealed to me to share his deep dislike for Spiritualists. Another said they weren't in a position to determine the factors that would need to be taken into account prior to testing particular phenomena, even though at the time they regularly used the press to debunk the reports of Spiritualist mediums. I wondered why one should get so emotionally attached to a viewpoint when all one needs to do is to apply a scientific method in the best way possible in the circumstances which prevail. If it were baseless then this could be clearly demonstrated and we would all be the wiser. I reached the conclusion that many of those involved weren't research scientists at all but ordinary people with normal prejudiced views employed in academic or medical positions. The extremes of both camps seemed locked into an antagonism towards each other which were clouding their views.

I had been taught to seek the truth as a scientist and to use my abilities to deeply understand aspects of our world. My work with disadvantaged children had taught me that initial results suggesting failure was only a starting point to look closer at what was really going on. I found that many scientists stopped investigating when negative findings first emerged. The most exhilarating moment for me, as a scientist, was a finding without an explanation. Science was an adventure in search of discovery and I for one was not going to abandon it in order to be part of a club, which held strong views one way or the other. In fairness, it must also be said that there were many balanced and critical enquirers from both the scientific and Spiritualist communities, who experienced the same types of reactions as I.

I also found that prejudice had spread to certain sections of the media. I was talking to an experienced film editor with a good friend Pete Miller, a film editor with whom I often worked. As often happened the conversation got round to the films we had made and the editor described the worst film he had ever worked on. The producer for the broadcast company had sent a director off to India to make a film about a well-known Guru. Upon his return the director and editor had edited the material into a rough-cut or preliminary version and the producer came to see it for the first time. On seeing this version he went into a rage and threatened to sue the director and make sure he never worked again in the industry. He explained that he had sent him off to make a film that showed that the Guru was corrupt and a fraud. The director explained but when he got there he found that the Guru was a really genuine man and there wasn't anything corrupt or underhand going on. The editor then explained how he and the director spent the remaining time making up a film from the material that showed the Holy man in a bad light. They both knew it was untrue but if they hadn't the director would lose his job and probably not work again for the broadcaster, and another editor would be brought in the do it.

Certainly, courage and clear thinking are vital tools of any filmmaker attempting to make a film in this area. I also heard an equally strange story from a very good friend of mine, Val Lundquist. She told me about her ex-husband, a documentary film-maker who wrote to Sai Baba, the Avatar in India asking to make a film about him. He got permission and shot the film and upon his return to England edited it. Once completed he showed it to an audience. When he went to show the film again he could not find it. He searched everywhere and eventually he went to see Sai Baba to explain his predicament. He told Sai Baba it had been shown once, but then apparently it had just disappeared. Sai Baba said he knew about the film and that it had been shown once and that it had achieved its purpose. Nothing more was said about it. The director believed that his film had been dematerialised and that was the end of it!

On hearing these stories I naturally thought, where does that place me? Indignantly, I thought, 'let them make my film disappear' if I made one, if it isn't good enough, but then how would I explain it to my backer! I would have to cross the bridge of possibly intimidating producers and dematerialising films when I got to it! I had to get back to reality. All I have are two proposals sent to the 'spirit world' but which was in fact still sitting in my desk drawer!

To my surprise a month or so after submitting my proposals while attending a Spiritualist Service in Hornsey Church, the medium came to me as I sat in the audience. She said she was being told that I had lots of very good ideas, that the spirit world were happy to work with me but they were saying it will take some time for them to organise things from their side of life, so I needed to be patient. I had sent a message and now I had received a reply. Part of me was surprised but I felt most pleased that my working method had apparently been supported. I had tried to gain the trust and the permission of those I wished to work with, and I had shown that I wished to do the subject matter justice. I had not told anyone about my proposal and I did not know the medium.

I contacted the Noah's Ark Society, who worked specifically with physical mediums and developing physical circles in the UK, in order to promote this form of mediumship. I met its founders George Cranley and Robin Foy and asked about their interest in making a film for television. They suggested I join the society, get involved and once they had got to know me they would make a decision. I joined the society and attended conferences.

After my first conference I joined a physical circle in Belsize Park run by a fellow member, Douglas Druce. Every Friday evening around a large oak table, a group of young people held hands in a blacked out room. After an opening prayer, we asked whether anyone was there. Then from the middle of the table raps could be heard. One tap for no, two for yes and three taps for don't know. Messages were tapped out. The number of taps representing each letter of the alphabet. I was very surprised by this phenomenon. I became personally convinced that the people present, some of whom became friends, were not acting fraudulently. I soon started to think long and hard about the types of questions a film-maker should ask a spirit. What do you ask a spirit?

After much thought, and naturally after being satisfied that the spirit was who they said they were, I concluded that the most important questions to ask a spirit centred on spiritual issues such as whether there was a God. If anyone should know whether there is a God, then spirits should, I reasoned. Every spirit I asked, replied that there was a God but not as we understand it. They explained there were many spirits who wanted to help mankind and they only wanted to be asked. We recorded these seances and I transcribed each one. Many purported spirits came through, tapped out messages and gave evidence about themselves which, when I researched the information, was verified. It was fascinating and Douglas was a wonderful host. I attended for many months and had many revealing experiences, but it did not lend itself to filming. I remember one evening prior to going to a conference the next day, to give an address about how one might go about filming physical phenomena, a message was tapped through the table giving me support and reaffirming that the spirit world would be with me the next day.

In the course of my research I also attended many seances conducted by physical mediums. Some demonstrations were events open to the public, Noah Society members or private affairs. I heard voices aloud coming from different parts of the room; saw trumpets lifting up and whizzing at high speed around the room and stopping in front of people; and heard voices of people they said they recognised coming through them. In one séance with Gordon Higginson I saw a very large cloud of white ectoplasm rise up from him, reaching a 9 or 10' ceiling, the width of his body. It remained in this position for some long time.

The majority of these seances were conducted in the dark, with the exception of luminous strips placed on the medium and the trumpets, so the audience could see them in the dark. Others were conducted in dim red light. In many seances I was personally satisfied that nothing fraudulent was occurring because either the trumpets flew over distances at such a speed that it would have been physically impossible for someone to do so in the dark and then produce recognisable voices for the appropriate individual. In others I knew the people or the location well, or I helped organise the seance. In other seances, the jury was out. In all cases, whatever an individual sitter's personal opinion may be, it bore no relevance to the criteria that needed to be adopted for a scientifically meaningful demonstration of physical phenomena, which then would be universally meaningful. The purpose of my research was to bring about such a demonstration and test.

The majority of mediums with whom I spoke were committed people who sincerely wanted to help other people and did so through their customary sittings. I thought how strange it must have been being a medium who goes into trance. Often they report having no memory of what had taken place after the demonstration was over. They only know what they are told occurred from those present. Often they are not given feedback in great detail. Even so, many sitters naturally judge them and questions (or accusations) about whether they are genuine or fraudulent are directed at them. This must seem rather peculiar and unfair if you are a genuine medium. You go asleep and when you wake up you are being judged, praised or accused of something you have no knowledge or memory of. No wonder they are often highly-strung and sensitive to other people's views. It seems that the only support genuine mediums have is the firm inner knowledge that they are not wilfully doing anything fraudulent, the support of their close friends, family and colleagues and a trust in the 'spirits' that they believe work with them. Placing your trust in someone from the media to fairly represent their mediumship is asking a lot. Many naturally feared that no good would come of filming, given a hostile media and they preferred to stay on familiar territory. It seemed that my request to film them also tested their trust in their 'spirit guides' if they were to support me.

I wrote an article for the Noah Ark Society's newsletter about filming physical phenomena and I was asked to address its London conference on my views on the topic. I discovered during the course of the conference, that the view of many on the executive committee was against filming. In the evening, in front of about 80 people, the physical medium Stewart Alexander was meticulously tied to a chair with lengths of cord with many ribbons tied doubly over the knots as seals. Luminous strips were placed on him, two trumpets and then the lights were turned out. Two trumpets levitated, flew around the room at great speed over distances of 10 to 15 metres, stopping in front of people, voices were emitted and discussions took place. Voices of relatives and friends were identified coming through the cylinders and evidence was given. Voices also came from the centre of the room. It was a remarkable demonstration. I was personally satisfied that nothing untoward was taking place given the speed, accuracy and distances covered in the dark, the information and recognition of voices of relatives. All I wanted to do was film it.

At one point a distinguished man's voice in deep, refined English was heard. He was apparently the medium's guide. He said to the assembled audience 'don't just think we are with you at the seances but we were very interested in the addresses and discussion at the conference about the filming project'. They said they knew their medium was against the idea but hoped he would change his mind. A short while later a voice called out 'Bob hold out your hands'. Immediately I did so, a man's jumper fell into them. When the lights were put on, I said it seemed like a used man's jumper. The woman next to me pointed out that the medium, who was only a few feet away, was now without his jumper. He was still tied in his chair, with the same complex bindings and double silk knotting around the knots, but in his shirtsleeves. Somehow his jumper had apparently been dematerialised and placed in my arms.

I inspected the knots and the ribbon bindings, as Stewart sat in the chair, coming back to consciousness and they all appeared to be in place. That incident produced much food for thought and I felt it was an act of support for my position, even though the Society and their leading medium who put on the demonstration held strong views against filming at that time. I later contacted Stewart and asked that if he ever changed his mind to consider my interest in filming his mediumship.

I went to a physical séance in the home of a friend, Val Lundquist. Colin Fry was the medium. A small group of people sat in a circle in a small room in complete darkness, the medium sitting in a curtained off cabinet. Soon a voice of a distinguished man emerged, asking who is the director here, the film director? I answered that it was I. 'Well' said the voice 'I have come here to inform you that I will be helping you with your experiment but I must tell you that you must be very patient because it is going to take a lot of time to organise from our side of life'. I thanked the person and I asked to whom I was speaking. The voice replied 'Ralph Richardson'. I enquired as to whether he might wish to give some evidence but he declined although he gave a communication about his son. Despite the varying factors that we need to be taken into account in such a demonstration, the communication interested me in case it was genuine and people in the spirit world wanted to help. Certainly if nothing else, the communication gave me encouragement to pursue the project further.

Similar support came from the purported guides of other physical mediums at seances. Generally physical mediums are very weary about being filmed given a hostile media and scientific community. Some were worried about the reaction of their local community towards their family and business, if it were known publicly that they were a physical medium. Others were firmly against the media and didn't want their mediumship filmed. There were stories within Spiritualism of some physical mediums experiencing serious harassment once their identity had become known. It was clear that presenting physical mediumship publicly did hold a number of important challenges and that the views physical mediums express are perfectly reasonable and need to be respected.

I contacted other developing physical mediums and circles. Some of these circles disbanded before any phenomena appeared. I met some individuals who had received purported spirit messages asking them to sit as a physical medium with a circle, but they declined. At first I felt a little disappointed about the difficulties inherent in the field but I also felt supported because in almost every instance the 'spirits' I spoke to at seances shared my view and they wanted filming to go ahead. They wanted to work together to present their phenomena for the benefit of mankind in order to demonstrate the truth of what was taking place.

Several aspiring physical mediums whom I met sat in development conscientiously each week, often for many years but did not have any phenomena to show. They wanted with all their hearts to be given an opportunity to help mankind. They were happy to be filmed if it might demonstrate the truth that there was no death. Unfortunately despite their best intentions and sincere dedication no physical phenomena was produced. Consistent with our agreement, after about eighteen months of being a member of the Noah's Ark, I rang Robin Foy and asked whether he had made a decision. He declined my proposal to conduct filming.

On further consideration I developed the view that although I was disappointed by my experiences, it seemed to me that I was not alone and that the 'spirit world' were equally disappointed. During all my research, I had not come across a medium whose guides did not want to be filmed, even though their medium, for one reason or another may have been reluctant. However surprised I was by this finding, at least my adopted working method was operating remarkably well. This seemed very good evidence, because if the medium was influencing the communication then I would expect an answer that matched his or her own views. Instead, whoever the medium was, the guides agreed with the need for filming and were happy to collaborate with me to undertake it. Furthermore, I got affirmative replies even when I did not intend to ask the question.

When sitting in a public demonstration of physical mediumship by Colin Fry, early on I saw a trumpet with a luminous strip lift up off the floor. It appeared to float from the centre of a room towards me, some 7 metres over the heads of two rows of sitters who were in front of me. It levitated right in front of me, at forehead height for several seconds.

A cultured man's voice then came from the centre of the room and said, 'Young man, will you take the trumpet and place it on the floor?' I did so. A short while later, the voice returned to me and said, 'The young man who took the trumpet, you have a question to ask and we would like to hear it'. I had no intention of asking my question on that occasion and resisted, saying the many people present were in a happy mood and they didn't want to hear my serious question. The voice insisted saying 'they' wanted to hear my question. I then made my request and the voice said that they indeed wished to be filmed but it would take some time. The voice explained that this was because at the moment the forms that were produced were made to produce sound rather than reflect the likeness to people. I was told that if filming took place now, the faces would look like 'porridge'. Much work would need to done before filming could take place. The voice turned to Colin's manager and asked him to arrange for me to attend the home circle so the proposal could be discussed further. Unfortunately the medium did not want the media to film his phenomena so the project went no further.

A fierce debate had started in the Spiritualist community and psychic press about filming physical phenomena. The debate became very passionate and it soon polarised between those wanting to demonstrate the truth of the phenomena to the wider society by filming while the Noah's Ark Society adopted a policy against filming and at one point declined to publish any further comment on the issue. As the number of physical mediums in the UK was very small and many kept to themselves or engaged in narrow networks, then getting access to them proved very difficult. I started to consider this situation and the difficulties inherent in such a project. As I spent my time and money trying to get a project off the ground I naturally started to consider the viability of continuing this work, although the communications I had received from mediums during this time had been supportive and encouraging.

I was sent one audio communication from a trance medium in the US who did not know me. A 'spirit' was telling a reluctant physical medium I was in contact with that the film maker who lives in London is part of 'their' organisation and that they wanted him to allow me to handle the public presentation of his mediumship. It seemed that if what I was experiencing was true then spirit world wanted their phenomena to be filmed as much as I did and, as such, I was part of a 'team' trying to achieve this end.

After all the research I had undertaken I had a personal commitment to undertake this work because I felt it was vitally important for people to be shown the truth about their lives, one way or the other. If there were spirits who wanted to demonstrate the truth and help mankind, then I reasoned that they must be as disappointed as I was at the situation. During my youth I had played a high level of football, playing for West Ham Utd. youth team, so being a team player was part in my nature. Given the difficulties inherent in the field and my own lack of resources, I decided that I was still committed and would continue to do what I could to help. This member of the team was staying and I would do as much as I could to help realise the filming project.

I had also spent some time researching the mediumship of Ray Brown and Paul, the purported spiritual surgeon who came through him. Ray and Gillian, his wife, were very welcoming and I was given complete access to Paul and his patients. I was so impressed by what I saw. Ray's mediumship was first class. Paul's work was remarkable and it seemed very important that his surgery and healing be documented, tested and demonstrated to the wider community. Paul welcomed a true test. I researched a film proposal involving some of Britain's leading doctors to test his work. I submitted a television proposal and Channel Four wanted to commission it. I was very excited, but then confirming many messages I had received saying I would go to the US to film physical phenomena, I received a number of messages from mediums to say the guides involved in filming physical phenomena wanted me to go to the US to work with a physical medium there, who had also received similar communications. Peter Grimsdale the Commissioning Editor agreed to put the film on hold until I returned.

I remember phoning Ray Brown to tell him of the delay. Gillian took the call and to my surprise she said she'd pass the phone to him so I could speak to Paul directly, who was beginning to entrance him. Paul explained that it was for the best that the Channel Four film was delayed because they were not prepared for the response that the film would generate in terms of new patients. He said they needed time to make the necessary preparations. I felt dreadful for Ray and Gillian, having taken the film project forward, only to have to postpone it when the commission was secure.

The trip to America was not successful. When I returned I endeavoured to get the film made but by then the Commissioning Editor had moved to another department and the new editor was not interested in the proposal.

Later I heard of a Scottish physical medium, named James McQuarrie, from my friend Val Lundquist. We both attended a workshop which James ran in London. James was a large, straight talking Scotsman with firm opinions. I introduced myself and asked him whether he was interested in being filmed and if so, maybe we could arrange a meeting to speak about the project and see what his guides had to say.

I was invited to his home in Wiltshire and enjoyed his hospitality with his enchanting wife Moira and young family. Later in the afternoon we sat together, James went into trance in his favourite armchair in front of his wife, two Spiritualist friends from Croydon and me, to hear what the 'spirits' attitude was regarding such a film being made.

The purported spirit, who communicated through James, spoke in a French accent and said he was from the White Brotherhood. He said that he knew of my ideas, the approach I wished to adopt and he explained it was their plan for me to film spirit phenomena produced by a group of physical mediums which they would bring together. They asked for this group to be named the 'Stella Polaris Group' and said they would bring this group together with James as a focus. He said that James, his wife and the other people present would belong to this group, that I would also be part of this group even though I was not a physical medium. The voice said that sometimes I would go away and then return to the group. They explained that first they wanted me to go away and make a drama-documentary film about Helen Duncan, but they said that I would return to the group afterwards.

I was a little reluctant to accept this proposal as I had come with the intention of filming physical phenomena I did not see the point of spending a great deal of time and effort on another project which did not involve doing this. I was also conscious of the many fruitless attempts I had had that had led to nothing. I suggested 'Why don't you get a feature director if you want to make a drama documentary because they would be more experienced than I with directing this type of film'. The voice replied 'we would like to ask you to undertake the project'.

I must also admit I knew little about Helen Duncan, apart from knowing that she was a famous medium whom older Spiritualists spoke about. The spirit who came through asked me to stay on another day to sit again with James, so he could clarify their plans further.

When James came out of trance he seemed to be aware of what had been said. I think he was disappointed at my reluctance to readily agree to the request that had been made, but he was unaware of my belief that filming spirit phenomena was of primary importance, and not a fictional documentary film that in my mind would resolve nothing of significance.

The next day we sat again, the same 'spirit' reappeared and explained that I would get help from two men in London for the fictional aspect of the film and financial backing would come to me! As one can imagine, it is quite unusual for a film director to be asked by a purported 'spirit' to make a film on a subject that one had no intention of making. This was a rather unusual commissioning process to say the least. The spirit also said that if I did not agree to undertake the project, they would get someone else to do it. I said I would go away and consider the proposal and let James know my decision.

Unlike the previous day, after the trance communication James seemed on this occasion not to know the content of what had been discussed. On being informed, he naturally seemed very pleased about Helen Duncan being referred to through his mediumship. Being a fellow Scot and someone who knew the history of Spiritualism, he knew the story of Helen Duncan far better than I did. James spoke about a journalist friend of his Michael Colmer and he was excited about heir plans to set up an organisation the British Society of Paranormal

Studies together.

Somewhat bemused, I returned to London to think about this unusual offer. I decided to go to a Spiritualist church to see if a medium, who did not know me, independently confirmed the message. Almost immediately, whilst sitting in a service at Hornsey Church, the medium came to me and explained she was being told that a project had been proposed to me which I was very sceptical about. She said they (the spirits) were suggesting that I give it a try, as it would be far more interesting than I anticipated. A short while later I received a phone call from a medium I knew, informing me that they had received a message saying that the spirit world wanted me to start research in earnest and that I had their full backing.

I checked up on who the White Brotherhood were. I read that the White Brotherhood were purportedly an ancient brotherhood who worked to help man in his spiritual evolution and search for truth. They work unceasingly for the spiritual unfoldment and advancement of humanity. They were a group of advanced spirits of men and women who supposedly drew close to earth again. Some writers stated they were a group of ascended masters or a group who have reached a level of spirituality which has brought them into close communion with the eternal spirit or God. Within Spiritualism the writings of spirit guides such as White Eagle and White Feather are purported to be members of the White Brotherhood. I have since read in some texts that the White Brotherhood is under the leadership of Christ, although I was unaware of this claim at the time.

I thought further about the other aspect of the communication that James had given. It seemed very significant and worthwhile that the spirit world wanted to bring together a group of physical mediums to work together for spiritual purposes under their guidance. Although the Noah's Ark Society existed, it now seemed from James' message that the spirit world wanted another group of physical mediums to work together un der their control. This was an exciting plan and one that I was naturally keen to see be developed, as it might allow for a body of evidence to be established about physical phenomena.

Like many freelancers who are developing several film ideas at a given time, I decided it would not put me out too much to undertake some preliminary research into Helen Duncan. She had died in 1956 so many of the people who knew her had passed and there did not appear to be too many books written about her. I decided to carry out the research as quickly as possible so my other film projects would not suffer. You will appreciate few directors would refuse such a film in case it was genuine. I immediately contacted James to let him know I had agreed to undertake the film project that the White Brotherhood had purportedly proposed through him. He advised that I contact Alan Crossley who had known Helen Duncan and had written a book about her and Helen Dunne, another Scottish medium who had been running a Campaign to get a

Pardon for Helen Duncan for many years, and he gave me their contact details.

WHO WAS HELEN DUNCAN?

I started to read accounts about Helen Duncan's life and the Old Bailey trial from books at the British Library and other archive sources.

Helen McFarlane was born on the 25th of November 1898 in Callander, Perthshire, Scotland. Her father was a master slater and he ran a long established company. She came from a family of eight and displayed mediumistic abilities as a child. At school she discovered answers to questions appearing on her slate which surprised her teachers and found she could occasionally see spirits. On one occasion when a local doctor went missing overnight in a snowstorm, the town's people went out to look for him. Helen told her mother that he was OK and only a short distance away. After being scolded she kept quiet, only to have her information verified the next day when he was found. In her teens she had visions of her future husband as a soldier in France and they later met and married. These types of spontaneous experiences continued.

She married Henry Duncan on the 27th of May 1916. He regarded her as quiet, kind girl. After her marriage, while she was in hospital suffering from pneumonia she saw a coffin with her mother-in-law's name inscribed on it with the date of death shown. She told Henry about what she had seen. As her mother-in-law was alive it was disconcerting. Her mother-in-law died nine months later on the day shown in the vision.

A similar incident later occurred with Henry's father. After apparently fully recovering from an illness and planning to return to work, Helen quietly confided that he wouldn't last the week. A few days later Henry and Helen were woken by his father's characteristic knock on their door, which was followed by an eerie wailing sound around the house. A short while later there was another knock on the front door and Henry was told his father had just died. Unlike her parents who suppressed Helen's psychic ability, Henry shared her interest in psychic and supernatural matters and he read many books on the subject. He also wrote on the subject but never published.

Henry started work as a cabinetmaker and joiner in Dundee but suffered from heart trouble. One day Helen knew there was something wrong and she rushed to his office and with the help of a policeman found Henry slumped over a desk having suffered from a heart attack. His heart trouble stopped him working and he received a small disability pension from the Great War of 12s 6d a week in 1932. Helen also suffered from diabetes, kidney problems, angina and eclampsia. She gave birth to nine children, three of whom died in infancy. Some of her children also suffered from ill health. Anne (known as Nan) had heart trouble, Bella had one eye and Georgina had a deformity in the right hand. Henry, Peter and Lillian were the other surviving children. They were a poor working class family, Helen was the main breadwinner. She developed her mediumship abilities at home, holding seances over three years often with her children present.

Helen invited friends to form a home circle in September 1925. First objects started moving and raps conveyed answers to mental questions. After introducing some trumpets into the séance room, on the first evening faint whispers were heard. In the next séance objects were thrown around the room and the voice of Matthew Douglas, a spirit control was heard. This started a period of independent direct voice. After 15 months the circle were asked to sit for materialisation. Fully formed human figures that could speak and think independently were produced at her seances. This coincided with the appearance of a control named Albert Stewart in 1929. He was a native of Dundee, who had died in Sydney, Australia in 1909 aged 34 and had worked as a pattern maker. He organised the seances from the spirit side of life initially along with another spirit control Dr. Henry James Williamson, another Scot, purported to be a former Unitarian Minister from Mint Street, Dundee. Henry claimed to have verified these details.

Later, Albert was to run the seances with a young girl form named 'Peggy' Hazzeldine. She had died a few weeks' earlier aged three years, and she claimed to know Dr. Rust, a family friend who had attended her. It was claimed that Peggy's mother and father, a market gardener from Kirkton Mains, Dundee were quite satisfied as to the identity of the child. Peggy's mother Lena Hazzeldine, of Dundee confirmed that Peggy was indeed her daughter who appeared in Mrs. Duncan's seances to her knowledge up to 1941, when Mrs. Hazzledine stopped sitting. Helen was also a very good clairvoyant and trance medium.

Her abilities started to be recognised by the Spiritualist movement, namely the main organisation the Spiritualist National Union as well as the Edinburgh College of Psychic Science. Soon she was giving public seances and travelled around the country while Henry looked after the family and home. Helen was a poor working class woman with no great intellectual ability but she had a canny understanding and was independently minded. Soon an uneasy relationship developed with the main Spiritualist bodies and colleges after she found that she received only a small share of the income they were making from her popular sittings.

Helen was fast gaining a good reputation and many people clamoured for a reading or a seat at one of her seances. Even the police called on her services. One day two policeman came and asked if she would hold a visiting card. Using psychometry she told them they were holding a man who had stolen a motorcycle from a shipyard. The number plates had been ripped off and now the machine was in a dealers shop in a narrow street close to a derelict factory.

Her reading was accurate and the police recovered the cycle.

The London Spiritualist Alliance sittings

In late October 1930 the London Spiritualist Alliance (LSA) started a series of sittings to test Helen's mediumship over a period of eighteen months. Although Helen had been psychically warned that a disaster loomed in London and she had repeatedly resisted going, she eventually yielded under pressure from Dr. Montagu Rust, a close friend of hers. She held over 50 sittings, in good red light and reports were published in the journal titled 'Light'. Ectoplasm emerged from her mouth and nose and sitters felt it. It slid slowly over the hands and around the room liked 'coiled snakes' and withdrew into the medium seated in the cabinet. She was tied into various sack-like garments and on occasions emerged from the cabinet without it, but leaving the sack and its seals still intact. On occasions she was tied into her chair and after the séance the seals were intact. Partial and complete forms were reported as appearing with varying degrees of developed features and many of the forms spoke and appeared to have personalities confirming what many Spiritualists had claimed to have seen at her sittings around the country. Unfortunately many of the seances were poorly recorded and they were not written up in a systematic and detailed way. From March 1931 more complete investigations took place. Many sitters confirmed fully developed forms appearing with recognisable features. Later seances proved more disappointing possibly due to Helen sitting too often and her ill health.

The LSA published a favourable report in Light May 1931 claiming the sittings demonstrate that Helen's mediumship is genuine.

Harry Price, the psychic investigator

Harry Price entered Helen's life in 1930 after he had heard about her mediumship. He was an ambitious, hard working, publicity-seeking psychic investigator and author, who had publicly denounced and 'exposed' a number of leading mediums as being frauds. He set up the National Laboratory of Psychical Research in 1923 and he was a long time member of the Magicians Club. He had initially competed with the LSA to engage Helen but had failed. He even found himself barred from attending the LSA public sittings even though he had rooms in the same building. He had offered Helen a large sum of money to undertake a series of test sittings with a group of distinguished sitters at his National Laboratory of Psychic Research in London, of which Mrs. Molly Goldney a friend and colleague of his was one. Although the LSA had secured an exclusive contract with Helen, by the end of April 1931 Price and Henry

Duncan were negotiating a series of sittings without their knowledge. Consequently Helen sat for them both during the same period.

Helen started sitting for Harry Price, from early May 1931 until June 4th. She sat five times and was paid around £50. With six children to support no doubt Helen and her husband was tempted by the financial inducement. The first sitting was on the 4th of May. The next day Helen sat for the LSA. At this séance Price's colleague Molly Goldney deliberately stepped on the ectoplasm that was moving near her chair. At that moment Helen Duncan gave out a loud painful scream even though she was in the cabinet, unaware of what occurred outside the cabinet. When the séance finished Helen had blood covering her face and when she got home she had two burns near her navel. The next day she was ill and she was vomiting all night.

Mrs. Goldney successfully accused the woman sitting next to her of doing it, who was a Spiritualist. Goldney's act was taken very seriously because it breached the undertaking given by each sitter to abide by the strict rules of the LSA that under no circumstances may ectoplasm manifested be touched without permission. This incident upset Helen and thinking that the LSA had failed to protect her, it shook her confidence in them and made her nervous and upset with them. Henry found a sympathetic ear with Price who he phoned the next day explaining what had occurred.

Whether Molly Goldney did it deliberately in order to interfere with Helen's relations with the LSA and push her further into the arms of Price, given she was a member of Price's competing body, we will never know, but that was the effect. She had attended Helen's first séance with Price the previous day. Later Goldney openly boasted of stepping on Helen Duncan's ectoplasm to colleagues at the SPR.

Helen's relationship with Price and his colleagues also soured. After coming out of trance in the fourth séance Helen had blood pouring from her nose and without warning Price asked to X-ray her. Henry had earlier agreed without informing her. When Helen saw the preparation of the formidable mass of equipment to be used, she became furious and after Henry approached her she became hysterical. She struck Henry in the face and aimed a blow at an eminent doctor standing nearby but missed. She fled screaming into the street in her black séance clothes, designed for the experiment. For half an hour she clung to the railings and reacted hysterically. Eventually she was induced to return, where it was found that her séance clothes were badly torn. She then completely changed her attitude and demanded to be X-rayed. Three X-rays were taken. She had a p. v. and throat examination. Nothing abnormal was found. Price then asked to search Henry as he had been alone with Helen for two minutes in the street, but he refused. This gave rise to further suspicion. That evening Henry phoned apologising for not allowing the search and offered to return the cheque. He claimed that he resisted being searched because he was wearing old underwear.

Still feeling very uneasy Helen attended a further séance but she was unwell and had a bad abscess on her arm. Things got worse when a doctor accidentally tore off a piece of ectoplasm he was holding instead of cleanly cutting it. Helen screamed and it led to a persistent nosebleed that led to the close of the circle, with her face again covered in blood. Two doctors insisted Helen go to hospital where she stayed for a few days to have the abscess lanced.

On the 11th of June a meeting was held between Henry and Price with other members of the Council conducting the study. They informed Henry of the finding that the sample of ectoplasm taken had been analysed was found to be paper. They also raised the question of Helen's hysterical conduct after rushing into the street and Henry's refusal to be searched, which had raised suspicions. Henry had no explanation of the analysis and raised a number of questions about the phenomena witnessed that the committee themselves had no answer. Eventually he could only suggest that if Helen did regurgitate articles it was done unconsciously due to an automatism of the will. He suggested that three further seances be held and different procedures be introduced in order to determine the truth. Members of the Council raised their suspicions about the genuineness of the phenomena and openly asked whether they should end the study. It was agreed that a further sitting should be conducted where Helen is taped to the chair, held by two persons with a net over her head.

The next day, the 12th of June, prior to a séance arranged in the evening for the LSA, Henry asked to meet the Research Committee who were conducting the investigation. He told them he had believed that ectoplasm may have been produced as the result of regurgitation and that three hours before seances Helen 'lost her will' and unconsciously secreted things in and about her person and retained them in her stomach.

Clearly Henry was convinced by Harry Price's theory, and felt it proper to give some account in those terms to the LSA, possibly anticipating what Price was soon going to make public. Henry did so rather than asking for (or believing) his wife's and Albert's, her control's, accounts of what took place. It seems the LSA also learned around this time what Price's findings were. The LSA agreed to terminate the seances and generously agreed to pay for the return of the Duncan's and their furniture to Dundee even though when they had discovered that their medium had been poached and they were extremely angry with Harry Price and Helen.

There was then a rush between the LSA and Harry Price to publish their findings, with the LSA fearing Price would scoop 'their' discovery. Certainly Henry's duplicity in breaking his agreement with the LSA and Helen's secret sittings with Price soured the relations between them. Added to Henry's further unexpected declaration that his wife may be regurgitator, is it any wonder that the LSA published a critical report in Light a month later, completely at variance with their earlier report, dismissing Helen's mediumship and accusing her of regurgitating material. Some observers believed that the LSA had not even considered regurgitation as an explanation before Henry mentioned it.

As the Duncan's prepared to leave Thornton Heath, Molly Goldney discovered that they planned to do so without honouring their appointment for a further séance with Price. She took Henry to see him. At a final meeting Price offered Henry £100 if Helen would swallow and regurgitate cheesecloth in good light in front of the council and be filmed!

Helen returned to Scotland the next day by ship and Price made great play of this exit taking this behaviour to show that she was a fraud who had something to hide, rather than the reaction of somebody intimidated by the heavy handed procedures adopted by him. Helen had been injured in four of the five sittings that led to their termination. Three ended because of nosebleeds and one when she was burnt on the face when Price's flashlight went off unexpectedly. She distrusted and disliked Molly Goldney, believing that she had placed incriminating items on her.

Helen was also quite unwell, as several of the council members observed. Albert said he was having difficulty controlling the medium and he got tired of persistent requests for phenomena while he was trying to cope with his medium who was bleeding profusely and not in a good physical or emotional condition. Henry was probably right when he said she needed a holiday. Given everything that had taken place it is understandable why Helen had had enough and returned home, rather than it necessarily reflecting the conduct of someone who was a fraud.

Not to be outdone in the race for publication Price sent his findings to the Morning Post two days before the LSA Report was to be published. To gain further kudos he claimed that despite holding over 45 seances at a cost of hundreds of pounds the LSA had been 'hoaxed' into believing the ectoplasm was genuine by one of one of the cleverest mediums, and that his research had discovered fraud. The LSA were furious and denied Price's claims.

A short time later Price published his full findings in a Bulletin titled: 'Regurgitation and the Helen Duncan Mediumship'. He concluded that Helen was a fraud who swallowed cheesecloth and regurgitated it in order to create the forms. He claimed to have chemically analysed the ectoplasm from a LSA sample and one taken in the 5th seance and found it was of two types, egg albumen and paper. Mr. Bacon of Sindall & Bacon, who analysed the sample taken at Price's séance and discovered it to be paper, worked for a company who worked predominantly for the paper industry. Interestingly he had been used before by Price to analyse a sample of ectoplasm taken from a medium named Eva C and again he found it to be paper. At face value it seems to be an uncommon coincidence that an analyst specialising in paper should find that two samples of ectoplasm given to him by Price just happened to be paper. Harry Price published photographs purporting to show that it was cheesecloth being used by Mrs. Duncan along with rubber gloves, picture cut outs, yet analysis of this ectoplasm did not find any evidence of cheesecloth. Price publicly declared that the course of five sittings had ended acrimoniously after Helen had rushed out hysterically and eventually fled back to Scotland.

Investigators hotly debated Price's theory and raised a series of objections from the smallness of Helen's throat and stomach, the ability to produce white ectoplasm after her consuming large meals and red jam to the impossibility of regurgitating and swallowing rubber gloves as Price proposed. A theory even abounded that mediums had a second stomach like cows, even though there was no evidence in support. Price's strongest evidence were photographs taken at the sittings in which he claimed the material being emitted from Helen was the same as butter muslin, with tears and crease marks apparent. He repeatedly presented this finding forgetting that egg white and paper are not cheesecloth and Yoga practitioners using the Dhauti cleansing technique have been swallowing fine muslin and regurgitating it (using their fingers) for centuries, only to find it is not white at all but very smelly and covered in mucous. Helen and Spiritualists also accused him of manipulating the images. The LSA had found that two samples of ectoplasm proved to be surgical gauze, but researchers noted that the samples were identical with a sanitary towel, which Helen had left behind one day in her dressing room. The LSA later said that no samples had been taken from the mass of ectoplasm produced, and some small samples had been taken for analysis from the medium's clothes after the séance. As no one had seen some of the actual samples come from the ectoplasm produced, it may not have been ectoplasm at all.

Like the LSA, Harry Price had made a complete about turn after first enthusiastically declaring that her phenomenon was genuine. He had initially written confidentially to colleagues describing amazing phenomena with Mrs. Duncan. After he had examined her in the nude he decribed streams of ectoplasm trailing around the room that sometimes enveloped her, all in good light. Correspondence also confirmed that chemical analysis of ectoplasm (the LSA sample) matched Professor Schrenk-Notzing's analysis[1] and Price rang Hannen Swaffer the journalist and dictated an article for publication in the Daily Express confirming these findings. It is also interesting that although one chemist concluded the sample of ectoplasm he analysed included egg white another said he could not positively say that the protein was egg white, but it was an albuminoid type. Price tried to replicate ectoplasm based on the chemical analysis he had received, and found by using egg white, ferric chloride, hot manganic acid from olive oil, phosphoric acid and stale urine thickened with Nelson's gelatine he could do so. The question was never asked as to how Helen

Duncan who had no scientific background, secretly prepared such a formulation before each seance, swallowed it and then regurgitated many yards of it in self propelling mobile streams then reabsorbed it along with a rubber glove. This is quite apart from explaining how it maintained its structure after residing in her stomach and notwithstanding that this concoction is not butter muslin! Furthermore no one seemed to want to further explore the findings that a protein, albumenoid in nature was a constituent part of ectoplasm. Albumen is a constituent of animal solids and fluids and is present in blood serum. It is also interesting to note that Price did not present this finding to Henry at the meeting, but only that ectoplasm was found to consist of chemical and mechanical wood pulp.

Many respected psychic investigators regarded Price as unscrupulous. Mrs. Sidgwick who ran the Society of Psychical Research denounced him and the SPR Council refused to deal with him. Many investigators also thought that his regurgitation theory was ridiculous, asking how could Mrs. Duncan make cheesecloth talk, move like lightening, take different shapes and have enormous force. Certainly Price's assertions were not always supported by the protocol of the séances. Whatever had precisely gone on during those sittings, it concluded with Price being publicly scathing in his comments about Mrs. Duncan and with him claiming to have exposed a notorious impostor. So Helen's trip to London had been disastrous in terms of the LSA and Harry Price, as she had been warned.

Just as Price's report criticised Helen's mediumship and Price's claims were repeated in the press, many Spiritualists wrote to newspapers and journals applauding Helen's phenomena and describing successful seances where relatives materialised. A significant report appeared supporting Helen's mediumship in January 1932 in Light. Dr. Margaret Vivian who had attended a LSA sitting in March 1931 could not reconcile what she had witnessed, with the LSA and Price's published findings. She and a group of investigators undertook a series of four sittings in Bournemouth with Helen and published her findings in support of her mediumship. She found snow-white ectoplasm was produced after making Helen swallow methylene blue dye pastilles prior to two séances. This finding offered no support for the regurgitation theory. The sitters had also assumed pseudonyms as names and the materialised forms soon gave their actual names. An apport occurred, different coloured lights and recognised materialised forms which spoke independently. Vivian's findings contradicted both the LSA's and Price's. She also noted that when a chair was accidentally knocked over during a séance the ectoplasm rushed back and the séance had to be stopped as Helen's face was burnt.

Price's theory was coming under increasing attack and some investigators even accused him of making British psychic investigations a laughing stock internationally. Nevertheless the press extensively publicised his views and it was against this background that one day a neighbour told Helen that a man had come to the area and had been asking questions. The man had approached neighbours and had asked whether they had been to one of her seances and whether any suspicions had been raised. The man eventually spoke to Helen's daughter Bella and maid Mary McGinlay in the street outside their home. He asked questions about Helen's work and mentioned shop dummies, masks and white material. When confronted by Helen, Bella and Mary claimed that they regarded it as a joke that they had played along with him and said these items were kept in the bathroom. The man made notes and seemed very pleased and he handed them £10. Helen was very upset but there was not much she could do. She suspected that Harry Price might be behind it.

This had obviously set Mary, the maid, thinking. Later after taking advice, she decided not to go to the newspapers but wrote to Harry Price saying that she was disgruntled at her treatment by the 'Duncans' and looking to make some money from her time in London with the 'Great Materialized Medium Mrs. Duncan'. Her attitude had completely changed towards Price as she had been 'nasty' to him during a phone call whilst in London with Mrs. Duncan.

Price paid for her to travel to London and she was put up in a hotel. She eventually made a statement in which she accused Mrs. Duncan of deception. She claimed that Mr. Duncan had admitted to her that Helen had passed him a roll of butter muslin in the street outside Price's laboratory and that is why he refused to be searched. According to her, Henry had confided in her that 'the game was all up now'. She claimed that she had been sent to buy cheesecloth for Mrs. Duncan prior to seances and asked to wash it afterwards. She also claimed that she discovered rubber gloves and picture cut outs, which Price had also claimed to find her using in his investigations. She also claimed to have identified the same actual piece of cheesecloth Price had photographed with the piece of cheesecloth she had bought for Mrs. Duncan a few weeks earlier.

Price presented these allegations publicly, with the signed statement from Miss McGinlay in February 1932. Price used this statement to bolster his theory of regurgitation and support his accusations of fraud. Price claims only to have paid Miss McGinlay her expenses. Certainly she asked Price for money and for his help to find work in London. Money and clothes were sent to her with the promise of further money if the information that she had was 'extremely interesting'. Soon after making her statement she asked for more money saying she was about to get married but Price declined. When John McIndoe the President of the SNU investigated, he reported that Miss McGinlay gave a completely different account to the one presented by Price. Many investigators noted that Miss McGinlay's statement happened to conveniently refer to each facet of Price's testing and it called for remarkable feats of memory on the maid's part. Many regarded the statement as another stunt arranged by Price.

Helen continued her sittings around the country and she still allowed herself to be tested. For example, the Sunday Chronicle invited famous magicians and doctors to a séance and reported positive results. She was repeatedly warned by prominent Spiritualists about sitting too frequently which will harm the quality of the phenomena and her health. Price's research had also created a lot of interest and many people wanted to discover the truth for themselves about the opposing claims. This led to heightened danger for Helen, as some sitters were liable to make a grab for the ectoplasm if it came near them.

Esson Maule enters Helen's life [2]

Esson Maule, a writer, wrote to Henry Duncan a month after the McGinlay scandal, in March 1932, asking for Helen to give a series of sittings for a book that she intended to write about her. Given the adverse publicity Helen had received from the LSA and Price, it was considered that benefits would accrue to Helen through such a publication. It was agreed that a series of seances would be arranged in Edinburgh most to be held at a Miss Taylor's flat in Brandon Street. This gave Helen a regular income and allowed her to remain closer to her family, thus cutting down on her travel away from home.

Miss Maule attended this series of seances along with other paying sitters during 1932 although her friend, Mrs. McLaren was banned because she had once seized hold of the ectoplasm, Helen had screamed fallen on the floor and had hurt herself badly.

At a séance in April 1932 Miss Maule also rose with the intent to inquire further. Different coloured lights were coming from the cabinet and as she pulled the curtain to the side and was about to put her head inside, she found herself gazing at a large lit up balloon face, that had just returned into it, within inches of her. As she rose to grasp it, it disappeared and the curtain was pulled from her grasp. She then received a blow to her forehead of considerable force that stunned her for several minutes and caused a nosebleed. Things got to such a point that Albert only allowed Helen to leave the cabinet at the end of the séance when Miss Maule had assured him twice that she would not touch Mrs. Duncan. Miss Maule had the habit of putting her head in and peering into the cabinet without permission and got a blow on her face or pulled hair for her trouble from whatever was inside.

Miss Maule was a very determined lady. On one occasion after failing to speak to Mrs. Duncan during the day and in order to ensure that a séance she was wanting to arrange was confirmed, she broke into the Duncan's house after midnight and woke Henry and Helen up.

During these seances Albert spoke openly about the events in London with Harry Price. He gave a vivid account of the suffering Helen endured under him. He said that it was little wonder that no decent woman would become a medium. Albert was directly asked what ectoplasm was and he gave a detailed breakdown of it to two doctors who were present. All Miss Maule would recall of the detail was it was albumen, urine and mucous of some membrane. Albert explained the rubber glove that was purportedly seen in London as his attempt to materialise a hand which when it first appears smells like rubber. He then went on to materialise a hand at the séance to demonstrate the point.

Albert customarily asked sitters to observe closely the amount of ectoplasm that was produced and use their judgement as to whether even Mr. Price could swallow and regurgitate it. Albert was particularly critical of Henry for standing by and letting Price internally examine his medium and for refusing to turn out his pockets when asked. Miss Maule had argued that Albert should have acted to prevent these problems, by intervening himself to cause Price to have appendicitis or turn Henry's pockets out himself, when he refused.

Albert made fun of Miss Maule, commenting on what a pair of conspirators Miss Maule and Harry Price would make. When she asked for a sample of ectoplasm she was told to ask Price to send her some. At the end of many seances Albert asked sitters whether anyone thought what they had seen was cheesecloth and regurgitated. No one did.

Apparently Miss Maule had taken a dislike to the Duncan's, their character, their life style and she was sceptical about the phenomena she had seen, even though the people who accompanied her at the seances were excited and extremely complimentary about it. This seemed to make her even more incensed and determined to show everyone that she was right. Miss Maule was a belligerent sitter and openly antagonistic to the guides and séance procedures. On one occasion she refused to sit with the other sitters, wanting to sit extremely close to the curtains so the séance could not proceed. She openly questioned the authenticity of the forms and time and time again she said that Albert was in fact Mrs. Duncan. To demonstrate to her that this was not the case, in two seances Albert appeared at the same time as Mrs. Duncan at the entrance of the cabinet to her and the other sitters present. Miss Maule reported that she saw both of them standing together.

Shortly after reading Price's book she became very interested in his theory, his accusations of fraud and she contacted him. She advised Price to come to the Theatre Royal in Edinburgh to see Kanichka, the human ostrich and professional regurgitator, perform. He went to see the human ostrich for himself in December 1932, although it is unknown whether they took this opportunity to meet. Whatever transpired Miss Maule was spurred on and she decided to set a trap to expose Helen. She consulted Price about the best way to do so and she spent sometime examining details of Scottish law so there would be no loophole, in order that she might get a conviction. In January 1933 she arranged for a group of sitters to attend for this purpose. She sent Mrs. Sowden to go the Duncan's home to arrange it the night before. Helen had received a warning from Albert, her guide, immediately prior to that séance, to take great care.

Reports differ, but it appears a plan was hatched for a séance to be held on the 5th of January 1933. Ten sitters attended. The plan was for Miss Maule to give a signal by knocking twice, at which point Miss MacKay would immediately turn on a powerful light she was holding. Unfortunately at a point when Miss Maule first grabbed the ectoplasm from the rear of a figure and had knocked twice, Miss MacKay paid no attention, as she was so absorbed in the séance and the scene of a male sitter embracing the form of his deceased wife. Miss Maule was getting increasingly frustrated as the séance was coming to an end.

After an hour of inactivity on the conspirators' part, it was only after Miss Maule had gone over and reminded Miss Mackay of their plan that an opportunity arose. Miss Maule made a grab for the form of Peggy, one of Helen's child guides. Miss Maule described a frantic struggle as the material was pulled away from her. She saw Mrs. Duncan stand up from her knees in front of the cabinet and eventually the material was pulled out of her grasp. She said that she felt it tear and a sitter said he heard the sound of a tear. She then rushed forward, pulled open the curtains and shouted that she had caught her in the act of fraud. She then called for her good friend Miss MacKay, a solicitor to put on the 120-watt electric light and she did so.

When the light was switched on the sitters saw what appeared to be Mrs. Duncan, on a chair, with her head hanging down, apparently trying to conceal some white material under her clothes. Mrs. Duncan was later to explain that when Miss Maule grabbed the form, she experienced the sensation of burning from her chin to her stomach and she was bending down with her hands by her side. Mrs. Duncan was then openly accused of fraud and Miss Maule explained that she had put her hand into the cabinet as each figure appeared and touched an empty chair. Helen flew into a rage. Helen picked up a chair and swung it over her shoulder at Miss Maule. She struck two male sitters and then threw a shoe at Miss Maule. Having completely lost her temper with Miss Maule she shouted 'I'll brain you, you bloody bugger'.

Eventually things quietened down and she was asked to disrobe in front of Miss Maule and two other female sitters. According to Miss Maule, a white cotton stockingette sleeveless vest fell to the floor as Helen disrobed. Upon examination it was discovered that her vest had been torn. Esson Maule claimed that had occurred when she grabbed the material that Mrs. Duncan was manipulating, in order to produce the appearance of Peggy. Helen repeatedly offered the sitters a free test séance to settle the matter but this was not accepted. After another period of rowdiness the police were called. No arrests were made and the police eventually left. Helen left leaving the torn sleeveless vest with Miss Maule. She decided to take the fee of £4 and signed a receipt, but then offered Miss Maule a pound to cover her expenses. Eventually she left a 10s note as this was considered to be a fair amount.

It is unknown what led Miss Maule to carry out what she did next, but it matched Price's desire to encourage people to make formal accusations of fraud against Mrs. Duncan, as he had done with Miss McGinlay. Esson Maule typed out a declaration claiming the sitters had detected a fraud and she outlined the evidence. She sent draft copies of the statement to Harry Price to read and suggest amendments. Eleven days after the séance she declared the agreed version before a Justice of the Peace. She then forwarded it to the Procurator Fiscal for consideration for a criminal trial. Five of the ten sitters who attended signed the declaration.

At the hearing held at Edinburgh's Sheriff's Court, many witnesses were called who vouched for Helen's mediumship and the defence asserted that Miss Maule had acted to satisfy her vanity and thirst for publicity. This accusation was no doubt founded upon the fact that most London newspapers turned up for the trial and covered it with front and inside page headlines.

Helen's case was dealt a blow when the law agent defending her, Ian Dickson, pleaded for clemency because she was 34, she had eight children, her husband had no income and that she had 'only once stooped to manipulation'. At this point Helen shouted out it was not true! Harry Price attended the whole trial and on May the 11th 1933 Helen was convicted of 'fraud' and fined £10.

The press had a field day. It is difficult to know what truly took place at the seance. Maurice Barbanell the editor of Psychic News claimed that Miss Maule had changed her story at the trial from the one she told him shortly after the incident. Different drafts of the statements also reveal subtle changes. The final statement was very carefully constructed and certainly there were a number of discrepancies in her account. In the sworn statement and its different versions, not one sitter confirms Miss Maule's account of what took place when she grabbed the form of Peggy. This is despite several sitters describing the forms that appeared during the séance and a covered 40-watt red light bulb and a candle illuminated the séance. No person said they saw Miss Maule put her hand into the cabinet as the forms appeared, grab the form of Peggy or the earlier form, see Mrs. Duncan get up from her knees, or see the material pulled from Miss Maule's grasp. Even Miss Maule did not describe Mrs. Duncan returning into the cabinet and back onto her chair even though this is where the sitters saw her when the curtains were pulled back and the light went on. Given that the statement carefully offers confirmation from the other sitters for every other event Miss Maule described, significantly it avoids any confirmation of the most critical moment when she made a grab for the form. The signatories obviously could not agree to what took place and so this was ignored.

The statement mainly focused its attention on the only white garment that Helen was wearing when she disrobed, a small cotton under-vest. Its appearance was viewed as proof that something underhand must have gone on. Miss Maule's accusation rests upon the fact that when Helen disrobed the white vest fell simultaneously with two other items and it did not come from over her head. She then put it on before the other garments as she got dressed, but then removed it separately without removing the others. It was deduced that as Helen had not removed it from over her head when she first disrobed but did so when she removed it a second time then in Miss Maule's view it must have been concealed under her clothes. Analysis of the sworn statement shows that slipping the vest off the shoulders could have taken place at a time prior to disrobing after Helen had gone behind the curtains, again in view of three of the women sitters. There is no logical reason why it could not have been slipped off for some other reason. This was in effect the crux of their case. It seemed to rest upon whether the vest was pulled over the head or not. They asserted that they had discovered the method of the deception.

The immediate question had arisen was how a large woman of 20 stone had covered herself in a small vest to imitate forms. It was also unclear how Miss Maule could be so sure she had created the actual tear on the vest, as she said the material she grabbed at the séance slipped from her fingers. Certainly the garment was torn in a number of places. Mrs Sarah Keith or O'Hara, Mrs. Duncan's housekeeper testified that the undervest was full of holes and that she had caused the tear on the vest when ironing it.

A number of unsettling features exist. Miss MacKay said that she could not identify the vest produced in court as Peggy. Sitters also described adult forms appearing at the séance in long white material. Some thought it was Mrs. Duncan with white material covering her head and dress. Sitters stated that the undervest was the only white material present that could have been used for fraud and Miss Maule admitted that the undervest was no more than eight to ten inches in length. Given the small size of the vest it would have been quite impossible for Mrs. Duncan to cover herself with it in the way described for adult figures. It was not long white material.

Miss Maule herself unwittingly and vividly demonstrated this impossibility. She went to the trouble of recreating; the type of figures that appeared at the séance and had a photograph taken of someone dressed as the type of form that appeared to demonstrate it and had sent it to Harry Price. It showed a figure covered in a very long piece of white material running almost the complete length of the body, from the top of the head to her knees with an open portion revealing the face.[3] This material could not have been a small vest. Miss Maule's photograph was not presented at court but it clearly contradicted her assertion that Helen had fraudulently produced figures by means of the only white material present and seized after the séance.

Other sitters contradict Miss Maule's claims that all the figures looked like Mrs. Duncan because at least two went up and embraced and kissed them. Surely they would not have done so if they believed it was Mrs. Duncan they were kissing. Half the sitters were not called to give evidence and they did not sign the statement.

Mrs. Sowden, an eventual prosecution witness who had called at the Duncan's home the previous evening to confirm the booking, had given a false name at the time, as a Miss Souls. Helen claimed that she had never agreed to go to Miss Maule's home and thought she was going to the Psychic Club next door, but when the taxi arrived she was led by a woman into Miss Maule's residence, next door. The taxi driver, William Watson, confirmed this account.

Whatever the truth, a very strong minded and motivated woman who disliked and despised the Duncan's and thought Helen was a fraud deserving exposure had set a trap at a séance and instigated a successful prosecution, after recovering material. After hearing of Harry Price's involvement Helen viewed him with the greatest suspicion and believed he was behind the whole unpleasant episode as did Maurice Barbanell the editor of the Psychic News. Price used the conviction to support his research findings and to further his claims that Helen was a fraud. A few months later, in July, Miss Maule had written in her book, describing the series of seances she attended. She gave it to Harry Price, so no one was able to refer to it and discuss the instances where Miss Maule's observations contradicted his theory and assertions or her own testimony. Clearly if Miss Maule had seen Albert and Helen appear simultaneously as she reported then clearly it undermined the case she instigated accusing Helen of imitating him and the other forms.

Miss Maule did not agree with Price that Helen regurgitated. She believed Helen hid the cheesecloth in her pelvic region as she claims occurs in 'female lunatic asylums' and during menstruation Helen hid it between her clothes and her skin. Her book shows that she was full of resentment, dislike and contempt for Helen, which makes it difficult to take it seriously as an objective record. Nevertheless some of the descriptions are revealing, as detailed accounts of Helen Duncan's mediumship that remain, are few. Harry Price and Miss Maule became firm friends and she helped Price in various matters in London whenever she had an opportunity and Price encouraged her to publish her memoirs.

Helen soon paid off the £10 fine by holding a few seances starting within hours of the conviction, much to the displeasure of Miss Maule. To the further dismay of Harry Price this prosecution did nothing to diminish the public interest and demand for Helen Duncan. Believing Price was behind the whole affair, the SNU returned Helen's certificate to allow her to continue working in their churches. Later that year using the pen name of Madame Victoria Duncan, she also had a regular Saturday full page spread devoted to her experiences in

'The People's Journal' newspaper, under the headline 'My Second Sight Secrets'. Her abilities were also regularly described in the Psychic press of the day.

Helen had gained a reputation among psychic investigators as being a clever and cunning woman with an innocent air. She was viewed by some as having a distasteful personality, which those more refined onlookers took offence to. She was very fat, weight ranging from 17 to 20 stone, 5' 6" tall, ungainly, had coarse features, enjoyed smoking and spoke in a strong Scottish accent. Like her husband she was also had a reputation as a heavy drinker.

Like other mediums on the road she approached engagements in a professional manner and did not make a great effort to ingratiate herself with many 'respectable' people who attended seances. Even some senior Spiritualists agreed with the view that she was a 'dreadful woman'. Negative views about her were no doubt entrenched in the minds of many by her breaking her word with the LSA and her tendency to lose her temper, to become hysterical and to use strong language when confronted or upset. The scene, after Price's séance when Helen swung a punch, rushed into the street, clung to the railings and screamed obscenities in front of eminent members of Price's laboratory, no doubt led to a firm view amongst members of the establishment that she was a coarse and unsavoury character. A similar incident at Miss Maule's no doubt confirmed this view in polite circles. In her defence it must be stated that many of those who spoke badly about her hardly knew her and also opposed the possibility of such a thing as genuine physical phenomena. It is probable that most working class mediums entering into intimate proximity with Harry Price and other sceptics like Molly Goldney would not have come out unscathed in terms of personal attack or criticism of some sort or other. Helen was to some extent an easy target for those with a critical disposition, as her appearance and temper led to negative qualities being attributed to her.

This view contrasted sharply with those who knew her more intimately. She was known to be a naive, truthful, warm, plain talking decent woman with a quick temper. People who knew her well repeatedly claimed that Helen was honest and would never cheat. She was also known for her acts of generosity and kindness. She was the main breadwinner for a large family, on the road for many months at a time, which she viewed as serving the 'spirit world'. Although she received a good income from her seances and had to support her family, she fed the homeless and took into her home young troubled girls from the streets whom she helped reunite with their families. One girl she met who was suffering from ringworm of the head and who had lost much of her hair, became part of the family until she got on her feet and eventually married. Helen was also a person who also gathered loyal friends around her. Like many people with a temper there was also another side to her character which was sensitive to those who were suffering and in need. Frequently those who could not afford the fees for her seances were allowed in for free.

Her loyal following no doubt grew because Helen was the only medium who was happy to be tested at each of her seances. She allowed herself to be stripped naked so she could be examined, to assure the sitters that she was not concealing anything. Sitters were also free to examine her clothes, the cabinet and room prior to her taking her chair in the cabinet. She travelled the country and reportedly materialised thousands of forms whose features, mannerisms and voices were readily identified by the attendant public. This activity and her willingness to be examined and tested made Helen the most popular and sought after medium, and, in the eyes of many the most courageous physical medium this country had seen. This life style went on for many years, whilst a housekeeper looked after the children in Scotland.

In May 1937 Helen again allowed a public examination of her mediumship to take place. The Evening News newspaper ran a Séance Inquiry. With a series of bold front page headlines 'I Argue with A "Ghost" At Glasgow Séance', 'Glasgow Séance Exposures', 'Special Investigator Sees Dead Resurrected', 'Séance Spirits Are Ingenious Fakes', their reporter and investigator Albert Mackie wrote a series of front page articles on seances held in the city. At first she was not named, although the presence of Albert and Peggy soon informed the reader who knew of Helen, who the medium was. Eventually Helen was named and the reporter received a torrent of criticism for his uninformed approach to the investigation. He said Helen was an ingenious fraud, whilst at the same time describing her as a rather ignorant woman who used rough language. He recognised and spoke to a deceased friend who appeared but then declared the form also looked like Helen. The reporter did not present any serious evidence and blandly stated that Helen used regurgitation to produce the effects but offered no critical insight or explanation. Replying to his critics he concluded by saying 'if the Spiritualists depend on her for their evidence, theirs must be a very poor case indeed'.

Portsmouth 1944

Helen travelled all over the country once the Second World War started, with hundreds of sitters recognising and speaking to their deceased relatives and friends. Portsmouth was a regular stop on Mrs. Duncan's travels. In January 1944 her daughter Gena pleaded with her not to go, following a disturbing dream, fearing something terrible was about to happen. Both Henry and Helen dismissed it. Helen travelled to Portsmouth having also forgotten the general warning mediums had received a year earlier that an attack upon them was anticipated. At an early séance it is reported that Albert warned the couple organising the seances Mr. & Mrs. Homer not to allow a gentleman dressed in

Naval uniform to attend a later séance. Later Albert warned the Homer's again not to let in three gentlemen who would apply the following week and one would be dressed in Naval uniform. He said these men meant harm to Mrs. Duncan.

A week or so later on the 19th of January Helen was arrested and charged again with fraud. Two Naval officers Lt. Stanley Worth and Surg. Lt. Elijah Fowler who travelled to The Master's Temple, a registered Place of Worship at 301 Copnor Road, Portsmouth on their bicycles, attended a séance. They were sceptical about what took place. Lt. Worth later complained to the local police and a raid was mounted on the 19th of January in which he took part. They used the same method as Miss Maule had done in Edinburgh in 1933. War Reserve Police Constable Rupert Cross (and bookshop keeper) jumped forward at a prearranged moment to grab the white form in front of the cabinet and as he did so Lt. Worth flashed a torch to increase the illumination on the scene. A third Naval serviceman sat next to them. Cross claimed he caught Mrs. Duncan red handed standing in front of the curtain as she was trying to push the white cloth that had been covering her, down to the floor. He claimed that someone then grabbed the cloth and pulled it into the audience at the moment he had got his hand on it. One of the sitters, Mrs. Lock claimed that she saw the cloth slip through his hand. A whistle was blown and more police officers rushed into the room. Even though the room was thoroughly searched and everyone present offered to be searched, no cloth was ever found. The police claimed, that as a doctor was not present, they were unable to search all the women present even though they had asked to be searched.

After Cross had rushed forward and grabbed Mrs. Duncan, he met up with Worth and asked whether Worth had seen the sheet. Worth replied that he hadn't and that it had gone. Then Mrs. Duncan retorted 'Of course it has gone, it had to go somewhere'. The prosecution eventually made great play on this statement believing that if the substance had been ectoplasm, Mrs. Duncan would have said so and refuted the suggestion that it was a sheet. The prosecution argued that this indicated that she acknowledged that it was a sheet and that it had been grabbed back by an associate in the audience. The prosecution further argued that if Mrs. Duncan was a genuine medium and the substance was indeed ectoplasm, then why didn't it return to Mrs. Duncan, as those who organised the séance and other experts stated it would.

The Spiritualist National Union set up a defence fund to pay for Helen to be represented by barristers. It attracted donations from throughout Britain. The defence was conducted by Charles Loseby and assisted by J. Simpson Pedler. Loseby was someone who had been very interested in Spirit phenomena for many years and who was active within the Spiritualist movement.

Initially Helen was charged under the Vagrancy Act and unusually she was refused bail. As Loseby, the Defence Counsel, had been part of the Spiritualist

National Union Deputation to see the Home Secretary in 1943, at the first hearing in Portsmouth he complained that the Home Secretary had promised not to use this act against Spiritualist mediums. Eventually the Director of Public Prosecutions dropped the charge under section 4 of the Vagrancy Act but replaced it with a serious charge of conspiracy.

Spiritualists also pointed out that the Chief Magistrate at the hearing was Sir Denis Daley, the Lord Mayor of Portsmouth since 1939, who was a very staunch Roman Catholic. He had been the first Lord Mayor to officially attend a service in a Roman Catholic Church since the reformation. At the magistrates hearing in Portsmouth in which the court clerk used a typewriter, war planes roared overhead and somewhere nearby someone tinkled on a piano running rapidly through dance tunes, the justices transferred the case to the Central Criminal Court in London starting on the 23rd of March 1944.

Early press reports ridiculed and pilloried Mrs. Duncan. When the trial arrived Loseby believed that the jury must have been aware that she was the woman who the police had 'laughably exposed'. This 16 stone medium was the 'ghost' that the police constable had grabbed and one of a 'group of charlatans' who staged seances in which 'shocking things' will be divulged, not least that they held 'fake seances to cheat war bereaved'.

Mrs. Duncan was eventually charged under the 1735 Witchcraft Act that carried a sentence of imprisonment if found guilty. She was also charged with conspiracy and fraud under the Larceny Act and with effecting Public Mischief. Mrs. Duncan, her assistant Mrs. Frances Brown, Ernest Homer and Elizabeth Jones, known as Mrs. Homer were charged on seven counts in the indictment. Mrs. Frances Brown of Houghton-le-Spring, Durham, who accompanied Helen and prompted sitters to identify the materialised forms showed a set of spirit photographs to sitters that the prosecution claimed were also fake. Mr. & Mrs. Homer ran the Church where the seances were held. Mrs. Homer prompted sitters in the same way Mrs. Brown did during the seances and Mr. Homer was the proprietor of a shop who ran The Master's Temple above his drug store at 301 Copnor Road, Portsmouth and took the money. Eventually during the trial only the first count remained referring to conspiracy under the Witchcraft Act.

It read: In the first count that between 1st December 1943 and 19th January 1944 you conspired together and with other persons unknown to pretend to exercise or use a kind of conjuration, to wit, that through the agency of the said Helen Duncan spirits of deceased persons should appear to be present in fact the said spirits were communicating with living persons then and there present, contrary to section 4 of the Witchcraft Act 1735.

The trial started on March the 23rd. in Court No. 4 at the Old Bailey. It took place over 8 days with packed galleries and a frenzy of press activity as witness after witness described the most amazing experiences during Helen Duncan's seances on the days in question and up to fourteen years earlier, back to the early 1930's. Helen was on trial at the Old Bailey charged under the 1735 Witchcraft Act, accused of being a trickster earning £112 for 6 days work from vulnerable grieving members of the public, as the bombs fell in London and the nation watched.

John Maude KC the Prosecuting Counsel was also conducting another trial starting in Court No. 1 starting five days later on the 28th, as Defence Counsel representing Harold Loughans. Loughans was a career criminal who was accused by the Chief Constable of Portsmouth Arthur West of strangling Rose Robinson in her bedroom in November 1943. Mrs. Robinson was a widow and licensee of the John Barclaycorn beer-house in Portsmouth. A jury had been unable to reach a verdict in the first trial and a retrial was scheduled for the Old Bailey. Loughans faced the gallows if convicted.

Maude, a legend at the bar, conducted both trials simultaneously leaving substantial parts of the Helen Duncan trial to his junior counsel Henry Elam, who was also the Recorder for Poole. Maude was the Recorder at Devizes. Maude chose to conduct the defence for Loughans free of charge, so it seems he decided to split his time freely between the two cases brought by the Chief Constable of the Portsmouth to the Old Bailey.

Maude arranged for Helen's former maid Mary McGinlay to come to London and be present during the trial, in case she was needed as a witness. Maude made the opening speech for the prosecution that set out their case and the tone of the prosecution. He ridiculed the séance and the forms that appeared and presented the implications of what was taking place as ludicrous.

For Maude, Albert the guide was in the advertising business and Peggy was his assistant, was acting as a sort of commissionaire. A parrot fluttering around from some Heavenly forest was called by Albert to come to Portsmouth. A grandmother was petulant and she was not going to stay but then sang a song in a language which could not be understood. Peggy 'this wretched Scotch child who had passed was still being tiresome; it had never grown up' had been asked whether it had taken some papers. She hadn't but she knew where they were. He concluded by saying that the dark room, the little red light, the traditional ghost appearing between the curtains, the perpetual prompting by Mrs. Homers and Mrs. Brown and the voices of a man and Peggy, the clearly bogus spirit photographs and the prayers were all the paraphernalia and the elements of fraud. He said the entry charge of 12/6d a person 'was very moderate if one was going to the ghost of Napoleon or the Duke of Wellington, but it was not value if you were going to see a bogus conjuring trick'.

He went on to say that 'At a time when the dead are anxiously sought after in prayer, such conduct as to pretend to conjure them up when it is a false and hollow lie is nothing less than a public mischief... One has turned the light on to the little room in Portsmouth; and finally it is not too much to say that the mockery of the dead will cease in the little room over Mr. Homer's shop'.

Loseby was aware of Maude's great skill as a barrister. He described him as 'tall good-looking and a fortunate possessor of a good voice'. He judged his opening speech to have been a 'contemptuous parody' based on Worth's version of events but spoken with such 'adroitness, skill and economy of words that any ill-informed person might well imagine that there could be no effective answer to the case as he set it out'.[4]

Maude allowed Elam to conduct the examination and present the evidence of eight of the most important prosecution witnesses. Maude examined four of the lesser witnesses although he took it upon himself to re-examine all his witnesses if required. He seems to have put his attention to considering and then countering Loseby's strategy. He then cross-examined Loseby's first six defence witnesses and Nurse Rust who was a strong defence witness plus two others. Elam was then left to cross-examine the remaining 36 defence witnesses for over two and a half days. It seems that once Maude had set the style of cross-examination he favoured, he was confident to leave Elam to follow his lead. He then gave a very short closing speech for the prosecution.

The Spiritualist press openly declared that the prosecution represented a great opportunity and Defence Counsel Loseby prepared to call 45 witnesses to testify to the genuine nature of Mrs. Duncan's mediumship. He said he could have called a hundred witnesses. He asked that his client be allowed to demonstrate her mediumship to the jury to prove her innocence. The Recorder Gerald Dodson rejected his request. Towards the end of the trial the jury also let it be known that they also did not want a demonstration. Loseby decided not to call Mrs. Duncan, Mrs. Homer or Mrs. Brown as witnesses, although he proffered Mrs. Duncan for cross-examination by the prosecution.

Loseby claimed that the police had acted dangerously in deciding to shine a white light and grabbing a spirit form during a séance as Lt. Worth and WRC Cross had done, as serious injury can occur. The prosecution made great play on the fact that no such injury occurred when this occurred. This supported their view that Helen Duncan was acting fraudulently and the restrictions placed upon sitters not to touch the medium or have better lighting was part of the arrangements put in place in order to deceive the people present.

The main prosecution evidence came from Lt. Worth and WRC Cross and a small group of people who supported Worth in saying it was likened to the Punch and Judy show. Worth had first got involved with The Master's Temple early in November 1943. He had gone to many services and joined development circles at the church. Important evidence came from a local long serving Spiritualist medium, Charles Burrell, who also testified against Mrs. Duncan. He was dismissive of her mediumship, believing that she was tricking the public. Although Mrs. Duncan had been charged for committing fraud from the 1st to the 19th of January, the evidence centred mostly on two seances held on the 14th and the 19th. The raid took place on the 19th.

Seating positions were arranged by means of cards with the names of sitters placed on their chairs. On the 14th Lt. Worth and Surg. Lt. Fowler inadvertently swapped seating positions when they arrived. Like most other sitters they had paid 12/6d. Worth testified that two figures appeared to him, one confirmed that they were his aunt, the other an uncle who saluted him. But his aunt was alive, he had two deceased uncles but he could not recognise either of them. Albert, the control of Mrs. Duncan, also said he had a sister who was in spirit, who had died prematurely, and he was asked to find out about this. Later Worth claimed there was no such sister.

Maude the Prosecuting Counsel put the failure of Lt. Worth to recognise these figures to him as being due to him swapping seats with his friend, which had confused Mrs. Duncan, in her attempt to carry out her deception. Loseby argued that such a proposal was far-fetched and too elaborate to build a case. No one bothered to ask Fowler whether he had an elderly aunt in the spirit world, a sister who had died prematurely or whether he recognised these two forms.

A number of other figures appeared to Lt. Worth at the séance on the 14th. Mrs. Duncan's guides came, Albert, an Australian with a refined voice and Peggy a young woman. Peggy a young guide danced in front of the curtains and sang a song. A form named Jarvis came, who was identified as the brother of one of the sitters and who spoke in a Yorkshire accent and used rough language. There was a mutilated young man with a stump of an arm, an elderly lady in her 90's and a policeman who purportedly appeared with a helmet. Worth considered all these figures to be Mrs. Duncan imitating voices, with a white sheet over her head. He saw no features at all on the forms. Animals also purportedly appeared including a cat, a parrot named Bronco and a rabbit, which he couldn't see and appeared to him to be inanimate white objects pushed through the curtain.

Defence witnesses who attended the same seance described several of the same figures coming from the cabinet as Worth but that they recognised their distinct facial features, voices, mannerisms and the information given.

On the 19th, Worth described a woman appearing from behind the curtains holding out her outstretched arms and the form of a young man, who WRC Cross rushed forward to grab. This initiated the start of the police raid to catch Mrs. Duncan red handed.

The other prosecution witnesses gave similar evidence regarding the forms they saw. Charles Burrell, a medium, referred to seeing an arm being poked through the curtains that he was sure was Mrs. Duncan's and instead of a materialised hand comprising of ectoplasm, a human hand that looked like it was covered in white cloth was holding a torch. He referred to a purported guide he did not know appearing, bowing to him; a missing airman, named Freddie, who he was told in one seance that he had survived a plane crash only to find out in another that this was untrue and he was dead. Mr. Lock, a pedlar, referred to his mother-in-law appearing, him shaking hands with a form purporting to be his sister Sally, but the hand was 'undoubtedly' human and similar to Mrs. Duncan's. His wife, Bessie described a form purporting to be her mother coming over three seances on the 17th, 18th and 19th of January, but she did not recognise it to be her mother. Mrs. Jennings, an experienced actress gave evidence about Peggy not liking Christine Homer's lipstick and her belief was Mrs. Duncan was using her voice to impersonate the different forms. These witnesses also believed these forms were nothing other than Mrs. Duncan running around with a sheet over her head in semi-darkness. Mr. Burrell was unconvinced by Mrs. Duncan's mediumship and gave evidence to say that he was unhappy with the seances and had told Mr. & Mrs. Homer so. Mrs. Homer said 'You, a Spiritualist, after all these years are not convinced now, when all these poor people who don't understand are'. He explained that the sitters were convinced because they didn't understand.

Even though Lt. Worth said he was unconvinced after the first séance, he told Mrs. Homer and Mrs. Brown that it was 'amazing'. After contacting the police, he returned to say that he had phoned his mother, she had informed him that he had had a sister who died prematurely. He later admitted that this was not true.

Defence witnesses gave impressive evidence supporting the genuine nature of Helen's mediumship. For example, Anne Potter, who attended on the 18th explained that her mother came out from the cabinet to look at her. She had the same distinctive features as when she was alive. She had died in 1925, with dark hair. The figure had the same features with the same bald spot, an inch from the top of the head. She said her face and voice matched that of her mother. Her father also emerged from the cabinet with the same prominent features he had when he was alive. He had white hair, a large Grecian nose and spoke in the same low Scottish Highland accent. She also recognised a friend from India appearing, a very slight woman, weighing no more than seven stone and speaking in the same polite Scottish voice she had had when she knew her.

Mr. Kirkby recognised his friend George Dobson who appeared to him. His friend had the same moustache, nose, shape of face, particular way of looking at him and the same smile. The form walked out in the same cramped, bent-up way he had when alive, as he had been paralysed due to radiation. Mr. Kirkby also recognised his friend's voice, mannerisms and way of speaking.

Loseby called witness after witness giving testimony supporting Mrs. Duncan. They gave evidence that they had recognised and had meaningful conversations with materialised forms of their close friends and relatives. By the forms that Mrs. Duncan materialised it was claimed she could not have known that Mrs. Barnes' father was a policeman, Mrs. Tremlett's husband had the habit of tapping his walking stick; that Mrs. Wheatcroft's husband called her by her second name Annie and that she called him Alfie when his name was Albsalom; that Nurse Rust's husband had suffered from rheumatism in his hands, spoke in a gruff voice, her mother had a mole in the hollow of her chin and her Aunt Mary spoke Gibreltese Spanish that was used in conversation at the seance; Mr. Branch's grandmother had hundreds of wrinkles on her face and spoke in a Suffolk accent; Margaret Lyons father had had a broken nose that meant it lent over to one side and that he called her Marget; Mr. Frank Spencer's brother had a small moustache, was 5' 10" tall and his Christian name was Merlin; Mrs. Bailey's mother was a very tall, slim woman, 5' 11", with golden hair and that her grandmother had a long nose; Mr. Dodd's first ever sweetheart Helen, waved in exactly the same way she did when he took her home after their last dance together, had hazel eyes, the same pallor on her cheeks....

Loseby was criticised for making the mistake of seeking to use the trial to prove Spiritualism and the genuineness of his client rather than focus upon the precise indictment she was charged with. It was argued, that indeed Mrs. Duncan may have been a genuine medium on other occasions, but the question was, did she act fraudulently on the dates cited in the indictment? Investigators had observed that even genuine mediums may resort to trickery on occasions to help things along.

Loseby decided that he would produce a wealth of evidence in support of her mediumship. The other 20 or so witnesses that Loseby called, who were not present during the dates covered in the indictment came from around the country. Each described their experiences of seeing and interacting with recognisable materialised forms. Mrs. Blackwell claimed to have sat with Mrs. Duncan over a 100 times and seen over 500 of her materialised forms. Likewise Mr. Smith had sat with Mrs. Duncan for over six years and Mr. Bailey claimed to have done so on many occasions. Mr. Dodd and Mr. Steabben had sat with her between 30 and 40 times, Mr. Ormesher, Mrs. Fry, Mr. Herres and Mrs. Woodcock between 10 and 20 times. Mr. Collins, Mr. Spencer, Mrs. Hurd and Miss Lyons between four and five times.

By introducing many witnesses who testified about their experiences at Mrs. Duncan's séances beyond the dates cited in the indictment, it led to many hours of repetitive testimony. This came to bore the jury but filled the newspaper columns, which focused upon all manner of stories which related to what occurred in Spiritualist seances. Calling witnesses who testified to their experiences in Mrs. Duncan's seances back to the early 1930's, also allowed the prosecution to raise the matter of the Edinburgh prosecution. Once this was done, it proved a fatal blow to the defence. The jury took less then 30 minutes to reach their guilty verdict.

On Maude's 43rd birthday, Mrs. Duncan was sentenced to nine months imprisonment in Holloway and Mrs. Brown to four months. Mr. & Mrs. Homer were given a conditional discharge. At the end of the trial the Chief

Constable of Portsmouth, Mr. Arthur West, stated that Mrs. Duncan had transgressed the security laws when she foretold the sinking of a warship, that she was a humbug and pest to society. It was also revealed that Mrs. Brown had a conviction for shoplifting.

When the verdict was announced a distressed Helen was led to the cells. In a croaking voice she shouted 'Why should I suffer like this? I have never heard so many lies in my life. I dinna ken why they should get away with thae lies'. As she left the dock, Spiritualists in the public gallery waved to her.

If you were a member of the public, unable to attend the trial then the press coverage was the only way you could know of what occurred. Here is a selection of what was reported in the press at the time. Many of the national newspapers used the same agency reports, so many of the selected accounts of each witness's evidence was repeated through the national and regional press:

THE TRIAL AS IT APPEARED IN THE PRESS [5]

"If the prosecution's case is proved, said Mr. Maude, "we shall have drawn the curtains back in the Master Temple, and the mockery of the dead will have ceased in the little room above Mr. Homer's shop."

Lt. Worth said Mrs. Homer told him the ectoplasm rushed back into Mrs. Duncan's body with great force. She said that Mrs. Duncan had had an operation and inside her body were found cigarette ends, match sticks and all sorts of rubbish from the floor. Mr. Elam: Like a vacuum cleaner? – 'Yes' a medium with a vacuum-cleaner action that sucked cigarette ends into her body…' [1]

These were the things talked about at the Old Bailey yesterday

In a corner, curtained off to make a cabinet, Mrs. Duncan appeared to go into trance. [2]

No sooner had the curtain been closed round Mrs. Duncan than a voice spoke from the cabinet. A white form a rather traditional kind of ghost, said Mr. Maude – appeared and Mrs. Homer informed the gathering that that was Albert, the medium's guide. [3]

Mr. Worth asked the spirit, which Albert said was for him, "Are you my aunt?" and a husky voice replied "Yes." That, said Mr. Maude was unfortunate, because all of Mr. Worth's aunts are alive. [1]

On January 18th a Mr. Lock was invited to shake hands with his dead sister Sally. He took hold of a fat, clammy hand which was undoubtedly human. [4]

Later, Albert said he wanted to "come to somebody who had put their foot on an animal."

A woman told how she had put an injured cat out of its misery. [1]

Later Albert said that was the voice, and there was the cat – and something whitish passed in front of the curtain and the people said 'Look at the pussy'..

Then the audience was shown a parrot called Bronco, which said 'Pretty Polly'. [5]

The next form was that of a policeman. A woman said: "Is that you dad?"

The figure replied: "Wait a moment while I put on my helmet".... [1]

In another incident Albert, who spoke with a cultured accent, said: "He had a young man who was horribly mutilated"

When a woman in the audience claimed him she was invited to come forward and touch what was said to be only the stump of his arm.

The voice said it had happened "out East, at Singapore." [6]

One figure leaned over and shook hands with a man in the second row, and in a Yorkshire accent said, "How are you Jarvis?"

"The spirit form" added Lieutenant Worth, said he did not think much of the medium because she is too fat.

"There was then a muttered conversation between the two, as though they were having a private joke, and 'I distinctly caught the words 'B—twister'. [1]

In the dock in Court No. 1 at the Old Bailey yesterday sat a burly, fur-coated woman "She is in a trance," said her counsel. As she sat there gazing ahead of her in the court.... [7]

Peggy, another guide, spoke with a Scottish accent, and after singing "Loch Lomond" said: "I'm gaun doon noo".

Peggy, a child guide who is alleged to have materialised at a séance and said that she had taken some scent from a bottle and tried lipstick.

John Maude prosecuting: 'What did Peggy look like – Helen of Troy or a pillow case? It was like a figure with a sheet over it. [5]

Spirits, which spoke in Spanish, recited nursery rhythms, and kissed members of the séance audiences were described yesterday by a procession of women. [8]

Mrs. Tremlett spoke of a spirit of her husband, who preceded his appearance with taps from his walking stick
She said that 'Albert' said "you don't need your walking stick here old man." That said Mrs. Tremlett "was a family joke as her husband would never be parted from his stick". [9]

Mr. Homer described the appearance of a woman's granddaughter "not more than 3' high".
The child went to her knees" he said "caught hold of her finger, and said 'This little piggy went to market' – just as a child would do" [10]

Mrs. Rose Cole said that at one meeting in the Master Temple a friend of hers, a Mrs. Allen, appeared and said, "Thank you for the orchids" – put in a wreath on the coffin when Mrs. Allen died just before Christmas. [11]

Her husband had been dead for 5 years, but had not altered – just a wee bit thinner. She felt his knobbly knuckles – he had had rheumatism. My husband kissed me right on the mouth" declared Mrs. Rust.[12]

A feeble voice was heard, and Mrs. Homer said "Is that you granny, darling?" The voice replied "Yes but I am not coming out this time." [1]

A witness in the seances trial at the Old Bailey yesterday said she had a guide named Rambeida. I should say he is a Red Indian. I can tell that definitely from his features", she added. ...The woman Mrs. Anne Potter, of Portsmouth, was asked by the Recorder (Sir Gerald Dodson) why a guide is necessary. She replied. "Even now I can hear my mother talking to me – a message from the other world. I should say I am a natural medium." [9]

On January 18 said Mr. Kirkby, one of his own guides a Chinese called Chan appeared. He had a moustache 20 inches long. [13]

An offer to swallow a length of cheese-cloth at the Old Bailey séance trial was refused by the judge.
The offer was made by Mr. Hannen Swaffer who was introduced to the jury by counsel as "a well known journalist and former dramatic critic."... During his evidence he was asked by Mr. C. E. Loseby, defending counsel, to take the

cheese-cloth in his hand.

The Recorder then declared: "I said he is not to have it in his hands if it is to be a question of any experiment. This court is not going to be reduced to the level of an exhibition."

Mr. Swaffer went on to say that if it was really swallowed muslin that came from Mrs. Duncan during the séance, it would have come out all sopping wet.

He said that he himself had a guide, an Egyptian. [14]

At a séance in Bootle in 1936 Mr. Dodd said he saw the living form of Helen, his first sweetheart aged 21. 'She stood and waved in exactly the same way she did when I took her home after the last social dance'. She came and stood before me, a living palpitating woman, the same hair I knew so well, dark and ruddy, the same eyes, hazel and shining with animation, the same pallor on her cheeks'. She spoke in the same cultured Scottish accent I knew so well'.

'Then there came out the living form of my grandfather. He was 6ft. 1in and very corpulent.

He looked round the rooms very critically until his eyes caught mine.

He then strode across the room put out his hand and grasped mine saying: 'I am very pleased to see you here in my native city'.

He held my hand so firmly that it ached for hours afterward. Later my grandfather walked back to the cabinet lifted his leg, and smacked his thigh and chest and said: "It's solid!"' [15]

The spirit of a woman named Mary who was beheaded 300 years ago tried to appear. [16]

'All Lies!' cry by medium. Police revelations do not shake followers. [17]

Humbug and Pest Says Police Chief [18]

Mrs. Duncan… collapsed moaning in the Old Bailey dock today when the Recorder, Sir Gerald Dodson, sentenced her to nine months imprisonment for her part in the Witchcraft Act conspiracy. 'Oh' I have done nothing!" she cried."Oh God!…Is there a God?" [19]

The press coverage focused mainly upon the experiences of the sitters rather than the specific issues relating to the case. At the time of the trial Spiritualists were highly suspicious about the true motives behind the case. They came to believe that the authorities had brought the case because Mrs. Duncan had brought through the form of a sailor who had drowned on a sunken British battleship, the HMS Barham. A sailor from the ship was brought through to his mother in a séance of Mrs. Duncan's in Portsmouth in 1941, at a time when the Navy had denied that it had been sunk. The Chief Constable referred to her disclosure about the sinking before the news had been made public Having news of their losses broadcast to the community created concern for the Navy at a time when secrecy was vital for the military effort.

Meanwhile in the other trial in Court No. 1 a sensational development had occurred. Loughans accused Chief Constable West of trying to frame him. According to Loughans, Chief Constable West had had a conversation with him where he admitted knowing that he had not done this murder but as it had gone too far he could not stop it. He said that West had told him it had to go the whole way. Loughans also said Det. Thayne of the Portsmouth police had also told him that he knew he had not done this murder.

Loughans went on to say that he had been taken to the scene of the murder and asked to go and look through the window in an attempt to get him to leave his finger prints on it. He also said he was given opportunities to escape by the detective with him, who he knew had a loaded revolver with him.

Loughans was found not guilty after the forensic evidence showed that the victim had been strangled by the murderer's right hand. Maude called an eminent pathologist who testified that his opinion Loughans could not have strangled Mrs. Robinson because he had a deformed right hand. Loughans' fingers on his right hand had been torn away after an accident as a youth and it could not fit around a neck. Loughans also had an alibi as four witnesses came forward who remembered talking to him in Warren Street underground air raid shelter in London at the time of the murder.[6]

The evidence points to the fact that Chief Constable West knew Loughans was probably innocent and that Maude would produce evidence to get him off. It was apparently helpful for Maude to have some time away from the court room, so he left some of the work to his junior counsel Elam. A relatively easy murder trial starting 5 days into the Duncan trial, where the outcome was assured suited him, especially as Chief Constable West in the view of the defendant apparently shared his view with regards his client's innocence.

After the Helen Duncan trial Loseby appealed on several grounds including the bias of Recorder Dodson. He argued that Lt. Worth had given a distorted picture and that he could be proved to have spoken falsely on every material point. He also submitted that the verdict of the jury was so much against the weight of the evidence and that the refusal of the Recorder to allow a demonstration of her mediumship was a denial of justice of the 'blackest kind'. The Appeal failed and Mr. Loseby was criticised within the Spiritualist movement for the way he conducted the case.

The Spiritualists also felt they were under attack from the police as police forces and local councils, such as the Surrey Police Force and Altrincham Council took action against meetings, churches and mediums after the conviction. Certainly their fears were founded as letters from the secretary of the

Magic Circle to Harry Price at the time of Helen Duncan's arrest in January 1944 show Scotland Yard were actively trying to gain prosecutions against other mediums. They were liasing with members of the Magic Circle to gather evidence and the executive of the Magic Circle was organising their local groups to trail particular mediums in order to assist the police to bring prosecutions.

Helen was pilloried in the press and sent to Holloway Prison. After her release she announced that was not going to sit again as a medium but some while later she gradually started working and resumed conducting her seances in between bouts of illness, first in Scotland and then around the country. The SNU who had organised the defence fund wanted to take charge of Helen's seances but when she refused they took away her certificate in 1945.

Eleven years later in 1956 the City Police in Nottingham raided another of her seances and like Edinburgh and Portsmouth someone jumped on the figures in an attempt to gain evidence of fraud. Two policemen and two policewomen had gained access posing as sitters. A ring on the doorbell signalled three of them to rush forward from the second row. They rushed forward with torches; tore down the curtains and two policewomen grabbed Helen and started to search her. One policeman stood on a chair, took photographs and then tried to switch on the light after which he rushed to the door. The police, who had been let into the house, rushed into the room. Again, they failed to find any cheesecloth, but on this occasion, the ectoplasm went back into Helen's body, as the Spiritualists had feared would happen in Portsmouth 1944. Mrs. Duncan, who was a diabetic, had a heart condition, was in deep shock and the doctor attending her, said she was 'very ill'. She had a large saucer sized burn on her breast and a larger one on her stomach. She died a month or so on the 6th of December aged 59 years after being in hospitalised in Edinburgh. Spiritualists claimed she died because of the injuries she received at the hands of the police.

On hearing of Mrs. Duncan's death Charles Loseby declared that 'Helen Duncan was murdered'. His statement appeared as headlines. He said any person who by gross negligence accelerates the death of another is guilty of murder. At Helen's cremation Rev. Thomas Jeffrey, a Church of Scotland minister described her as 'Scotland's Joan of Arc'. She was viewed as a modern day martyr by Spiritualists who had been persecuted by the authorities and eventually killed by them. If her mediumship was genuine, then clearly this claim is accurate.

Continuing My Research

As I continued my research into the Helen Duncan trial I was surprised at the headlines from the Psychic World newspaper that read: Mediums Declare "We Demand Redress For Helen Duncan's 'Murder'". James McQuarrie and Michael Colmer, the Assistant Editor of the 'Psychic World' newspaper had begun a campaign to get a pardon for Helen Duncan. In the article which outlined the case against her they appealed to radio and television researchers and production companies to consider it. It gave James' address, which I had visited a few weeks earlier in Iford, Bradford upon Avon. James and Michael had set up a pardon fund and a web-site to publicise their campaign.

During this time I was busily conducting research into the trial and going to Portsmouth to talk to relatives of those involved. Unusual incidents continued to happen. I visited Alan Crossley in Runcorn, the author of a book on Helen Duncan and someone I have met before from the Noah's Ark Society. He had known Mrs. Duncan and he was a respected medium himself. He described his experiences with Mrs. Duncan and outlined her story to me. Like other Spiritualists, he was convinced that the government conspired against Helen Duncan because she was a security risk. He described how she had brought through a sailor from a sunken warship the HMS Barham in 1941, when the authorities were trying to keep it a secret. Quite unexpectedly midway during our discussion Alan said 'hold on a moment some spirits are here'. After a moment or two of silence he went on to tell me they (the spirits) are telling you not to have anything to do with a particular film company or a certain person with regard to the film. After some thought I said 'I think I know what they may be referring to' and said that I did not intend to but that I would keep it in mind. They replied through Alan: 'good, we didn't think you would, but we wanted to make sure because we don't want you associated with these people if they contact you'! As you can imagine such an experience reinforced my belief that I had truly been commissioned by the spirit world to make the film they wanted, in the way they wanted!

I followed up another contact James had given me, Helen Dunne a Scottish medium who had been running a Campaign to get Helen a pardon. She was in the process of getting the Criminal Cases Review Commission to reconsider the case. Helen Dunne was a charming woman who had tirelessly and almost single-handedly tried over many years to raise the issue of Helen Duncan's case and get the authorities to pardon her. She told me that Helen had come through her for several years, which Alan Crossley independently confirmed. I was shocked when she told me she had been told of plans for a film almost a year before from the spirit world. She told me she had been told that the spirit world intended to materialise people who would talk to camera in order to set the record straight.

When I returned to London I started to look back at the other messages I had received over the previous year, that may have related to Helen Duncan and to Portsmouth, where the raid took place. I looked through my research note book and saw that in July of the previous year at Wood Green Spiritualist Church, the medium Michael Lennon gave me a message saying I would be studying a murder. He told me the spirits were saying 'Go to Portsmouth. You know why. Go to Portsmouth'. I did not know why but it seemed to tie into the proposal I'd now been given, as much of the activity centred on the city. I was also spending time trying to discover the link between the Portsmouth case and the Nottingham raid twelve years later.

I also had stored away in my home a portrait I had received from the well-known psychic artist Tony Katz, in which he had referred to the person who wanted me to have their portrait. When drawing the portrait he clairvoyantly picked up a message that referred to Portsmouth and Albert. Tony had made this portrait for me some seven months before I had met James and the Helen Duncan project had ever been mentioned. He drew it when I attended a demonstration of psychic art at Finchley Spiritualist Church although I did not recognise the man in the portrait. I had always wondered who this man was. It seemed strange that 7 months later I should be researching incidents that were centred on the city that were associated with this person. I also remembered that Albert was also the name of the spirit guide of Helen Duncan. Possibly this person had some involvement in the Helen Duncan case.

I checked other messages I had received and made a note of one from an outstanding medium Jackie Jenkins. She had given me the name Phyllis Davies. The name meant nothing to me but my friend Dilys Davies a psychologist from Wales. I asked whether it was her. 'No' replied the medium she (the spirit) is saying Phyllis Davies from Northampton. This name remained with me because it was similar to my friend's name. As I spent many hours in the Colindale Newspaper library in London reading the press coverage of the trial, suddenly to my complete surprise I spotted a familiar name in a 1944 April edition of the Daily Mail . Below the headline 'A Maid Saw Through Mrs. Duncan's Claim to be a Medium – Faith Racketeer', was printed 'by Phyllis Davies'. This was the same name I had been given months earlier, which I could not then place. Was it a coincidence? I decided to trace details of her through the NUJ and found that Phyllis had died a month after I had received the portrait of the unknown man. The only other information I had of her from the medium was a connection with Northampton. I eventually got Phyllis Davies' death certificate and found that she had indeed lived in Northampton at the time of her death. Had Phyllis Davies genuinely tried to make contact with me through a medium, knowing I would be researching the Helen Duncan trial and reading her work?

I wrote to James McQuarrie to let him know how my research was progressing and that I had met Helen Dunne. I informed him that she had confirmed the communication that he had given that a film had been planned about Helen Duncan, that she had told me that she had learned of it apparently from the spirit world. I reminded him about the message he had given me to go away, make that film and then return to the group. Having heard that he was talking to broadcasters about making a film, I requested that he ask the guides to clarify the situation so their intentions were not compromised. I was concerned that we should not do anything that might jeopardise the plans of the 'White Brotherhood' that he communicated to me.

As I researched the case, my ideas about a possible film started to take shape. The priority one has when researching a film is to think creatively about its structure. Anxiety seems to grip me as a director until a structure falls into place. Considering the subject, I realised that the truly profound question at the heart of the case was not whether a conspiracy had taken place, but was Helen Duncan's mediumship genuine. Admission of a government conspiracy does not prove Helen Duncan's innocence, only that the government tried to prevent information from being leaked, in order to protect the lives of our servicemen. However misguided it may have been, most members of the British public would understand that, at that critical time in the Second World War, in order to save the lives of Allied Servicemen and women, some action may have needed to be have been taken. The method used was highly questionable but the intentions of many of those involved were probably humane and patriotic.

The balance in wartime, as supporters of the government might argue, was between imprisonment for one woman for 9 months against risking the lives of possibly thousands of allied servicemen and thus possibly the future course of the war. It seemed clear to me that at that time, reading Harry Price's research bulletin, with his photographs of Mrs. Duncan and the London Spiritualist Alliance's final report, it would have convinced most intelligence officers reviewing the matter, that Helen Duncan was indeed a fraud. It was not my position to judge others but to tell the story and allow the audience to make up their own minds.

Spiritualists believe the information Helen received about the sinking of battleships came from the spirit world whilst sceptics maintain she was a spy or that prior to the seances she gained the information from the families of the deceased sailors. The only genuine way to show that Helen Duncan was not a fraud is to demonstrate that she was a genuine medium. Showing there was a government conspiracy does not prove she was a genuine medium, only that it is likely that she would not have been convicted in 1944 of being one. As a director, I preferred to also explore this added dimension of her genuineness because the public were very familiar with TV documentaries that show governments and intelligence services do underhand things in wartime or that the police sometimes wrongly charge people.

I reasoned, if Helen Duncan did truly allow people from the spirit world to communicate, then logically she must be alive in the spirit world today. I started to ask Spiritualists whether Helen Duncan had ever returned in seances since her death. They replied that she had many times. Alan Crossley told me about the wonderful evidence provided through Rita Goold's mediumship. Helen Dunne, the Scottish medium who has campaigned for Helen's pardon for over 8 years, told me she had brought her through several times. She also said she had been told from Helen that a film was planned in which she would come through and that other people involved in the conspiracy were also to communicate in it. She told me these people have not been allowed to progress in the spirit world until they put the record straight.

The film then started to tie up with my original interests to film physical mediumship. Might it be possible to make a film about the Helen Duncan case and in it interview Mrs. Duncan herself in a seance, precisely in the way hundreds of people attested that she had brought their loved ones through when she was alive! I also thought if true, this intriguing possibility would be a fitting tribute to her life and a poignant and powerful demonstration of the truth she espoused and eventually suffered for. It would demonstrate once and for all that she was not a fraud and it would be far superior to the usual investigative or historical documentary .

A mutual friend told me that James was now speaking to broadcast companies about making a documentary film about Helen Duncan. I spoke to him, raising the difficulties that his collaboration with other film companies would create for the film project which I had been asked to develop, through his mediumship. James offered to give me the money he had received for the pardon, but I declined, because I had been asked to make a film about Helen Duncan, not specifically to campaign for a pardon. I asked him to consult his guides and let me know what they said. All I wanted were the plans from the purported spirit world to be implemented.

It now seemed that the film project that the spirit world had wanted to develop was being placed in direct competition with the activities of the medium who had first given the message. From my point of view, James' initial message had been very encouraging and we should do our best to carry it out. It seemed a really good idea to bring together a group of physical mediums to work together. Also the Helen Duncan part of the message, asking that I go ahead and make a film, had received some independent confirmation from Helen Dunne and Alan Crossley. This seemed to confirm that this was a plan they wanted to undertake.

As the weeks went on the 'Helen Duncan Campaign' run by James and Michael Colmer through their organisation, the British Society of Paranormal Studies, had gained strength and had sparked a lot of press activity and support from within the Spiritualist community. National newspapers were now running the story with bold headlines and local radio stations around the country were interviewing the campaigners. ITN news ran a 5-minute news item and Radio 4 referred to the trial. Alan Crossley was also being interviewed by the print and broadcast press. The story had also reached foreign papers.

An announcement in the press by the writer and medium Dorothy Davies asked for information about Helen Duncan for an intended biography, which the writer believed was being directed by Helen herself. I contacted Dorothy and discovered that the press coverage was not completely accurate, as Dorothy was not convinced that Helen had truly communicated with her.

As I beavered away researching the case, a friend of mine, Val Lundquist started to phone me with messages about the project. She was as surprised as I was, saying she had got a message for me from the spirit world to do so and so e.g. seek publicity for the project etc. It seemed that I had become immersed in an adventure. I had to see it through, however challenging, dramatic and bizarre it had become. Whatever my personal reservations, it seemed clear from all the different messages I had received that the purported 'spirits' wanted me to carry on with the film research and development. Each time I did as I was asked it seemed I discovered quite revealing clues to the events that took place in 1944.

Soon I knew a broadcaster would decide which film they wanted. I offered my considered professional view to 'them' that in these circumstances the possibility of being able to get 'their' film commissioned by TV was very slim. I could not get any publicity because of the campaign and my status, as a freelancer was much weaker than the larger broadcast companies now attracted to the story. I was also being rushed into researching a complicated story and submitting a proposal that needed time. It would have been so much easier if I could have quietly researched the film without any interference. It was clear to me that the spirit 'commissioners' knew the type of film they wanted and I needed to have a clear picture of what that might be. As a film director wishing to film spirit phenomena one is necessarily dependent upon the 'spirit world' about what phenomena would be produced, who would appear and what would be said. I naturally needed to know their intentions for the film before I could submit a proposal to a broadcaster in an attempt to make it.

I had discovered new and very interesting information about the trial and some of the people involved. I had supposedly achieved a commission from the 'spirit world' but without any backing in 'this world'. What could I do?

I sat down and reviewed the situation and the many issues and difficulties I was facing. After much thought I concluded that if Helen Dunne was right and 'spirit' truly wanted Helen to materialise for the film then I could possibly avoid the difficulties that I faced in terms of competing with British TV production companies. If I was unsuccessful in getting the film commissioned in the UK I could go to a friend who is a feature director in Hollywood or other US producers in order to try and get US finance and put the film on the US cinema circuit. He had expressed an interest in this type of project when I saw him in

LA but he naturally wanted to see footage first. This would produce a far better quality image and film and hopefully avoid the issue of editorial control by English broadcast companies over such controversial material.

I also concluded that I needed to apply my working methodology again. I thought that if the spirit world wished to make a film about Helen Duncan then the person I needed to speak to was Helen herself! A short while later, as if by confirmation, Val contacted me and told me 'they' wanted me 'to register my interest' and so I put an ad in the press. What was I doing running around researching events in an effort to realise a film proposal from the 'spirit world' when I had little real idea about what I might be allowed to film and when the person I need to speak to may be alive in the spirit world? Presuming that James McQuarrie's, Helen Dunne's, Alan Crossley's and Val Lundquir's messages were genuine then I needed to speak to the Helen Duncan herself, to find out what was going on and what was the best way to proceed. Like all film directors I needed to talk to my subject and discover who and what I might film, before I could start to plan the film and submit a realistic proposal.

I duly composed a letter and sent it to the editor of Psychic News asking that it be published in the letters page. I explained in the letter that I was a documentary film director researching a film about Helen Duncan and I asked if a medium or circle had recently been bringing her through.

A week or so later to my surprise I was contacted by a circle in the north of England. I was told that Helen Duncan had been coming through for two months, telling the group that there is an important project that the spirit world wished to develop and she had asked for their help. Helen had promised she would bring a man to them. Upon seeing my advert they wondered whether I was the man! We agreed that I should travel to their circle to speak to Helen. The medium through whom these communications were being made was Mrs. Sandy Sinclair, a well-known Yorkshire medium who had also been invited to participate in this project, as the medium Mrs. Duncan wished to use in order to communicate in the film.

And so a relationship developed between Sandy, the medium, the circle, and the personality purporting to be Mrs. Duncan and myself. During this period I continued my research into the trial in preparation for the eventual film and sought ways to develop the project, not least by seeking evidence to demonstrate that the personality speaking through the medium was indeed Helen Duncan.

I conducted a lot of research into the case from the time I had first been asked to make a film from James McQuarrie's message. I had held back publishing these findings because I felt the greater good would be served if this material were integrated in the proposed film. In the meantime other journalists and writers have discovered some of this information and revealed parts of the story.

Unfortunately there was some long delay and several setbacks due to difficulties and family problems that prevented the medium from completing her physical mediumship development in the way that was planned. Eventually it was suggested that I should go ahead and publish the work I had undertaken for the project that relates to the trial and my research for the film. Accordingly a further book describing my research after I travelled to meet Sandy and the group is being prepared. I had been a film director without a film for several years as I waited to undertake my role. Hopefully Sandy's physical mediumship development will soon be complete, so the film project proposed by the 'White Brotherhood' can be made and everyone can see for themselves the truth, that is at the heart of the Helen Duncan case.

I have told the first part of the story of what occurred in my attempt to carry out the communication that I received from various mediums and the adventure that followed. I am confident that 'Helen' and the purported 'spirit world' in due course will clarify any points that may arise, when they can speak for themselves via Sandy's physical mediumship, for those Spiritualists and readers that may have questions that only they can answer. For those readers I am happy to wait until they have an opportunity to be heard.

CHAPTER ONE

Pre-production And Casting

Was it a government conspiracy?

As a documentary film director researching a film about Helen Duncan my primary focus was an examination of the proposition that there was a high level conspiracy to imprison her because she posed a security risk, having leaked secret information about the sinking of HMS Hood and HMS Barham. This is what Helen's family and friends and the Spiritualist community had claimed for many decades. My natural starting point then, is to first consider what would be the requirements necessary for the government to carry out such a conspiracy.

Certainly the security services, police, military and the judiciary would need to be involved along with prosecution witnesses willing to testify against Helen Duncan and her co-defendants. One might also need the judge to be involved to ensure that the trial goes the way the authorities desire. It seems if one has got all these powerful figures in position, the least of the conspirators concerns would be a jury, in this case six anonymous men and a woman who may or may not have been randomly selected. Such a trial would certainly attract public attention, so any conspiracy would necessarily need to take into account public reaction. Efforts would need to try to control the public's perception of the trial. If it can be shown that the authorities acted in such a way as to conspire against Mrs. Duncan, then it is clear that if the jury had been aware of this feature and this was the true reason for bringing about the prosecution, then she would not have been convicted. In order to examine the credibility of a conspiracy all these factors needed to be examined.

As the trial took place many years ago it is helpful to examine what some of those involved have had to say since and the evidence which showed that the prosecution represented an attempt by the state to imprison Helen Duncan because she disclosed secret information.

In a BBC Radio 4 programme titled: 'The Last Witchcraft Trial' broadcast in 1979,[1] Mr. Arthur Charles West OBE, the Chief Constable of Portsmouth, who oversaw the investigation against Mrs. Duncan and the other defendants, talked about the case. In the interview Mr. West confirmed the intention and direct involvement of the government and Admiralty in the prosecution, stating that they wanted Helen Duncan out of the way. Mr. West: 'Oh, they wanted her out of the way because she was a danger'. He confirmed that he knew the

Admiralty were quite satisfied about the course the Director of Public Prosecutions took, that they and the government did not want a song and dance made of the thing. He felt that the Admiralty emphasised too forcefully the fact that Mrs. Duncan had got hold of secret information.

Mr. West elaborates upon his statement made at the trial itself, confirming that she was a viewed as a security risk because in 1941 Mrs. Duncan had been 'reported as having transgressed the security laws'…'when she foretold the loss of one of His Majesty's ships before the fact was made public'. This sinking related to HMS Barham, which was sunk on November 25th 1941 but the government only made it public on January 28th 1942. Mr. West confirms that Mrs. Duncan was considered a serious security risk because once she had communicated this secret to 30 or so people, it was immediately broadcast throughout Portsmouth, at a time when the military authorities and government wanted to keep this information secret.

The difficulties the government faced for withholding the public announcement of the sinking of HMS Barham is confirmed in a confidential Home Office Police Appreciation Report of January 1942. Under 'Censorship & Publicity' it states that 'critical comments have been reported on the long delay in announcing the loss of HMS Barham, despite the official explanation'.

Brigadier Roy C. W. G. Firebrace, the then Head of Military Intelligence of the Scottish Command confirms the view that Mrs. Duncan was prosecuted because she leaked secrets. He revealed that Scotland Yard and he had discussed how she could be stopped from giving out 'authentic information'[2] and that the authorities regarded her as a somewhat dangerous person. Brigadier Firebrace's daughter Margot Walker confirmed this point in the Channel 4 documentary, 'Witch Hunt' broadcast in 1998, disclosing that Scotland Yard had consulted him about how to prevent these leaks of information.

Brigadier Roy Firebrace had been present at a séance conducted by Mrs. Duncan in Edinburgh in May 1941 when Albert, Mrs. Duncan's purported guide announced that a great British battleship had been sunk. He speedily left the séance and phoned the Admiralty. They assured him that nothing of the sort had occurred. Later he received a call confirming that HMS Hood had sunk earlier in the day. Mrs. Walker confirmed that her father had gone to the séance and he had reported the message that HMS Hood had sunk to the Admiralty, which made him consider that Mrs. Duncan was a splendid medium, 'splendid but dangerous'.

Henry Elam, the junior prosecuting counsel, later to become Judge Elam, also confirmed in the 1979 BBC Radio 4 programme that he believed it was the fact that Mrs. Duncan was a security risk which led to her prosecution. He admits however that the prosecution did not wish, and were very careful not to raise the security issue at the trial, although he believed this was the true reason for the prosecution being brought. This accords with Mr. West's statements that the Government and the Admiralty did not want the aspect of Mrs. Duncan being considered a security risk and the background relating to it being raised at the trial.

Another senior security officer in the government Abdy Collins CIE confirms this view. In two letters written in April and May 1944 to Harry Price at the National Laboratory of Psychical Research, Mrs. Molly Goldney refers to what she had been told by Mr. B. Abdy Collins CIE, an Assistant Secretary at the Ministry of Home Security (and a retired magistrate and Judge in India). Records show that Adby Collins' senior position allowed him to attend Security Executive Meetings during the war. Mrs. Molly Goldney states that Adbdy Collins told her that the Admiralty was 'behind the whole thing. Apparently a materialised form of a sailor informed a sitter, his mother, that he had been torpedoed. He happened to be on HMS Barham, and, in fact, this ship had been torpedoed and at that time it was imperative this should not be known. It left us without a major ship in the east Mediterranean and the Italian Navy did not know this'.

This information has since been confirmed from documents released following the war. British Intelligence knew from decrypted Enigma messages that the Germans did not know they had sunk HMS Barham and they confirmed the Italians were equally in the dark. This allowed the Mediterranean battle fleet precious time to reorganise, consequently it was essential that the news of the sinking was not disclosed to the British public.

Given the accurate and secret nature of Abdy Collins' information, it was clear that it could have only come from senior sources within the Government or the Military at the time. Abdy Collins' statement made in 1944 was further confirmed by Mr. West's and Judge Elam's accounts some 35 years later, that the reason for the prosecution was to deal with the security risk posed. Like Chief Constable West, Adby Collins refers to the role of the Admiralty in seeking to imprison Mrs. Duncan.

Accounts describe that the news of the sinking of HMS Barham spread throughout Portsmouth like wildfire after the séance, and it meant tragedy for many families in the Naval port. Apparently the mother of the sailor who was given this information, had checked with the Admiralty. She later received a visit from two senior officers from it, who questioned her about how she had come by this information.

Mr. Percy Wilson the then President of the Spiritualist National Union reports that immediately following the séance Maurice Barbanell, editor of the

Psychic News newspaper was informed, who in turn informed him. The following day Mr. Wilson, a Principal Assistant Secretary in the Ministry of War Transport recalls asking his colleagues whether they had heard of the sinking of HMS Barham, but none had.

Ernest W. Oaten the editor of the Two Worlds journal was also told of it at the time but security regulations prevented him from disclosing details. He later reported in the Two Worlds journal that Mrs. Duncan's guide Albert had repeated the statement about the sinking of HMS Barham throughout the week she had been in Portsmouth, during November 1941, which breached security regulations.

It is also worth noting that Molly Goldney refers to Abdy Collins saying the prosecution team tried to secretly negotiate with the defence counsel with regard to dropping the prosecution, if Mrs. Duncan were to agree to being locked up over the coming offensive. Such a suggestion implies that the Defence team was also fully aware of the security dimension to the case. In this case, any review of the conviction would necessarily need to seek evidence as to the contact and influence that the authorities had on the Defence team.

In summary, evidence exists that shows that the prosecution was instigated by the State and Military authorities to imprison Mrs. Duncan because she was a security risk. This evidence comes from the statements of a) Chief Constable of Portsmouth Police who mounted the police operation, oversaw the investigation and instituted proceedings against her b) an eminent judge Henry Elam who was a Prosecution Barrister in the case c) Brigadier Roy Firebrace the Head of Military Intelligence in Scotland who was asked by Scotland Yard for his help to devise an operation to stop Mrs. Duncan from giving out information and d) Mr. Adby Collins who as an Assistant Secretary at the Ministry of Home Security stated that this was the reason for the prosecution and gave a detailed account at the time of the circumstances involved which was confirmed later.

Given this situation, it is not surprising that authorities were particularly sensitive to public opinion surrounding this case. The Portsmouth police, the DPP and Home Office collected extensive press cuttings of the pre-trial hearings and the trial and referred to the public response in their correspondence. Regular cuttings were sent to the DPP and the press coverage of the pre-trial hearings was sent to prosecution barristers prior to the trial. With an active and vocal body of Spiritualists, and the controversial charging of a famous medium under the Witchcraft Act of 1735, the authorities closely monitored the public response and managed it the best they could.

Prosecuting Counsel: MI5 Officer and Captain in Military Intelligence at the War and Cabinet Office

Confirming the reasons given by Chief Constable West, Judge Elam, Brig. Firebrace and Abdy Collins CIE it has emerged that the Prosecuting Counsel assigned to the case was John Cyril Maude KC who was a senior MI5 officer who had been in charge of dealing with such matters as raised by Mrs. Duncan disclosing sensitive security information. John Maude had been in charge of MI5 'B' Division section B19, which dealt with tracking the source of rumours. During the war, and in the run up to D Day, the military authorities were very sensitive to rumours as they tried to keep their preparations secret. Chief Constables immediately reported matters of special security interest. Maude had been a Regional Security Liaison Officer (RSLO), part of his job was working closely with Regional Commissioners, local Army Commanders and Chief Constables. Nigel West in his book titled: 'MI5' lists John Maude's position within MI5 as head of B19 and a RSLO and it contains an interview with him about his MI5 work to do with tackling rumours and leaks.

During this time like other senior security service personnel, Maude was given the lowly title of a Temporary Civil Assistant to the General Staff of the War Office however in June 1940 has was given a commission in the Intelligence Corps, as Acting Major. The Army Lists two years later confirm that he held the rank of War Service Captain (& Temp. Major) in the Army Intelligence Corps during the time of the preparation of this affair. For official purposes, moreover from April 1941, for a year or so he was officially listed as only a Second Lieutenant. His obituary published in the Times on 20th August 1986 confirms this connection to the War Cabinet.

John Maude was put in charge of a section dealing with rumours and leakage of information in December 1939. Maude travelled extensively to investigate the source of leaks. In April 1940 this section was named B19 where Maude was assisted by Major J. C. Phipps and twenty months later it was renamed B.1.K. Major John Phipps was also a barrister and he had been Maude's junior prior to the war, where they developed a close personal friendship and successful working relationship. Phipps also worked as a RSLO for MI5.

In September 1939 MI5 appointed Colonel William Edward Hinchley-Cook responsible for advising upon the prosecution aspect of cases that had to be investigated primarily from the intelligence and security standpoint. In 1941 MI5 set up a legal section called S.L.B under Hinchley-Cooke and Lt. Col. Edward Cussen, a trained barrister, that liased with the DPP and armed services legal sections to ensure that intelligence and security investigations operated in such a way to prepare for prosecution. Hinchley-Cooke's S.L.B. section and Maude's sections worked closely to ensure enquiries were made that could lead to criminal proceedings under the Official Secrets Act 1911-1939 or Regulation

3 of the Defence (General) Regulations 1939. In preparation for D Day and the security threat it posed in terms of leakage's of its plans, in May 1943 B.1.K was absorbed into the S.L.B. section and called SLB2, while the prosecution section was known as S.L.B.1.

Nigel West regarded 'B' Division as the most important MI5 branch, being responsible for counter-espionage, counter sabotage and counter-subversion. It is clear that given his position within MI5 that John Maude and John Phipps would have been in contact with Chief Constable West in the course of his investigations over security breaches and when dealing with the risk Mrs. Duncan posed. Maude would have met Brig. Firebrace, in the course of his investigation of the leak of the information about HMS Hood in 1941, as Firebrace had raised the matter and had attended her seances. Army lists from 1942 reveal that while Maude was working for MI5 he had been listed as a War Service Captain in the Intelligence Corps. In October 1942 he was given the rank of Temporary Major in the Intelligence Corps, under Special Employment, based at the War Office. In 1942 he was also attached to the Offices of the War Cabinet. It is interesting to note that Maude was joined at the War Office by Firebrace, who had been moved from Scottish Command as a General Staff Officer 1st Grade. Firebrace was soon promoted to acting Brigadier in Military Intelligence undertaking Special Employment between September 1941 and January 1942.

Clearly, Arthur West as Chief Constable for Portsmouth would have been fully aware that Maude was a high level MI5 officer, as well as the security issues involved and any proposed action against Mrs. Duncan to deal with the risk posed. As West was a senior police officer in charge of the investigation which led to the security risk Mrs. Duncan posed being neutralised, then logically he must have known of, and been part of any plan the authorities put into action to remove her. Charging Helen Duncan under the Witchcraft Act allowed for such a prison sentence.

This action coincided with the preparation of the Allies for D Day, where the need for secrecy was of the utmost importance. Portsmouth and its surrounding area were crucial in the plans for D Day as thousands of troops were camped in the woods and forests of Hampshire and they intended to use the nearby beaches to launch the invasion. The Invasion HQ was located near Portsmouth. Mrs. Duncan's detainment and imprisonment for nine months removed a security risk for the six months up to D Day on the 6th of June 1944 and it also prevented her presence in the town that was central to the invasion. This rationale was indirectly confirmed in a statement attributed to Mr. Abdy Collins by Molly Goldney, that the authorities had privately tried to negotiate with the defence that Mrs. Duncan be locked up for six months until June 1944. There is no evidence to confirm that such an offer was ever made.

The involvement of John Maude in the Helen Duncan case brings the affair to the heart of the murky world of the security services. Maude had been a senior and well-respected MI5 officer, involved in running departments, developing and controlling agents, sometimes without the knowledge of his colleagues, as Guy Liddell's published diaries show. He had originated the idea of MI5 using domestic staff as agents and it raises the incidental question whether he got that idea from Harry Price's use of Mary McGinlay. He had been responsible for setting up the MI5 section responsible for dealing with leakages of information and no doubt he had considerable influence in developing the policy which the security services adopted in tackling this difficult problem.

Maude also had most powerful friends, such as Guy Liddell who was in charge of MI5's Counter Espionage 'B' Division, Lord Rothschild, MI5's advisor on sabotage and scientific issues and Maxwell Knight MI5's spymaster. He also had contacts throughout the security services. His senior status is demonstrated, when on his return from working for the MI5 in Washington, he went to work for the War Cabinet, under the title of acting Major then Captain in the Intelligence Corps.

It was accepted practice that in cases of leakage of information, before any proceedings, the case should be referred to the DPP, and they would seek advice through S.L.B section of the Security Services. A circular had been sent to all Chief Constables asking them to follow this practice. Although Mrs. Duncan had not been charged for leaking information, if this was the true reason for the prosecution then it is clear that the DPP would have played a central role. Guy Liddell confirms this to be the case in his diaries. He discloses that counter-intelligence officers Col. W. Edward Hinchley-Cooke and Lt. Col. Edward Cussen of S.L.B section investigated Helen Duncan's leak of the sinking of HMS Barham in Portsmouth after séance was held.

The story had reached the desk of the Director of MI5's 'B' Division that a drowned sailor named Syd had been recognised by several people in Mrs. Duncan's séance and he had said that he was one of the crew. The involvement of the S.L.B section demonstrates that legal action was being considered soon after the séance in Portsmouth in 1941.

Hinchley-Cooke was a veteran MI5 officer with over 30 years experience working in counter espionage. He was their top interrogator and MI5's silent observer at all pre-war spy and espionage cases and he occasionally gave evidence as their representative. Lt. Col. Cusson was later to become head of the section responsible for leaks in the run up to D Day in 1943, when it appears they put into operation a prosecution to prevent further leaks from Mrs. Duncan. The S.L.B. section worked closely with Gerald Paling the Assistant Director of the Public Prosecutions and First Legal Assistant at the Ministry of Home Security, in bringing the cases they had investigated to trial. It seems reasonable to assume that it was decided at the time that it was not possible or helpful to bring criminal proceedings against Mrs. Duncan for leaking information in a séance because the source of the information, the 'spirit world', was not supposed to exist but that some future action might have been planned by the MI5 officers involved in this work.

Correspondence between the Director of Public Prosecutions and Theo Mathew of the Home Office after the trial on 11th April 1944 supports the view of the vital role one such MI5 officer John Maude played. The DPP held John Maude personally responsible for taking the highly unusual step of using the Witchcraft Act to prosecute Mrs. Duncan and her co-defendants. The Director of Public Prosecutions wrote explaining that Maude KC and Elam were nominated by the Attorney General as prosecution counsel and that the usual instructions were sent to them to settle the Indictment for the purpose of the trial. He pointed out that it was Counsel, in the process of pursuing the affair that made the conspiracy to contravene the provisions of Section 4 of the Witchcraft Act 1735, the principal part of the indictment. He pointed out that, he generally left the decision of choosing the indictment in the hands of Counsel, and where a leader had been nominated, he would not ordinarily object to it.

The DPP's stated position that it was the Attorney General who nominated Maude and Elam as Counsel, by implication that Maude as leader had independently decided upon the indictment may be viewed as misleading, because it was the DDP themselves who asked the Attorney General to nominate Maude in the first place, at little over a month earlier on the 1st of March. When requesting Maude and Elam, they explained to the Attorney General that it was a 'case of some difficulty relating to alleged fraudulent Spiritualist Seances. The defence will strenuously contest the issue ...' They proposed Mr. Elam as junior and asked the Attorney General to consider nominating Maude 'as he was likely to handle this rather unusual case with ability'.

This discrepancy raises the question why the DPP were trying to play down their influence on the proceedings and choice of an MI5 officer as counsel. It will be observed that with Maude working for the War Cabinet at the time, his choice or acceptance by the Attorney General to handle the prosecution would be expected. This suggests that the DPP's request for Maude and Elam may have been influenced in the first place, from on high. This accords with the DPP's position that the Attorney General wanted Maude to handle the trial and Chief Constable West's statements in the BBC Radio 4 programme when he confirmed that the government was involved in the attempt to get her out of the way.

The DPP maintained their position, in response to the Home Office, when they tried to obtain information in order to answer the Churchill's questions about the affair. After the conviction, on the 3rd of April Prime Minister, Winston Churchill sent a personal minute asking questions about why the Witchcraft Act of 1735 was used in a modern court of Justice. He also asked what was the cost of the trial to the State, of bringing and maintaining witnesses in London for a fortnight. Churchill wrote 'the recorder was kept busy with all this obsolete tomfoolery, to the detriment of necessary work in the courts'.

In answer to the question about bringing the trial to London, Herbert Morrison was told by the Home Office that the Justices in Portsmouth were responsible for sending it to London, otherwise it had to wait a long time till the next Assizes. Also, as many of the witnesses lived in London, this was convenient for the defence. This answer to the Prime Minister again misrepresented the situation. Only eight witnesses came from London compared to 29 from the Portsmouth and the surrounding area. Indeed almost as many witnesses came from Scotland (seven) as came from London.

The true reasons for applying the Assize Relief Act 1889 that allowed the Justices in Portsmouth to commit the trial to the Old Bailey instead of being heard at a later Quarterly Sessions was sent by Mr. B. J. Tay, the Clerk of the Justices at Portsmouth to the Central Criminal Court. He claimed it had been done for a 'special reason' and there were 'special circumstances' that made the case 'unusually grave' and a difficult one. He explained that delay and inconvenience would result if it were left to the Quarter Session to be held later in the year. It is clear that Herbert Morrison did not refer to the actual reasons.

What were those 'special' 'unusually grave' and difficult reasons, and what inconvenience would ensue if a delay occurred in waiting for the Quarter Sessions that the Justices were taking into consideration when transferring the trial to the Old Bailey? This document strongly suggests that the Justices at Portsmouth were fully aware of the security issues involved in the case. This confirms Elam's admission that he also was aware of the security issues involved, which leads to the obvious conclusion that more senior members of the judiciary, including the DPP and the Recorder, must also have been aware and whose actions were influenced by these considerations, as the Justices had.

Malcolm Gaskill, the author, described when he viewed the file at the DPP that on it was written the word "SPECIAL". The question is raised as to why the DPP regarded Helen Duncan as special and different from other cases, when publicly they declared it was an everyday case of fraud. Publicly, the police and judiciary referred to the case as anything but special, it being a case of common fraud. Contrary to this public position, privately they referred to the 'special' and 'grave' circumstances involved. Given Arthur West and Henry Elam's later admissions, it seems clear that the special nature of the trial referred to its security aspects. As in reality, this feature affected the speed at which it was heard, it seems probable that this feature related to the security aspect of the trial. This was the impending allied invasion of mainland Europe, planned for June. If the jury had known that the prosecution was regarded as 'special', it would have allowed the defence to enquire what had made it so and what were the 'unusually grave' circumstances involved. This would have led to the security aspects of the trial being revealed.

The Director of Public Prosecutions asks Recorder Dodson to hear the case

In a Personal and Confidential letter from the Director of Public Prosecutions Tindal Atkinson to Recorder Gerald Dodson sent a week before the trial,[3] he asked Dodson to hear the case. Although the DPP had no right to make such a proposal, it would be considered quite improper for the prosecution to try and select the judge they wanted, this is what they did. They asked the person who they wanted to hear the case, just as they asked for the Prosecuting Counsel. They kept quiet about the latter and officially denied doing the former and claimed they knew nothing of the forthcoming indictment under the Witchcraft Act. Their attempt to distance themselves from the appointment, and the actions of Maude and Elam, whilst at the same time having a hand in all the major decisions, begs the question why they were acting covertly and what they actually knew. It seems clear that any conspiracy to imprison Mrs. Duncan by the state, as admitted, would need to involve the DPP and these irregularities and misrepresentations are consistent with such an act.

The personal background of the Recorder, Sir Gerald Dodson may give some insight into the decisions made at the time. The DPP's request for him to hear the case may have been no accident given that that had served in the Navy. In the First World War he served as a Lieutenant in the RVNR Hydrophone Service, tracking German submarines. He developed a very strong affinity with the men of the sea following his training on a Scottish trawler with ordinary seamen and in his time in the Navy. A trawler-man saved his life after a wave almost flung him overboard. He regarded seaman as courageous, bold and daring and he wrote the lyrics for the popular song 'The Fisherman of England' as a tribute to them. He later wrote in his memoirs[4] that the song applied equally to seamen in the Second World War.

Dodson personal affinity with seamen was demonstrated again in 1941. He appeared in a film to promote Savings, being the Chairman of a War Savings Committee in Surrey. He scripted a stirring speech soon after the sinking of a British battleship, which had led to a great loss of life. The release of the film suggests that his speech might have referred to HMS Barham, the actual ship that Mrs. Duncan's leak referred. In the film he paid tribute to the dead and delivered an earnest and solemn invitation to everyone to follow the example of sacrifice made by those heroes who had given their lives for their country.

Dodson also wrote some verses in tribute to the young men who fought in the Battle of Britain published in newspapers in 1940. If he had been aware of the security issues involved in the case, as the police, the DPP, the prosecution and defence were, then given his background it would have made him highly sympathetic to the prosecution in securing the conviction of Mrs. Duncan in order to protect the lives of Naval servicemen. This was a subject he had passionate feelings about. His reputation as having a complete knowledge of criminal law and practice gave him all the skills necessary to successfully conduct a trial under these circumstances.

The DPP's position on using the Witchcraft Act was later spelt out in a letter to the Law Office in September 1944. They pointed out the advantage of using the Witchcraft Act is that the prosecution, having proved a conjuration of spirits does not need to prove a deliberate intent to defraud which would be necessary in an ordinary common law misdemeanour. Maude made the same point when the appeal was heard. Certainly the DPP regarded the use of the Witchcraft Act as a perfect Act to prosecute Mrs. Duncan. The Witchcraft Act also had the advantage of giving heavier penalties that would allow the prosecution to imprison Mrs. Duncan for a period decided by the judge if convicted, compared to the Vagrancy Act, whose maximum penalty was only three months imprisonment. This suited the security aspects of the case. It is important to note that this was an exceptional case as it was one of the few occasions that the Witchcraft Act was used in a case of alleged fraud by a Spiritualist medium or any so-called psychic during the 20th century. It was not unique however, that is contrary to what some commentators have asserted.

The Involvement of Commander (Sp. Br.) Ian Fleming of Naval Intelligence

Chief Constable West and Ministry of Home Security officer Adby Collins assert that the Admiralty wanted Mrs. Duncan out of the way, for informing the public about the sinking of their ships. Richard Deacon in his book 'The Silent War' asserts that as Personal Assistant to Admiral Godfrey, the Director of Naval Intelligence (DNI), any reports of Mrs. Duncan leaking sensitive Naval information would have immediately come to the attention of Commander Ian Fleming (Special Branch). Given Ian Fleming's role in the Naval Intelligence Department (NID), Deacon believes he would have almost certainly had some input in the formulation of any proposed action to deal with it. Fleming was a senior figure in the intelligence services, knowing more and having more power than most of the senior offices in all the three services with whom he came into contact. He frequently represented Admiral Godfrey at interdepartmental meetings and he took over intelligence planning. He also had close contacts with MI6 and MI5 being responsible for the NID's relations with all sections of the secret intelligence services. He was also the NID liaison officer with the wartime heads of the Secret Service through the Joint Intelligence Committee. He acted as an intermediary with other branches of intelligence, whilst at the same time sorting out difficult situations. He had a reputation of coming up with many far fetched ideas but also being an unfailing source of brilliant constructive ideas and knowing how to apply them in a practical way.

Fleming had been specifically selected to fill the role that Claude Serocold had played in the NID as PA to Captain Reginald Hall, a former DNI. Serocold, a stockbroker at the same company as Fleming, had carried out all sorts of unofficial and unorthodox tasks for Hall with outstanding success, and they wanted Fleming to continue this role. Admiral Godfrey trusted Fleming, and so allowed him enormous scope to run operations, with a licence to pursue his own initiatives. Admiral Godfrey always insisted, however, that Fleming 'fix every detail down to the last button'. Fleming had a finger in everything being a skilled fixer, vigorous showman and 'war time executive par excellence'. Admiral Godfrey saw Fleming as the son he never had and after the war he paid him a tribute by saying that Fleming should have been the DNI and he, his Naval advisor. Many of the most effective war winning operations came from Fleming's inventive mind, even though he allowed others to take the credit.

He had a wide range of influential contacts in society, journalists and in the City, becoming someone who was educated at Eton and Sandhurst and whose grandfather, Robert Fleming, was a millionaire who owned a merchant bank and the Scottish American Investment Trust. His father Valentine was a land-owner, barrister, the Sheriff of Oxfordshire and popular MP, who died a war hero in the great war, when Ian was a child.

Fleming was friends with many of the most influential people in society, wining and dining them in London's exclusive restaurants. He was good friends with the press barons of Fleet Street, in particular Lord Kemsley and Lord Rothermere with whom he regularly played bridge and accompanied them on their yachts and was a frequent houseguest. Godfrey had paid close attention to establishing close relations with the press and held regular press conferences with the proprietors and head of news agencies, where a valuable exchange of information was created. Fleming took on this role being responsible within NID for day to day liaison with press proprietors and editors.

Consistent with Fleming's brief he soon established a reputation of carrying out espionage affairs outside his department and going over the heads of his immediate superiors. Ian Fleming was a man to initiate immediate action once a solution had been proposed to deal with an intelligence problem and any assessment of the Helen Duncan trial needs to seriously consider his role in the conspiracy, as it is most likely that he would have had a key role in determining how the security threat she posed was dealt with.

Fleming, like many other intelligence officers drew on his own experience in mounting operations. A close look at his background suggests the likely source of the idea to deal with the problem Helen Duncan posed. Fleming's first assignment and big break as a young correspondent for Reuters was to cover a show trial in Moscow in March 1933.

Six British engineers working for Metro Vickers were charged by Stalin's OGPU agents with espionage, wrecking and bribery. The arrests caused uproar in Britain and created a crisis for Anglo-Soviet relations. The trial became a major news event in Britain and generated considerable excitement, with the British government threatening a trade embargo on Soviet goods.

The seven day trial allowed Fleming to witness the operation of the State police at first hand, as witnesses came forward to give false evidence in order to convict their friends and colleagues. The pattern of Stalin's show trials as Fleming's biographer John Pearson describes were 'sudden arrests, the startling accusations, the fantastic confessions undisclosed until the prisoners appear before a military judge, whose major task in court was to demonstrate their guilt to the world'.

Although Fleming was the most inexperienced journalist there, he took up the challenge with all the vitality and imagination he could muster. Like the competitive sportsman he had been, he became obsessed with beating the other agencies. He knew that the British public had an insatiable appetite for news about the crisis and what he lacked in experience, he made up for by cabling a series of imaginative background stories prior to the trial and then sought to get the story of the events at the trial out before his competitors. He sent more frequent cables reporting the unfolding events at the trial than any other correspondent. This was no mean achievement given the censorship restrictions, bureaucratic obstacles and lack of lines available to correspondents. By using his ingenuity he displayed complete control of the press and he got the news of the verdicts back to Britain at such speed that his performance as a young journalist was complimented by the more senior seasoned correspondents covering the trial. He did not know it at the time but it was the brilliance he displayed as a journalist at the show trial that brought him to the attention of the British Security Service chiefs via the reports they received.

Two of the engineers were convicted to imprisonment for 2 and 3 years, three were deported and one acquitted. The trade reprisals threatened by the British government had caused Stalin to back down and within a couple of months as a result of a deal the two convicted men were freed. This experience of seeing first hand and reporting about how a show trial is conducted in its fine detail was a landmark in his life according to his friends and one of the few periods in his life that he fully engaged his personality in a complete and most satisfying way.

Despite his lack of journalistic experience Fleming had learnt the ability to carry millions of British readers with him as he charted the course of events prior to and as they unfolded during the trial in his reports. This ability would prove vital if he were to mount a successful operation to prosecute Mrs. Duncan. As the source of some of British Intelligence's most inventive and ingenious operations, calling upon his experience of witnessing one of Stalin's show trials gave a ready made solution to the risk posed by Mrs. Duncan. It may have been no accident that those in Naval Intelligence Department at the Admiralty in Room 39, who were likely to be behind the trial, chose this particular method once it was clear that it was not possible to use existing security regulations to silence her. One could not charge her with being a spy or of spreading gossip when the source of the information could only be identified as the spirit world, which was not supposed to exist.

Ian Fleming would also have had close links with John Maude at MI5 because Fleming was a fellow MI5 operative. Fleming had been recruited to MI5 by Major Maxwell Knight prior to the war and they were close friends. Max Knight and John Maude were also close MI5 colleagues. [5]

Knight was MI5's spymaster and had ran many agents from the mid 1920's and he had considerable influence with the intelligence hierarchy and personally with Churchill, through Desmond Morton, Churchill's personal assistant for intelligence and security matters. Knight effectively ran MI5's Espionage B Division along with Guy Liddell.

Knight ran B5(b) section that monitored political subversion from an office in Dophin Square. He had successfully used his agents to infiltrate the British Union of Fascists, the Communist Party and Trade Unions and he had contacts throughout the country. Knight, who had also served in the Navy in the same anti-submarine Hydrophone Service as did Recorder Dodson, although it is unknown whether they met while in the service.

One can get an idea of Fleming's and Knight's relationship because Maxwell Knight was known in his section as 'M' and Fleming based a good deal of the 'M' character in his James Bond films on him. In 1944 Knight ran B2 section that had responsibility for agents and he had also placed many 'part-time' agents in institutions as part of his MI5 network.

Ian Fleming had also been a member of the Society of Psychical Research; he had a great interest in astrology and the occult, which he drew upon in his intelligence work. Fleming's interest in astrology started in the mid 1930's through his friendship with Vanessa Hoffman, a musician who played in the Munich orchestra. She was a well respected friend and their relationship continued for many years. She introduced him to the idea of book collecting and although he never spoke much about it, he came to respect the subject of astrology and take it seriously.

The degree to which Fleming was an occultist himself is unclear but he always referred to his friend, the occultist and 'black magician' Aliester Crowley, as 'Master', and was friends with others involved in the occult, Denis Wheatley and Ellic Howe. Fleming's occult contacts may have come through Knight, who was an old friend of Wheatley, as they both shared a deep interest in the occult, had been cadets on HMS Worcester and both had written crime thrillers. They attended Crowley's magical ceremonies and both applied to Crowley as novices and were accepted as pupils. Wheatley's wife worked at MI5 and Knight had recruited Wheatley's stepson Bill Younger to MI5 as an agent, who was also interested in the occult. At his wife's suggestion Wheatley offered his services to the Ministry of Information in 1943. Wheatley became one of Churchill's special staff officers and an officer on the Future Operations Staff, where he worked with Fleming on planning intelligence operations. So Fleming like Knight was a good friend with Crowley and combined his personal interest with a view to the potential benefits for the security services.

Fleming and Knight worked closely together on a number of intelligence operations involving the occult. In some operations Fleming recruited the help of Crowley who had earlier acted as a spy for the British and the Americans, Dennis Wheatley and Louis de Wohl an astrologer. Knowing from Vanessa Hoffman that leading Nazi's were interested in and relied on astrological predictions and many were members of the occultist order, the Order of the Golden Dawn, Fleming conceived of an operation that fed back false horoscopes to them. Hess was purported to be Hilter's personal astrologer, and after the war Crowley reported that Hilter himself was a practising occultist. Fleming, not wanting to be considered a crank by his superiors, by-passed the NID and went to his friend Max Knight at MI5. They worked together in planning the operation. Accordingly Knight and Fleming started by using Louis de Wohl, who was a Major in the Psychological Warfare Department to chart the exact moments when Hilter might be open to 'ruses and feints'.

Fleming's idea was to set a trap and let it be known that the 'Link', a pro-German organisation whose leaders had been interned, had been driven underground and they had enough influential support to overthrow Churchill and negotiate peace with Germany. Fleming and Knight fed back this information to Hess via a Swiss astrologer who had infiltrated the occult circles frequented by Hess in Germany. At MI6's suggestion it was also made known that the Duke of Hamilton, who was working for the RAF in Scotland, was willing to meet Hess and act as a peace negotiator. Hess received further encouragement in January 1941 when he was informed that the planetary alignment on May 10 was a good portent for the meeting.

As part of this operation Fleming attended long complex occult rituals that Crowley conducted, along with two German officers in Ashdown Forest, Sussex in an effort to influence their decisions and lure Hess to Britain. Fleming fully participated in the ceremony probably wearing occult robes as most of those present. Fleming was a friend of Crowley, he used Crowley's expertise in astrology and magick to assist the operation.

Hess took the bait and his landing in May 1941 in Scotland was according to his biographer Richard Deacon, one of Fleming's outstanding achievements.

Although Fleming preferred that Crowley interview Hess, his superiors refused, even though interrogators were finding it difficult making sense of what Hess was telling them. Firebrace was appointed to the task. He shared Fleming's and Hess's interest and knowledge of astrology and the occult, having being tutored by a German astrologer himself. Fleming may well have known Firebrace as they were both in Moscow in 1939 when Fleming accompanied a trade mission as an MI5 agent masquerading as a Times journalist and Firebrace worked there as a Military Attaché. Firebrace would have provided the means by which Fleming and Knight could carry out their intention and use astrology and knowledge of the occult to help in the interrogation of Hess.

The idea of using the occult to entice Hess to Scotland would have found a sympathetic ear with Knight, because he had used a similar method to trap Anna Wolkoff the German spy in 1940. Knowing Wolkoff believed in the occult, he arranged for his agent a 'Miss Z' to get particularly close to her by proclaiming that she possessed special psychic abilities. She gave character readings to her and her friends on the basis of a specimen of handwriting. This allowed Knight to influence Wolkoff's relationships with others including his agents.[6] Fleming also used pendulum prediction, detection and radiesthetics in some of his other plots.

As a member of the SPR (Society of Psychical Research) Fleming would have been familiar with Harry Price's research report about Mrs. Duncan's mediumship, which presented evidence purporting to demonstrate that she was a fraud. Vice Admiral Hon Arthur Charles Strutt, the officer in charge of Dartmouth at the time and second son of the Baron of Rayleigh was also a senior figure within the SPR, also was available to give relevant advice. Equally Brig. Firebrace who liased with Scotland Yard to deal with Mrs. Duncan, would have been familiar with Harry Price's research, as he also had an active interest in psychic research and physical mediumship. Firebrace had actually attended one of Mrs. Duncan's seances in 1931 at the LSA. Both Fleming and Firebrace were to work as senior liaison officers within British Intelligence while Fleming was already an experienced MI5 operative and a close friend of Knight's.

Knight also regularly worked with John Maude, the prosecuting counsel, in investigating British fascists and in developing networks of agents. It seems probable that the idea of using a show trial would have come from Fleming as it bore all the characteristics of his showmanship and imagination to solve difficult problems, while he worked with Knight and Maude employing their skills in the planning, selection and development of the agents to carry it out. Their mutual interest in the occult (and astrology) suggests a close affinity between Fleming, Knight and Firebrace in their intelligence work and it is likely that they worked together in considering how best to deal with the security threat Mrs. Duncan posed.

In support of the involvement of Naval Intelligence in the conspiracy, there is evidence to show that Naval Special Branch made contact with Harry Price very soon after the sinking of HMS Barham with a view to requesting his help in getting the police to prosecute Mrs. Duncan. This confirms Firebrace's statements on the matter and Fleming's involvement.

Naval Special Branch officer Lieutenant James Sheffield Jones sent a letter to Harry Price, dated 18th December 1941, written within one month of the sinking of HMS Barham, that occurred on 25th November 1941. Confidential Naval Lists show that Lt. Jones was a Special Branch Officer. Naval documents further confirm that Lt. (Sp) Jones was, at the time of undertaking these actions, officially carrying out his duties for the Navy of an Executive nature on the Mainland. His letter acknowledges his earlier acquaintance with Harry Price. Price had publicly denounced Mrs. Duncan as a fraud on numerous occasions, had contributed evidence to the prosecution brought against her in Edinburgh in 1933 and was widely believed to have been behind this successful prosecution.

Lieutenant Jones' correspondence enclosed a letter he claimed to have received from Mrs. Marion Gray[7] purporting to be an outraged woman who had attended a Helen Duncan séance and felt she had been defrauded. Jones claimed Mrs. Gray's contact was through her son Surg. Lieut. Peter H. K. Gray, stationed with him on HMS St. Vincent, at Gosport. It turns out that Mrs. Gray was the wife of Colonel Mark Ker Gray DSO (formerly of the Royal Marines based in Portsmouth), and part of a well-established military family.

Mrs. Gray's letter confirms Jones' intention and refers to her determination to pursue a course of action that would lead the police being 'called in' to deal with Mrs. Duncan. Lt. Jones' own attitude towards Mrs. Duncan is made clear when he referred to her as 'a most repulsive and unpleasant woman as well as a fraud'. Such comments can only have been included if he knew Price shared these views. Mrs. Gray matched this views stating 'I went with another woman to a bedroom to search Mrs. D. A coarse and immensely fat woman, partly naked, was sitting on a chair smoking the fag end of a cigarette. The very sight revolted me'.

Jones asked Harry Price to send him any documents and information in connection to his investigation of Mrs. Duncan's mediumship, which he claimed he intended to pass on to Mrs. Gray. Mrs. Gray's correspondence with Price continued throughout the period of the government's nondisclosure of the sinking of the Barham.

Jones' letter shows the involvement of Naval Special Branch soon after the sinking of HMS Barham complaining about Mrs. Duncan and seeking expert advice and information in preparation to mount a police action against her, not in terms of the security threat she posed but in terms of fraud. These letters confirms Firebrace's statements that there was an intention to involve the police after Mrs. Duncan had been identified as the source of the leak of sensitive military information. The timing of Jones' actions also coincides with MI5's S.L.B. section officers investigating the matter with the intention to mount a prosecution. Seeking to charge Mrs. Duncan with fraud cleverly avoided any reference to the security aspects of the situation, as fraudsters are seldom associated with such matters. It should not be forgotten that another Naval Special Branch Officer Lt. Worth made the eventual complaint of fraud that led to the prosecution of Mrs. Duncan in 1944.

Further confirmation of the link between Naval Special Branch and Harry Price is demonstrated by the presence of a letter from Maurice Barbanell, Editor of the Psychic News newspaper to the same Mrs. Gray, dated 10th February 1942, which is contained in The Harry Price Collection sited at London University. This original letter was sent on to Harry Price presumably by Mrs. Gray, showing that information was being exchanged relating to the efforts involved in investigating Mrs. Duncan following the sinking of the warship and that these investigations continued into 1942.

When placed in the context of other letters, it confirms that Harry Price was actively helping the department of the Director of Prosecutions, the police and the prosecution lawyers in preparation for the magistrates hearing and Central Criminal Court trial in 1944. Many letters were exchanged between Price and Chief Constable West, referring to sending information, his research findings and photographic evidence in February and March 1944 after Helen Duncan's arrest. Harry Price also received correspondence from leading prosecution witness War Reserve Policeman Rupert Cross in early March (letter dated 6th March 1944) and whom he met, to brief him prior to the trial. The letter from Lt Jones shows that Harry Price was sending information that could assist Naval Special Branch from the time immediately after the sinking of HMS Barham in late 1941.

This evidence shows that a Naval Special Branch officer was involved in investigating Mrs. Duncan and seeking information about her soon after she had been reported for transgressing the security laws following the sinking of HMS Barham, as would be expected. It also shows that they may have used the mother of a fellow Naval officer as a way to gather information about Mrs. Duncan from various sources. This allowed them to conceal the true purpose and use of the information, in preparation for their attempt to prepare for the police to be called in or as Mr. West, the Chief Constable who brought the prosecution confirmed to 'get her out of the way'. It will be appreciated that these intentions were eventually realised following the police raid, trial, successful prosecution and subsequent imprisonment of Mrs. Duncan.

The role played by Lt. (Sp Br) Stanley Worth

Confidential Naval Lists show that the leading prosecution witness and the person responsible for the instigation of the police action and subsequent prosecution of Mrs. Duncan, Lieutenant Stanley Raymond Worth was also a serving Naval Special Branch Officer. He joined the Navy as a Sub. Lt in Naval Special Branch on the 4th of December 1941. This was shortly after HMS Barham was sank and a couple of weeks prior to Lt. Sheffield Jones' letter being sent to Harry Price, seeking help to call in the police to prosecute Mrs. Duncan. Worth was later stationed at HMS Excellent in Portsmouth 6 months later on 22nd of June 1942 and he was appointed Lieutenant (Sp Br) exactly a year after entering the service.

Lt. Worth became the person instrumental in establishing the case against Mrs. Duncan, as he was the leading prosecution witness whose testimony about the seances formed the basis of the Crown's case against her. This being the case, when the Chief Constable Arthur West asserts that the trial took place because government and Admiralty wanted Mrs. Duncan out of the way because she was a security risk, he is in reality referring to the instruments the authorities used to do so. These instruments are namely John Maude an MI5 officer and Captain in Military Intelligence attached to the Cabinet and War Offices, Lt. (Sp. Br.) Stanley Worth RNVR the principal prosecution witness and himself as Chief Constable, who was in charge of the police prosecution.

It will be recalled that Lt. Worth had attended ordinary Spiritualist meetings and had actually joined a mediumship development circle at the 'The Master's Temple' in Copnor Road in November 1943, the same place that Mrs. Duncan was to hold her seances. There he had got to know two of the defendants, Mr. & Mrs. Homer, and so gained access to the seances where the subsequent police raid took place. These activities including the actions of Lt. Worth throughout the period were referred to at the trial. This occurred at a time when Lt. Worth was officially referred to in confidential Naval documents as an officer qualified for and undertaking duties of an executive nature on shore for the Navy. Given Lt. Worth was on active duty for Naval Special Branch during this time it is understandable why the Government and Admiralty did not want a 'song and dance' made of the background to the security issues and the 'story of the trial' and why Judge Elam explained the prosecution were so careful not to raise it. Had they done so, it may have alerted the defence to investigate the backgrounds of the prosecution witnesses themselves, which would have shown at least one and possibly more were acting on the instructions of the military authorities and government departments against Mrs. Duncan and her co-defendants.

The Recorder in his Summing Up emphasised the critical importance of judging Lt. Worth as a witness. Addressing the jury he said: 'if you accept his evidence in the main, in substance, of course, it is absolutely fatal to this case so far as Mrs. Duncan is concerned'…'You have had an opportunity of seeing Worth and judging him. ….At one time I think he won even the counsel from the defence the tribute of being a wonderful witness. Whether he deserved that epithet is a matter entirely for you'.

The evidence shows that Lt. Worth was a serving Naval Officer engaged on duties for Naval Special Branch. This directly contradicts testimony he gave at the trial and in his sworn statements made prior to the Old Bailey trial when his role in the prosecution of the defendants was raised by Mr. Loseby, the Defence Counsel. In a signed Police Statement and the sworn statement signed by Lt. Worth (dated 29th Feb. 1944) he stated 'I have not had any connection of any kind with the Police Force here. I have not been paid for the part I played in this. I have received no money at all'. At the trial itself in answer to the question posed by Mr. Loseby, the Defence Counsel: 'Were you connected with the police force anywhere else (apart from Harlington where he had served as a Special Constable)' Worth answered 'No, Sir'.

Stanley Worth has since publicly contradicted this statement in an interview in the Channel 4 Secret History documentary entitled: 'Witch Hunt' where he admitted that he was, in fact, a close family friend of the Chief Constable of Portsmouth, Arthur West and his wife. Mr. Worth stated in an interview that he knew Arthur West and his wife although they never discussed the matter of Mrs. Duncan. Worth's statement in the programme clearly shows that he made a false statement at the trial. He did have a connection with the police in Portsmouth at the time. He had a good friendship with the leading police officer of Portsmouth.

A person could hardly have a more intimate connection with a police force at the time of a trial than being a good friend of the Chief Constable who is personally overseeing the investigation in which he is the leading prosecution witness. This demonstrates that he indeed had highly placed friends in the police and that he made false statements in his testimony.

If he had told the truth and informed the jury he was a friend of the Chief Constable then his testimony would have been discredited and the Chief Constable would certainly have been called to ascertain the nature of their relationship, why they had both kept it secret and how it had influenced the course of the prosecution. It is also difficult to believe that the matter of the arrest, charge and prosecution of Mrs. Duncan in which he was the chief Prosecution witness, was done without the collaboration of the Chief Constable and his staff. It was also the policy of the security services to inform the Chief Constable if an agent was working in their district. It is difficult to believe that the person instrumental in bringing the case against Mrs. Duncan, a known security risk, would not have discussed the matter with his friend the Chief Constable who knew of her via the security services. Given the evidence presented it can be reasonably assumed that Lt. (Sp) Worth and the Chief

Constable's close relationship was established for the purpose of the intended plan to 'get Mrs. Duncan out of the way'.

Furthermore Stanley Worth's sister Mrs. Madeleine Sylvia Pierson informed me that Lt. Worth had also befriended War Reserve Policeman Rupert Cross, the policeman who mounted the raid with him, during his visits to his bookshop in the war. Duncan Gaskell also reports it in his book 'Hellish Nell'. One might ask why Lt. Worth did not disclose that he was also good friends with WRC Cross but state he had had no connection 'of any kind' with the police in Portsmouth, prior to January 15th 1944. Cross was the policeman who attended the séance with Lt. Worth and who together co-ordinated the police's attempt to interrupt the séance, seize Mrs. Duncan, any incriminating evidence and signal the police raid, which led to Lt. Worth becoming the chief prosecution witness. So, contrary to Lt. Worth's claim that he no contact 'of any kind' with the police in Portsmouth, in fact he was a close friend of the Chief Constable and the other leading prosecution witness who mounted the raid with him, WRC Policeman Rupert Cross. Their friendship developed to such an extent that Lt. Worth eventually married Rupert Cross's sister-in-law, Alice, they became brothers-in-law and both later resettled in New Zealand.

The relationship between the two leading prosecution witnesses representing a policeman who was selected to mount the raid on Mrs. Duncan's séance with a former London Special policeman and Naval Special Branch Officer was never revealed to the jury. Given that the prosecution case rested critically on their combined testimony, as the Recorder observed in his summing up, and that their testimony differed significantly from the accounts of other witnesses on crucial points, their relationship and actions in preparation of the raid, subsequent hearings and trial is of crucial importance.

Lt. Worth also had a very close friendship with Detective Constable Reynolds who was one of the first officers to enter the séance room. He became Lt. Worth's best man when he married Rupert Cross's sister-in-law in Scotland.

These close relationships represents a completely different picture to the one given by Lt. Worth and the police at the trial. They led the jury to believe these witnesses had no prior contact and they were genuine people acting independently and brought together by the circumstances described by Lt. (Sp) Worth from the seances he attended from January 14th 1944 and not prior to that date. Lt. Worth stated he was an honest enquirer with a genuine interest in exploring Spiritualism who had gone to the police for the first time after experiencing a séance with Mrs. Duncan. He had gone to the police on Saturday the 15th of January, four days before the raid. In fact we now know he had had intimate contact with the policeman involved in the case well before January 1944.

If Lt. (Sp) Worth was carrying out orders for the Navy in his relation to Mrs. Duncan, as the Navy lists of the time clearly indicate, then it has crucial significance for the case. As a Serviceman employed by the state to convict Mrs. Duncan he cannot then be considered a member of public in the eyes of the court.

Conditions necessary to bring a prosecution not fulfilled

Although each case brought under the Vagrancy Act by the police depended upon its own circumstances, prior to November 1943, as 'a bottom line' police forces had been following a policy to prosecute impostors exploiting credulous members of the public. But they also took into account that this was complicated during the war by the claims of being in touch with missing relatives. Proceedings were usually taken under Section 4 of the Vagrancy Act of 1824 that stated: 'every person pretending or professing to tell fortunes or using subtle craft, means or device of palmistry or otherwise to deceive or impose on any of his Majesty's subjects shall be deemed a rogue and a vagabond and shall be liable to three months imprisonment'.

Confirming the view that it was the authorities who conspired to bring the prosecution about, there is evidence to show that the Portsmouth Police did not follow Home Office guide lines when bringing about this prosecution. This refers to the Home Office circular letter sent by Sir Frank Newsam to Chief Constables issued on the 29th of November 1943. Mrs. Duncan had been charged under section 4 of the Vagrancy Act of 1824 on the 19th January 1944. At the court hearing on the 25th of January, Defence Counsel Loseby rounded on the Portsmouth police, pointing out that they had followed precedent, as mediums had been treated with 'similar arrogance and harshness' by other police forces throughout the country. He went on to declare that their action had also broken the assurance made by the Home Secretary to a Spiritualist National Union deputation a few months earlier, not to use the Vagrancy Act with Spiritualist mediums. The press reported this matter and many Spiritualists felt persecuted and publicly objected to the prosecution of Mrs. Duncan on these grounds.

This came at a very bad time for the Home Secretary as Loseby had been part of the SNU deputation that had seen him. Loseby along with other members of the SNU deputation were in correspondence with him prior to the arrest and Loseby had in fact written to him about this subject on December 21st 1943 and was waiting for a reply.

The Hampshire Telegraph[8] quoted Loseby 'During the first months of the war the Home Secretary under his own signature had given the undertaking to persuade the police not to adopt the pre-trial machinery under Section 4 of the

Vagrancy Act in the trial of Spiritualist mediums'.

The chairman of the local county bench Sir Grimwood Mears K.C.I.E, immediately wrote to the Home Secretary[9] complaining about Loseby's comments at the hearing, that the Home Secretary had given the assurance that he would not use the Vagrancy Act against Spiritualist mediums, when the procedure has not been repealed.

The Home Office claimed Loseby's comments were without foundation and the police had acted properly because mounting a prosecution under this Act was permissible if a prior complaint had been received by members of the public, that the person was an impostor and money had been exchanged.

After Mrs. Duncan had been charged J. A. R. Pimlott Private Secretary to the Secretary of State of Home Affairs replied to Sir Grimwood Mears (on the 25th of February) confirming this position. He wrote 'The Secretary of State made some enquiries and found it was a common practice for police forces in cases of this kind to instigate proceedings only against persons whose activities have been the subject of complaint by members of the public, and where there is evidence that the person is an impostor and is taking money or other valuable consideration'. He resisted Sir Grimwood Mears' request to make a public statement to counter Loseby's statement. The Parliamentary Under Secretary of State Rt. Hon. Osbert Peake MP confirmed the official position three weeks before the trial[10] regarding the reasons for instigating proceedings using identical wording, when replying to Miss Eleanor Rathbone MP, who had written on behalf of an irate constituent.

A week after Sir Grimwood Mears' letter, Francis Graham-Harrison of the Home Office asked Arthur West the Chief Constable of Portsmouth for his observations. West reported that all the conditions had been met in the prosecution of Helen Duncan confirming that Helen Duncan's activities had been complained about and that there was clear evidence that she was taking money and was an impostor.

Only after the trial did confirmation come that these conditions also formally applied to the Witchcraft Act. In a Metropolitan Police document presented by A. G. Ralph Deputy Assistant Commissioner "A" Division dated 9th March 1945 it stated that the police should only institute proceedings against bogus mediums under the Vagrancy Act 1824 or under the Witchcraft Act 1735, when all the conditions are present.

The first condition so frequently cited to justify the proceedings stated that there has been complaint by member(s) of the public, the second was that there was evidence that the person was acting as an impostor and the third that the person is taking money or other valuable considerations. What is omitted from much of the correspondence is the full text of the second condition as specified in the Home Office circular. The SNU had made representations to the Home

Secretary arguing that their mediums had no intent to deceive and that the Vagrancy Act was hampering the administration of their church and psychical research. The condition relating to imposture (in response to the point raised by the SNU deputation) described by the Chief Constable of the Metropolitan Police on the 1st March 1945 and as being applicable at the time of Helen Duncan's arrest is as follows. It states that there must be evidence that the person is an impostor and is pretending to have powers, which he or she is conscious of not having. This follows the point made by the SNU that had been accepted by the Home Secretary and reflected in the Home Office circular to police forces that stated some mediums exercise their powers in good faith and without the intent to deceive. Unless there is evidence to show they are pretending to have powers they are conscious of not having then it doesn't bring these Spiritualistic activities within the scope of Section 4 of the Vagrancy Act. Clearly the Under Secretary of State declared 'not every medium is an impostor'. Certainly the DPP sought to play down the full extent of the second condition that the Home Secretary had referred to, as it raised a number of complicated issues. Mrs. Duncan believed that she was a medium, she advertised herself as such, made her living as a medium, had been tested by psychic investigators and journalists as being one on many occasions and satisfied thousands of people that she was one.

The Home Secretary Herbert Morrison referred to the same conditions contained in this circular to Chief Constables in answer to Churchill's question about why the Witchcraft Act was used. It seems clear that the Home Secretary applied his conditions to both the Vagrancy Act and the Witchcraft Act in 1944, in fact any prosecution against Spiritualist mediums undertaken by Chief Constables. Consequently Loseby had a point in complaining that charging Mrs. Duncan did appear to breach the suggestion given by the Home Office in its circular to police forces.

It is interesting that the DPP dropped the charge under the Vagrancy Act and that the full text of the circular relating to one being considered an 'impostor' was never quoted in correspondence to those who raised questions, including the Prime Minister. It may also explain why Maude introduced the Witchcraft Act without the apparent knowledge of the DPP.

Under the Witchcraft Act the prosecution did not have to prove a deliberate intent to defraud so the issue of knowingly being an impostor was neatly avoided. Introducing the Witchcraft Act at a very late stage also prevented representations from being made before the trial from Spiritualist bodies in the same way they had done over the initial use of the Vagrancy Act and similar unwelcome press coverage. Adopting the Witchcraft Act avoided those sensitive issues being raised that may have led to further political embarrassment for the government and accusations of religious persecution. For good measure Maude also charged the defendants under the Larceny Act and on three counts of effecting a public mischief contrary to common law.

The result of using the Witchcraft Act made Spiritualists feel doubly betrayed and persecuted by the Home Secretary, for not only did he breach his undertaking towards Spiritualist mediums under the Vagrancy Act but then the authorities replaced it with a far more stringent Act that also introduced notions of witchcraft and the occult to modern day Spiritualist practice.

It should be noted that The Witchcraft Act had been used at the Portsmouth Quarterly Assizes in 1939 to prosecute a gypsy named Bessie Birch for unlawfully pretending to exercise witchcraft by undertaking to remove a spell from a ring. Mrs. Birch took jewellery and money from her victim and was bound over for 2 years. Having used the Witchcraft Act it did not come as a complete surprise to those in Portsmouth that it should be used again and it set an important legal precedent.

It is interesting to speculate what would have occurred if Loseby had not complained about the use of the Vagrancy Act. Possibly Maude might not have been forced to consider what other legislation to charge Mrs. Duncan under. In this case the use of the Witchcraft Act may not have been intended but was used in response to the public objections made by Spiritualist to a medium being charged under the Vagrancy Act given the Home Secretary's suggestion to Chief Constables that Spiritualist mediums should not. Conviction under the Vagrancy Act would have removed Mrs. Duncan from circulation until after D Day and the Witchcraft Act allowed for the same. It appeared to hold many advantages in terms of securing a conviction and avoiding political embarrassment but it would also generate added public interest in the case which would need to be handled.

Another condition also seems to have been overlooked. Chief Constable West had claimed that Helen Duncan had been arrested after a complaint from a member of the public. In the letter that was sent from the Private Secretary of the Home Secretary, Frank Graham-Harrison to Chief Constable West on the 10th of February 1944, it refers to Sir Grimwood Mears statement made in a letter sent a week earlier.[8] It stated that Mr. West had told him the case had aroused much public interest from all over the country and Mr. West had based this statement on letters he had received. As the Home Secretary's attention had not previously been drawn to this case, he requested the facts of the case and West's observations. The file contains letters and police statements.

Chief Constable West forwarded a letter of complaint he had received from Mrs. Varina Taylor a schoolteacher from Southport dated the 1st March 1944 to Edward Robey, the Prosecuting Counsel at the DPP. It turns out that Mrs. Taylor was the wife of a serving police officer. He also sent a statement made by Mrs. Dorothy Evelyn Evans to Det. Insp. Ford of the Portsmouth police made on the following day. Mrs. Evans' complaint was about Llewellyn Rosser a medium who gave her a disputed message at the place of worship that Mrs. Duncan was eventually arrested at. Interestingly the DPP also forwarded a letter to the Home Office which they had received directly (dated 7th March 1944) complaining about Helen Duncan. It was from a former opera singer Harold Bealey of Paddington, who co-incidentally had long experience of performing in operas like Robey, Dodson and Gerald Paling the Assistant Director of Public Prosecutions. It is unknown however whether Bealey had connections with any of these men through opera. It is clear however from the complaints sent to the DPP and Home Office, that Chief Constable West (and the DPP) had not received complaints from the public prior to the arrest of Mrs. Duncan, apart from Lt. Worth who was a serving Naval Officer. The ones forwarded were all dated after the request for these letters was made to Chief Constable West and well after the comment he had made to Sir Grimwood Mears that he had received many letters. This suggests that West may have urgently sought letters of complaint against Mrs. Duncan that supported his position and that he could then forward to the Home Office.

The trial transcripts also confirm that the police action had been prompted solely upon the complaint they received from Lt. Worth made on the 15th of January 1944. At the trial, after outlining Mrs. Duncan's 1933 conviction, Mr. Maude asked Chief Constable West whether there had been any complaints since? West replied that no complaints had been received and that Mrs. Duncan had not been in trouble. Later Chief Constable West stated that Mrs. Duncan had transgressed the security laws, again in a Naval connection, 'when she foretold the loss of one of His Majesty's ships long before the fact was made public'. If Lt. (Sp) Worth was serving in the Armed Forces and carrying out duties in respect to dealing with a security problem presented by Mrs. Duncan, as Chief Constable West has stated, then Lt. (Sp) Worth cannot be regarded as a member of the public and by definition in this instance the prosecution would have no legal basis for being brought. Certainly Lt. Worth agreed that he had been acting under police instructions on the 19th, and he said at the trial that he had acted on police instructions on the 16th when he spoke to Mr. Homer, to falsely claim that his mother had confirmed information when she had not. Later he withdrew this statement.

One reason why the law acted on complaints by members of the public and not other instances was because prosecutions under the Witchcraft Act had been brought by individuals with a vested interest against mediums, such as Sir Alfred Harmsworth of the Daily Mail in 1904. The Daily Mail, through Harmsworth had forced a prosecution of a medium in order to generate a story to demonstrate a point they were publicising and sell more newspapers. This occurred even though no member of the public had made a complaint   against the psychic in question and the police and DPP did not wish to prosecute. This proviso prevented people or institutions from using the Act for their own interests as the Daily Mail had done through Sir Alfred Harmsworth. Even in 1904 the Witchcraft Act was being called 'old and obsolete'. In the Helen Duncan case the security considerations that led to the prosecution by Naval and police personnel acting under instructions can, like the Daily Mail, be seen as contravening this important condition. Also each of them did not act independently of the institution to which they belonged, they received instructions and were paid. It is interesting that Worth specifically referred to not being paid for his part in the arrest of Mrs. Duncan in his magistrates statement, as if he was aware of this point in law.

If the witnesses had openly and truthfully declared their knowledge that the chief prosecution witness was a close friend with the Chief Constable then the defence could have been able to question Worth further and the Chief Constable himself. The Chief Constable's assertions that the prosecution had been brought based upon complaint from a member of the public would be been questioned and his observations made to the DPP, restated. More accurately the Chief Constable of Portsmouth would have observed that the prosecution had been brought on the basis of the subject of complaint by 'my very good friend Stanley Worth'. He did not choose to inform the DPP or the court of his relationship with the leading prosecution witness, nor correct the false statement made by Lt. Worth in his testimony about his connections with the Portsmouth police. Such a fact would have completely undermined the prosecution, the truthfulness of the testimony of Lt. Worth and his own comments to the court after sentencing.

Significantly Lt. Worth, stated on oath at a pre-trial hearing and that he was not a spy for the police but 'spying on my own account'. Against the background of the active preparation for taking action against Mrs. Duncan by Naval Special Branch and MI5, the fact that Worth was a serving officer of that Branch engaged on active duty for the Navy, acting under their instructions and a close friend of Portsmouth Chief Constable then it clearly discredits his testimony and himself as an independent reputable witness. If he is acting under Special Orders as his status indicates then he cannot be considered to be a member of the public, upon which basis a prosecution can be brought. This is especially so given the admission by the Chief Constable that the trial took place because the government and Admiralty wanted Mrs. Duncan out of the way. The person who actually got her out of the way was West himself, one of his officers WRC Rupert Cross, and his friend Lt. (Sp Br) Worth aided by John Maude, the Prosecuting Counsel and MI5 officer who had been responsible for dealing with the type of security risk Mrs. Duncan posed. Had the jury and the defence counsel known these facts it is clear the defendants may well have been acquitted and probably the trial would never have started.

Lt. Worth's close contacts with the police and other senior officials

Given the role of Lt. Worth and Naval Special Branch in seeking to get the police called in and Brig. Firebrace's admission that Scotland Yard had been consulted and asked for its help, it is worthwhile noting Lt. Worth's own close personal relations with other senior police officers at a local and national level. Most significantly Lt. (Sp) Worth's uncle was Percy Worth MBE who was one of Britain's most senior police officers. He was the then senior Superintendent of the Metropolitan Police Criminal Investigation Department at Scotland Yard and was popularly known at the time as one of the 'big five'. It is likely that he would have known of any official contact between Scotland Yard with Brig. Firebrace of Military Intelligence. Lt (Sp) Worth's own father Leonard Raymond Worth was a long serving Metropolitan Police Sergeant who along with his uncle Thomas Vincent Worth, a Metropolitan Special Branch Officer (later Sub-Divisional Inspector) had served for some time in the Portsmouth Dockyards. This was during the time that the Metropolitan Police was responsible for security in the dockyards. Lt. Worth's other uncle Albert Stanley Worth had also been a Metropolitan Police Detective. Lt. Worth's family had serving metropolitan policemen and policewomen going back several generations before 1879. Prior to joining the Navy Lt. (Sp) Worth had been a Special Constable for 6 months in the Metropolitan Police in Harlington, London.

Worth's evidence at the trial about 'spying'

Knowing now that Lt. Worth had close connections with officers involved in the investigation prior to the 15th of January when he told the court he first went to the police, it throws new light on some of his testimony, which was challenged during the trial. At the trial itself much attention was paid to Lt. Worth's actions and statements leading to the police raid. Mr. Loseby cited instances where Lt. Worth's testimony contradicted itself and other witnesses.

Lt. Worth had been told during the séance that a sister had been born prematurely and had died. At the time Lt. Worth had told Mr. Homer that he had phoned his mother to check to see whether a sister had been born prematurely and she had confirmed this was correct. In fact Lt. Worth had not done so, and could not have done so, as his mother did not have a telephone and he later claimed she had not confirmed that a sister had been born prematurely. Lt. Worth explained himself for being untruthful to Mr. Homer, saying 'acting on police instructions I said that'. Later when challenged again to explain what point the police would have to do so, he asserted that the 'police could tell you that, sir…. And 'Whatever I may have caused I am not worrying'. When pressed further for a third time, Lt. Worth confirmed to the court that he had said what he is purported to have said.   Later in the trial he reversed his position and changed this testimony saying he had stated this untruth to Mr. Homer by his own free will 'in the interests of justice to allay any suspicion they (the defendants) might have of me'.   He changed his answer asserting that the statement was not made upon instructions of the police.

This demonstrates that Lt. Worth had made a material false statement on three occasions and then changed it. In the light of the current knowledge that he had very close links with the Chief Constable (and WRC Cross), who was bringing the prosecution, prior to meeting Mrs. Duncan, then acting on police instructions about what he did and said to the defendants accorded well with this relationship. Deceiving the defendants in order to gain their trust and to gain admission would necessarily have been called for in such circumstances and if the jury had known of this situation then the credibility of his testimony would have been severely diminished.

Lt. Worth also admitted he had lied to Mrs. Brown when she asked him how Surg. Lt. E. Fowler (a prosecution witness) had felt about the séance he had attended. He falsely stated 'No need to trouble about the doctor, he believes it'. Given Lt. Worth was an active Naval Special Branch Officer and a close friend of the Chief Constable, the jury would certainly have viewed these inconsistencies in his evidence as part of his activities needed to successfully carry out the conspiracy against Mrs. Duncan. Having admitted that he had made false statements to the defendants on the 16th of January 1944 when acting on police instructions, after falsely claiming this was the first time he had had any contact with the Portsmouth police, then it is reasonable to assume he had done the same on previous occasions, now it is known he had been in contact with the police prior to that date. He had no credible basis to deny such a possibility, given he has now admitted lying about these two central features of his evidence.

Naval Special Branch was composed of untrained civilians brought in to undertake Special Duties justified by their jobs and experience. By definition Lt. Worth was in Special Branch because he held qualifications for specific duties. A man with senior and very strong family connections with the police at Scotland Yard and Portsmouth and who himself was a Special Constable was well qualified to undertake the types of duties called for. That is closely and covertly collaborating with another police force in order to conspire to bring about the imprisonment of Mrs. Duncan who was the source of leaking sensitive information. It is also worth noting that intelligence officers were placed in RNVR Special Branch as Ian Fleming's Special Branch rank demonstrates.

In 1940 Admiral Godfrey (DNI) made a request that civilian Naval Intelligence officers be granted commissions in the RNVR (Special Branch) because as the war progressed many intelligence officers felt the need to get involved in the fighting services and were getting restless. Some highly trained intelligence personnel who were doing good work were leaving the NID to join the services and he asked the 2nd and 4th Sea Lords to agree to grant these gentlemen commissions in the R.N.V.R. (Special Branch). He argued that the Army and Air Force did so and that this took place in the First World War. It was Ian Fleming, his PA, who was personally charged with appointing RNVR officers to the Naval Intelligence Department. Had the defence known that Worth was in Naval Special Branch it would have been able to determine what those qualifications were, in the context of the security risks posed by the defendant.

Examination of Lt. Worth's status and connections in the light of existing knowledge would have necessarily meant disclosing and investigating his close contact with the police at Scotland Yard who had contacted Brig. Firebrace for advice about how Mrs. Duncan can be prevented from giving out security information. Brig. Firebrace confirmed after the war that Scotland Yard had targeted Mrs. Duncan. Disclosing Worth's close friendship with the Chief Constable of Portsmouth again would further allow the defence to investigate his relationship with Arthur West who had instigated the prosecution and publicly declared his view that she was a danger.

On being examined after the verdict and before sentencing he stated Mrs. Duncan had been reported on one occasion in 1941 as having 'transgressed the security laws, again in a Naval connection, when she foretold the loss of one of His majesty's ships long before the fact was made public. I can only describe this woman as an unmitigated humbug who can only be regarded as a pest to a certain section of society'. In the BBC Radio 4 interview he stated, 'Oh, they wanted her out of the way because she was a danger'. This information would have been crucial in revealing the preparations to create the circumstances necessary for the eventual successful prosecution of a civilian who was considered a danger and serious security risk. Investigation of the links of people close to Lt. Worth might also have allowed the Defence to trace the possible contacts between Worth's father, Leonard Raymond Worth, uncle Thomas Vincent Worth who had worked in the Portsmouth dockyards. This in turn would have allowed questioning about their contacts with Charles Burrell, William Lock and other key prosecution witnesses who had also worked in the same dockyards.

It is also of interest to note that WRC Rupert Cross, the other main prosecution witness had close personal links with the local judiciary. Apart from being a policeman and an active freemason in Portsmouth, his father, Conygham Cross was a long serving Justice of the Peace in the Naval port. We have seen above that documents suggest that the local judiciary were aware of the security aspects of the case. Cross' father-in-law, Ernest James Nichols was also an Admiralty Overseer. Consequently Worth and Cross who jointly carried out the raid had close personal ties with the police and the local judiciary who were to initially hear the case.

With Lt. Worth's uncle as one of Scotland Yard's most senior police officers at the time and military intelligence liasing with Scotland Yard about how Mrs. Duncan might be prevented from giving out information, this no doubt led to the need to recruit a Portsmouth police officer who was similarly reliable and trustworthy in terms of any action of this type. Had this information have been known it may have well supported the view of the jury that Lt. Worth and WRC Cross were not reliable witnesses. Lt. Worth certainly had close personal contacts with people in important positions that would aid the carrying out of sensitive intelligence work between the police and Navy, whilst giving the authorities the confidence that he could be trusted not to disclose the conspiracy. Clearly such evidence may have also spurred the defence to find out the role of the other Naval Officers like Petty Officer Foster who met up with Cross and Worth on the night of the raid.

It is clear that if the above evidence had been presented to the jury they might have understood more accurately the reasons for the prosecution and that the prosecution witnesses they thought were acting on their own account, were in fact acting and giving evidence on the instructions of the military authorities and state. In this regard there is some good reason to believe that they would reasonably be expected to reject the testimony of Lt. Worth viewing him as an unreliable witness (and Rupert Cross who accompanied him) and that his testimony was tainted. Certainly both these witnesses testimony differed significantly from many other witnesses present at the same séance and the Recorder in his Summing Up stated that the prosecution case really all focuses itself down upon the jury being satisfied as to Worth's and Cross's testimony. Their personal friendship developed on visits to the bookshop and the knowledge of Naval Special Branch's prior involvement may also have seriously questioned the validity of the other prosecution witnesses.

'The Oxford Leak'. The conspiracy nearly becomes unstuck.

The evidence indicates a conspiracy to prosecute Mrs. Duncan by the Navy and State, using Lt. Worth, is strongly supported by other events referred to at the trial. This involved a reported leak of information about the conspiracy in early January 1944.

Approximately two weeks prior to the police raid Mr. William Lock's son, Launcelot David Lock, placed a bet in Oxford in which he declared that in two weeks time the police will raid Mrs. Helen Duncan's forthcoming séance in Portsmouth. He bet that she will be charged and that a Naval Officer named Worth would be involved. Loseby raised this matter in court when cross-examining Lt. Worth and Mrs. Lock.

Launcelot Lock worked as a storeman at Morris Motors, Cowley in Oxford and lived in Ashton Road, Cowley with his wife Nora. Launcelot Lock had visited his father, William Lock (a prosecution witness) in Portsmouth with his wife for Christmas 1943 and returned to Oxford. There he placed the bet on January 3rd. with William James Spencer of 46 New Street, St. Abbey's, Oxford. Mr. Spencer was a foreman in charge of welding at Morris Motors making Army Reconnaissance vehicles. He was also a long serving member of the Spiritualist Church held at the Reform Club at New Inn Hall Street, Oxford, along with his wife, Marion. Mr. Spencer and his wife regularly held seances at their home and invited mediums from around the country to stay and demonstrate. Their son Mr. Eric Spencer informs me his mother Marion Spencer was a practising medium and that his father William was a Spiritualist healer.

This incident is reported in Mr. Loseby's notes (in the SPR Archive at Cambridge University) and by Richard Wilson in a letter to Donald West, after the trial. He had acted with his brother Geoffrey as unpaid members of the defence team who spoke to Mr. Spencer and took a signed statement from him. They refer to Mr. Lock being called John Lock, but in fact he was born Launcelot Lock. He was probably referred to as John by the defence team because he was known as 'Jack Lock'. The nickname of Jack was used throughout his life, and it originated because he had the reputation of being a 'Jack the lad'. Richard Wilson describes how he was told that a conversation took place at the works between Launcelot Lock and Mr. William Spencer while stocktaking was taking place. It was witnessed by Mr. Reginald C. White a welding charge hand of Dorridge, Lashford Lane, Dry Sandford near Oxford and Walter Frederick Surman who worked as a crane driver and who lived in Berrick Salome. Many people came to hear of the bet.

A conversation took place between Mr. Spencer and Mr. Lock, as they worked, and the subject of Spiritualism and materialisation came under discussion. The name of Helen Duncan was mentioned. Lock contended that she was a fraud. Spencer upon the other hand, who had sat with her, said that he knew she was genuine. When challenged Lock offered to bet Spencer that Mrs. Duncan would be summoned and convicted for fraud at Portsmouth, within the fortnight. Lock remarked that he knew that this was so, because a certain Mr. Worth whose name was not at this time known to Mr. Spencer, had joined the Spiritualist church three months previously with the intention of catching Mrs. Duncan. The bet was fixed at 5/-. Lock immediately realised he had said too much and despite further attempts from Spencer to get more information out of him, he said no more.

When the arrest of Mrs. Duncan was announced in the newspapers, Mr. Lock, in the person of Mr. Reginald White, endeavoured to collect the bet. It was pointed out, however, that Mrs. Duncan had not been convicted. After the arrest Mr. Spencer told Wilson that an Inspector McDougall showed him the report of the arrest in the 'Herald' newspaper.

Mr. Launcelot Lock was a man with a criminal record and had served a term of imprisonment. He had been prosecuted for stealing and receiving stolen goods and his own family describes how he also stole meat from Portsmouth Education Authority, when he was delivering as a butcher. He also had a conviction for receiving stolen goods, a silver milk jug and tiger skin rug. He was also convicted of stealing oats from a farm in Fareham where he was working as a rat catcher. He gave the oats to his father, William Lock to feed the chickens, ducks and sheep he kept. He and his brothers also worked as pedlars selling gold on doorsteps from door to door.

His wife Nora also confirmed in an interview that such an act as placing this bet was consistent with the nature of the man, being someone who would use any opportunity to make money. She explained: 'this is precisely the type of thing Lance would do, taking every opportunity to make money'. She continued: 'I only ever knew what was occurring when the police called at the home'. She described him as a 'tearaway' and that she never knew from one minute to the next where he was or what he was up to.

It is inconceivable that Launcelot Lock, a known petty criminal at the time, could have accurately predicted such an event as a police raid and the name of the Naval officer involved unless he had come to learn of the precise details of the conspiracy to 'get Mrs. Duncan out of the way'. This being the case it supports the conspiracy that Lt. Worth as Special Branch Officer was instrumental in organising the raid with the police. It also points to people who were to become prosecution witnesses being recruited well beforehand and that at least some of them knew of the plans of Lt. Worth and the police to raid Mrs. Duncan's séance and for her to be charged.

Although Mr. Loseby had a statement from Mr. William Spencer, the man who had accepted the bet and was ready to be called as a witness, Mr. Loseby chose not to call him. Such a failure raises the possibility that he had been influenced by the security issues involved, as Mrs. Goldney's letter suggests. It is quite possible that like the prosecution and the Justices at Portsmouth, Loseby was also aware of the security issues surrounding the case. Certainly one of his defence witnesses Abdy Collins asserted that the Admiralty was behind the prosecution and so it is likely Loseby was also aware of this background. He may have been caught in a dilemma because while fully exploring these issues may have been helpful to his clients it may have also alerted the enemy to the reasons behind the case being brought, which would not have been in the interests of the country. We can only guess at what private discussions took place between the parties on how the trial should be conducted.

At the trial Worth and Mrs.Lock claimed never to have heard of each other when Loseby cross-examined them on the matter of the leak. His decision not to proceed further by calling Mr. Spencer or cross-examining Mr. Lock on the matter suggests that the security issues involved may have inhibited him. With the allied invasion coming up there was obviously some security risk involved in exploring the conspiratorial and related security aspects of the case openly in such a high profile trial. Loseby was probably forced to tread a difficult path between defending his clients and risking revealing sensitive security matters in the process. He chose not to play the powerful cards that he held in his hand which would have certainly been detrimental to Stanley Worth and Naval Special Branch whatever the outcome of the trial. No wonder Loseby looked under enormous strain during the trial.

When knowledge of the bet became known after the arrest, Launcelot disappeared. People who enquired about his whereabouts were told he had gone to Africa. Unexpectedly a key witness who had disclosed details of a state conspiracy had left his job and had gone to Nigeria with a meat company at the height of war. At least this was the story his wife, Nora, had been told to explain her husband's sudden disappearance. Certainly if the jury had been given the opportunity to hear Mr. Spencer's testimony it would have clearly undermined Worth as a witness. It was inconceivable that men in Cowley, Oxfordshire had been told of Mrs. Duncan's arrest and Worth's involvement by the son of a prosecution witness unless it had been planned prior to the 3rd of January, which is something that Worth had denied. Loseby was to become highly suspicious of the incident involving William Lock's son and noted after the trial that apart from Cross and the Lock party, Worth received no support from the other witnesses.

It is worth noting that in the Channel 4 documentary about Helen Duncan, Richard Wilson claimed that the leak occurred in a pub in Portsmouth six months prior to the arrest of Mrs. Duncan, involving a Mr. Spencer. Wilson's hand written letter, made at the time, and Loseby's own notes about the trial, correct this more recent recollection.

Links between the prosecution witnesses

Clearly such evidence of a bet being placed that predicted future events castes serious doubt on the testimony and independence of the other prosecution witnesses, it being obvious that any conspiracy to imprison a person would require witnesses willing to give false evidence against the accused. Comparison of the trial transcripts, original police statements and sworn police court statements show that the strong links that existed between Charles Burrell and many of the other prosecution witnesses Mr. & Mrs. Lock, their daughter Ena Harris and Mrs. Violet Lonsdale Brosman were removed over the course of the proceedings by careful editing. Early statements clearly showed that prosecution witness Mr. Charles Burrell was instrumental in arranging for the majority of the prosecution witnesses to attend the seances at Copnor Road and that he had a significant influence over them with regard to psychic matters.

Mr. Burrell lived with Mrs. Lonsdale Brosman at 77 St. James Road, Portsmouth, yet when they are called to give evidence their relationship is not referred to or that they lived together at the same address. Mr. Burrell went to see Mrs. Duncan with his partner on the two occasions, the 17th and 18th of January and he confirmed this in his signed Police Statement. Burrell said that he went with her and Mr. & Mrs. Lock. However in his sworn February 29th statement and when under cross-examination at the trial he stated he only went with Mr. & Mrs. Lock. Examining the changes to the pre-trial statements of these witnesses show all links with Mrs. Lonsdale Brosman were edited out. Similarly Mrs. Lock in her police statement stated that on the evening of Tuesday 18th January 1944, she went again went to the Temple with her husband and Mr. Burrell and Violet Lonsdale Brosman, who she referred to as Mr. & Mrs. Burrell. But in her later sworn February 29th statement she also states that on 17th and 18th she went only with her husband and Mr. Burrell.

Charles Burrell visited the Lock family at 1 Stubbington Avenue on a weekly basis in order to give mediumship and trance messages to Mrs. Bessie Lock and her daughter Mrs. Ena Nichols Harris. Mrs. Dolores Callender was a child at the time and granddaughter of Mr. & Mrs. Lock and daughter of Mrs. Ena Harris. She confirms that such was her mother's and grandmother's faith in Charlie Burrell (who was a family friend), with regard mediumship matters, that 'if he (Charlie) declared Mrs. Duncan's mediumship to be fraudulent then they would unreservedly agree'. Mr. Burrell can then be said to have influence over four prosecution witnesses with regard such affairs (Mr. & Mrs. Lock, Mrs. Harris and his own partner Mrs. Lonsdale-Brosman). Furthermore and contrary to his testimony, he had brought three prosecution witnesses to Mrs. Duncan's séance, not two, the third person being his partner Mrs. Lonsdale-Brosman.

Mrs. Callender's recollections also contradict Mrs. Bessie Lock's testimony which asserted that Mr. Burrell did not come to the family weekly, only occasionally. Her granddaughter clearly remembers Charlie Burrell coming each week and it was something the women members of the family regularly looked forward to. Mr. Burrell's son Reginald Burrell also contradicts his father's statements. Charles Burrell stated in his witness statement that he was a Spiritualist medium who gave readings but that he never accepted money for them. His son states that getting money for clairvoyant readings was one way his father got money to supplement his income. Mr. Burrell's testimony was vital at the trial as quite unusually for a Spiritualist medium he was willing to give damning evidence against a fellow medium. Mrs. Callender also remembers that the family referred to the rumour that 'Mrs. Duncan was a German spy'.

She also recollected that the rumour continued that the 'ectoplasm was not real and that she was a fraud'.

Recorder Dodson was also seriously mistaken in his summing up, when emphasising the significance of Mr. William Lock's testimony against Mrs. Duncan.   Recorder Dodson stated: 'This is evidence of a man who is a sympathetic Spiritualist and himself a medium. He came to the conclusion that this demonstration on the 17th was not a genuine one. Mrs. Lock his wife, corroborates her husband'. In fact the Lock family confirm that William Lock was not only not a Spiritualist or a medium but he was a staunch sceptic, holding the view that all such matters to be a 'load of rubbish'. He had nothing to do with Charlie Burrell's weekly visits to his home to give Spiritualist or trance messages and he dismissed his wife's and daughter's interest. Given these facts, it is difficult to fathom how Recorder Dodson could have made such an error, unless he had got confused with Charles Burrell, but then he is not married to Mrs. Lock!

If the Recorder was referring to Mr. Burrell then his role in any conspiracy deserves particular focus. It is worthy to note that for a prosecution of fraud to occur money or other valuables need to be exchanged. Although Charles Burrell offered to pay everytime he attended, Mr. Homer declined to accept payment because he had helped him with the service. This probably also refers to the appreciation felt by the organisers knowing that Charles Burrell had been responsible for repeatedly bringing several paying sitters to the seances and meetings held over the previous few days.

The question also arises why William Lock, a pedlar, who had shown no interest in Spiritualist mediumship when presented weekly in his own home, should pay 12/6 on the 17th of January and attend again on the 18th of January and no doubt fund his wife's many visits. William Lock's sudden interest and expenditure on Spiritualism should be viewed critically in the context of the above information. It should not be forgotten that he is the most likely source of the leaked information given to his son, Launcelot, before the police raid, who tried to capitalise on it by placing a bet. His family recall that William Lock described himself as a wide-boy, and the available evidence points to him being involved in the case at the behest of Lt. Worth or someone working closely with him, as Lt. Worth's name was referred to as part of the bet. It is also of interest to note that Mrs. Lock and her daughter Ena Harris although not wealthy, repeatedly arranged to return to the meetings between the 17th and 19th of January as paying members, even though they were 'still not satisfied'. Mrs. Lonsdale Brosman's statement of the 9th of March 1944 indicates the degree of influence of Mr. Burrell had over her. Mrs. Lonsdale Brosman said that it was obvious to her that both 'shows' were a fake and that she was perfectly willing to give evidence to say so. She went on to say that she attended both meetings with Mr. Burrell, and was willing to corroborate what he says. If Mr. Burrell were to unexpectedly changed his testimony as he did, then Mrs. Brosman might become something of a liability and so need to be edited out. If all these facts had been correctly presented to the jury then the recruitment of witnesses for the prosecution could have been explored as well as the person who had arranged for them to attend the séances, Charles Burrell, and so undermined their status as reliable witnesses and their testimony.

The trial also failed to reveal that Mr. Burrell had also served in the Navy, having joined at the age of 14 in 1903 and trained at the Naval College in Greenwich. He had been such a handful as a child that his mother had sent him to the Navy in order to put him 'straight'. He went on to serve in the Navy from the age of 16, leaving in 1921 after 15 years service. He was receiving a Naval pension at the time of the trial. From the 1920's to 1939 he had also served as a member of the Territorial Army Coastal Defence Royal Artillery.

He had also worked since 1924 in Portsmouth dockyards, during the same time Lt. Worth's father Leonard Worth who had worked there from 1920 to 1927 as a policeman.[11] His uncle Thomas Worth had also worked there during this time as a Special Branch officer in the Metropolitan police.[12] William Lock another prosecution witness who was brought to the seances by Charles Burrell had also worked in the Portsmouth Naval dockyards as a boiler maker rivetter for many years. Knowledge of the fact that Charles Burrell, a long serving worker in the dockyards who may well know Lt. Worth's uncles who also worked at the same time and for many years in the same establishment, might have reduced the significance of his testimony. Cross-examination may also have demonstrated the links between this witness and Lt. Worth and family in his involvement in the preparartion of the raid and eventual prosecution of Mrs. Duncan.

Naturally it would also raise questions in their minds about any relationship between Lt. Worth and the other prosecution witnesses and whether any payment may have been made to them for acting in the way they did. Charles Burrell's son Mr. Reginald Burrell has told me that his father was quite poor, being on a small Naval pension of £2 3s 6d per week of which he had to give his wife, Gertrude, from whom he was separated at the time, £1/week. His financial circumstances were not helped with his reputation within the family as someone who spent money as soon as he received it. Reginald said in his opinion his father would have lied regarding the case if he had been offered money but would have also have been sympathetic to any request made by the authorities to aid the Navy regarding the security threat posed by Mrs. Duncan. Burrell's niece Joan Wellington said that he was considered as a rogue in the family and described him as the black sheep. He had a reputation for making up things, always telling stories, and having the 'gift of the gab'.

So two male prosecutions witnesses either described themselves or were described by their family as a 'wide-boy' and a 'rogue' who enjoyed making up stories.

Harry Price

The involvement of Harry Price by the Director of Public Prosecutions, the Portsmouth Police and Naval Special Branch in preparing the prosecution against Mrs. Duncan and contacting and briefing WRC Cross prior to the case is significant. Firstly I understand it is quite improper for the police to bring in experts to brief their own officers who are about to be called as leading prosecution witnesses. Moreover their officer was being briefed by a person who had earlier been approached by a Naval Special Branch officer to assist in calling the police in about Mrs. Duncan. If the jury had known about the above, then they would be aware that the witness had been coached and their testimony possibly unduly influenced. This is especially significant given the unusual nature of the circumstances in which the purported offences took place, a séance room, and the central question in the trial referred to the vital piece of evidence which the prosecution's case rested upon, but which the police had failed to find. That is, the material used to make up the forms emerging from the cabinet, in which Mrs. Duncan was sitting. It may also be significant given that witnesses at the séance reported WRC Cross being extremely shaken by the experience in the séance.

Harry Price was considered an expert who had studied Mrs. Duncan's mediumship and had concluded she was a fraud. Harry Price's contact and exchange of information with the Portsmouth Police which in turn was forwarded to the DPP from shortly after the police raid to the trial, is significant. It can be shown that he had a vital role at the trial in influencing the testimony of Cross, a layman in psychic matters, and the approach of John Maude, prosecuting Counsel. Significantly in his sworn statement and at the trial Cross refers to the substance making up the white figures ('ectoplasm') in exactly the same terms that Harry Price had described in his publications, as 'similar to butter muslin', even though he claimed to have held it for the briefest of moments.

This is interesting given the other lay witnesses' descriptions of the substance (prosecution and defence) are far less precise, describing 'a white mist in front' (Mr. Lock), 'a transparent sort of stuff (Mr. Gill), 'a white form', 'living snow' and many witnesses describing how it 'disappeared into the floor'. This is the first time this material has been mentioned at the trial. Immediately Prosecuting Counsel Maude referred to the substance in the same terms and from then on in the trial, he conducted his cross-examinations holding and presenting a piece of butter muslin. This clearly represents Harry Price's influence in getting Cross to refer to muslin, which then allowed the prosecuting counsel to utilise it in front of the jury. Maude stopped doing so after Hannen Swaffer, the journalist, attempted to swallow it in order to show how ridiculous Price's regurgitation theory was.

Harry Price was the psychic investigator who first asserted that the substance known as 'ectoplasm' in Spiritualist circles was, in the case of Mrs. Duncan's mediumship nothing other than butter muslin or cheesecloth. Harry Price sent his book, negatives and prints of photographs showing Mrs. Duncan being tested to Chief Constable West soon after the raid. One cannot dismiss the possibility that Harry Price's involvement with the DPP, police (and Navy) prior to the trial influenced the actions of the officers involved and their testimony in the carrying out of their conspiracy against Mrs. Duncan. This is in contrast to the other witnesses who describe the substance more vaguely and refer to unusual features of the substances making up the forms such as the texture of ectoplasm as being unlike butter muslin, but like silk or like touching a 'spider's web'. This point is relevant when considering that the prosecution had failed to find any incriminating muslin sheet and only had Cross's evidence supporting this quality of the material, having stated he had briefly held it. Mr. West confirmed in the BBC Radio interview that the latter point was the only 'concrete' evidence the prosecution had. It is clear that the testimony given about this vital piece of missing evidence had been coached by Harry Price. Loseby later disclosed that he had suspected that the prosecution witnesses had been coached.

Had the jury known Harry Price's involvement in preparing the prosecution team and its witnesses then they would have been allowed to consider whether testimony had been contaminated. This disclosure would also have allowed the jury to consider the evidence on which the prosecution based their case, this being the similarity between butter muslin and the substance that was used to create the forms at the séance. They would have been able to consider the views and research of many other scientists who had investigated Mrs. Duncan and criticised Harry Price's research. They may have been asked to consider how it is possible for the 'white forms' to appear at the séance as all the witnesses reported if butter muslin was in fact used, given that butter muslin under the red light used at the séance would appear pink or red! They may also have had the opportunity for the prosecution to explain how Mrs. Duncan could have produced forms with butter muslin when experiments with other scientists had shown forms had been produced when she and her hands had been tied down. It would also allow them to explain how the material could be similar to butter muslin if as Harry Price had claimed in his research reports that a sample he had taken and analysed of Mrs. Duncan's 'ectoplasm', had comprised of paper or an albumen type protein! How is it possible for paper or a substance similar to egg white to act in the way the witnesses described and the prosecution asserted?

The jury may also have been given an opportunity to consider other 'evidence' Harry Price had published of Mrs. Duncan's mediumship and sent to the police including photographs Mrs. Duncan taken while conducting her mediumship. Expert opinion has since claimed that some of the photographs published by Price appear faked and 'brushed' in. Significantly since the trial, investigators have discredited other published research of Price's, stating he had faked his findings (T. Hall in 'Search For Harry Price' 1978).

Harry Price's 'highly confidential' letter to Professor J. C. Flugel in May 1931[13] clearly describes a different picture and suggests Helen Duncan's mediumship was in fact genuine. In it Harry Price described a séance which he attended in good light with Mrs. Duncan, in which: 'the medium produced streams of 'teleplasm' (another term for ectoplasm), which trailed about the room and sometimes enveloped her'. This letter clearly contradicts the prosecution's version that Price himself had helped construct but which directly supports the evidence given by all the defence witnesses. How it is possible for streams of 'ectoplasm' or butter muslin or 'paper soaked in egg yoke' to trail about a room and even envelop a medium in good light unless something 'amazing' was occurring. This letter clearly suggests that the substance was doing this 'trailing' without any influence from the medium. Such interference would have been clearly visible and so completely contradicts any account, which suggests Mrs. Duncan created these figures or movements of ectoplasm fraudulently by going around a room with a sheet over her head.

Although the prosecution team used Harry Price to prepare its case, significantly Price did not want to be called as a witness. They did not present any evidence upon which their case was based nor inform the jury of his role. Had the jury been informed then they could have well considered WRC Cross's vital evidence to be tainted. It would also be interesting to ascertain how much the DPP paid Harry Price (WRC Cross and the other prosecution witnesses) for his assistance.

Lt. Worth's Naval Special Branch Unit

Chief Constable West and Abdy Collins both confirm that the Admiralty was instrumental in bringing about the prosecution of Mrs. Duncan. We know that Lt. Worth was the instrument the Navy used and so is there any evidence that his unit also played a part?

Naval lists of the time show that the day before the first séance on the 11th of January 1944 and eight days prior to the police raid on the 19th of January

1944 three newly appointed Special Branch officers arrived at Lt. Worth's unit on HMS Excellent. They were Acting Sub Lt.'s (Sp Br) Alan Maurice Hyman, Maxim Phelps Anderson and Alfred Terence Bishop. These three men were professional scriptwriters. Hyman called himself a film writer, Anderson a script technician and Bishop a writer director. Anderson and Bishop were also documentary film directors who had been transferred from making films for the Ministry of Information (MOI) to Worth's unit. Let us consider the possibility that Worth's Special Branch unit on HMS Excellent may have been engaged in the preparation of the case against Mrs. Duncan.

Of the new recruits Max Anderson was a distinguished documentary director who up to then had been directing films for the Realist Film Unit and MOI. His films include:

1938	'God's Chillun' GPO Film Unit (Editor)
1941	'Out of the Night' British Council/Realist Film Unit Film about welfare of blind in Britain's teaching of blind children in special schools and of blind people for careers
1942	'Victory Over Blindness' MOI & Realist Film Unit (work of St. Dunstans)
	'The Harvest Shall Come' MOI & Realist Film Unit (with John Slater)
	'Canadian In Britain' Canada Film Board Canadian soldiers training in Britain
1943	'Clamping Potatoes' MOI/Ministry of Agriculture/Realist Film Unit
	'Dustbin Parade' ICI Film/Realist Film Unit (Producer)
	'Words And Actions' Realist Film Unit/Gas Council. Application of democracy to everyday affairs and about the need for total co-operation in wartime
	'The Anaesthetic Series' ICI

Max Anderson was a leading director working for the Realist Film Unit and he had been described in the press in 1942 as one of the best documentary directors to emerge for many years. He also held a responsible position within the industry, being an active and senior trade unionist. He was a member of the General Council of the Association of Cine-Technicians (ACT) where he mixed with the other leading film-makers of the time. He would have known Terry Bishop, who had been the ACT representative at Merton Park Studios and the other filmmakers involved by this means as well as working in and being at the hub of the small film making community for many years and working for the MOI.

Max was a humanist and lifelong Communist so he was highly unsympathetic to mediums and tricksters seeking to exploit the grief of the families of servicemen. Although he was a communist he was regarded as a democrat, as his film 'Words And Actions' made in 1943 demonstrates. He was a highly respected man within the film industry and colleagues described him as a quiet, reserved man and most loyal friend. Edgar Anstey, the producer, described him as a 'scientific humanist'. After studying history at Downing College, Cambridge he entered the film industry and trained as a film editor and worked at the GPO Film Unit. He became an outstanding film director with a reputation of being meticulous, of knowing what he wanted and someone who never liked to compromise. His father was Stanley Anderson OBE, RA, RE the famous engraver, etcher and watercolour painter.

Alan Hyman was transferred to Lt. Worth's unit having served as a scriptwriter at the Royal Navy Film Section as a Leading Photographer based at HMS Vernon in Brighton. Hyman was a talented scriptwriter famous for adapting a successful British crime mystery movie 'The Arsenal Stadium Mystery' in 1940. He also had a feature film story credit for 'Trouble Ahead' aka 'Falling In Love' made in 1935. After the success of 'Falling In Love' he was given a contract to be a scriptwriter for Gaumont-British.

Hyman was essentially a scenario writer and adapter. He was someone with a vast experience within the film industry having been involved in the making of many feature films when working with his cousin Michael Balcon, the famous film producer of the day, who ran Gainsborough Pictures, Gaumont British and later Ealing Studios. His wide experience covered such a range of roles as continuity, assistant producing, scenario writing, PR while working with Balcon and he had also been involved with documentary production. He was also an experienced journalist having worked for the Daily Sketch and Sunday Graphic in the 1930's. He had experience of writing for the radio, with 'Spotlight On Tunesmiths' and 'Pioneers of Jazz' on the BBC and he wrote sketches and lyrics for war time Revue's in Marylebone, 'Funk-Hole Follies' in January 1940.

There are also possible links between these men and John Maude, the prosecution counsel. It is important to consider that at that time MI5 officers often drew colleagues from the social world they occupied and they were familiar with. Maude's social contacts were many and he frequently appeared in the Court Circular and Court and Social columns of The Times during the 1930's – 40's. Any examination of the proposition that there was a conspiracy against Mrs. Duncan would need to consider the possible links between other people who may have played a role and John Maude.

John Maude came from a highly distinguished theatrical dynasty the Maude's and Emery's. This included a rich theatrical and military family heritage, being descendants of Sir Conwallis Maude, 1st Viscount Hawarden, Hon. Francis Maude (Royal Navy), his grandfather was Captain Chas. H.

Maude (Army), grandmother the actress Winifred Emery. His father Cyril Maude was an actor and the manager of the Playhouse Theatre and later the Haymarket and his mother was the actress Winfred Emery. His sister Margery Maude better known as the actress Mrs. S. W. Burden, and other actresses Joan Price Maude and Elizabeth Maude and actor John Emery were cousins. His aunts and uncles were also distinguished actors including Charles Maude, John Emery, Georgina Waldron and Nancy Price, who also managed the Little Adelphi Theatre in the West End. John Emery a Hollywood star had recently divorced Tallulah Bankhead.

It is also worth noting that the other prosecuting counsel involved in the case Edward Robey was the son of George Robey, who had connections with several of these Special Branch officers. Incidentally George Robey had also come under criticism from Spiritualists nine years earlier in 1935. He was accused of making unnecessarily offensive references to Spiritualism in a BBC variety programme. Many Spiritualists objected and complained to the BBC. Robey had made humour about a table séance and the rapping that occurred and had introduced a character named Mr. Horace Mopper. Mr. Hannen Swaffer the journalist and avowed Spiritualist had taken offence and the BBC was forced to issue instructions to its variety department that in future no reference be made to Spiritualism. How this episode went down in the highly conservative Robey household can only be imagined.

The family background of the last of the new recruits Terry Bishop, like Alan Hyman's matched those of John Maude's. Alfred Terence Bishop known, as Terry Bishop was a leading young director who like Anderson had made many films for the MOI during the war. Bishop began his career in the film industry in 1932 at the age of 20. After working as a sound assistant he worked at Twickenham Studios in the scenario department when in 1939 he became a writer director, joining the Film Producers Guild. He moved to Merton Park Studios and became one of its leading documentary writer-directors known as a determined and highly competent documentary director and developing talent. His films included:

1941	'Kill That Rat' MOI & Ministry of Agriculture/Publicity
	'Steel Goes To Sea' British Council/Merton Park Studios (Scriptwriter)
1942	'Down Our Street' MOI & National Savings Committee/Merton Park Studios promoting the National Savings Committee
	'Western Isles' British Council/Merton Park Studios The story of Harris Tweed
1943	'More Eggs For Your Hens' MOI & Ministry of Agriculture /Merton Park Studios
	Jablo Wood Blade: Its Manufacture & Repair'

'Out of the Box'
'The Royal Mile Edinburgh'

Like Maude, Terry Bishop also came from a famous theatrical dynasty, the Bishop and Lohr's. His father was the distinguished actor George Harold Bishop who had also acted with George Robey (in the film 'The Rest Cure' 1923, who wrote and starred in it) the father of the Counsel acting in the prosecution for the DPP, Edward G. Robey. Bishop's grandfather had been the leading actor Alfred Bishop, his grandmother the actress Rose Egan, his uncle the actor Charles Bishop with leading actresses Marie Lohr and Jane Prinsep as cousins. He was also related to the leading actress Margaret Bannerman. His grandmother's side of the family listed famous actors. Like John Maude he also had theatrical managers in the family Anthony and Valentine Prinsep, Frank Egan and James Woulds further back. Marie Lohr and Anthony Leyland Prinsep had managed the Globe Theatre together from 1918 to 1927. His father George also produced a number of West End theatre productions. Terry Bishop changed his name from Alfred Terence Bishop to Terence Egan Bishop. He was remembered around that time as a lively congenial character who enjoyed a reputation for enjoying the company of women.

Alan Hyman also came from a very wealthy family who were also steeped in the London and international theatre scene and had relatives who were theatrical managers. Hyman's wealth came from his father who had been a stockbroker similar to Ian Fleming's family and it is well known that Naval Intelligence liked to recruit officers via city stockbroking contacts.

Like Fleming and Maude, Hyman and his family also appeared in the 'Court and Social' newspaper columns of the day. He loved the theatre himself and his two uncles were famous in that world. Sydney H. Hyman had been a famous London theatre agent, booking acts and actors throughout Britain and the Empire and in particular the music hall. He was also the sole booking manager for the Empire Theatre Company in South Africa, who was responsible for many thousands of English actors and actresses undertaking work there, including George Robey. Alan Hyman's other uncle was Edgar Hyman who had been the manager of the Empire Theatre of Varities in Johannesburg.

Within the small world of London theatre there is little doubt that Hyman's family had close contacts with the Robey's and the Maude's in the course of their business and social world, who in turn were well acquainted with the Bishops – Lohrs. Hyman had also been more personally involved in a film whilst at Gainsborough Pictures titled 'Marry Me' with George Robey in 1932. Hyman's wife's family had connections with the British Intelligence Service as her father Major James Carr Gypson had worked for them in Persia.

The links did not stop there. Alan Hyman's cousin Michael Balcon had worked with John Maude's father Cyril Maude when he produced the film 'Orders Is Orders' for British Gaumont in 1933, and Maude's cousin Joan Maude in 'Jew Suss' in 1934, when Hyman was working for the production studio.

Waiting to welcome the new recruits in Worth's Special Branch Unit on HMS Excellent was Lt. (Sp.) James Drever. He was a psychologist and teacher of philosopher, soon to be appointed Professor of Psychology at Edinburgh University in the summer of 1944 in succession of his father. Drever had been educated at the Royal High School Edinburgh, Univ. Edinburgh MA 1932 Hons Philosophy, MA Cambridge 1934 (Moral Science Tripos). Between 1934-8 he was a FRSA Assistant in the Dept. Philosophy in Edinburgh and from 1938-41 lecturer in Philosophy & Psychology Kings College, Newcastle. He had joined Naval Special Branch in July 1942 as a Sub Lt. (Sp Br) and by early September he was at HMS President at Middle Temple Lane undertaking duties for special and miscellaneous services whilst there. A month later he was promoted to Lieutenant (Sp Br) and he joined Worth at HMS Excellent a month later in December 1942. Eventually he became a Lieutenant Commander in Naval Special Branch. Being a psychologist this background would have been helpful in analyzing complex psychical research studies and in weighing up evidence that emerged from the type of demonstration that Mrs. Duncan was engaged in. If one were going to organise a conspiracy having a psychologist, teacher and researcher in philosophy would seem to be most advantageous. James Drever was also an arch sceptic. He stated his main duties related to the selection of personnel. Whether his role was related to the selection of personnel for the preparation for the Helen Duncan trial we do not know.

Drever's father was a most distinguished psychologist and a member of the Advisory Committee of Psychologists for Personnel Selection at the War Office. He had been the Professor of Psychology at Edinburgh University since 1931 and had been the President of the British Psychological Society from 1935-8.[14] One of his staff from his department at Edinburgh University Boris Semeonoff also worked at the War Office in personnel selection, selecting spies and secret agents. James Drever Jnr. had also been taught psychology by Professor Bartlett, a close family friend and who served on the same advisory committee in the War Office as his father.

So two Prosecuting Counsels John Maude and Robey and two Special Branch officers Terence Bishop and Alan Hyman brought to the unit about to be involved in a raid on Mrs. Duncan, interestingly all had rich family and theatrical traditions and connections in common. The other Special Branch officer Max Anderson was an experienced director and scriptwriter who had worked for the MOI and who had achieved some recent success that gave him the reputation of being one of Britain's leading documentary directors. He also held strong humanist views. One was the nephew of one of Scotland Yard's most senior policeman with police and family contacts in Portsmouth, Stanley Worth. Another was the son of a distinguished Professor of Psychology who worked with senior military figures at the War Office regarding selecting personnel and who was about to be made Professor of Psychology at Edinburgh University, Lt (Sp.) James Drever.

It seems clear that someone may have carefully selected the personnel who arrived at Worth's unit which was in the process of organising a raid on Mrs. Duncan. As the evidence also points to a MI5 officer and Intelligence Officer John Maude being instrumental in organising the prosecution and investigating leaks of information then links with him need to be considered. This is especially so as having a team of script writers and directors would seem essential if one were going to effectively manage a convincing trial. Any such trial would need to be presented to the public in the same way a successful fictional documentary film needed to be constructed and presented. The demands were the same. Realism, good writing, good direction, well rehearsed characters who know their lines and who can improvise when necessary. Certainly knowledge of the specific assignment of scriptwriters and in particular a successful crime mystery writer and journalist and two writers-directors to Stanley Worth's unit eight days prior to the raid would have allowed the defence to cross-examine the officers involved. In so doing it could be determined why they were sent to the unit, what special abilities and Special Orders they may have been obeying and what role they had in the affair.

Records show that Max Anderson left his director's job at the Realist Film Unit around November 1943[15] at the same time that Worth got involved with the activities of The Master's Temple Spiritualist Church in Portsmouth in preparation for the raid on Mrs. Duncan. This might indicate that Anderson was researching the viability of such an ambitious project and approaching the work in a similar way he would have tackled a documentary film. It should not be forgotten that following the great success of his film 'The Harvest Shall Come' in 1942 where he used actors in a most realistic way and setting, Max Anderson had been attributed with making a most significant step forward in film making at the time. His film had been 'the first genuine film story made with the documentary purpose and by documentary method'.[16]

Such a method fitted exactly with what was required in the operation to convict Mrs. Duncan in a realistic way, in order to remove any sign of a conspiracy and convince the public of the story that the prosecution, through Worth and Cross presented. A story had to told in a documentary way, and Anderson had successfully done so in film, so now all that was required was for the method to be applied to the trial.

Anderson, Bishop and Hyman were highly talented men with accomplished and well-respected work to their name. Two were suddenly taken from leading positions in the film industry in working for the Ministry of Information and the other the Naval Film Section and transplanted as Naval Special Branch Officers in Worth's unit the day after Mrs. Duncan had arrived in Portsmouth to start her engagement and eight days prior to the raid on her. Surely if the security services were to present a convincing show trial then a team of writers with documentary and drama experience was a necessary asset. These were men of the highest calibre. These men's work had been critically acclaimed and Anderson and Bishop were later to receive an Oscar in 1949 for best feature documentary they produced and directed together, 'Daybreak At Udi' for the Crown Film Unit. They also received a BAFTA in the same year.

Waiting for these three film-makers at HMS Excellent was another Naval Special Branch officer, the experienced director and scriptwriter Lt. (Sp Br) John Paddy Carstairs. Carstairs father had been the famous impersonator, actor and popular broadcaster Nelson Keys. Nelson Keys like the father's of both prosecution counsels Maude and Robey and Terry Bishop was a part of the theatre establishment and so had close contacts in the theatrical profession and film industry. He had also worked and appeared with Robey's father George Robey on numerous occasions at society gatherings, Maude's mother Winifred Emery and Bishop's cousin Marie Lohr in the theatre and films as far back as 1915 up to 1939.

Carstairs had joined the Royal Naval Film Section in the late summer of 1943 and worked at the small Royal Navy Film Unit on the base but as he was a distinguished director he was still involved with and worked on major British feature films, while serving at Excellent. It is unclear whether his status as a trusted and more accomplished director led him to have some role in the preparation and selection of this small scriptwriting and directing team that joined Worth's unit. It may have been the case but as he was a distinguished film director putting him in Worth's unit would have clearly drawn attention to itself. Certainly Carstairs knew the officers, because he said so in a tribute when Max Anderson died. Carstairs and Max Anderson also shared a mutual friend, the actor John Slater, who was Max's best man when he got married.

Carstairs had a close connection to Alan Hyman and his cousin Michael Balcon. Michael Balcon, the Head of Ealing Studios had produced three British propaganda films with John Paddy Carstairs. These three films were about the problems of careless talk during wartime and their disastrous effects. They were titled: 'Dangerous Comment', 'Now You're Talking' and 'All Hands' and all shot in 1940. He also directed 'Telefootlets' the following year for the MOI promoting the message of not gossiping on the telephone. Given the nature of the security threat Mrs. Duncan posed especially in the Naval port they were based, it is interesting that Carstairs was there committed to the issue of preventing rumours. These films were made at the same time when Maude was running MI5's section responsible for dealing with rumours and he was well have instigated these films. With their family connections in common, Maude may have taken an active interest in their making as they gave a powerful message about the dangers of leaking information. It is interesting to note that Max Anderson also directed a film on a similar theme of total co-operation in wartime in 1943.

Carstairs also personally knew the new recruit, Alan Hyman. He had worked closely with him on the film 'Falling In Love' in 1935 where Carstairs was one of the scriptwriters and Hyman wrote the story. So Alan Hyman had close relations with both the producer, Michael Balcon and the director John Paddy Carstairs of these three wartime films related to the same threat that he was recruited to deal with, careless talk and leaks of information. A short time after Carstairs joined the Royal Naval Film Section in 1943 and had met up again with his former scriptwriting colleague, Hyman had been promoted from Leading Photographer to Sub. Lt. and transferred as a Special Branch officer to Worth's unit at HMS Excellent in Portsmouth

Alan Hyman had also worked with Herbert Wilcox who was a very close family friend of Nelson Keys and a former business partner and who had sponsored Carstairs at Repton in 1924. Wilcox directed a series of feature films with his friend Nelson Keys in the late 1920's and had also employed Carstairs. Miranda Miller, Alan Hyman's daughter told me that Herbert Wilcox had also worked with her father on the 'Three Maxims' in 1936, 'Victoria The Great' in 1937, which no doubt strengthened the link between the two men. So we had in place another trusted Special Branch officer on the base whose family belonged to the same theatrical establishment with strong links between them as well as personal working relations. Carstairs was a high profile character with close connections with Naval Intelligence.

Carstairs in his diaries[17] refers to working with Lt. Commander George Clairemonte RNR who was the Head of Naval Intelligence for the Southern Area and his aide was Lt. Com. Chris Sutton RN. Like Maude, George Clairemonte was also a barrister. Carstairs must have been engaged in significant work, as such contacts place him with figures at the Military Southern Command HQ, which was based in Portsmouth. The secret world of the security services is apparent when one sees that one of the Britain's most senior intelligence officers Clairemonte is officially listed as a relatively lowly Paymaster Lieutenant at the Admiralty. Carstairs recalls a comment Clairemonte made to him about Operation Overlord when he said that the security is so good for D Day, that even God hadn't heard about the invasion plans.

Carstairs was also good friends with, and from his diaries, in contact with another scriptwriter and director Donovan Pedelty who had indirect links to Helen Duncan. Donovan Pedelty shared the writing credits with Esson Maule for a film, 'Flame In The Heather' in 1935, which he directed after adapting her novel 'The Fiery Cross'. You will remember that Esson Maule was the person who had organised the raid on Helen Duncan at a séance in 1931 along with Harry Price, which had led to Mrs. Duncan's conviction in Edinburgh for fraud. In many ways the 1944 raid used the same methods 'successfully' applied by Maule and Price. Pedelty was a talented journalist, writer, film director, a radio presenter who used the name Robert Shafto and who also worked for the MOI at the time prior to and during the time of the police raid. Pedelty and Hyman both had worked for BBC Radio prior to 1944. It was a small world and the links between these fellow officers in terms of friendship, family, theatre and film connections are plentiful. It is interesting to note that Pedelty was released from serving as a Second Lieutenant in the Royal Fusiliers at the HQ of the 177th Infantry Brigade soon after the sinking of HMS Barham between January and April 1942 after which he worked in the media and for the Ministry of Information.

It is also worth noting the background of Maude's assistant at MI5, John Phipps. Phipps was a barrister who had acted as Maude's junior for several years before the war where they established a successful close working and personal relationship. This close relationship continued in the Security Services during the war, in the MI5 section dealing with leaks. Phipps was also a RSLO and his family were also part of the establishment. His father Sir Edmund Bampfylde Phipps had been a former General Secretary at the Ministry of Munitions during the First World War, where he had been seconded from the Board of Education, where he became Deputy Secretary. His mother Lady Margaret Phipps served as the Mayor of Chelsea from 1929-31 and his grandmother Jessie was the first woman to chair the London County Council Education Committee.

John Phipps was socially well connected and he appeared in the same society columns of the broad sheets as John Maude. Their good friendship extended to their families, and they both attended each other's family events. Phipps also shared similar family show business connections to Maude and the other Special Branch recruits. His brother was the established stage and screen character actor and writer, Nicholas Phipps, and Joyce Grenfell (nee Phipps) was his cousin and 'exact contemporary'.[18]   The Phipps social network was extended further as Nancy Astor was Joyce's aunt and they shared in many of the activities at Clivedon.

Ian Fleming would also have known John Phipps, as Fleming was part of a tight social circle in the late 1920's that included the Phipps'.   He was particularly close to Phipps' cousin Joyce Phipps, who became Joyce Grenfell. Part of this close social circle also included Celia Johnson, a close friend of Joyce's from school days. Celia Johnson went on to marry Ian's brother Peter in 1937, who also happened to work for Military Intelligence and was Literary

Editor of the Spectator. The close links between the Phipps' and the Flemings' was demonstrated again in 1938 when Joyce's father Paul Phipps designed 'Merrimoles', Peter Fleming's family home, set in 20,000 acres of land.

It is tempting to speculate that private meetings took place at the Dorchester or Carlton Grill of the type described when Ian Fleming was recruited to a senior position in Naval Intelligence. In this instance between senior figures in the world of Naval intelligence, MI5, theatre and film in order to recommend the writers, directors and the production team for the mystery crime thriller to run for a limited season at the Old Bailey involving Helen Duncan. If this was the case then the challenge for the security services was to select able, talented people with trusted, close family and personal connections able to mount such an operation. Secrecy was essential and these men had close relatives who were the most powerful figures at the top of their profession in the theatre and film worlds and some had received Royal honours. It seems highly improbable that these talented men with their varied and close connections should come together at the same time at the same location and so close to the Helen Duncan trial purely by chance.

The connections of these men with John Maude suggests that it was a combined operation between MI5 and Naval Intelligence and that it was thought best to draw on his theatrical links to recruit the personnel and give it the flavour of a top secret show business enterprise, undertaken to assist the nation. It seems most probable that Ian Fleming's idea to run an operation for a 'show trial' in order to get Mrs. Duncan 'out of the way' was taking shape. This likelihood is further supported when we know that Ian Fleming was personally responsible for the final selection of Naval Intelligence officers to Special Branch.

Some of the Personalities Involved: [19]

The Recorder Sir Gerald Dodson

The Recorder, who heard the case, Sir Gerald Dodson was born to the Sheriff of Norwich John Dodson in August 1884 and he was educated at Downing College, Cambridge. He was called to the Bar, at the Inner Temple in 1907. He was known as a deeply patriotic man prepared to do what he could to help the war effort and who had a close affinity with the men of the sea. This developed while he was in Navy during the first World War and his strong Christian faith made him someone who would have been highly sympathetic to the patriotic sentiment behind a plot intended to save the lives of allied servicemen.

He also shared a deep involvement in the theatre like Maude, Hyman, Bishop and Robey. Dodson's interest in theatre had developed before and during the First World War when he with his wife Emily promoted and produced weekly concerts for the troops based near Sandown Park. He managed to attract many well-known and respected London music hall artists to appear in these productions. It is not known whether George Robey actually performed at one of Dodson's concerts but it is certainly likely that he knew him and Hyman's uncle who was also a leading figure in Music Hall.

Later he met the composer Montagu Phillips in the Navy and they were to write the musical opera 'Rebel Maid', which appeared at the Empire Theatre, Leicester Square in the West End in 1921 and was performed all over Britain and is still performed today. This success was matched by the song he wrote for the opera titled, 'The Fisherman of England', which was sung and broadcast all over the world. The song was a tribute to the fisherman of Britain. Prosecuting Counsel Edward Robey and Gerald Paling Assistant Director of the Public Prosecutions and his wife, also shared his love and active involvement in Opera, performing in productions for various operatic societies.

He also had some involvement in the film world for a short time. He wrote a script for a film encouraging war savings in the early 1940's and appeared in it giving a stirring speech in tribute to those sailors who sacrificed their lives for their country. When the film was shown at cinemas audiences started to giggle which led to uncontrolled hilarity. In good humour he recognised himself appearing as a haggard old man apparently with a single tooth. A ray from one of the film lights had struck one of his teeth, which made it appear as if there were a beacon illuminating a moonless night everytime he opened his mouth. Dodson laughed along with the rest of the audience but he requested that the film be withdrawn immediately. So ended his career in film.

Dodson's legal career also flourished. He was Counsel to the Treasury at the Central Criminal Court from 1925 until 1934, and was Recorder at Tenterden from 1932-34. He was appointed Judge of the Mayor's and City of London Court from 1934-37. The holder of that office is also the Commissioner when sitting at the Central Criminal Court. He became Recorder of London and High Steward of Southwark in 1937 until 1959. He was Knighted in 1939.

Brigadier Roy Firebrace

Brigadier Roy Firebrace was the Head of Military Intelligence in the Scottish Command who attended Helen Duncan's séance in May 1941 when she reported the sinking of HMS Hood which was later confirmed by the Admiralty. At the time of the séance he was a Colonel, but he was soon promoted to acting

Brigadier attached to the War Office in London. In January 1943 he was appointed Chief Liaison Officer for Military Intelligence for the Russian Liaison Group and by July 1943 he was Deputy Director of the Liaison and Munitions Section of the Department of the Chief of the Imperial General Staff at the War Office. In this capacity he may have liased with the police and other armed services in the run up to D Day and no doubt with his knowledge of physical mediumship and seances, it was in this capacity that he liased with Scotland Yard about Mrs. Duncan.

He had become an authority on psychic phenomena having studied it and sat with distinguished mediums prior to the war. When he was Military Attaché to Estonia from 1931 to 35, he sat with his wife and a Russian psychic and the circle produced direct voice phenomena in which he claimed Red Cloud spoke through the trumpet. On his return to the UK in another circle Red Cloud came through again confirming his appearance in Estonia. Before going to Riga he had sat with Helen Duncan in 1931 at the LSA.

From 1939 to 1940 he was Military Attaché in Moscow, after which he returned to London to work for the Inter-Services Security Board. Firebrace would have been an ideal person to assist in the prosecution against Helen Duncan, with his impeccable military intelligence credentials, his knowledge of physical phenomena and his position as Deputy Director of Liaison for Military Intelligence. Firebrace was an excellent and qualified Military interpreter speaking Italian, French and German fluently. He had also served as a Quarter Master General and Department Assistant Adjutant for Western Command.

Colleagues from an organisation Firebrace co-founded after the war, the Astrological Association publicly revealed in their journal 'Transit'20 that he had been involved in the arrest and prosecution of Helen Duncan. This suggests that Fleming and Knight of Military Intelligence used Firebrace's experience in the field of physical mediumship to help secure a conviction, with his position as Deputy Director of Liaison for Military Intelligence at the War Office aiding this role with the various armed services, government departments and the police.

It is also interesting to note that Brig. Firebrace joined the Society of Psychical Research on the 24th of March 1944, the second day of the Helen Duncan trial where he was to meet another person who was to play a role at the time of the Appeal. As an intelligence officer Firebrace would have understood that the SPR represented an important body in terms of how the trial would come to be seen and he might gain valuable information from experienced psychic researchers about the impact of the prosecution case. Moreover any considered response from members of the SPR to the trial was likely to gain the attention of the press and influence post trial public opinion. The response of academic and psychic researchers to the trial was obviously an important matter for any intelligence operation if it was to be successful and Firebrace's membership of the SPR at the start of the trial cannot be seen at purely accidental.

Chief Constable Arthur West

Arthur West joined the Hampshire Police Force in 1921 and was promoted to Sergeant in 1930. Six years later he reached the rank of Superintendent for Andover Police District and in August 1940 he was appointed the Chief Constable of Portsmouth. He was awarded the Kings Police Medal for distinguished service a few days before Helen Duncan arrived in Portsmouth, on the 1st of January 1944.

Defence Counsel Charles Loseby

Defence Counsel Charles Loseby was the son of a solicitor in an old established legal family in Leicestershire. He was one of thirteen children. He began his career as a schoolmaster. He went to South Africa and worked in the Educational Department of the Transvaal Civil Service and got involved in politics. He was offered a seat in the South African Parliament but refused it. He returned to the UK and was called to the Bar at Grays Inn in 1914 and joined the Inner Temple later.

During the First World War he served as a Captain in the 2nd Battalion of the Royal Lancashire Fusiliers and on the staff of the 86th Brigade. He became a war hero, winning the Military Cross, when those who were present felt he deserved a VC. His bravery was unquestioned. In 1918 he was elected as a conservative Member of Parliament for East Bradford but lost his marginal seat in 1922. He gained a reputation as the ex-serviceman's champion in Parliament, gaining an increase to their pension and fighting many causes on their behalf. For this work he became known as the 'Soldiers M.P.' He was a friend of Churchill and was an unsuccessful Parliamentary Candidate for a seat in West Nottingham in the 1929 General Election.

He worked on the Midland Circuit from 1918 to 1945 and opened a successful chamber's. Around 1934 he became interested in Spiritualism and set up a Society for Psychic Research in Leicester which he was President for ten years. He also represented the Spiritualist National Union in deputations to see government ministers. Those close to him believed his practice suffered as he became absorbed by the idea of proving survival. He loved playing and watching cricket and was a member of the Leicester County Cricket Club. Those who knew him well regarded him as a colourful, courageous personality who put great enthusiasm into everything he did. At the time of the Trial in 1944 Loseby was in his 60's.

Summary

Considering the criteria that were set for a conspiracy to have been staged, we see that the case of the Spiritualists is very strong. The plot matches the type of operation devised by one of the most powerful men in Military Intelligence, Commander (Special Branch) Ian Fleming who was personal assistant to Admiral Godfrey, DNI and senior MI5 officer John Maude. We have senior people involved at the time disclosing that there was a government conspiracy to imprison Mrs. Duncan for security reasons, that was actively pursued by the Admiralty, which would involve necessarily Naval Intelligence. They are the Chief Constable Arthur West and Abdy Collins a senior person in the Ministry of Home Security. Henry Elam, prosecuting counsel also discloses that the trial was brought for security reasons. The State Security Services are represented by John Maude who prosecuted and who had been a MI5 officer responsible for setting up the section dealing with leaks and rumours. He settled the indictment against Mrs. Duncan and controlled the conduct of the prosecution. Brigadier Firebrace also of Military Intelligence confirmed that Scotland Yard was seeking to prosecute Mrs. Duncan and he was brought to the War Office after bringing Mrs. Duncan's first leak to the attention of the authorities. It has also been stated that he played a part in her arrest and prosecution.

The instruments by which the conspiracy was implemented was through a Naval Special Branch Officer Stanley Worth, nephew of one of Scotland Yard's most senior officers Percy Worth and who had family connections in the police in Portsmouth. He was also a friend of the Chief Constable of Portsmouth and he was an officer in Naval Special Branch where Naval Intelligence Officers served. There is also evidence that initially Naval Special Branch through another one of their officer's Lt. Sheffield Jones sought to get the police called in to prosecute Mrs. Duncan soon after the sinking of HMS Barham was leaked in 1941.

The judiciary is represented by Maude but also the DPP proposed that Maude and Elam conduct the trial and they even sought to assign Recorder Gerald Dodson who heard it, who was also a former Naval Officer. The DPP also tried to distance themselves from their influence in the important decisions that were made.

The witnesses necessary to give evidence against Mrs. Duncan were Worth the Naval Special Branch Officer, his friend and War Reserve Policeman Rupert Cross and the rest was organised through another former Naval man of 15 years who understood the subject of mediumship, Charles Burrell. He was personally responsible for bringing the majority of the remaining prosecution witnesses to give evidence against Mrs. Duncan and he had some considerable influence over them, although the prosecution tried to play down the extent of this link.

In support of the conspiracy, details of it that were supported by future events were disclosed two weeks before the arrest of Mrs. Duncan, by the son of a prospective prosecution witness, who had a criminal record as a petty criminal.

Finally, having the need to get a conviction and effectively stage a trial that would convince the public, a team of scriptwriters and documentary film directors who had family connections to the prosecuting counsel and MI5 officer Maude and the other prosecuting counsel Edward Robey were brought in. They arrive at the leading prosecution witnesses Special Branch unit, prior to the operation starting. So certainly everything necessary for a conspiracy is in place. The proposition that the security service, military, judiciary and police sought to get Mrs. Duncan convicted seem well supported and the instruments of their effort were the Chief Constable, a Special Branch Naval officer and War Reserve Policeman whose close relationships were kept secret at the time. Later, one of these men admitted to the Government and Navy acting to get Mrs. Duncan 'out of the way'. Let us now see how the prosecution was conducted and whether there is evidence to show that false evidence was presented in order to achieve a successful result and imprison Mrs. Duncan.

CHAPTER TWO

Staging And Performance

Examination of the testimony and statements of the prosecution witnesses is helpful in considering the proposal that the authorities conspired to imprison Mrs. Duncan. Any conspiracy needs evidence to be presented in order to convict the prisoner and some of that evidence needs to be false. The analysis undertaken looks at the evidence of those witnesses who attended the seances specified in the indictment from the 12th to the 19th of January 1944. According to Mr. Homer who was the organiser, thirteen seances took place between those dates. The analysis will seek to focus particularly on the evidence of the prosecution witnesses with regard to the features of the case. It will examine a range of issues such as the light, the seating arrangements, the evidence regarding the forms that the prosecution referred to and the attempt to grab a form on the 19th when the defendants were arrested.

Many other witnesses called by the defence testified as to the genuine nature of Mrs. Duncan's physical mediumship and some offered expert testimony. Many of these witnesses referred to events that occurred before the period specified in the indictment and consequently in terms of the case, had little or no bearing on the evidence that was relevant to whether Mrs. Duncan acted fraudulently in January 1944. Consequently the analysis will only examine the statements of those who attended Mrs. Duncan's séances in January 1944 which formed the basis of the case against her.

Summary of the evidence of the prosecution witnesses:

All the prosecution witnesses repeated the same basic account. Lt. Stanley Worth saw a white sheet, shrouded bulky figures with no features, all the voices were husky which he didn't recognise and the forms went back into the cabinet. He accused Mrs. Duncan was playing 'bogey-bogey' with a sheet over her head. Charles Burrell saw muslin covered white forms, figures dressed up in white cloth. He couldn't discern faces, features or figures. Four times he said it was as if someone put on a sheet of muslin or a white sheet. Mr. William Lock repeated the same. He saw no features but a large person or figure under the sheet that looked like Mrs. Duncan and the hand he touched felt like Mrs. Duncan's. Mrs. Bessie Lock distinctly saw a white robe sitting there, just white forms. She didn't see a face except once distinctly. She saw Cross's hand on the cloth. She did not recognise the voice purporting to be her mother. Mrs. Kitty Jennings saw no definite shape and no features. She saw figures in white material and thought Mrs. Duncan was doing voice impressions. War Reserve Policeman Cross just saw a white blur and confirmed that the substance looked and felt like butter muslin. He saw Mrs. Duncan covered in white sheet, pushing it down to floor. Mrs. Lonsdale Brosman was not asked about figures and Mrs. Ena Harris couldn't see anything. Although Surg. Lt. Elijah Fowler was sitting next to Worth he was not asked to corroborate Worth's testimony. He said he saw both slim and bulky figures but this was created by the impression of curtains open or not. His scepticism increased.

In summary the prosecution witnesses claimed no distinctive features were apparent and that all the materialisations could have been Mrs. Duncan covered or manipulating butter muslin.

At the time the prosecution witnesses gave their first witness statements a definite pattern emerged. Mr. Burrell was the straight talking disgruntled Spiritualist. He was a medium and genuine believer in Spiritualism who had complained about the racket Mr. & Mrs. Homer were running at their church by charging high fees. He was dissatisfied at paying 10/- for a 15-minute reading when Mrs. Homer knew the same information about him. This complaint is unusual given he was a serving medium at the church himself. When Burrell threatened to call the police the Homer's returned his money. The prosecution suggested this was relevant on the question of guilty knowledge on the part of the Homer's.

Burrell also claimed he complained about Mrs. Duncan's sittings in terms of satisfaction, genuineness and cost, although he was allowed in free of charge whenever he attended. He stated he distinctly saw it was a sheet. A figure he described went through sitters pockets without permission, he saw an arm which looked human and said he was sure it was Mrs. Duncan's. He saw a spirit hand, which he was sure, was a human hand with muslin covering it. He also saw an animal, like Worth and had the same sceptical reaction. He stated Albert's voice was similar to Mrs. Duncan. He openly expressed his dissatisfaction to Mr. & Mrs. Homer about what he witnessed at the seances. He offered a theory about how Mrs. Duncan created the illusion and his testimony was used as an explanation about how the fraud was produced. He said the Homer's passed Mrs. Duncan a sheet in the dark and that she used methods similar to stage illusionists.

Mr. & Mrs. Lock's role seemed to be to do with touch. This is clear because on every occasion a form appeared for them, they asked it to touch them. Only one form did and Mr. Lock claimed it was not a spirit hand even though he had never touched one before. Mrs. Lock repeatedly asked to be touched by forms that presented themselves to either her or her husband, but none did. Her major role in the prosecution case was seeing the white material in Cross's hand when he leapt forward to grab a form. She was the only witness to support Mr. Cross's evidence and she was therefore a very important witness in terms of material evidence, given no cloth was found when the police searched the room. Mrs. Lock also said the face she saw of a spirit was similar to Mrs. Duncan's.

Mrs. Emma Jennings came on the scene later. The Portsmouth police recommended her as a witness for the prosecution in early March 1944 and it seems her role was principally to do with the voice. Claiming to be an experienced actress she said that in her view the voices she heard could well have been Mrs. Duncan doing impersonations.

Prosecution witnesses each had a part to play in covering the main features of the evidence. These related to the shape, features and texture of the forms, the voice, the information provided and an explanation of the illusions created. Each accused Mrs. Duncan at some point of being the form they saw, touched or spoke to. Worth set the agenda and the other prosecution witnesses followed and supported it.

Loseby's approach

Loseby, the defence counsel, made attempt to dispute the prosecution witnesses accounts of what occurred, except in terms of presenting his own witnesses who asserted the opposite, namely that they positively identified the forms as being their relatives or friends. Loseby adopted a strategy that led him to ignore all technical points that might favour his client. He wrote 'She (Helen Duncan) might have pleaded Not Guilty, have put every possible technical point and hoped for the best. I may say in passing, that I am satisfied that if she had done so it would have availed nothing'... 'In the course of a long trial, in fact, no technical point was taken upon her behalf. She replied only that "she did not pretend". She said that at Portsmouth, and indeed at other places, she had alleged that through her, the spirits of deceased persons not only showed themselves but did so, at times, in full physical form and in such a way that they could be clearly and plainly seen and identified. This, she said, she would prove'. Loseby's strategy then was to present an endless stream of witnesses who vouched for the authenticity of Mrs. Duncan's, which implicitly contradicted the accounts of the prosecution witnesses.

The defence witnesses:

The defence witnesses who witnessed what took place between the 12th and 19th of January consisted mostly of local people with varying degrees of interest and involvement in Spiritualism and psychic phenomena. Mrs. Dorothy Gill, Mrs. Bertha Alabaster, Miss Christine Homer (a nurse in an Institute of the Aged), Mrs. Ivy Stammers, Mrs. Rose Cole, Mrs. Ellen Barnes (wife of a retired Indian Army Captain) and Mrs. Mary Wheatcroft (from London) described themselves as Spiritualists. Mrs. Dora Jopling and Mrs. Tremlett had been interested in Spiritualism and psychic phenomena all their lives, although Mrs. Tremlett had only attended the church once before. Marine Horace Clayton and George Barnes, a retired captain of the Indian army had been interested between four to six years, while Mrs. Ada Sullivan, Ann Potter (wife of a retired Army officer) and Mrs. Irene Taylor (wife of an Army Captain) had been going to The Master's Temple between one to three years. Walter Williams (a collector for Portsmouth Corporation) was the witness with the least experience having been interested for only two months.

Other witnesses described themselves as investigators of Spiritualism. Mr. Basil Kirkby (a retired businessman) had come from London and he had carried out research into Spiritualism and psychic phenomena for over 20 years and he had conducted research with Sir Arthur Conan Doyle and Sir Oliver Lodge. Wing Commander George Mackie regarded himself as an investigator and a Survivalist, but not a Spiritualist. He had become personally convinced of the authenticity of materialisation after attending a séance of Mrs. Duncan's three months earlier.

Other local investigators included Harold Gill (an Approved Society official), William and Annie Coulcher who ran a shop together, who had only been three or four times before and Nurse Jane Rust. She was a retired midwife who for many years had been a 'sceptical' investigator but like Wing Commander Mackie, she had become convinced about the truths contained in Spiritualism since attending one of Mrs. Duncan's séances six months earlier.

Sitters Known To Have Attended the Seances in January 1944

Wednesday 12th
      Mrs. Cole, Mrs. Coulcher, Mrs. Lock, Mr. Gill, Mr. Branch,
Thursday 13th
      Mr. Barnes
Friday 14th
      Lt. Worth, Surg. Lt. Fowler, Mrs. St. George, Mrs. Cole, Mrs.
      Tremlett, Mrs. Sullivan, Mr. Homer, Mrs. Homer, Mrs. Barnes,
      Mrs. Taylor, Mr. Mackie, Mrs. Jopling, Mrs. Stammers,

Mrs. Nuttal,Mr. Ineson, Mrs. Mackie

Sunday 16th Service

Lt. Worth, Mr. Barnes

Monday 17th

Mrs. Lock, Mr. Lock, Mr. Burrell, Mrs. Lonsdale-Brosman,
Marine Clayton, Nurse Rust, Mrs. Coulcher,

Tuesday 3pm   18th

Mr. Kirkby, Mrs. Wheatcroft

7pm 18th

Mrs. Lock, Mr. Lock, Mr. Burrell, Mrs. Lonsdale-Brosman
(Mrs. Wheatcroft, Mr. Kirkby, Mr. Williams, Mrs. Potter,
Mrs.Shepherd unknown which séance on 18th they attended)

Wednesday 3pm 19th

Mrs. Harris, Mrs. Jennings, Mrs. Trimboy, Mrs. Ayres,
Miss Homer

7pm 19th

Lt. Worth, WRC Cross, Mr. Coulcher, Mr. & Mrs. Gill,
Mrs. Alabaster, Irene Taylor, Daphne Taylor, Mrs. Doughty,
Mr. Williams, Miss Homer, Mrs. Bird, Mr. & Mrs. Green, Mr. &
Mrs. Brown, Chief Petty Officer Foster, Mr. Bush, Mr. White,
Mrs. Johnson, Mrs. Lock, Ena Longshaw, Mrs. Waite, Mrs. Bert,
Mrs. Harris, Mr. Pickett RNVR, Mr. Jacobs RNVR, Nurse Rust

Mr. Homer, Mrs. Homer and Mrs. Brown attended them all.

The Room

Mr. Homer gave details of the dimensions of the séance room in his testimony. A recent inspection of the séance room supports the following dimensions. The room was 18' long, 14' wide and 9' high. It had an 8' long window seat which was around 2' 4" deep, with an 7 or 8" high and 11" wide footrest that ran beneath it that is set into the recess suggesting that it did not protrude into the room to any great extent. A 7' long curtain rail was placed across the corner of the room with two 3' 6" brown curtains running on rings along it to create the cabinet. The rail was 8' high. The edge of the window seat was around 4' 6" from the wall behind the cabinet, and between 8" and 1' from the edge of the cabinet curtains. This suggests that the 7' curtains were at a slant to the corner of the room and not symmetrical. There was a rostrum at the other side of the room on which a small writing desk was located at the front of the rostrum with a ceiling light just over the desk, which shone a red light that illuminated the seances. This ceiling light was 4' 1.25" from the chimney breast. As this light was located over the front edge of the rostrum, this places the rostrum approximately 5' from the wall and 4' or so from the chimney breast. This seems to be a reasonable width for a platform on which a chairperson and medium would be seated for a service. There was also another ceiling light in the middle of the room, which shone a white light and a wall light shining a green light whose location is unknown. The walls behind the cabinet were draped with dark blue curtains and carpet was on the floor with an 18" gap of board to the end wall. Mrs. Duncan sat on a Jacobean armchair, which had a removable leather seat within the cabinet.

A diagram showing the features of the plan of the room that was presented to the court by the police is presented on page 210. The police plan is not to scale and the basic dimensions of the length and width of the room are not proportional. This makes the room appear approximately 1' 6" longer than it actually was. Items within the room are drawn consistent with the scale used to depict the width of the room. Some other points need to be taken into consideration. The length of the curtain rail is shown as approximately 6" shorter than its 7' length and the width of the rostrum is shown as only 3' from the chimney breast and not 4'. This in turn means that the red light source was a foot or so nearer to the cabinet than suggested by the plan. The greater width of the rostrum also suggests that the sitters filled the remaining floor space, rather than being seated in the narrow band of seats shown. Applying the scales used in the police diagram suggest that the three rows of sitters were seated within a width of seats 5' 7" to 5' 9", which is probably unreasonably tight given the space available. The suggestion that all the rows ended with space to spare along the window seat towards the rostrum is also unlikely. The police plan also omits the footrest, which runs along the base of the window seat.

Depending on the séance either two or three rows of chairs in the shape of an arc faced the cabinet. On the 14th there were two rows and on the evening of the 19th three rows of chairs. Nurse Rust estimated people in the front row were about 3' from the curtains and Wing Commander Mackie and Marine Clayton estimated people in the second row were 8-9' from the curtains.

The Séance Procedure

After making a prior appointment when people started to arrive at 301 Copnor Road, Portsmouth they were shown into a waiting room at the rear of the druggist shop. Here they paid 12/s 6d if they had not done so already, although several sitters were allowed into the séance free of charge. On average three or four people were allowed in free at each séance over the course of the 13 sittings in January 1944. New sitters were told what to expect and Mr. Homer needed to be satisfied that they would not cause a disturbance as this might have drastic consequences on Mrs. Duncan, who was suffering from a weak heart. Once the sitter had assured Mr. Homer that they would remain calm and everyone had arrived, then they were led upstairs to the séance room and conducted to the chair where a card bearing their name had been placed.

Mrs. Homer then called for three men to volunteer to conduct a thorough search of the cabinet. Then the clothes that Mrs. Duncan was going to wear, were passed around members of the audience for inspection. These consisted of a pair of black leather court shoes, a pair of black silk knickers with elastic in the waist and legs, a black slip and dress. Mrs. Homer asked for three female volunteers to leave the room with her and dress Mrs. Duncan with her clothing. After a short while they returned with Mrs. Duncan and they returned to their seats. Mrs. Duncan stood at the front of the audience and explained that she had been searched by these three women and dressed and then asked the women to verify that they had done so.

Mrs. Duncan then went into the cabinet and sat in a wooden Jacobean armchair and when she had relaxed to go into trance, Mr. Homer closed the curtains. Mr. Homer asked for a blessing on the meeting and opened with a prayer and then led the audience in saying the Lord's Prayer. During the Prayers the white light was turned off leaving a green and red light. Then the green light was switched off leaving the room faintly illuminated in a red light at the end of the prayers when the sitters opened their eyes. Mrs. Brown removed the white light bulb from its socket to prevent it being switched on during the séance.

Then a man's voice emerged from the cabinet who was identified as Albert, Mrs. Duncan's guide. Then Mrs. Duncan and the form of Albert were shown to the audience. This part of the séance will be examined in detail later. After the audience had expressed their satisfaction that they had seen Mrs. Duncan and the figure of Albert at the entrance of the curtains and Mrs. Duncan had returned to her chair, the séance started.

The method by which purported spirit forms appeared was as follows. The voice of Albert would describe the features of the spirit waiting to appear. This usually related to the sex of the spirit, the way the person had died, any medical conditions they were suffering from, their occupation or their relation to the person in the audience e.g. sister, brother, mother. Albert might also say that the spirit form is for someone seated in a particular part of the room.

Mrs. Homer and Mrs. Brown prompted the sitters to call the forms out, by saying 'Is it for me?' If it was not for that person Albert said 'That is not the voice'. If the appropriate person called out, Albert would say 'That's the voice'. 'Will you please call him/her out'. The sitter then said 'Will you please come out if you are for me' or words to that effect and the form emerged between the curtains or came out in front of the curtains.

The Light

When a séance was held a group of up to 30 or so people would be facing the cabinet and seated in two or three arc rows, each within foot or so of their neighbour. They viewed the same events from a range of touching distance to as far as 10' away. Those in the second and third rows were allowed to stand to get a better view. The lighting conditions are naturally very important and it became a central issue in the case.

Mr. Homer stated that the seances were illuminated by a red light bulb of 25 to 40 watts hanging from a ceiling light just over the writing desk at the front of the rostrum. Under examination he said he was not definite about the wattage of the bulb. He states that nothing covered this light on the 14th and 19th of January, although a red silk handkerchief was sometimes used to cover it if it was deemed by Albert to be too bright.

Maude in his opening speech for the prosecution asserted that the red light left a very faint glow and that the room was very dark indeed. He continued 'if you choose to do things in the dark it is very much easier to do conjuring tricks than if it in the light'. By innuendo he also suggested that Mr. & Mrs. Homer collected the torches prior to the séance because light would have exposed the fraud. This ignored the fact that witnesses described two instances where forms actually took torches and shone them onto their faces so they could be recognised and seen by the audience. Sitters would have brought torches because of the black out arrangements during wartime and Mr. Homer explained that they were collected for fear of the light from a torch injuring Mrs. Duncan. All the prosecution witnesses, Worth, Harris, Burrell stated it was too dark to see clearly. Fowler's unsigned witness statement states there was just sufficient light to distinguish the position of the curtains in the corner from the front row. The prosecution's position was clear, their witnesses could not see clearly at all.

The problem for the prosecution of taking such a stance is the argument that if you could not see clearly then how do you know Mrs. Duncan was operating a fraud and the figures were not identifiable. It is interesting that during the presentation of their testimonies prosecution witnesses were confident about that what they saw and almost no reference was made about the light. How could you assert that the figures had no features if you could not see them? In this regard it was very important that all the prosecution witnesses kept to the same story. If prosecution witnesses also claimed they could see features of the forms, obviously there was enough light to see by to identify features then the discrepancies between their identification testimony and all the other witnesses who claimed to have distinctly seen facial details has some basis for comparison. In turn the question of the differences of the features recognised and their likeness to Mrs. Duncan becomes a critical issue.

For the prosecution, the forms had no features and although it was very dark

Top: Helen Duncan

Left: Seance photograph taken by Harry Price using a flash in May 1931

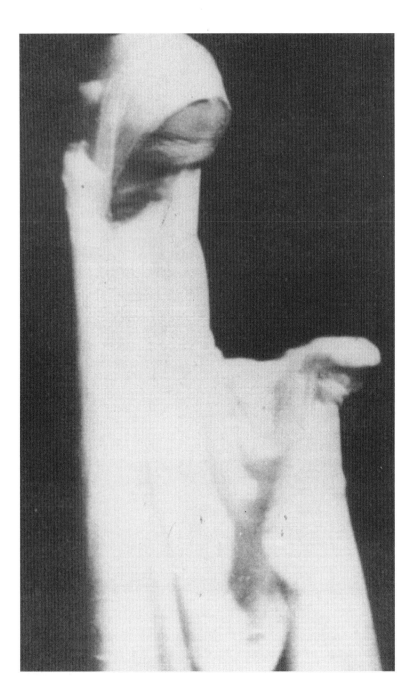

Left: One of
Helen Duncan's
materialisations, photo
taken by John Kinsella

Top: Esson Maule's
reconstruction of a
materialised form
(Jan. 1931)

Right: Mrs. Duncan's
undervest. The only
white material seized
by Miss Maule at the
Jan. 1931 seance

Opposite page:
From top left to right:
Sir Gerald Dodson,
John Maude KC,
Henry Elam,
Chief Constable Arthur
West

Right: Lt. Worth &
WRC Cross on way to
Old Bailey

Bottom right:
Bessie & William Lock

Below:
His Master's Temple

Top left: Ian Fleming

Top right: Max Anderson

Right: Alan Hyman

Right: Charles Loseby

Below: William Spencer
(he took the bet at
Cowley, Oxford on
January 3rd 1944)

Bottom right:
Harry Price

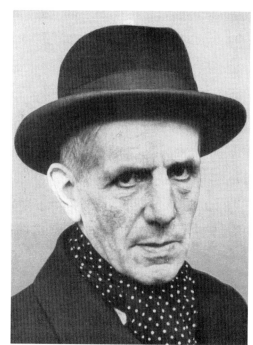

Portrait drawn by Tony Katz (psychic artist)

they could see that they had no features. So there was enough light to determine the forms had no features and the material was a sheet of cloth covering Mrs. Duncan but there was not enough light to answer any discrepancies about reports from other witnesses who claimed to have seen something different.

The only time prosecution witnesses brought up the question of light, or the lack of light during the trial was when they were being cross-examined. They were then asked to account for the difference in evidence between what they saw and what the other members of the audience saw. Burrell when claiming he clearly saw that the forms were clearly made of cloth did not mention light in his testimony. Being in the best position to see what was going on in the front row, he said that although he was in a position to see clearly, being within a foot of the figures and the curtains, there was insufficient light to see by.

When Worth was challenged about the contradictory testimony of other witnesses who described the features of his aunt, when he had claimed the form was featureless, he answered: 'I defy anyone to say that she was a little old lady, because it was so dark you could hardly see anything at all and all you could see was this shrouded figure which did not look an old lady'. It is interesting that when Worth arrived at the séance on the 19th with WRC Cross he asked that Cross be given a 'good seat' in the front row. This naturally begs the question how could it be termed a 'good seat' if he could not see anything as he claimed!

William Lock described how the white cloth purporting to be his sister Sally disappeared towards floor and the figure disappeared towards the curtain. He said the white curtain seemed to disappear down to the ground. When challenged how a figure of Mrs. Duncan's size seemed to go back and also disappear through the floor, he said 'well I could not see where figure disappeared to because of the light'.

Neither the Recorder nor Counsel suggested that any of the defence witnesses gave false testimony at the trial. They have been regarded as people giving genuine reports of what they saw. This being the case it is worthwhile examining what they saw given the lighting conditions that prevailed.

Naturally people who were closer to the forms that presented themselves are in a better position to see what appeared whatever the lighting conditions. The prosecution questioned people about the identification evidence they presented and what distance they were from the figures described. As expected witnesses stated the closer they were the easier it was to identify and recognise details of people they knew when presented to them by the forms that emerged between or from the curtains. Estimations of between 1-3 feet was stated as the optimal distance to clearly recognise and see facial features that appeared in the facial area of the forms.

Chart No. 1 summarises the evidence of those witnesses (defence and prosecution). The chart shows that there are 30 instances where witnesses seated in the front row recognised forms. Although some witnesses stated they could

Seating Position	Date	Closest Recognition Distance	Viewing Distance	Estimated Best	Recognised Forms/Features
Front Row					
Mrs. Cole w/s	14th	right up	to end of rows		Albert, Mrs. Allen (right up), Shirley, Worth's 'aunt'
Mrs. Alabaster	19th		across room	3-4' OK	
Mr. Williams	18th	1'			Mother, Mrs. Duncan (2')
Mrs. Tremlett	2.4.1941	right Up			Husband, Girl, Albert
" "	14th	Curtains	in front row		Shirley, Mutilated man, Peggy, Peggy, Cat, Parrot, Worth's 'aunt', Policeman, Old Lady, Albert
Mrs. Sullivan	14th	Curtains			Shirley, Mother, Policeman
	Undated				Father, Elderly Gentleman
Ann Coulcher	12th	2-3'			Cousin
" "	17th	touched			Mother
Mr. Homer	14th	1'		3'+	Worth's 'aunt', Albert, Policman
					Shirley, Mrs. Allen, Mrs. Homer's, Grandmother, Mrs. Duncan
" "	Jan. 1944				Mother
Mrs. Wheatcroft	18th	3' - curtains			Husband, Mrs. Allen, Chinese Guide
Mr. Gill	12th	2' 6"			Nun
" "	19th	2' 6"	see faces to 3 seats away		Boy, three forms (did not specify)
Mrs. Potter	18th	'close'			Mother, Father, thin Friend
Mr. Branch	13th	1' (2' from curtains)			Grandmother
Mrs. Barnes	14th	touched			Shirley, Father (1')
Mr. Barnes	13th	1'	3-4'		Son (3-4'), Shirley (1')
Mrs. Gill	19th				Young Man, Albert
Mrs. Cole	12th	within reach			Son, Albert
Mrs. Jopling	April 1942	2'			Husband, Girlfriend
Nurse Rust	17th	touched	to end of rows	2'	Mother (T), Husband (T), Aunt Mary
	May 1943	right up			Daughter-in-law, Daughter, Mrs. Duncan
	undated	3'			Airforce serviceman
	19th	curtains			Man
Mr. Kirkby	1934	'close'			Peggy
Mr. Fowler	14th				Mutilated man
Mrs. Lock	18th				Mrs. Duncan, Bird
Ada St. George	14th				Mutilated Man, Mrs. Duncan
Mrs. Harris	19th 3pm				Mrs. Duncan
Second Row					
Mrs. Taylor w/s	14th				Worth's 'aunt', Shirley, Policeman
Mr. Mackie	14th		3-4'		Mother, Policeman, Parrot
Mr. Mackie	Sept. 1943 3-4' apart				Mother. Brother, Sister
Mrs. Jopling	14th				Worth's 'aunt', Shirley, Policeman, Cat, Parrot
Mr. Kirkby	18th	3-4'			George Dobson, Budgerigar, Guide
" "	undated				Mother, Albert
Mrs. Alabaster		could see faces from 2nd row			
Marine Clayton	17th	1' 3" (touched)			Grandmother
" "	1943				Grandfather
Mrs. Sullivan	undated				Father, Elderly Friend
Mrs. Lock	17th				Airforce officer
Third Row					
Burrell	18th				Mrs. Duncan's/Mrs. Allen's arm
Ena Harris	19th				Mrs. Duncan
Standing at back					
Irene Taylor	19th				Lady carrying baby

Key:
T - Touched

Table showing forms recognised for each row in seances for sitters attending between 12th -19th January 1944

see beyond 3-4' and several forms came out towards the sitter and on occasions even touched them, the evidence shows that being in the front row allowed the vast majority of people to adequately see features on the forms that appeared at the curtains. Witnesses estimated that the distance to the curtains was between 3-4'. There are also eleven instances where people seated in the second row also managed to recognise forms or features that presented themselves. These witnesses include prosecution witnesses who were seated in this row. This indicates that people seated in the second row could see clearly enough to recognise features, although some of the sitters at the end of the row stood up to see more clearly. These findings support the common sense view that working people who were paying 12s 6d to attend a séance would not agree to sit in a room so dark they could not see anything. The chart shows that for all the defence witnesses and three of the prosecution witnesses, they paid their money and were able to see clearly enough to recognise features on the forms that appeared.

The descriptions of the other witnesses who reported seeing recognisable features on the faces of the forms at a distance further away from where Worth, Fowler and Cross were seated, suggests, that Worth should also have been able to recognise these features. People seated next to him or just behind him described the same features on the forms that Worth claimed to have been unable to see. Moreover the light was such that he confidently declared that the other people around him were deluded if they claimed to have seen recognisable features.

A number of witnesses also gave general descriptions of the lighting conditions that prevailed. The person in the window seat was the closest to the curtains and as they were seated at right angles to the other sitters, then much of the time their view would be across the room. Mrs. Cole who sat in this seat stated 'We can all see by the red light, you can see quite plainly by the red light. If on the windowsill I could see the faces of people at the other ends of the rows of seats. I could see everybody in the room, not distinctly at the other ends of the chairs, but I could recognise them'.

Nurse Rust agreed it was a dull light but not a bad light. She agreed with Mrs. Cole that you 'could see across the room and recognise people seated at other end of row'. This would be at an estimated distance of 12' (if eight or nine seats in a row).

Mrs. Alabaster concurred stating it was 'not difficult to see living people by red light'. She sat in the second row and still saw their faces. 'The light was not absolutely dark, you got used to it and you can see people the other side of the room'.

Mr. Gill said he could see face of a member of audience next to him and the next one on the same row of seats, but any further not clear.

A good standard to adopt in these instances would be the perception of people rather than disputed forms. The example of a person, such as Mrs. Duncan, standing at the curtains at the start of the séance provides a good measure of what members in the audience could see in those red light conditions. Worth, in his witness statement, stated 'certain members of the audience agreed' they could see Mrs. Duncan standing at the front, at the trial he agreed it was murmured assent. Mr. Homer who sat in the front row next to him claimed, at the start of the séance when Mrs. Duncan was standing at the side of the curtains, that everyone said 'We can see the outline of her face clearly'. Burrell supports this account when the question was posed aloud 'Can you see Mrs. Duncan', people in the audience said 'Yes'. Cross who was sitting in the 2nd row next to Worth, confirms in his police statement that the audience agreed when asked by Albert whether they could confirm that they could see Mrs. Duncan at the curtains.

If we examine the prosecution witnesses' various statements, describing what they saw at the seances, from the witness statements, statements given on oath at the pre-trial justices hearing and later on oath at the Old Bailey, then this may given us further insight into this matter. The room conditions seem to have got darker in the course of Lt. Worth's accounts. In his first statement when he was in the first row next to Mr. Homer, he stated that when Albert invited Mrs. Duncan to come to the curtains, he saw the outline of Mrs. Duncan's face and neck in the opening between curtains. Although he reports not to have seen any features on Albert he could make out enough features to recognize Mrs. Duncan.

In his next statement, given on oath in late February to the Portsmouth magistrates, all he managed to report was a visible dark form. It was very dark but he could see the faint outline of a face, which could have been Mrs. Duncan's. At the trial all he could see was a dark shape which he gathered was Mrs. Duncan. So from describing seeing the outline of Mrs. Duncan's face and neck in his first statement made in January, the lighting gradually deteriorated in his memory, to the extent that he only saw a dark form which could have been or he assumed was Mrs. Duncan.

Another prosecution witness Mrs. Lock directly contradicts Worth's account. She was seated in a similar place to Worth, next to Mr. Homer in the front row on the 18th. She claimed in her police statement to have seen Mrs. Duncan at the front of the curtains. She agrees with most of the defence witnesses about the general lighting conditions, claiming that one could see quite distinctly if one was standing at the end of the 2nd row near the door. This position would be around 9-10' to the front of curtains.

On the 17th whilst in a similar position in the 2nd row next to her husband, Mrs. Lock reports distinctly seeing the facial features of a figure who pulled the shroud away from their face revealing black hair and a very red complexion. Whilst in the same position as Worth was on the 18th, in her witness statement she made the point that the bird she saw looked like a real bird. It is interesting that from the same seat next to Mr. Homer, Worth failed to see any animal forms, but Mrs. Lock saw green in the flowers that she identified as chrysanthemums from two feet away. Mrs. Lock clearly saw both Mrs. Duncan and the features of spirit forms from the front and second rows. In cross-examination in answer to the question that she might be able to see well from the 2nd row on the left she answered 'You could see quite distinctly, in fact Mr. Homer gave permission to stand up. You could not see distinctly if sitting'.

It is difficult for the prosecution to dispute Mrs. Lock's eyesight under these conditions because they claim she was the one witness that confirmed Cross's account of seeing the white cloth pass through his fingers when he grabbed Mrs. Duncan. Mrs. Lock's evidence contradicts Worth's testimony about what one could see at the seance, while at the same time her ability to see clearly is used to support his account with regard the white material in Cross's hand.

In Mr. Fowler's unsigned witness statement it states there was just sufficient light to distinguish the position of the curtains in the corner. He couldn't distinguish very well the outlines of people unless they we very close. At the trial he agreed that as he was in the front row in front of the curtains he was in a good position, so when he was asked whether he saw everything fairly clearly, he replied 'Yes'.

He described Peggy as being like the size of a 16 or 17 year old girl. However when Loseby asked for any more details about the form, he said he couldn't see the figure well enough for that. He was in a good position and he agreed he could see everything clearly but he was unable to describe anything clearly! Interestingly in his unsigned witness statement, Fowler described how he distinguished the features on the face of a mutilated soldier, which clearly contradicts his assertion that he could not see clearly because of the poor light.

Mrs. Jennings, who was sitting in the middle of the second row, claimed in her evidence for the afternoon séance on the 19th of January that she saw no features on the forms, such as Peggy or other forms that got as close as 4' to her in her estimation. She claimed 'the room was dark, it was a very dark room'. When asked how Mrs. Duncan who was twenty stone could have danced like or imitated Peggy as she had inferred, she answered 'You could not see anything at all very plainly'. When Loseby provoked her and said that you could not see anything very plainly that she was not near enough to form an opinion, she retorted 'I was quite near enough to see what was going on. The whole room was not a large room'. She then concluded her evidence by describing in detail something that had interested her during the séance, how the figures disappeared. She explained she was interested and stood up to see the head portion disappear first, then from the shoulders down and last thing was a bit of white on the floor. Mrs. Jennings who described that the room was so dark you couldn't see anything 'very plainly' then plainly describes events that she saw and states she could see 'plain enough'!

Ena Harris, Mrs. Lock's daughter attended two seances on the 19th of January in the afternoon and evening. In the evening séance that Worth and Cross attended, she was seated in the third row directly behind Worth. At the trial Ena Harris announced 'You couldn't see nothing'. Her comment became much quoted by the journalists present. Her witness statements reveal a different picture however.

In the afternoon seance that Mrs. Jennings also attended, Mrs. Harris was seated in the front row. She described clearly seeing Mrs. Duncan's features when she came to the entrance of the curtains. She saw her face; a bluey red complexion with her dark hair brushed back, and closed eyes as she stood next to Albert. You will recall that Burrell and Fowler's unsigned statement reported they couldn't see Mrs. Duncan at all from that position and Worth changed his account to match theirs. All three reported not seeing Mrs. Duncan and Albert standing together, while Mrs. Harris claims, like other defence witnesses, that she clearly had.

When Ena Harris was seated in the third row behind Worth in the evening séance she again stated she recognised Mrs. Duncan at the curtains. Even though she was seated behind Worth, like other defence witnesses seated next to or behind him, she distinguished features he claimed he was unable to distinguish. At the trial Worth defied anyone to see the features of a form a foot or so away from him, due to the poor lighting conditions. Well, two other prosecution witnesses, Mrs. Lock's and Mrs. Harris's statements certainly challenge him. He is the one witness that needs to account for why he states that he did not see features which virtually everyone else did (including both other prosecution witnesses), one of whom gave crucial evidence seeing white material in Cross's hand.

Clearly, Mrs. Harris's account regarding the lighting, changed radically like other prosecution witnesses, from the time of making her witness statements to the time she gave her testimony at the Old Bailey. Contrary to her statement made at the trial, she 'couldn't see nothing', she was quite able to recognise features from the front row and while at the back, which is consistent with the reports of other people present at these seances.

Burrell was one of the most articulate prosecution witnesses regarding the nature of the light during the seances. He saw no features on the many forms that appeared on the 17th and 18th of January. The conditions were also too dark to spot any possible deception of Mr. Homer passing something to Mrs. Duncan as he closed the curtains. Even though Burrell was in a front row seat, in front of the curtains, seated next to Mr. Homer, forms came to within a foot of him and his head was at times only a foot away from the curtains he could not discern properly. At a distance that many other witnesses described seeing features in detail, the darkness meant he could not discern properly. He said he was in a position to see clearly but there just wasn't sufficient light to see by. In spite of these conditions, in an apparent contradiction, he did claim to see the form of a hand emerge holding a torch covered in a cloth.

The next day Mr. Burrell was in an even worse position in see. He was standing many feet further back in the third row. Consistent with the lighting conditions he describes, he didn't see the bird purported to be on Mrs. Duncan's hand that others present claim to have seen. He saw no features on Peggy, or the silvery hair other members of the audience claimed to have seen on the head of a figure of an old man that purportedly appeared. But when standing at the back he saw an arm poked through the curtains, which he described it in detail. He saw a well-defined 'nice arm' that was white and flesh-like in colour. It was a big fat arm from bicep down to wrist and he had no doubt it was Mrs. Duncan's.

Although he said it was so dark he could not see features from the distance of a foot when seated in the front row, he now claimed he distinctly saw details of an arm while standing at the back in the third row. He was so certain from the details he would see that he had no doubt that it was an arm but also that it was Mrs. Duncan's arm, as his witness statement reports. He stood between 8.5' to 9.5' from the curtains yet despite all his claims that it would have been quite impossible to see clearly at one foot, he now claims to have seen clearly a part of an arm in a position nine times that distance.

Mr. Burrell's evidence, like many other prosecution witnesses is clearly self-contradictory and he uses the lighting to support whatever statement he wishes to make. At one time it is too dark to distinguish features at a distance of a foot when he is challenged to account for differences between his evidence and other sitters, then when it suits him he can distinguish features on much smaller forms when he is around 9' away in the third row. In both instances he assuredly claims his recognition was accurate and in both instances he accuses Mrs. Duncan of fraud.

These inconsistencies represent the type of error characteristic of a conspiracy. In order for the prosecution to conspire to convict Mrs. Duncan they have to stick to the position that no features were apparent on the forms she produced, yet there was enough light to see things that indicate that Mrs. Duncan was acting fraudulently. This position is double edged as we have seen. It seems clear that those behind the conspiracy had not completely thought through all the aspects of presenting such a position from the very start, hence the changing statements of the prosecution witnesses. It seems that Worth and

Burrell were prepared to make false statements from the start as their accounts are self contradictory and in complete contrast with all those people seated around them. But Cross and Fowler's descriptions did not quite fit the strict position that needed to be maintained. Clearly the light was sufficient to distinguish and identify the features of Mrs. Duncan standing at the curtains and certain recognisable features of the forms that emerged from the curtains. This had to be denied as we have seen the prosecution try to do, in order to discount the sheer weight of evidence against them by the numerous defence witnesses who recognised people they knew well. The inconsistencies of the testimony of Burrell and the Lock's show the type of error that will undoubtedly occur when trying to maintain an untenable position.

It is difficult to understand why the prosecution or the defence did not ask for the actual red bulb that was used to be called as an exhibit. Mr. Homer had the bulb locked away in a safe. Both may have felt that their case might be weakened if the actual brightness was known. The prosecution managed to paint a picture of darkness when in fact the actual wattage of the bulb might have demonstrated that as many defence witnesses asserted it was bright enough to see details of forms from different parts of the room. Loseby's strategy did not endeavour to raise 'technical' matters in challenging the prosecution case which he felt would lead to defeat. If he had done so he would have established that the red light was only 11' 6" from the front of the curtains. Possibly he was happy that the issue regarding the amount of brightness held a degree of uncertainty, as he may have feared that the lighting conditions were too low in the jury's view. We will never know. Loseby also failed to take the opportunity to raise the question of lighting in support of his client when scientific investigations of Mrs. Duncan's mediumship were referred to. Lighting was never cited as a problem, and eminent researchers including Harry Price tested her phenomena in very good light where one was able to read a newspaper. Price even reports a séance when he suggested lowering the lights and Albert refused saying he liked working in the light, 'everybody should work in the light'. There were also many other reports of Albert repeatedly asking for increased illumination under scientific testing conditions. Harry Price had even claimed in the press on the day he publicly denounced Helen Duncan as a fraud, that Helen's reputation as a medium had been enhanced because she performed in the light. Certainly the evidence of the witnesses strongly suggests that an objective demonstration of the brightness would have been in the defendant's interests and may have highlighted the discrepancies and contradictions inherent in several of the prosecution witnesses testimony.

The Preliminaries

Evidence of Forms and Mrs. Duncan being seen at the same time

One of the most telling pieces of evidence that occurred in full view of every member of the audience at the beginning of each séance, clearly counters the prosecution case. It is the arrangement by which Albert presented both himself and Mrs. Duncan to the audience at the same time. He accompanied this presentation with the question to the audience: 'Now can you see both of us?' This presentation shows to everyone present that Mrs. Duncan and the form known as Albert are separate and so this form is not Mrs. Duncan conducting an impersonation. This occurred at the beginning of every séance and the proceedings only commenced when the audience answered that they would see the two of them together. Dissenters were given an opportunity then to make their views known.

The prosecution team was clearly aware that this powerful demonstration undermined their case. A diagram shows the sequence of these events asserted by the defence and the varying accounts given by Lt. Worth. Mr. Homer described the customary opening of each séance. First of all he heard Albert's voice. From behind the closed curtains a voice says 'Is anyone going to say how do you do'. Albert himself opened the curtains and having asked Mrs. Duncan to stand up he holds the curtains open for her to appear. 'There we saw Mrs. Duncan standing at the side of the curtains. Albert asked each sitter whether they could see the outline of her face and everyone said 'We can see the outline of her face clearly. Albert was 9" to 1' away and I could see them both plainly'. Mrs. Duncan was in deep trance.

Other sitters confirmed that Albert had asked the audience to confirm 'Now can you see both Mrs. Duncan and myself'? (Mrs. Harris, Worth, Fowler). Then he said 'Mrs. Duncan can sit down there as a good girl and have a rest'. It is unclear from Mr. Homer's account when this statement is made, because he was interrupted during his testimony by questions about his actual seating position and his distance from the cabinet. Loseby was very critical of the Recorder's interventions, which he regarded as continuous.

As Albert opened the curtains for Mrs. Duncan to emerge, logically it was before Mrs. Duncan was seen. The only unclear aspect of Mr. Homer's testimony was whether Albert asked Mrs. Duncan to stand up and show herself from inside the cabinet or when he is outside the cabinet.

Mr. Homer sequence is shown below for the séance of the 14th

1) Voice from cabinet 'How do you do'
2) Albert opens curtains and appears
3) Albert asks Mrs. Duncan to stand up and Mrs. Duncan appears
   (Albert standing behind her a foot away)
4) Albert asks the audience whether they can see the outline of her face?
5) Albert asks the audience 'Now you can see both Mrs. Duncan
   and myself?'[1]
6) Albert asks Mrs. Duncan to sit down

When Worth gave his first police statement about the opening presentation
he described how the voice issued from the cabinet saying 'How do you do'. The
form of Albert then appeared by means of the curtains parting a little and a white
form rose up in the opening and remained there for a few seconds. The head
was covered completely in a shroud revealing the outline of a face. The voice
then stated that Mrs. Duncan was here. In dim light he saw the outline of Mrs.
Duncan's face and neck in the opening between curtains. The voice then
announced that here is 'Mrs. Duncan and myself'. Worth said that he saw the
figure of Albert but he could not distinguish Mrs. Duncan. The voice then
asked Mrs. Duncan to please sit down.

Worth's sequence for the 14th from his witness statement is shown below

1) Voice from cabinet 'How do you do'
2) Form of Albert rose up in the opening of the curtains for a few seconds.
3) Here is Mrs. Duncan and Mrs. Duncan appears between curtains
4) 'Here is myself and Mrs. Duncan'. Only Albert is apparent.
5) 'Please sit down Mrs. Duncan'.

In terms of what is said, Worth's account matches Mr. Homer's, but what
Worth claims to have seen at each point varies from the logic of the statements
and requests for confirmation that were made. The illustration showing the
different accounts highlights the contrasts. At the stage when Albert asserted
that he and Mrs. Duncan were visible, strangely Worth could not see Mrs.
Duncan even though he had recognised her and she had had been standing in
front of him a moment before and he had not mentioned that she had retired.
Worth also doesn't explain that Albert came forward again but this is presumed
since Worth states he only appeared for a few seconds at the beginning. Fowler's
unsigned witness statement supports this assumption, when he states Albert
reappeared. Both Fowler's unsigned statement and Worth offer no explanation
why Mrs. Duncan should not be seen when Albert reappears, given they do not

139

Diagram showing sequence of events conducted by Albert at the start of every seance in Mr. Homer's and Lt. Worth's accounts.

Notes:

V: refers to Albert's Voice
1 V: 'Now can you see both Mrs. Duncan & myself?
Mrs. D refers to the statement 'Mrs. Duncan'.

Homer's Trial Testimony

V: 'How do you do?

Curtains open Albert appears. V: 'Mrs Duncan stand up'.

Mrs. Duncan appears V: 'Can you see Mrs. D's face?' cont. 1

Mrs. Duncan leaves to sit down leaving Albert

Worth's Police Statement

V: 'How do you do?

Curtains open White form rises up for a few seconds

V: 'Here is Mrs. Duncan'. (unclear if closed or not)

Mrs. Duncan appears V: 'Here is Mrs. Duncan & myself'.

Albert present V: 'Please sit down Mrs. Duncan'.

Worth's Magistrates Statement

V: 'How do you do?

White form appears V: 'Pleased to see so many familiar faces'.

V: 'I'm going to ask Mrs. D to come foward so you can see her'.

Dark form appears V: 'Sit down Mrs. Duncan'.

Curtain closes

Worth's Trial Testimony

V: 'How do you do?

White form appears & walks back

Curtains close V: 'Here is Mrs. D for you to see'.

Dark form appears V: 'There is no doubt about it being Mrs. D. Sit down'.

Curtains close V: 'Mrs. Duncan & myself'.

White form appears

Curtains close quickly

describe her moving away after appearing a moment earlier. Fowler and Worth assert that then Albert's voice tells Mrs. Duncan to sit down even though in their accounts she was not there.

In the following sworn statement Worth made at the Magistrates Court he changes the order of events still further

1) Voice from cabinet 'How do you do?'
2) Form of Albert appears between curtains
3) Voice says Pleased to see so many familiar faces amongst the audience
4) Albert retires
5) Voice asks Mrs. Duncan to come forward so that you can see her
6) Dark form appears
7) Voice asks Mrs. Duncan to sit down
8) Curtain closes quickly

In the magistrates statement Worth omits the announcement of Mrs. Duncan and Albert appearing together. In this account Albert and Mrs. Duncan are only presented separately to the audience and Albert fails to return.

Worth stated that a refined man's voice from cabinet started by saying 'How do you do'. He looked towards the curtains and saw a white form, which appeared between them. He could not distinguish any features but there was a space where the face would be. The figure said he was pleased to see so many familiar faces amongst the audience and then the form retired. The voice then said that he was going to ask Mrs. Duncan to come forward so that you can all see her. Worth heard the sound of someone getting out of chair, the curtains parted slightly and then a dark form was visible. He said it was very dark but that he could see the faint outline of a face, which could have been Mrs. Duncan's. The Voice asked Mrs. Duncan to sit down and then the curtains quickly closed.

By the time of the trial Worth had changed the order of appearance yet again:

1) Voice from cabinet said How do you do?
2) White draped figure appears between curtains which slowly parted
3) Albert went back into curtains and curtains closed again
4) Voice 'Here is Mrs. Duncan for you to see'
5) Dark shape appears between curtains we gathered was Mrs. Duncan
6) 'There is no doubt about it being Mrs. Duncan, is there?'
   Waits for audience response
7) Voice asks her to sit down
8) Voice said 'Mrs. Duncan and myself'

9) Curtains parted and Worth saw a shrouded white figure but not
   Mrs. Duncan
10) Curtains closed again quickly

In Worth's trial version after Mrs. Duncan comes forward she is now asked to sit down again. Then Albert announces 'Mrs. Duncan and myself' and the curtains open, but as far as Worth states Mrs. Duncan isn't there. Under cross-examination he admits that several people in the audience said they could see Mrs. Duncan standing next to Albert when the curtains parted. Fowler's unsigned witness statement also states that several people in the audience said they could see two figures standing together at one time.

Worth's original account matches Mr. Homer's account most closely. It is quick and straightforward. Albert asks Mrs. Duncan to stand up and as she appears he asks the audience whether they can see her and then asks whether they can see both Mrs. Duncan and him standing together. In Worth's original version Albert disappeared and reappeared again, while in Homer's version Albert is standing there all the time. In Worth's magistrate's statement account Mrs. Duncan is asked to sit down after she appears and the demonstration of them standing together between the curtains is completely omitted. At the trial Worth had introduced the addition of asking Mrs. Duncan to sit down after she first appeared only for her to be asked to stand up again to reappear at the curtains and then sit down again.

It is clear from the changes to Worth's account that the prosecution had a problem they needed to overcome but they may not have been sure which was the best method to use. The nature of the inconsistencies suggests an attempt to present a picture of Albert and Mrs. Duncan as not being present at the same time. First Albert appears and he is recognized and then he retires. Then a disembodied voice calls Mrs. Duncan to show herself and then after doing so she retires into the cabinet. Then the disembodied voice announces Mrs. Duncan and myself, suggesting they will both come to the entrance of the cabinet at the same time and what happens, only Albert is seen. This sequence is designed to fit the prosecution's case as closely as possible. Mrs. Duncan is the only figure conducting the fraud and so she is never seen with another figure at the same time. The fact that this contradicts the audience's reaction and the statements of other witnesses, is put down again to the failure of other members of the audience and 'believers' to critically question what they are seeing. Ironically, any critical analysis shows it is Worth and Cross's version that fails to stand up to scrutiny when such an analysis is applied, because it lacks consistency and it is contradictory.

WRC Cross's version for the 19th basically fitted Worth's second account with two exceptions. Albert appeared between curtains first of all and then said 'How do you do', whereas Worth said the voice from the cabinet was the first thing that was noticed. Secondly Cross states that Albert clearly stated after Mrs. Duncan had come forward 'there is no doubt about that being Mrs. Duncan, is there?' Many witnesses assert this statement was made so then again this feature accords better with Mr. Homer's version than Worth's. Cross's version like Worth's omit any reference to both Mrs. Duncan and Albert being asked to stand together or any such announcement being made. Ena Harris's account for this séance agrees with Cross's although she agrees with Mr. Homer's for the afternoon séance.

At the trial Mr. Homer said everyone in the audience agreed they could see Mrs. Duncan standing between the curtains. He said Albert was 9" to 1' away from Mrs. Duncan and he could see them plainly. He described Mrs. Duncan as being in deep trance and that he could even see ectoplasm in her mouth. Ada St. George who was present on the 14th January said in her police statement that she saw 'Mrs. Duncan standing at the same time as the white figure' that she knew as Albert.

Prosecution witness Ena Harris's account for the afternoon séance on the 19th of January made in her initial witness statement is a case in point. Sitting in the front row she asserted that after Albert had appeared he asked whether everyone could see him. Everyone answered 'yes'. Then the voice asked whether the audience can see Mrs. Duncan and then the face of Mrs. Duncan showed through the curtains by the side of Albert. Mrs. Harris could see Mrs. Duncan's face. She saw her bluey-red complexion, her dark hair and that she had her eyes closed. Albert then asked whether the audience could see them both. Humorously, he added that as long as you can see him, he was the one that mattered.

Mr. White describes, at a Mrs. Duncan séance at the same venue 4 months earlier, the same sequence of events when Mrs. Duncan joined Albert at the entrance of the cabinet so they are seen together by the audience. His witness statement confirms that he attended the 19th of January séance and that he witnessed a similar performance. Mr. Bush in his police statement confirms Mr. Homer's and Mr. White's account. Mr. Bush was seated next to Worth. After Albert appeared between the curtains he asked Mrs. Duncan to show herself at which point something dark appeared which he took to be Mrs. Duncan face. Mr. Bush noted the difference in height between Albert and Mrs. Duncan. Mr. Bush like Mr. Homer and Mr. White does not describe Albert going back into the cabinet after he asked Mrs. Duncan to show herself. Ena Harris who sat in the third row changed her account for this séance saying that after Albert appeared he called Mrs. Duncan to the curtains and then withdrew after which Mrs. Duncan appeared. She retired and the white form reappeared.

Other double sightings

There were several other instances during the seances when Mrs. Duncan and a white figure were seen together. Loseby in his cross-examination of Worth claimed the curtains were pulled wide apart and Jarvis (a form representing the deceased brother of one of the sitters) and Mrs. Duncan was seen separately, quite apart from one another. Worth acknowledged that Jarvis had pulled the curtains apart a little way and said 'there she is in there' but Worth claimed he could not see anybody. He claimed he could not remember whether other people said they could see them both at the same time.

On the 18th January John Williams explained that he actually put his head into the cabinet and stood talking to his mother whilst at the same time seeing Mrs. Duncan in the chair. Mr. Williams stated they were 2' apart. His mother was standing in front of Mrs. Duncan just inside the curtain.

Nurse Rust who was present at a number of seances during January, including the 19th January séance with Worth, also describes an instance where she saw her husband materialize over the top half of Mrs. Duncan who had been brought to the opening of the curtains. Both Mrs. Duncan and her husband could be seen together, with him shown head and shoulders above and Mrs. Duncan's body below. Mrs. Duncan's head and shoulders had been transfigured into Nurse Rust's husband. Her husband then bowed to her.

During cross-examination by junior Prosecuting Counsel, Mr. Elam asked Mrs. Coulcher to describe what occurred when a torch was used with a form that had come to her. Mrs. Coulcher explained at a séance with Mrs. Duncan the previous September sitters had asked Albert whether it was possible to light up the features of a materialized person. He then asked a woman in the audience who had a torch in her handbag to give him her torch. Then he lit up the 'whole of the features' of a materialized lady who was standing next to him. Upon further questioning by Mr. Elam about this matter Mrs. Coulcher then described another instance at the same seance in which her cousin appeared as a form. She had a 'spirit light' in her hand (similar to the light emitted by glow worm) and Albert stood behind her, held a real torch high above her and switched it on at the same time that her cousin had the spirit light on. We have here two instances of two forms being clearly seen in front of the cabinet with clear illumination provided by white light.

Two forms were also visible at the same time on the 18th of January according to Mr. Burrell's witness statement and sworn police court statement. Burrell said he saw the white form of Mrs. Allen outside the curtains at the same time her swollen arm materialized and was pushed through the curtains. Mrs. Homer had held Mrs. Allen's arm and after she had said 'God bless you dear', both the white form and the arm disappeared. Naturally it would be quite impossible for Mrs. Duncan to put her arm through the curtains at the same time as she is impersonating Mrs. Allen in front of the curtains, covered in a white sheet and talking to people as the prosecution alleges. This anomaly reflects the tangle Burrell probably got into in his inconsistent and contradictory testimony. Its ridiculous nature suggests that it probably never actually occurred, but if we take Burrell's testimony at face value this is what he described.

It seems a serious oversight by Loseby not to make use of the wealth of evidence available from the witnesses supporting the observation that Mrs. Duncan and the forms she was accused to have been operating herself were seen together at the same time. He assumed that as several people had said that the audience had agreed with Albert that they were seen together, then the jury would view the matter clearly. It is worth noting that Albert stood 6' tall and Mrs. Duncan only 5' 4" so Loseby had every opportunity to explore the issue and put the prosecution to the test, to try and explain how Mrs. Duncan achieved such a distinctive double presentation. Maude tried to confuse the issue of the double sighting by stating that although Albert asked the audience to agree that Mrs. Duncan and he were seen together, the way Maude described it, clearly made this request nonsensical, as Mrs. Duncan was said not to be present at the time.

The Recorder appeared to be aware of the significance of the double sighting, because he examined witnesses who described this occurring or whose descriptions led to this possibility. He did so when Worth, Mr. Williams, and Mr. Barnes gave evidence. The Recorder also interrupted those occasions when witnesses were about to develop what they saw on these occasions. When Worth was being asked about the sequence of events leading up to the double sighting, the Recorder interjects. He also encourages witnesses not to repeat the preliminaries to the seances, even though he must have been aware that the double sightings they saw were crucial. Only on a few occasions did Loseby seek confirmation of this double sighting from the witnesses, even though he could have done so with every witness. The prosecution tried their best to present a completely different picture, through Worth's testimony and by not referring to the double sighting announcement by Albert. It is interesting that the purported 'spirit world' operating the seance seemed to have a procedure at the beginning specifically designed to silence those who suspected Mrs. Duncan is conducting a fraud, yet Loseby failed to understand the significance of it and capitalise on it. The prosecution did not ask their witnesses to describe this phase of the séance and when it did arise they all said they could not recognise Mrs. Duncan when she was presented to be standing beside Albert.

The statements of prosecution witness Mrs. Bessie Lock most dramatically showed the changes that occurred in accounts about what took place. In her police statement Mrs. Lock states that on two occasions she saw both Albert and Mrs. Duncan standing together. On the 17th January when she is in the second row she describes how Albert's voice asked whether the audience could see him. She confirmed that the audience answered that they could. She then saw Albert bring Mrs. Duncan to the front of the curtains where she saw Mrs. Duncan and a taller white form standing at the back of her, although she couldn't distinguish any features.

The next day, when in the front row she describes the same occurrence. Albert's voice asked whether the audience could see him. She saw a tall white form showing no features. Then when the curtains were pulled back and she saw Mrs. Duncan upper body. 'Above her I could see a form taller but no features'. She stated that she did 'in fact' see both the form and Mrs. Duncan standing together and then together they both retired. She described the opening of the meeting on the following day as being the same as the previous two occasions. By the time of the trial her story had changed completely.

At the trial under cross-examination by junior Defence Counsel Mr. Pedler, Mrs. Lock was asked whether she had seen the curtains open and both the figures seen separately. She answered 'No'. At no time did she see curtains open except when the time when the hand appeared with a bird on. This directly contradicts her police statements, however, it now accords with Worth's account and the prosecution's overall position.

The same level of misrepresentation about the double sighting of Mrs. Duncan and the forms can be seen in the Recorder's summing up. The Recorder states for the 14th of January that Mr. Homer said that he heard the voice and he saw the spirit form of Albert and 'this face with a beard'. Albert asked whether the audience could see him and Mrs. Duncan standing there together. The Recorder goes on to assert that Mr. Homer said he clearly saw Albert in ectoplasm and then Albert asked Mrs. Duncan to sit down and have a good rest, having invited her to stand up. Then Albert took over the running of the demonstration. The Recorder's account clearly misrepresents Mr. Homer's evidence. Mr. Homer had testified that he saw Mrs. Duncan come forward and everyone in the audience agreed they saw the same and that he saw Mrs. Duncan and Albert standing together 9" to 1' apart at the same time. The Recorder's account presents the same incomplete and misleading picture as the prosecution did over this crucial piece of evidence. Given that Recorder Dodson had specifically asked questions of witnesses about these very matters, it raises serious questions about why he misrepresented it in the way he did.

Separation of Voice from the Location of the Forms

We have charted the way the prosecution changed their account to try to present a picture of only one figure being seen between the curtains at any one time. There is another important feature of evidence that is involved in this process, which the prosecution attempted to play down.   Not only is evidence of Mrs. Duncan and figures being seen together at the same time is very damaging to the prosecution case but also instances where the form or Mrs. Duncan can be seen but the voice emanates from somewhere else.   Worth's complicated sequencing of figures appearing and retiring creates it's own set of problems because as the voice is always Albert and Albert isn't (in Worth's account) always visible then it is essential he speaks when Mrs. Duncan is also not visible.   This is not always easy to assert given the order of events he describes.   Worth's account has a further peculiar feature which involves Albert asking questions to the audience 'Can you see Mrs. Duncan?' 'Can you see Mrs. Duncan and myself?' before the forms are actually there to be seen.   He isn't always successful in doing so and witnesses describe other instances that reveal the voice does not come from the figure that is visible to the audience.

Mr. Homer's account of Mrs. Duncan being seen standing 9" to 1' apart from Albert at the same time that Albert is speaking and Mrs. Duncan in trance with ectoplasm in her mouth, clearly demonstrates the impossibility of Mrs. Duncan also being Albert.

During his testimony Worth describes Mrs. Duncan being shown as a dark form then retiring, he agrees at that time a voice asked the audience 'There is no doubt about it being Mrs. Duncan is there?'   It is unclear from Worth's testimony whether this occurred when the dark form was present or after it retired. Fowler's and Cross's police statements for the 14th and 19th of January seem to clarify the picture. Fowler's unsigned witness statement asserts that when Albert disappeared he declared that Mrs. Duncan was here and then he saw the outline of Mrs. Duncan.   While she appeared at the curtains, Albert's voice coming from inside the cabinet   declared that here is Mrs. Duncan and myself afterwhich the white form reappeared.   Cross's statement describes the face of Mrs. Duncan being visible between the curtains when Albert's voice is telling the audience that there is no doubt about that being Mrs. Duncan, to which the members of the audience agreed.   Clearly in both Fowler's and Cross's accounts the voice and Mrs. Duncan are separate.

Mrs. Lock's and her daughter Ena Harris's police statements further confirm this fact. Mrs. Lock describes how on the 17th of January, as she saw Albert and Mrs. Duncan standing together between the curtains, Albert asked the audience whether they could see Mrs. Duncan. He then asked for confirmation whether they could also see him. In the afternoon séance of the 19th of January Ena

Harris described seeing Albert at the curtains and then clearly seeing Mrs. Duncan appear, she saw her facial features in detail. Albert confirmed this occurrence saying 'Now you can see both of us'.

Mr. Burrell's witness statement describes a moment at the start of the séance on the 18th where Mrs. Duncan is visible to the audience at the curtains and the voice of Albert asks the audience whether they can see her. Burrell states that the people in the audience confirmed aloud that they could.

There are further examples of this voice and figure separation occurring in the course of the seances. Mr. Kirkby recalls hearing Mrs. Duncan breathing in the cabinet at the same time as being within 2' of a figure outside the cabinet. Both Worth and Fowler's unsigned witness statement describe an elderly aunt in her 90's being called out to meet her niece, whereupon a conversation takes place between the niece and Albert about the age of the form.

The best example of this occurring was on the 14th of January. The form of a young man who had a mutilated arm appeared. Albert informed the audience that this boy could not speak. All those witnesses, both the prosecution and defence described this incident and assert that while the form was outside the cabinet the voice of Albert from inside the cabinet spoke instructions and gave information. Prosecution witnesses Worth and Fowler describe this occurring. Even so, Worth's accounts from witness statement to trial testimony changed dramatically. Both he and Fowler's witness statements assert that while the form was out of the curtains the voice asked the lady sitter, who had identified the form, to come forward to feel the stump of his right arm. Ada St. George's police statement confirms this took place. She described how she saw this form, with a scar on the face and an arm without a hand, while the voice of Albert was talking.

At the trial Worth's version had changed considerably. He asserts that everything that was spoken took place between the voice in the cabinet and the lady, prior to the form emerging. That is, it relates to describing the conditions of the young man, the conversation about where the explosion occurred with the lady who had claimed him, that the young man would not speak, the request to call him out and touch his stump. All of what happened next, according to Worth, was that the form came between the curtains, a lady came forward and touched the stump, it then returned.

This account contrasts sharply from his and Fowler's earlier account, but matches the consistent editing of statements by the time of the trial, to separate Mrs. Duncan from the forms, in terms of voice and visibility. Ada St. George's witness statement describes seeing the figure at the same time the voice was speaking. She agrees that the request to come and feel the arm was made while the figure was visible but she mistakenly says the form made this request. As the other witnesses Worth (police statement and at trial), Mrs. Tremlett (trial) and Fowler (unsigned police statement) agree, that as the form could not and did not speak, then this request must have occurred from within the cabinet at this time.

During the trial Loseby failed to ask his witnesses any details of what took place when this mutilated figure was announced. He asked his witnesses about many other occurrences that took place on the 14th January, but he avoided any reference to this figure. It is clear from the evidence available that if he had explored the versions of events a little closer, he would have been able to show not only that Worth's account had no support, but that it was another instance where the voice and form were separate. Its importance cannot be underestimated, as it was quite impossible for Mrs. Duncan to be the figure whilst at the same time creating the voice from inside the cabinet or the figure standing next to her. Presenting this evidence would have forced the prosecution to explain how this might have occurred.

Dodson's role in this misrepresentation is shown when in his summing up of Worth's evidence he states there was a mutilated form of an arm. When a lady went forward to touch the arm, the form to which the arm belonged asked the lady whether they had felt the stump. Neither Worth or any of the witnesses claim such an event ever took place. It is significant that in an instance where the voice and form were separate, Dodson asserts that the form spoke, when clearly it did not. This is similar to his misrepresentation of Mr. Homer's description of Mrs. Duncan and Albert appearing and being seen together. Dodson states Albert said to Mrs. Duncan: 'Sit down, Mrs. Duncan – having invited her to stand up 'and have a good rest'. Because Dodson never acknowledges that Mr. Homer actually saw Mrs. Duncan and Albert together, then his description of Albert asking her to sit down and have a good rest avoids placing the comment being made at the same time they were both clearly visible together. These types of editing, changes and subtle misrepresentation are necessary when people conspire to paint a picture, which is required by definition to distort the truth of what took place. Tracing these changes and errors show that they are not arbitrary. They are related to crucial evidence which could show that the prosecution case is unfounded if focused upon by an intelligent juror, observer or journalist. When conspiracies are asserted, analysing the errors and inconsistencies can help lead you to the truth.

Recognising Forms

The way materialisation evidence can be assessed is mostly critically demonstrated by those manifestations that are known to the sitter and that show themselves. Indeed, the police themselves use next of kin to formally identify bodies of deceased people. Interestingly, the police dismissed such evidence when relatives identify their loved ones, even though if the person were 'dead' this identification evidence would be actively sought and accepted. Consequently, examining what occurred when Albert brought forms to Worth, Burrell and the other prosecution witnesses, and how they described their experience, is most insightful.

Typically, the forms had the facial part of the veil cut away and in this area, according to many witnesses, recognisable facial features were apparent (see photographs). Even Worth, who saw no features, described this feature in the forms that presented themselves. If the prosecution was correct and Mrs. Duncan was moving around with a sheet over her head, then each face should have been Mrs. Duncan's.

Discrepancies between Worth's and most of the defence witnesses do not rest solely on the quality of the lighting or whether two forms were seen at the same time. There are discrepancies in terms of what he claims to have heard, seen and remembered.

Let us examine in detail Worth's description of the seances he attended and the forms he saw, which formed the basis of his evidence against Mrs. Duncan and her co-defendants.

Séance 14th January
Lady brought through to Worth

It was stated at the trial by Recorder Dodson that the case for the prosecution rested upon Worth's testimony and that it differed markedly from practically all the other witnesses present at the time. No one corroborated his testimony for the 14th and only WRC Cross corroborated his testimony on the evening of the 19th.

Probably the most talked about and damning evidence to the defence occurred when Lt. Worth claimed a form appeared who confirmed that it was his aunt, when in fact he didn't have an aunt in the spirit world. This incident was covered in every newspaper and it set the tone of the prosecution case along with the other two forms that were presented to him.

At the trial Worth described how his first contact with Albert came when a voice from the cabinet said 'I have here a lady who passed with a problem to the lower part of her body and the bowels'. The voice asked someone to call this lady out Worth was prompted by Mrs. Homer and Mrs. Brown to do so. Worth asked who it was. He was told the type of question should be phrased 'Is it for me?' and when he did so the Voice in the cabinet confirmed 'that's the voice'. Worth then asked the form to please come out. A white shrouded shape then stood between the curtains. Worth asked the form: Are you my aunt? The form replied, in a husky voice, that it was, then it went back into the curtains.

The form came down to the ground giving the impression of a large person beneath. During cross-examination, at one point Worth agreed that the figure came out of the cabinet, then he said the figure stood between the curtains and only partly outside, but that she never came completely out.

Other witnesses describe something very different occurring, but they all agree that Worth said 'Is it my aunt?'

Mrs. Jopling said Albert declared 'I have a spirit form here for the gentleman on my left', and he asked him to ask the female form to please come forward. Mr. Homer confirmed this account asserting that Albert said 'he has here an old lady for a sitter on Mr. Homer's right'. Homer testified that there were only two Naval gentlemen on his right and Surg. Lt. Fowler spoke first and Albert said 'That is not the voice'. Then Mr. Worth asked whether it was for him and for it to please come out. A lady came out of the cabinet 3-4' right up to Worth and peered into his face. Worth then asked 'Are you an Aunt of mine'? or 'Is it my aunt'? Then the lady looked right at him and said 'You are trying to act strange, aren't you? She then disappeared right in front of Mr. Homer and Worth. Albert observed aloud that 'she didn't get much of a welcome'.

This account is clearly very different from Worth's in terms of where in the room Albert said the recipient was located, what the form said, what it looked like, where it went to and how it disappeared.

The other witness descriptions tell the same story:

'of a sweet old lady' (Rose Cole (window seat), Irene Taylor (sitting next to Rose Cole), Mr. Homer (sitting next to Worth in front row), Mrs. Tremlett (seated towards the back), 'coming right out of the cabinet to Mr. Worth' (Cole, Taylor, Tremlett, Dora Jopling (second row)), 'looked Worth right in the face' (Cole, Mr. Homer, Tremlett) and said 'You are trying to be strange are you not' (Cole, Taylor, Mr. Homer, Tremlett, Jopling)

The form was very thin and slender (Tremlett, Mr. Homer), rather bent and stooping. (Tremlett, Taylor), with long features (Taylor), a pointed chin (Tremlett, Taylor, Mr. Homer), a very old face, greying hair and just over 5' 1" to 5' 2" tall (Mr. Homer)

According to the other witnesses, after the form spoke, it then dematerialised, disappeared (Tremlett), sank through the floor where it stood (Jopling, Homer).

It is clear that the differences between the accounts are not due to lighting. Completely different accounts are given, in terms of the features that were seen, the actions that took place and what was said.

What is interesting in Worth's witness statement is his explanation for mentioning an aunt when he later claimed he knew he did not have an aunt who was dead. He said he thought quickly in order to place a lost relation and could only think of an aunt of his mother. In the next statement he gives no explanation merely saying he could not place this relative and said 'Are you my aunt?' At the trial he changes his position stating 'all my aunts are living'. Worth was the first person to mention an aunt. Why did he do so knowing he did not have an aunt whom had deceased? Loseby made much play of it, as he was the person who introduced a fictitious deceased aunt and only he claims the lady replied 'Yes'. All the other witnesses asked about the encounter contradict him and say the lady never confirmed that she was his aunt but declared that 'You are trying to act strangely'.

If you are an intelligence officer attempting to imprison Mrs. Duncan it is essential that none of the manifestations brought to you be verified. So deliberately misidentifying them is an excellent strategy to adopt. A form of a lady he possibly recognises approaches him and he misidentifies her - whoever approaches he has to reject it.

Wing Commander Mackie (seated in the second row behind Worth and Fowler) did not contradict Worth's testimony about the 'Aunt' figure. Mackie stated he was not too clear on point and could not recollect that the figure came out. Mackie said that Worth had said he had not got an aunt.

This is very interesting because Mackie's version doesn't fit any of the accounts, neither Worth's nor the other witnesses. Worth never said at the time 'I have not got an Aunt'. This was only said afterwards by way of explanation away from the seance room in the press and at court hearings. If there was a conspiracy to convict Mrs. Duncan then it would be expected that some pressure might have been applied to Mackie not to dispute Worth's central testimony because he was a fellow officer. Mackie's unusual error in stating he heard Worth say 'I don't have an aunt', certainly suggests that Mackie heard or read this comment in another context and transplanted it to his general understanding of Worth's position regarding the encounter.

The prosecution and the press made great play that because Worth and Fowler swapped the cards with their names on the seats, then the figures that went to Worth were intended for Fowler. It was claimed that Mrs. Duncan would remember where in the room people were seated and accordingly direct forms to them. As Loseby pointed out this calls for some great feat of memory. Mr. Homer asserted that in the case of a lady being ready in the cabinet to be identified by Worth, when Albert described the medical condition he stated that Fowler actually spoke up and he was told it was not the voice. This evidence contradicts the prosecution's assertion.

It is unclear why Loseby did not question Fowler about his aunts if as he claimed it was for him. Furthermore all the witnesses give the same account of the procedures followed in the seances. When a form was ready Albert gave a description of the condition of the person at the time of passing. When the voice of the sitter is recognised then the form came out of the cabinet to be claimed. Homer explained it does not matter where one sits because this method relies on the vibration or sound of the voice and not any particular seating position. Indeed many people may call out seeking to claim a form and if the prosecution were correct Mrs. Duncan would need to be able to distinguish the relevant voice from several calling out behind curtains knowing the appropriate position the voice emanated from. Given the curtains were closed during this time and so Mrs. Duncan has no opportunity of looking out, this suggestion seems highly improbable. It is worth noting that Wing Commander Mackie also stated he swapped his seating card with his neighbour when he attended a séance but identifiable forms still appeared to him.

It is interesting to note that Fowler's original unsigned police statement asserts that Albert said to Worth that he was not a Spiritualist but that he was interested, although he was 'very materialistic'. Ivy Stammers and Wing Commander Mackie confirm that Albert said to Worth that he was not a Spiritualist. Worth replied that he wasn't, but that he was interested. Mackie also said Albert repeated the question to Worth as to whether he was a Spiritualist before Worth concluded that 'well', he was an investigator or enquirer.

Dodson sums up pointing out Worth said once the figure had came out 'Are you my Aunt?' And he got the reply Yes? He has not got an aunt who is deceased. All his aunts are living. Dodson mentions that Fowler was not asked about the aunt and so in that respect Worth's evidence stands by itself. What is interesting is that despite all the testimony on this incident by both Worth and 5 defence witnesses, Dodson emphasises the matter in the case of Wing Commander Mackie.

Dodson, when summing up Wing Commander Mackie's evidence for the 14th said that Lt. Worth did 'undoubtedly' say that he did not have an aunt and that Mackie did not remember any figure coming out of the cabinet. The statement is misleading. Worth, from his testimony, nor any of the other witnesses present heard this statement, apart from Mackie, who said he had no recollection of a figure coming out (when everyone else does remember). To his credit he did say he was none to clear on the point of Worth's encounter with the lady.

Dodson highlighted a piece of evidence that had no support from Worth or the other witnesses. Yet clearly it would have the affect of strengthening the prosecution's case in the jury's mind, by giving the impression that Worth had rejected the figure of the aunt that had been presented to him. Such an argument is ridiculous because it was Worth who asked whether it was his aunt and not those operating the séance, consequently in this instance Worth would be rejecting his own false assertion. Worth stated that the figure answered 'Yes' but at no time did Worth then state at the séance 'Well I haven't got an aunt'. Asserting that Mackie 'undoubtedly' said something that is disputed by everyone else present is misleading and adds further to the flippant nature and the disregard the Recorder gives to the defence's evidence in his summing up.

It is interesting that Worth's most recent statements about what occurred matches Mackie's statement. He said in a Channel Four interview in 1998 that after asking the figure whether it was his aunt and the figure replying yes, he had said that's 'funny' because none of my aunts are dead. Clearly this later account bears no relation to his testimony but conveys the ridicule he wishes to express about the seance.

Loseby used this incident to cross-examine Worth most strenuously but it is unclear why he did not refer to what Worth had said originally that he thought it might be an aunt of his mother's. This provided a clear rationale to explain Worth's conduct instead of allowing him to assert that all of the aunts he can think of were living when clearly they were not.

Press Headline
Mystery of An Aunt
Daily Mirror 24.3.44

Worth's Uncle/Sailor

Worth claimed another form then appeared to him. In his account he claimed Albert referred to a man that had passed with trouble to his chest and that the form was for him. Worth asked if it was and Albert replied 'That's the voice'. Worth said please come out and a figure appeared before the curtains. Worth then asked whether it was his uncle. A husky voice said 'yes' and then the figure saluted and disappeared. Worth then sat down. Worth's version in his witness and police court statements are essentially the same.

At the trial Worth said he did not know whom to think of, so he just said 'Are you my uncle'. He claimed he had two deceased uncles one who was in the police and the other who had not been in the services. He said the salute could have been a cab drivers salute.

This incident again got much press coverage along with the form that said she was his aunt when he didn't have one. Now there was an uncle he couldn't recognise who saluted him!

No other witness recalls any such event occurring. Witnesses also specifically stated under cross-examination that no uncle ever appeared for Worth or saluted (Tremlett, Homer). They all assert that after the first lady came to Worth, the next figure intended to be claimed by him was not an uncle but a sailor.

Albert said there was another person for Lt. Worth, a sailor. Worth replied 'I know no sailor' and so the sailor did not show itself. Albert then reminded Worth that there was 'no rank and file' on their side.

Many witnesses were certain of this taking place. There was sailor for Worth (Mrs. Cole, Mackie, Mrs. Taylor, Mr. Homer, Mrs. Tremlett, Mrs. Jopling)

'Worth replied 'I know no sailor' (Homer, Mackie, Cole, Taylor, Jopling, Tremlett). The figure did not materialise (Cole, Homer, Jopling). Albert said 'There is no rank and file on our side of life (Mackie, Taylor, Homer, Tremlett, Jopling), or distinction on our side (Cole).

Mackie thought Albert's comments were a reproof for Worth and he thought Albert believed Worth was standing on his dignity. Mrs. Tremlett thought Albert raised the subject of Worth not being a Spiritualist while other witnesses thought this occurred after the first figure appeared for Worth. Understandably witnesses may be confused about the actual timing of this statement but all are in agreement regarding the subject matter.

So we have a situation where six witnesses either sitting next to Worth, in the row behind or along the window seat report that Worth's version of his uncle appearing and giving him a saluting never actually occurred. They all agree that quite another encounter occurred at that time regarding a sailor who Worth rejected and which Worth alone refutes.

Dodson in his summing announces we can disregard the uncle. Surely in an instance where not one other witness corroborates Worth's testimony but moreover completely contradict it, it is worthy of some summary. Dodson chose to disregard it, so it was disregarded, which of course assisted the prosecution and acted against the interests of the defendants.

It is clear that Worth being a Naval officer for over two years would have known many sailors, so saying that he knew no sailor was clearly false. He must have known scores of sailors and so a reasonable response would have been that he knew sailors. Worth's remark supports the view that as an intelligence officer it was essential that he reject forms that might appear to him and know him. If he had called it out there is every likelihood that information linking him with the form may have been given or other naval personnel present may have recognised the form. Certainly if a Naval link had been given then this information could have been checked and it would have been extremely damaging for any conspiracy to imprison Mrs. Duncan.

Worth's Sister

Albert then referred to a prematurely born sister of Worth's as being present, but Worth's mother denied she had ever had a prematurely born daughter. Apparently Worth's sister was alive and driving an ambulance in London.

Worth's version given at the trial goes as follows. Albert said he had a sister for the same gentleman. Worth replied 'I have only one sister who is alive'. The Voice repeated that the form was his sister. It explained that perhaps Worth didn't understand that she was premature'. Worth said that he was 'quite certain there were no premature children in our family'. The voice replied 'You can ask the question' then Worth sat down.

Other witnesses described a slightly different version, Albert said that he had a 'baby sister here for Lt. Worth in the spirit world' (Homer, Taylor, Tremlett), 'a premature baby who was his sister' (Taylor, Tremlett, Cole, Stammers). Worth replied that he had 'no baby sister' (Mr. Homer), 'that he never had a sister' (Cole, Tremlett), 'that he did not know her' (Stammers, Taylor). Albert then asks Worth to do something for him (Homer) and to get in touch with your mother (Homer, Cole, Taylor, Tremlett, Stammers) and Worth said that he will (Homer, Taylor, Tremlett).

There are two discrepancies between Worth's account and the other people who were seated around him. Not one witness agrees with Worth when he states that he said 'I have only have one sister, who is alive'. They all agree that he said either he did not have a sister or he did not know her. The witnesses also do not agree with him that he said 'I am quite certain there are no premature children in our family'.

Worth's earlier witness statement presents a slightly modified picture. He claimed Albert raised the issue tactfully, wondering aloud about how he might approach the subject. He said to Worth that he had with him a young girl who is his sister. Worth was puzzled replying that he only had one sister, who was still alive. Albert then asserted that this was definitely his sister and that she was a premature child. Albert explained that he may not understand now but that Worth can ask a question. It is only later in his magistrate's statement that Worth includes the comment about being certain there were no premature children in our family.

The three statements display a lessening of diplomacy on Albert's part, and the inclusion that Worth is quite certain there were no premature children in the family. Fowler's unsigned police statement also fails to recall Worth ever making the remark about him being certain there were no premature children in his family. These features suggest this comment was included later after some consideration.

Certainly such a statement is a challenge to Albert in stating the figure he has behind the curtains does not relate to him. It also matches the attitude Worth conveys during the trial as someone who experienced something very different to all the other witnesses and was able to see through the fraud.

What explanation can we find to explain why Worth said that he did not have a sister (alive or dead), as the other witnesses assert? Well if Worth was conspiring to convict Mrs. Duncan it would be important for him to reject the figures that were presented to him. He could hardly accept them and then accuse Mrs. Duncan of being a fraud. Naturally if he adopted that approach during the séance but he did have a sister, then he could not admit to having denied it in any trial, as the presence of a sister would demonstrate that he is being untruthful. In that regard Worth's final account has to declare he has a sister. It is strengthened further if he states she is alive. Whether he actually said it given six other people never heard him make this comment and some specifically denied he had done so under cross-examination (Taylor, Tremlett) is for others to make up their minds about. Certainly it shows again that at each stage of the proceedings there is an enormous discrepancy between Worth and the other witnesses. It also shows that further changes occurred to his accounts over the course of the different statements he made that strengthen the rejection of the assertions purportedly made by Albert and accords with the style he adopts during the trial.

After this séance Worth reported Mrs. Duncan to the police and the following day, the 16th when he saw Mr. Homer he stated that he had phoned his mother who had confirmed that she had had a premature birth of a sister for Worth. He claimed three times during cross-examination that he returned on police instructions and lied to Mr. Homer about his prematurely born sister based on these instructions. His mother did not have a telephone. He said he did so because he thought Mr. Homer had misled him and he should get a taste of his own medicine. Loseby denounced Worth as a liar and went on to say all of his evidence should be rejected. At the start of proceedings the next day when being re-examined by Elam, Worth was asked whether he lied to Mr. Homer on police instructions. He then changed his testimony and denied he had acted on police instructions but had acted on his own free will because it was necessary in the interests of justice to allay any suspicions they might have of him.

Dodson in his summing states the nature of the evidence for what it is, either Worth pointed out he had not got a sister or not one to which reference was made. He added that he did not have a prematurely born sister but did not mention that this was disputed. In summing up the evidence regarding Worth's lie to Mr. Homer, Dodson explained that when Worth had said he was acting on police instructions he only meant it in a general sense and he corrected it afterwards and said it was his own mistake.

Jarvis

Worth's account of the figure appearing named Jarvis introduced an element of bad language and ill-mannered conduct to the proceedings. The voice in the cabinet was identified by the medium Taylor Ineson who was sitting behind Mr. Homer in the second row. Taylor Ineson asked whether 'Is that you Jarvis' and Albert replied 'That's the voice'. A bulky figure the same size as the others came out and leaned over the first row and shook hands with his brother, who was by now standing in the 2nd row. A jovial sort of conversation took place. Taylor Inseon said 'How are you getting on?' Apparently the spirit said, 'He did not think much of the medium she is too fat'. He said he did not like her and she was too fat. He then asked 'Why have you got all these people with you, why don't you come here' (indicating the cabinet). Taylor Ineson declined. Then there was some muttered conversation between the two as though they were having a private joke and Worth distinctly caught the words 'bloody twisters'. Afterwards Taylor Ineson said 'Did you hear him swear at me?' And as Worth had heard word 'bloody twisters' he said 'Yes I did hear it'. I heard the words 'bloody twisters' in a Yorkshire dialect. After the séance Ineson told Mrs. Homer that Jarvis had sworn at him.

During cross-examination by Loseby, Worth agreed that at one stage Jarvis opened the curtains a little way and said 'she (Mrs. Duncan) is in there'. Worth said he did not see anybody there, although Loseby asserted that several people in the audience saw Mrs. Duncan at the same time as Jarvis. Loseby never raised this matter with any other witness so there is no evidence to support it.

Worth's account of Jarvis was very damaging to the defence. It led Loseby to give a lengthy explanation in his introduction. He explained to the court how spirits can swear even though they are in the spirit world and the séance started with a prayer. He explained that uncouth, abrupt, and foul-mouthed people can be good people and if uncouthness was their distinctive feature, then if they returned without these features they would not be recognised.

If the 'spirit' insulted Mrs. Duncan as Worth states, then one might wonder why, if Mrs. Duncan was conducting a fraud she would insult herself by saying the figure did not like her or insult her by calling herself fat. It would seem a very unusual thing to do and so in a strange way it can be viewed as good evidence that she was not doing so. On the other hand such swearing and insults would strengthen any prejudice against Spiritualists or people undertaking a fraud in the jury's mind, which would also be damaging to Mrs. Duncan.

Loseby did not ask any of his defence witnesses about the Jarvis encounter. Mr. Homer was cross-examined about it by Maude. Mr. Homer was sitting next to Mr. Worth, who was on his right so they were within a foot or so of each other. Mr. Homer stated he heard a quarrel between Taylor Ineson who was sitting behind him and Jarvis who had come out about 2' 6". Taylor Ineson leant over Mr. Homer's left shoulder and as Jarvis bent forward he heard him say 'You were always bloody sly'. He did not use the word twister. Jarvis then asked his brother Taylor into the cabinet but he declined.

To confuse matters further Maurice Barbanell, the Editor of the Psychic News, who attended and reported on the trial, in his book titled: The Case of Helen Duncan' (1945) reports that Homer testified that Jarvis used the expression 'you are always bloody slow' and not the phrase 'bloody sly'. The

Daily Mail dated 28.3.44 under the headline 'Albert's Ghost As 'Witness' and the Daily Express of the same date and under the headline 'Test Séance For Jury Rejected' agree with Barbanell. These reporters did not hear Mr. Homer say 'bloody sly' but 'bloody slow'. So to conclude, the expression Worth claimed to have heard 'bloody twister' is contested by Mr. Homer. The expression that the trial transcripts quote Mr. Homer as saying, that Jarvis actually said is further contested by the press who reported his testimony. The court transcripts do not reflect what the press heard the witness actually say.

Examination of Worth's witness statement (he did not mention Jarvis appearing in his magistrates statement) and Fowler's unsigned witness statement describe a much more jovial and less acrimonious encounter, although amid a mumbled conversation Worth asserts that he distinguished the words "bloody twisters". Fowler's unsigned witness statement while describing much of what occurred in identical language to Worth's statement offers no corroboration to Worth's assertion that the 'bloody twisters' comment was made. It states he could not distinguish what was said.

Mr. Homer's and Fowler's witness statement have none of the insults that Worth later said were made about Mrs. Duncan or reference to Taylor Ineson claiming that he had been sworn at. It is altogether a lively banter between two Yorkshire brothers. Surely as Jarvis spoke to his brother over Mr. Homer's left shoulder, Mr. Homer was in the best position to hear what was said compared to Worth who was seated on the other side of him. It seems to represent nothing other than probably a lively encounter. However Worth managed to convey it in a most damaging way, by adding further insults that were only included at the trial itself. Worth referred to swearing and later introduced offensive remarks, lacing it together with a word referring to swindlers or dishonest people, which Mrs. Duncan was charged with. It is good if people don't use the word bloody but many men do. Nevertheless it is extraordinary to suggest Mrs. Duncan would be so stupid to refer to swindling if she was conducting a fraudulent enterprise and acting the role of Jarvis who made the accusation as the prosecution suggests. How she also opened her curtains to reveal herself sitting in a chair at the same time shows the degree of expertise and manipulation one has to imagine in order to accept the prosecution case. This is not withstanding that they asserted that Mrs. Duncan, imitating the form, invited the sitter into the cabinet, which would have demonstrated to everyone present that she was not in there and so clearly demonstrated that she was acting fraudulently.

Dodson in his summing up refers to the encounter between Taylor Ineson and the spirit form Jarvis. Dodson includes a statement questioning whether Taylor Ineson is his right name when nothing has been raised to suggest it isn't. This only fuels a further sense of the underhand regarding those present at the séance and other mediums in particular. Dodson concluded by saying if it was a very convincing demonstration, all one can say is Lt. Worth was not convinced.

Press Headline
Says he heard a row between "ghost" and medium –
You're Too Fat, said Spirit – and a muttered "twister" followed
Daily Mirror 24.3.44

Mutilated Young Man

The aspect of the use of voice separate from the form has been discussed above. Worth describes a mutilated young man who appeared. Unfortunately Loseby made no attempt to challenge Worth's testimony about this incident in the same way he never did Jarvis's appearance.

In Worth's first witness statement he describes how Albert announced to the audience that he had a young man who passed over with violent mutilations to his body, which was not caused directly through the war. They occurred in China. Albert asked someone to claim him. A lady stood up saying she knew a young man who was in Shanghai when she had last heard of him. The voice confirmed 'that is the voice', but it was Singapore, not Shanghai. The woman explained that she knew that he had moved but that she didn't know where. The voice explained that the form cannot speak to you, as he is terribly mutilated, but that he will now let him come out.

A form appeared with most of its face shrouded. The lady asked if it was George and the form nodded. The voice of Albert then asked the lady to come forward and feel the stump of his right arm, which the lady duly did. The spirit then vanished and the lady sat down. The voice then asked if the lady had felt the stump of the arm and she replied that she had.[2]

In Worth's magistrate's statement the order is changed, with the request to feel the stump occurring before the form appeared. Albert announced him in the usual way, a lady stood up and claimed him. Albert explained that this young man could not speak as he was 'so terribly injured' explaining his arm was only a stump. He then asked a lady to come forward and feel the stump. A shrouded figure appeared and a lady went forward and touched something. Albert said that the injury had occurred out east in China. The lady asked if it was Shanghai and Albert said it was not, but it was Singapore. The form then went back into curtains. And voice behind the curtains asked if she felt the stump of the arm and the lady said that she had.

Clearly the account has been changed subtly. The encounter between the lady and Albert now refers to where the injuries occurred and it refers to the ignorance on Albert's part suggesting that he thought Singapore was east of China, when we know it is west of China.

In Worth's police statement Albert's mention of Singapore may relate to the lady's last knowledge of the man. While the second statement moves the request to feel the stump from when the form is outside the curtains to before the form has left the curtains, discussion still takes place between Albert and the sitter about where the injuries occurred, when the form is outside the cabinet. This is would be impossible if Mrs. Duncan was impersonating the young man, as the prosecution asserts, as well as creating the voices.

It is interesting that Fowler's unsigned witness statement matches Worth's word for word for the first seven sentences. This occurs in several places in their original witness statements which indicates that authentic individual statements were not produced for these officers but a fabricated statement was constructed to fit them both for whole sections. Nevertheless there is an interesting addition. Fowler's statement describes seeing a white figure appearing with part of face shrouded. It states that he could see an uncovered portion of a face but that he could not associate it with any face that he knew. Fowler completes his statement in the same way Worth does.

Ada St. George[3] also states she saw facial features, a scar on the face of the young man and an arm without any hand. This is significant because it is one of the few occasions where a prosecution witness[4] refers to seeing a face or actual facial features on the forms. At the trial all prosecution witnesses denied ever seeing any features. They report only seeing what they thought was Mrs. Duncan covered in a white sheet.

Worth's testimony changes the scene ever further, he now asserts that everything that was said was spoken by the Voice from behind the curtains and the lady in the audience when the form was behind the curtain and not visible.

It is impossible to determine whether any of Worth's statement occurred or not, as Loseby decided not to cross-examine him on it and he did not examine this incident with his own witnesses. If he had done so he would have discovered that Wing Commander Mackie recognised the young man as his nephew. The lady who came forward and touched it was Mackie's wife. In a letter Wing Commander Mackie sent the Two Worlds journal on the 4th of February 1944 he stated that his nephew was a young civil servant out in the Far East at the time of Japanese successes in Hong Kong and Singapore. All efforts to contact him had failed. Albert explained that he had been badly mutilated in an explosion. He stated that his nephew then appeared at Mrs. Duncan's séance, showed his handless arm and actually placed his stump in the hands of his wife, who clasped it with both her hands. Mackie said he clearly identified his nephew. Wing Commander Mackie's description goes a long way to counter the description that the appearance and touching of this man was 'shocking bad taste' as the prosecution had described at the pre-trial hearing and that was repeated in the press.

The major change in the statements is the one referred to in the voice and figure separation. Worth's earlier statements and Ada St. George's witness statement describe seeing the figure at the same time the voice was speaking. She agrees that the request to come and feel the arm was made while the figure was visible but she mistakenly says the form made this request. As the other witnesses Worth (police statement and at trial), Mrs. Tremlett (trial) and Fowler (unsigned witness statement) agree the form did not speak then this request must have occurred from within the cabinet at this time. It is interesting that the apparent ignorance about geography contained in the earlier statements is missing. Worth refers to an explosion out east, when in the earlier statements he mentioned it occurred in China or east of China, and that was not Shanghai but Singapore.

Dodson's summing up misrepresents the evidence when he states the figure with the stump asked the lady whether she felt the stump. This adds to the general nonsense and lack of seriousness that the Recorder gives the evidence, implying that a figure would not know if they had been touched or not. By stating that the form had spoken when all the trial witnesses explained the form had not and was unable to speak, distracts the intelligent juror from understanding the significance of the evidence that the voice in the cabinet and the form was located in separate places.

Old Lady in her 90's

Worth refers to another incident, indicating that what took place was irrational and nonsensical. He states that a woman seated at the far side of the room claimed the form of an old lady, whom Albert described as being well into her 90's. The woman asked whether it was her auntie. Albert said that's the voice and a shrouded figure appeared between the curtains and after something was said between the two the form disappeared. The sitter then said to Albert that her auntie was 75, not 95. Albert replied that he did not say 95, but he had said that the lady was well into her 90's.

Loseby nor Maude presented any other evidence to dispute or corroborate Worth's account. It could have happened or it would have been a complete invention. Fowler's unsigned witness statement describes a similar occurrence, except that the irrational discussion occurred whilst the figure was outside the curtains. In this version the discussion was even more nonsensical with Albert concluding it by saying that the lady must agree 'that 75 is well into the nineties'.

Worth's police statement matches his testimony. In this account, after the lady points out that her aunt was 75 not 95, Albert declares that he did not say 95, but well into the nineties. Worth concluded it struck him as strange because his interpretation was 'well into the nineties' is 90 or over.

At the trial Worth similarly concluded that 'we were left wondering after that'. It seems given the way Worth appears to make up encounters that no one else verifies and change his accounts at will, one is left wondering whether this is another one of Worth's inventions or whether it actually occurred.

Dodson in his summing up simply reminds the jury that an old lady in her 90's appeared who someone spoke to.

Albert

Worth described seeing Albert, Helen Duncan's guide, at the seances, as a white draped, shrouded figure with a dark patch that seemed to be cut away in the material, which could have been a face (see photograph). It was as if a piece of cloth 'was being held by somebody who floated'. The cloth went down to the floor. At the trial Worth described Albert's voice as rather high pitched and asserted it could have been a man's voice.

Mr. Homer described Albert quite differently. He claimed to have seen Albert and Mrs. Duncan standing together 6" to 1' apart like other witnesses. Homer described Albert as being over 6' tall with a thin face and a beard. Mrs. Cole description of a very tall gentleman, dark with a beard and longish face matches Mrs. Tremlett's who described him as being very tall, with a thin bearded face. Mr. Kirkby described Albert as tall, about 6', fairly sharp features with a slight beard. It is interesting that little was said at the trial about the height discrepancy between Albert, who was over 6' and Mrs. Duncan who was reported to be between 5' 4-6". Chief Constable West in 1979 explained the way Mrs. Duncan produced Albert was by wearing high-heeled shoes, although no such shoes were ever found at the séance or in any of the reported seances that Mrs. Duncan held.

Homer described Albert's voice as cultured Australian. Mr. Branch and Mrs. Jopling thought it was an cultured refined Oxford accent. Ida St. George and Mrs. Tremlett confirmed that it was a refined voice, while Horace Clayton said Albert spoke in very good English. Mr. Kirkby thought the voice had a moulding of the BBC, Canadian or Australian accent. Even Cross described his voice as a good tenor voice while Fowler said the voice was certainly not the normal speaking voice of Mrs. Duncan.

Worth's assertion that Albert's voice was high pitched represented a change from his Police Court statement, also made on oath when he described Albert's voice as a sort of refined man's voice. Worth was not alone amongst prosecution witnesses in changing their statements and views about Albert's voice.

In Burrell's police statement he stated that the voice of Albert was definitely that of Mrs. Duncan. He goes on to say he could distinguish the voice of Mrs. Duncan at both the meetings of the 17th and 18th of January.[5] He explained he had heard Mrs. Duncan speak before and he knew her voice well. So the prosecution had a witness in January 1944, who was prepared to testify that they recognised Mrs. Duncan's voice when Albert spoke.

Another witness thought they also noticed the similarity between Mrs. Duncan's voice and Albert's. Mrs. Jennings having heard Mrs. Duncan say a few words when she asked the audience whether they were satisfied with the examination of her clothing and the cabinet, thought she was disguising her voice in order to create Albert's. She explained that the timbre of Albert's voice was the same as Mrs. Duncan's. Mrs. Jennings had appeared on the stage and so had some experience of having to disguise a voice. Mrs. Jennings made the same assertion at the trial and stated her initial feeling was when hearing Albert's voice that it was definitely Mrs. Duncan. Loseby naturally questioned the basis of Mrs. Jenning's judgement, given she had only been to a single séance and had heard Mrs. Duncan speak for only a very short while. Loseby also raised the issue of the possibility that Mrs. Duncan, an uneducated woman, speaking in a refined voice or in several other accents and languages.

One may have thought that as Mr. Burrell, had already accused Mrs. Duncan of impersonating Albert's voice in his witness statement that he would be called to confirm Mrs. Jennings' opinion. At the trial however he had changed his account and asserted that Albert now had a rather nice masculine voice and he made no mention of his previously strong held belief that the voice was produced my Mrs. Duncan. Worth however, had moved in a reverse direction between the time of making his witness statement and his appearance at the Old Bailey. He had stated that Albert had a sort of a refined man's voice but then at the trial, contrary to every other witness, he stated that Albert had a 'high pitched voice which could have been a man's voice'. This cleverly suggested that it was probably a woman's voice and it fitted well with Mrs. Jennings' statement that she thought Albert's voice was Mrs. Duncan impersonating him. This assertion is far from the position of his other co-prosecution witness, WRC Cross who described Albert as having a 'good tenor voice'.

It is clear that prosecution witnesses changed their position as readily as Mrs. Duncan was supposed to change her accent with each of the impersonations she was accused of performing. These inconsistencies, by two leading prosecution witnesses point to a situation where prosecution witnesses were ever ready to change their testimony to suit the demands of trying to get Mrs. Duncan convicted. The result of Mrs. Jennings asserting that Albert's voice was definitely that of Mrs. Duncan's, given her background as a stage actress and coupled with Worth's assertion that Albert had a high pitched voice gave the jury a misleading impression of Albert's voice. Worth's description of Albert's voice was contrary to all other available evidence but it supported Mrs. Jennings in her opinion. Mrs. Jennings' evidence had dealt with the voice aspect of Mrs. Duncan purported fraud, so Mr. Burrell no longer needed to support her, he could be used to cover another aspect of the prosecution case.

Press Headlines

Albert's Ghost As 'Witness'
Daily Mail 28.3.44

SPIRIT GUIDE HAD BEARD
Evening Standard 28.3.44

SORT OF COMPERE
Daily Express 25.3.44

Peggy

The other guide who regularly appeared during Mrs. Duncan's seances was Peggy. It had been reported that she had been appearing at Mrs. Duncan's seances since the late 1920's. She tended to come forward some way into the proceedings and encouraged the audience to sing as she danced about in front of the cabinet. Mrs. Jennings described how Peggy came out some 18'" from the cabinet and danced in a light, breezy and airy manner although she had no definite form. Nurse Rust describes her as dancing like any child of her age and that she comes right out in front of the curtains as does Mrs. Lock. Mr. Burrell described Peggy as a cloth, singing and throwing itself about[6] and who at the end of the song, disappeared. He described her voice as being full of 'vim and vigour'. Mrs. Jennings noted she kept up a continuous flow of chatter.

Peggy was described as a young woman ranging in age from 16 to 21 years. At the trial Fowler described her as a 16-17 year old in height, about 5' tall. When he was asked to describe whether Peggy was a slim or fairly substantial figure Fowler stated that he could not tell because some figures appeared bulky and others appeared slim. He explained that those figures who came out of the curtains usually took some of the curtain with them making them appear bulky and if the curtains were draped down the front of the figure the form appeared slim. Given none of the other witnesses including Worth describe this occurring to Peggy (or any other form) when she danced in front of the cabinet, it is difficult to see how Fowler's explanation adds anything apart from him avoiding having to give testimony that directly contradicts Worth's.

Mrs. Tremlett thought Peggy was aged 18-20, while Burrell thought she was

21. She had a girlish, high pitched feminine voice with a broad Scottish accent. Mrs. Lock described Peggy's voice as very childish. Mrs. Tremlett said she was not fat and Mr. Lock agreed, describing her as very slim when she came out of the curtains. Mr. Burrell said she was like a fairy in a Christmas pantomime.

Worth agreed with many of the characteristics ascribed to Peggy given by the other witnesses. He said she had a high pitched feminine voice with broad Scottish accent,[7] that she was about 5' tall and jumped about. The only differences between Worth's description and all the other witnesses (with the exception of Fowler who could not tell) was that Worth said Peggy was bulky in form, she did not have a small girlish figure and that he heard her feet banging on the floor as she hopped about.

Worth's description of the sound made by Peggy's heavy footed dancing bear no relation to the descriptions of other witnesses, who described her as jigging about in a light and airy manner like a young girl (Mrs. Jennings, Nurse Rust, Mr. Burrell). Even Burrell described her as a fairy in a Christmas pantomime. Many witnesses were asked whether they ever saw Peggy's feet and not one said they did or heard any sounds of footsteps outside the curtains.

Loseby stated in his closing speech that Worth's description of Peggy as bulky was his great slip because he had said in the court below (at the magistrate's pre-trial hearing) that a 'child form' had come out of the curtains. Loseby claimed this was Worth's only slip 'from beginning to end'. Loseby's memory of what Worth had said is not reflected in the written statement he gave on oath at the pre-trial hearing. Worth makes no mention of a child form coming from the curtains. Did Loseby get it wrong or so there another explanation? Possibly he said it at the hearing but it was not recorded.

Whatever the answer may be, Loseby pointed out that Peggy had been seen hundreds of times, in Mrs. Duncan's seances and she had always been described as slim. This is borne out with the witnesses who attended the January 1944 seances, for Peggy was, according to all other witnesses who saw her clearly and separate from the curtains - she was not bulky.

It must be remembered that Worth identified all of Mrs. Duncan's forms as bulky at the trial so Peggy was described similarly. It is clear that Worth painted a picture of all forms being bulky because he suggested Mrs. Duncan was impersonating them all. The other adjustment to his account that fits into this general pattern was that Peggy made heavy foot thumps as she danced about and returned to the cabinet once she had finished her community singing and dance routine. This does not accord with Worth's first witness statement that makes no mention of Peggy making thumping sounds as she danced and asserts that Peggy had disappeared under the curtain. Fowler's unsigned witness statement also described this type of exit in the same terms. Mrs. Jennings, who took a special interest in how forms disappeared, said that Peggy disappeared by falling to the floor.

It is clear that Worth's account has changed yet again, on this occasion in terms of the disappearance. Soon after seeing her at the séance he gave a statement to the police saying Peggy had disappeared under the curtains. Later at the trial when Peggy had now assumed bulky (20 stone) proportions, the form now went back through the curtains. Worth having changed his account to describe Peggy was bulky and thumping heavily around in front of the curtains could not reconcile that picture with the possibility that she could disappear under a curtain. This feature of his statement was changed, because although jurors could easily imagine Worth's scene of Mr. Duncan dancing ridiculously in front of the curtains as he claimed, no one could be expected to think she could also disappear beneath the bottom of the curtain and especially without it moving.

Dodson in his summing described Peggy as having a high pitched voice saying something in a Scottish accent and pointed out that Mrs. Duncan has a Scottish accent. Peggy came and sang a song Loch Lomond because 'Annie Laurie' was too high and then declared that she was 'going down now' after which she disappeared. Dodson then went on to assert that nearly all the forms disappeared downwards towards the floor. This is true with the exception of the leading prosecution witnesses Worth, who did not describe a single instance of this type of exit for forms.

Press Headlines

Peggy – The Child Spirit
She sang "You Are My Sunshine"
Evening News 24.3.44

Ghost Sang 'South of the Border'
Daily Herald 24.3.44

'Fairy Form at Séance'
Jigged Before Curtain
Daily Sketch 25.3.44

'Spirit' Called Peggy liked Lipstick
Daily Sketch 24.3.44

The Animals

Worth's testimony in which he described a number of animals appearing at the séance was portrayed as a Monty Python type scene. Once a member of the audience had identified an animal, a Voice said from the cabinet 'That's the voice, here's the animal' and a hand thrust out the animal through the curtains, which Worth could not see. It was comical in its description.

Cat

Witnesses agree that Albert announced that an animal was waiting to be claimed. He explained that someone 'had put their foot on an animal at sometime or other'. Mrs. Homer asked whether it was done in a friendly way or not. Albert replied 'definitely friendly'. A woman in the audience explained that she 'once put a cat out of its misery by holding it in a bath of water' with her foot 'because it had been run over'. Then the form of a cat came from between the curtains for the audience to see.

At the trial Worth claimed that before the cat came out something meowed from behind the curtains and a small object the size of a cat of white material was pushed though the curtains, but only half way out and a voice said 'Here is the cat'. He could not see what the cat was held by. People in the audience made comments like 'How wonderful. How nice it is'. He said it was as if someone behind the curtains threw the object forward at the level of their hands. Worth could not determine whether it was a cat or not, despite being in the front row.

Worth's witness statement doesn't have the comic quality of his trial statement. A small white object was partly held out from the curtain and there was delight from members of the audience. The form could have been anything to resemble a cat but the light was too dim for him to be sure. The cat then disappeared.

Worth's account had changed by the time of the Police Court hearing. He claimed the Voice said here is the cat and a small light object was thrust between the curtains. Then Mrs. Homer and Mrs. Brown exclaimed that a cat was here and a meow issued from the curtains. Fowler was asked questions by the Recorder about the cat and he confirmed what was stated in his unsigned witness statement that the cat appeared and made the noise of a cat when the image of a cat appeared. His witness statement differed little from Worth's with the exception that cat made the meow sound when it came out which to him seemed to be a human voice imitating a cat. He said he saw the image of a cat.

Three other witnesses were asked about the cat. Mr. Mackie said a cat 'built up' which suggests it was not thrust from between the curtains but then he said he could not see from his position. Fowler's testimony also doesn't mention a cat being pushed out but that an image of a cat appeared. The other remaining witnesses, Mrs. Tremlett and Mrs. Jopling claimed they saw a white cat, the former saying she saw its face. Mrs. Jopling heard a meow but could not tell where the sound came from. At the trial Fowler said the cat disappeared behind the curtains.

Dodson in his summing said a cat appeared to meow from behind the curtain and a white cat was pushed through the curtain about middle height.

Press Headline
Dead Cat Mieowed
Daily Mirror 24.3.44

Bronco the Parrot

After the cat, a parrot appeared. Wing Commander Mackie was somewhat of an expert about parrots because he had one at home. He said he was amazed that a parrot appeared. He was very familiar with their movements and actions. He claims the parrot built up. By this he means by this that the figure of a parrot built up in form in front of the audience from the base. Mackie said he had a very good view of it when the light seemed to strike it, it was a pretty friendly parrot and it started ducking its head in parrot fashion and it acted in the correct parrot type fashion. He stated it was not made of muslin. Mrs. Tremlett who was not seated in the front row said she also saw the parrot clearly. She claimed she saw its beak and eye and body, it was white in colour and it moved and said 'pretty Polly'. When Mrs. Jopling was asked about the parrot she also said she saw its outline and it said 'pretty Polly'.

All the witnesses (including Fowler at the trial) agree that a lady in the audience claimed the parrot and said its name was 'Bronco'. Worth's witness statement reports that a woman said 'It must be old Bronco' and something that looked like a parrot bowed from between the curtains and mumbled some unintelligible words in a parrot voice. This produced some enraptured remarks from Mrs. Homer and Mrs. Brown. Fowler's unsigned witness statement described the incident in exactly the same words.

The parrot was not referred to in Worth's sworn magistrates statement. At the trial Worth portrayal had modified. He claimed a guide announced 'Somebody lost a parrot'? A woman claimed the parrot saying it must be old 'Bronco'. The voice said 'that's the voice and here is the parrot' and he saw something pushed through the curtains again. It was held at an angle. He could hear a voice talking rather like a parrot saying 'Pretty Polly' and 'things like that'. He said the white object could have been a parrot, but he claimed again that he was not close enough to see. It was presented at the same height as the cat.

The obvious discrepancy that appears between Worth's two statements and the other witnesses is that those who were seated behind Worth distinctly saw the features and characteristic parrot movements that Worth said he was not close enough to see. As Wing Commander Mackie was very familiar with parrots he would seem to be an ideal witness for such an appearance.

Worth's testimony is also at variance with Wing Commander Mackie's in terms of how the figure first appeared. Like the cat Mackie claimed the parrot figure built up for the audience to see while Worth claimed it was pushed through of the curtains. Worth's witness statement[8] makes no mention of a parrot being pushed out between the curtains, but merely described how something that looked like a parrot bowed between the curtains and that it spoke some unintelligible words. Worth had described another figure 'building up' at this seance. In his witness statement Worth stated that Albert had built up between the curtains when he first appeared to him. Reference to any form building up during the seances he recounted was removed from all subsequent statements. By the time of the trial Worth had claimed 'Somebody had lost a parrot' rather than it just appeared for someone to claim. Also the unintelligible words Worth and Fowler's earlier statements had claimed emanated from the parrot had now become intelligible. Worth's parrot had learnt to speak English from the time of making his witness statement to giving his Old Bailey testimony, saying 'Pretty Polly'!

In Dodson's summing up continuing the same method of presentation as Worth described at the trial he said then the parrot came. He made no reference to what Wing Commander Mackie, Mrs. Tremlett and Mrs. Jopling had seen that contradicted Worth's account.

Press Headline
A PARROT, ALSO A CAT APPEARED AT SÉANCE
Evening Times 24.3.44

Rabbit

Worth and Fowler claimed a rabbit also appeared but the other witnesses who were asked about it claimed they vaguely recollected a rabbit, none could recall the matter clearly enough to give any other information.

Policeman

Next Worth described the appearance of a policeman. The form was for Mrs. Barnes. She explained that the voice from the cabinet announced that it had a policeman coming for someone on its left. When the form came out Mrs. Barnes, who recognised it as her father started to speak but he asserted 'Oh, you are always the same, you did all the talking'. Mr. Homer and Wing Commander

Mackie confirm that a conversation of this type took place. Mr. Homer said Mrs. Barnes' father, who stood about 5' 10" tall, asked his daughter to please stop talking. He said he had come here to talk to her and asked to be given a chance. Wing Commander Mackie recalled that while the form was talking someone mentioned aloud to the person sitting next to them that he had been a policeman whereupon he said 'I will go back and get my helmet' and with that he went back into the cabinet and returned wearing what Mr. Homer identified as a white Indian helmet or topee. Mrs. Barnes confirms that her father said 'Wait a moment while I'll fetch my helmet. I have forgotten my helmet'. Mrs. Barnes saw him return from the cabinet wearing a white tropical helmet with a black band around it. Her father had served in the Madras police force at some time.

Other people seated around Worth said they saw the helmet although the details varied a little. Mrs. Tremlett and Ms. Sullivan said they saw a dark helmet like Mackie who remembered it as being blue. Mrs. Sullivan noticed the helmet was not like the one's our policemen wear. Mrs. Tremlett said she could not see it clearly but she noticed two light bands on a dark helmet. Mrs. Jopling said she saw the helmet distinctly and it was white with a dark coloured band. Mrs. Taylor also said she saw the white topee with a dark piece around it and it stood 6" above the head in height. These descriptions match Mrs. Barnes'. We have 6 witnesses who saw Mrs. Barnes' father go back into the cabinet and return with his Indian style helmet.

At the trial Worth described how the voice said 'I have a policeman here who passed over and a lady said 'Is that you dad?' The voice said 'That's the voice' and a form appeared between the curtains and then went back and said 'wait a minute while I put on my helmet'. Then the form reappeared and Mrs. Homer said 'look at the helmet'. Worth in the front row said he looked very hard but he could not see any helmet. He said the form spoke in a husky voice but he could not say it was a man's voice.

The only difference between his testimony and his sworn magistrates statement is that he acknowledged in the earlier statement that several people said they could see the helmet when at the trial he said only Mrs. Homer made a comment. Worth's signed witness statement was again identical in wording to Fowler's unsigned witness statement with regard to the policeman incident.

In these statements Worth and Fowler use the same language to report that the voice from the cabinet asked for his daughter to wait a moment while he puts on his helmet. Then a bulky figure appeared at the right hand side of the curtains and came out through the middle again wearing a helmet that several people said aloud that they could see a helmet. This description is quite different from the one he made later. In this account putting on the helmet takes places before the figure comes out of the curtains. The account is a little confusing and it may have been written in error, as it describes the figure appearing and then going back and coming out again through the middle of the curtains. What is unusual however is if an error has occurred in both Worth's and Fowler's statements then any error that is present is identical for these two prosecution witnesses. It seems clear that in several instances the same witness statement was written for both Worth and Fowler to sign and therefore they do not reflect what both parties actually said when they were interviewed. It is quite impossible for two people to use the precise same wording to describe events in sentence after sentence as their witness statements show. This further demonstrates if errors are present in the text these will be replicated as well.

Again we have a marked discrepancy between seven witnesses' consistent descriptions of the same event and what Worth reported he saw. Worth who was in the same room, seated next to one of them, closer to the events than many of the others claims he did not see the same article of attire, a helmet or topee than the other seven people around him saw.

Dodson in summing up Worth's evidence said a form came out and returned for his helmet and when he came out Mrs. Homer said 'look at the helmet'. Of the seven defence witnesses who testified only Mrs. Sullivan's and Mr. Homer's evidence are referred to. Dodson said Mrs. Sullivan remembered the policeman, she thought the helmet was dark in colour. He doesn't make any comment about Mr. Homer's evidence as such but simply states that there was an incident of a policeman wearing a white helmet. Out of seven witnesses' evidence that contradict Worth's, the Recorder mentioned two in the briefest manner. It is also interesting that in spite of the fact that the importance of the evidence regarding the helmet related to the difference in the evidence presented by Worth, Dodson sums up the evidence in detrimental terms to the defence. He summarises evidence in terms of the differences in the details reported by some defence witnesses about how the helmet looked, ignoring the more significant point that other witnesses around him again give a different account to what occurred.

Mrs. Barnes described that before her father disappeared he told her that he had brought with him Mrs. Barnes' three-year-old granddaughter called Shirley. The encounter between Shirley and the people witnessing the séance became a talking point in the trial. This is described below.

Those events that occurred in this séance, which Worth claimed to have no recollection of, can be found in Appendix.

Press Headlines

Dead policeman, cat and parrot were "brought back" in store temple
Daily Herald 24.3.44

P.C.'s "SPIRIT" put on helmet
Evening News 29.2.44

Shirley

The encounter between Shirley and the people at the séance in Loseby's view provided some of the best evidence of Mrs. Duncan's mediumship, as no none seriously believed Mrs. Duncan could impersonate a three year old child to its grandmother in full view of an audience. Worth had been happy to contradict the evidence given by other witnesses throughout the trial, in this instance where his picture of a twenty stone woman masquerading with a cloth over her head completely fails to account for the occurrence, he claimed under cross-examination to have no memory of it ever occurring and so he could not answer questions about it. This is inspite of the fact that he recalled what Shirley's grandfather had said and done a moment before. He did acknowledge that if Shirley did appear then this is something that would need to be told if one is to have a fair picture of the séance that day.

Mrs. Barnes described what occurred. Shirley in white came out of the curtains on the extreme left side. She came right up to her to about a foot away and took hold of her hand and asked where her grandfather was. Shirley pronounced the word 'grandfer'. Mrs Barnes explained that he was at home. She said that her grandfather used to say the nursery rhyme 'This little Piggy went to market, this little Piggy stayed at home, this little piggy went for a walk'. Mrs. Barnes then said that she wished her mother was here to see her and with that Shirley looked to the ground and disappeared. Shirley had on a long robe, she was about 3' tall. Mrs. Barnes could not make out distinct features in the face because she was short sighted.

The details of Mrs. Barnes description are supported by every other witness who attended the séance with the exception of Worth who said he couldn't remember any such occurrence. Mrs. Taylor and Mr. Homer also said that the form of Shirley was 3' tall while other witnesses said she was the size of a very small child (Mrs. Cole). Mrs. Tremlett and Mrs. Jopling thought she looked like a 3 year-old in age and size. Mr. Homer, Mrs. Cole, Mrs. Tremlett, Mrs. Jopling and Mrs. Sullivan all saw Shirley go up to Mrs. Barnes and take hold of her hand. Mrs. Jopling said Shirley ran in and out. Mr. Homer, Mrs. Jopling and Mrs. Sullivan mentioned that the child form came out from the side of the curtains and Mrs. Cole estimated that the child came 1-2' away from the curtain. She went up to Mrs. Barnes knee (Mrs. Taylor). Shirley touched Mrs. Barnes finger (Mrs. Sullivan, Mr. Homer, Mrs. Taylor) and Mr. Homer, Mrs. Cole, Mrs. Sullivan, Mrs. Taylor, Mrs. Tremlett and Mrs. Jopling saw and heard the child sing the nursery rhyme 'This little Piggy went to market...' Mrs. Sullivan who was sitting next to Mrs. Barnes on the window seat saw the child's small hand. All witnesses describe the voice as being a young child's voice or baby voice. Mr. Homer saw the child disappear through the floor.

Again we have seven witnesses who describe the same incident that occurred in the séance in detail yet Worth who was in a good position to see what happened said he has no recollection of a young child coming from the cabinet. This is inspite of Worth giving a detailed account of what had occurred a moment before when a figure of a policeman appeared wearing a helmet for the same sitter. Worth's witness statement, sworn pre-trial police court hearing statement and Fowler's witness statement also fail to mention it.

Dodson described the matter when summing up several witnesses' evidence. He said Mr. Homer remembered Mrs. Barnes granddaughter who appeared with a baby voice. She ran to Mrs. Barnes side, took her hand and said 'this little piggy went to market' and repeated the nursery rhythm. He said Mrs. Sullivan remembered Mrs. Barnes and the granddaughter incident. Mrs. Taylor also remembers the child coming to Mrs. Barnes. Mrs. Barnes was there on the 14th. She tells you about her granddaughter Shirley. She said, she came very close and touched me, she repeated the rhythm and disappeared. She could not see her feet and she had a robe that reached the ground. There is no mention that Worth had failed to recall any part of it. Similarly the press generally gave Shirley's appearance little or no coverage compared to the other forms that appeared.

Voice box [9]

After Lt. Worth had finished describing the policeman incident the Recorder asked him if that is all he can remember. Worth agreed with the exception of saying that at the end of the meeting the curtains parted slowly and he saw what appeared to him to be a clenched fist in the air. Mrs. Homer explained it was a voice box. The Voice then asked the gentleman sitting on Mr. Homer's right to count the number of seconds it takes for Mrs. Duncan to appear after it had stopped talking. This person was Worth and Mrs. Duncan very quickly came out of the curtains.

In his witness statement he said the larynx was about 5' from the floor. Fowler's unsigned statement is a little different. In this statement the form of the larynx appeared between the curtains, then the voice referred to Mrs. Homer, saying, 'You see what I have here Mrs. Homer, yes, it is a voice box'. The statement asserts that the voice asked the person on Mr. Homer's right to start counting from the time the voice box disappeared and Mrs. Duncan reappeared from the cabinet. This took about 2 seconds.

A Form Worth acknowledged under cross-examination

Mrs. Homer's Grandmother

After Lt. Worth had finished describing the policeman appearing the Recorder asked him if that is all he can remember and Worth said that he had covered most of the afternoon séance.

During cross-examination Loseby raised the matter of Mrs. Homer's grandmother appearing and they singing a duet in Welsh together.   Worth remembered the occasion. He agreed that he heard Mrs. Homer sing a duet in a language that may have been Welsh, with an old lady who had come for her, who was behind the other side of the curtain. Loseby asked whether Mrs. Duncan spoke Welsh and Worth said he did not know.   Worth said a feeble voice was heard from inside the cabinet and Mrs. Homer stood up and said 'Is that you darling?' Yes came back the answer but it continued to say that it was not coming out and they commenced to sing a song in a language he could not understand. He said it may have been Welsh and she sat down when the song finished.

Worth mentions the same incident in both his witness statement and sworn pre-trial statement. In the former Worth describes the Voice saying that it had a very old lady who passed over some time ago and gave a brief description. Mrs. Homer then asked the form whether it was her darling grandmother. A halting voice came from within the curtains and commenced to sing a song in Welsh. Mrs. Homer joined in and they sang a short duet together in the same language. The voice declared that they were not coming out this time and Mrs. Homer sat down. Again Fowler's description in his witness statement is identical in every way and with every word to Worth's.

When Mr. Homer was asked about this incident he described what happened somewhat differently. Albert announced that he had an old lady for a lady sitting on the door side. He heard the old lady singing from within the cabinet before she came out.   Mrs. Homer recognised that it was her grandmother and she walked from her seat to the centre of the curtains. Her grandmother was still singing and they met at the front of the curtains by the centre. Mrs. Homer harmonised with her grandmother in a little Welsh hymn. Mr. Homer described the features of the old lady. The form was 5' 3" tall, she had an aquiline nose, grey hair parted in centre, bluey grey eyes and mole on right side of the nose.

Again we have substantially different accounts by two people seated within a matter of inches from each other in the same room under the same lighting conditions. Homer said that the form came out of the cabinet while Worth said it didn't. Worth presumably did not offer this encounter in his evidence because it showed that different languages were being spoken at the séance and Mrs.

Duncan did not speak Welsh.

Dodson said Mr. Homer said Mrs. Homer's grandmother came. She was singing a Welsh hymn. Mrs. Homer and the grandmother met in front of the cabinet and there was a mole on Granny's face on the right hand side of the nose, and she was in ectoplasm.

The form of Mrs. Allen was also acknowledged by Worth under cross-examination. This account can be found in Appendix, along with two other manifestations that he failed to recall Wing Commander Mackie's and Mrs. Sullivan's mothers.

Surg. Lt. Fowler

Surgical Lt. Elijah Fowler who was from Banff in Scotland, claimed to have been a friend of Worth's for two years prior to the trial. His testimony and statements will be considered in relation to the different forms that appeared. What is very interesting is that he never signed a lengthy nine-page witness statement in his name and was transferred away from HMS Excellent the day after the police raid, on the 20th of January 1944.

At the trial Worth's friend, who had cycled with him to the séance and sat next to him, as not asked a single question to corroborate him. This was most unusual. While numerous defence witnesses contradicted Worth's testimony, Fowler was not called upon by the prosecution or cross-examined by the defence on the central features of the prosecution case, Worth's testimony.

Fowler's unsigned witness statement supports Worth's version of events. But when he later appeared at the pre-trial hearing at Portsmouth in late February he only gave a short statement briefly acknowledging that he had attended on the 14th, and that when Mrs. Duncan came out of the cabinet he felt her pulse and she claimed to recognise him. He stated that Mrs. Brown showed him a number of spirit photographs and that he understood from Mrs. Duncan's expression that he didn't believe what had taken place. Although at the trial he claimed to have been sceptical about the séance, he stated in February that he was curious to take her pulse having seen the phenomena that he had seen. This is a curious action to take and to refer to having seen phenomena, if he had been sceptical about what had occurred and claimed not to have seen any.

It seems clear that Fowler was not prepared to support Worth's testimony otherwise he would have been asked to do so. At the trial junior Prosecuting Counsel Mr. Elam took him briefly through his pre-trial statement and a conversation he had had with Mrs. Brown which referred to Peggy. Unusually Loseby followed the same line of questioning as Elam concentrating purely on topics covered in Fowler's police court statement and what he had said to Elam moments earlier. He made no attempt to cross-examine him to determine whether he corroborated Worth's testimony or not. When Loseby probed a little for some detail about what he saw when Peggy appeared, Fowler was noncommittal, saying he could not see well enough.

Interestingly enough it was the Recorder who interjected and who took over the questioning from Loseby and asked Fowler almost as many questions. He moved from questioning him about Peggy to the animal forms that had appeared and he confirmed that his scepticism had increased as a result. Maude then asked whether Fowler could go and Dodson agreed.

So the person that the press had stated was one of the two Naval Officers who had felt themselves tricked by Mrs. Duncan and had initiated the course of events that lead to the most famous trials in English legal history, when it came to giving evidence on oath or putting his name to a statement, declined to corroborate his friend, Lt. Worth. Det. Insp. Ford originally applied for a warrant to arrest Mrs. Duncan, naming Fowler as being deceived by her along with Worth, but at the time of the Police charges, Fowler's name was not referred to. The day after the raid Fowler was transferred from HMS Excellent to HMS Tartar. On February 2nd Ford stated in a report that Fowler had earlier given him a statement but it is clear Fowler refused to sign it when he eventually saw it.

Dodson seemed aware of this difficult situation for the prosecution and that the defence was playing along with. It raises some questions as to why he took over Loseby's questioning and directed much of Fowler's time in the witness box after Elam had examined him. Fowler concurred with Dodson that he had been present throughout the whole of the proceedings on the 14th. Inexplicably, Dodson then said it was quite right that he hadn't been taken through all the details.

In his summing up Dodson acknowledges that Fowler was not asked about what Worth claimed he saw related to himself on the 14th and directed the jury that Worth's evidence stands alone on those matters. Again, Dodson puts a positive spin on Fowler not being taken through all the details of Worth's evidence, explaining perhaps it was for the 'sake of brevity'. Dodson then twice gave a sympathetic explanation to the fact that a leading prosecution witness did not give evidence in support of his friend, who had been branded a liar by the defence and whose account had been contradicted by the majority of people present.

If one examines the witness statement prepared for Fowler to sign the wording is identical to the wording in many places to Worth's witness statement. This is particularly apparent when inspecting their witness statements regarding Albert's statements, Worth's uncle, aunt, sister, the forms of Mrs. Barnes father the policeman, Mrs. Homer's grandmother, an old lady in her 90's, Jarvis, the mutilated young man, the appearance of Peggy and Bronco the parrot. Every time speech is quoted as occurring during the séance from Albert, a form or a sitter, Worth's and Fowler's witness statements are identical. There are 52 identical matching word for word quotations of what was said during the séance. There are 62 matching phrases or complete sentences involving over 683 words. Even an apparent error in the text is replicated. It is interesting to note the observations of Judge Justice Cassels in the other trial that Maude was conducting simultaneously at the Old Bailey, defending Harold Loughans against murder charges. Loughans had accused the Portsmouth police of trying to frame him claiming the two police officers had concocted the confession stating he had admitted to the murder.

Justice Cassels comments made in the nearby courtroom, apply equally to parts of Worth's and Fowler's witness statements, which were similarly prepared by the Portsmouth police. He referred to the identical notes taken by two Portsmouth police officers of the conversation they purportedly had with Loughans when he was supposed to have confessed to murder.

Judge Cassels said: 'That to anyone who had practised in the courts over many years, it had always appeared remarkable that two police officers, not in collaboration were able to produce an identical note of a particular conversation. Why police officers were not content to make their own notes and stand by them, even if they disagree, was difficult to understand'.

The same argument applies to Worth's and Fowler's statements and it appears that the same flaw in the police's preparation of witness statements carried over to this case. Fowler however had refused to sign the witness statement, which suggests he was also not prepared to go along with the fabricated statement prepared for him by the Portsmouth police and Worth's version of events. This being the likely explanation, Dodson's comments to the jury misled them as to the true circumstances behind Fowler not being examined on the same events that Worth referred to in his testimony.

The Sunday Service

Worth went to a church service on Sunday the 16th of January. During the service Mrs. Duncan speaking in the voice of Albert, addressed the congregation encouraging them to aspire to a more spiritual life. In the middle of Mrs. Duncan's delivery she suddenly stopped and looked down towards her right hand and said 'a little girl had got hold of my hand and that her name was Audrey'. Mrs. Duncan went on to describe how the girl had run down the room to a gentleman sitting at the end of the row at the back and that she is standing by a man indicating that she knew him. Mr. Barnes who was in this position announced that his daughter's name is Shirley, not Audrey. Mrs. Duncan replied saying that she was sorry that she had made a mistake and that she should have said Shirley. She said that she had got the name wrong. This struck Worth as a glaring mistake and the story was covered extensively in the press. Under cross-examination Worth admitted that if the name of Shirley was given in the séance of the 14th then Albert would know the name.

Mr. Barnes account of the incident brings a completely different perspective to the incident. When Mrs. Duncan referred to Audrey and brought this to the attention of Mr. Barnes, he explained to her that his daughter's name was Shirley. He said this is because he assumed it was Shirley. Mrs. Duncan replied speaking in Albert's voice that it sounded to her like Audrey. Mr. Barnes denied that Mrs. Duncan had said that she had got the name wrong and that she ought to have said Shirley. Mr. Barnes explained that, as Shirley had been very young when she had passed over she had had a slight speech impediment. This was apparent because she had difficulty in pronouncing the word 'show'. For example 'show me' sounded like 'ow me'. Shirley had not mastered the 'sh' sound. Mr. Barnes understood the error in terms of Shirley being unable to pronounce her name properly. This type of error would be quite unusual if as Worth suggested Mrs. Duncan was operating a fraud. It would have been relatively easy for Mrs. Duncan to remember Shirley's name and her relationship with the husband of Mrs. Barnes if as Worth suggested Mrs. Duncan had imitated her when going to Mrs. Barnes on the 14th.

It is interesting that in Worth's witness statement whilst repeating most of the dialogue at the trial, he actually agrees with Mr. Barnes in asserting that Mrs. Duncan's immediate reply was that she did not catch the name at first. In his next statement made at the Police Court hearing he changes this position stating that she said that she was sorry that she had got the name wrong and that she should have said Shirley. It is also interesting that Edward Robey the prosecuting counsel at the Portsmouth Police Hearing is reported as describing this incident in the same way as Mr. Barnes and not Worth. The News Chronicle (1.3.44) and The News of the World (5.3.44) quote Robey as asserting that Mr. Barnes had said that 'My daughter's name is Shirley' and that Mrs. Duncan immediately apologised explaining that she did not quite catch the name.

So we have the ironic situation where Worth in his witness statement and the Prosecuting Counsel at the Police Court Hearing agree with Mr. Barnes' point about Mrs. Duncan referring to the name that she heard given, but when the police court hearing and trial came Worth's version had changed. Robey naturally repeated the account he had heard or read from Worth but then the account had changed by the time the trial came. Ironically Loseby was faced with the task of arguing the same point at the trial against the prosecution, that had been asserted by the prosecution at the Police Court hearing.

Dodson covered this incident in his summing up. He said that Mr. Homer opened with prayer, Mrs. Duncan in Albert's voice conducted a sermon and she said a little girl Audrey had got hold of her hand and run down to Mr. Barnes. Mr. Barnes said his daughter's name was Shirley not Audrey, whereupon Mrs. Duncan said she had made a mistake in the name. Dodson said it was a very minor incident but then afterwards Mrs. Brown said she could see spirits.

Although Mr. Elam cross-examined Mr. Barnes on this incident and Dodson described the incident earlier in his summing up with reference to Worth's evidence, when it came to summing up Mr. Barnes evidence he omits any reference to it. The jury then is only left with one version of events, the prosecution's, as far as the Recorder's summing up was concerned.

Press Headline

LITTLE AUDREY AT A SÉANCE

Apologised

News Chronicle 1.3.44

Mr. Burrell's evidence

Mr. Redman Incident and Mrs. Lonsdale-Brosman

Mr. Burrell stated at the police court hearing that in August 1943 he had threatened Mr. & Mrs. Homer that he would go to the police after paying 10s 6d for a reading he had received from a Spiritualist medium Mr. Redman at their church. He said he was far from satisfied and that he wanted to stop this money racket. Mrs. Homer said she did not want her church ruined or herself. Mr. Burrell claimed he said he did not have a grievance against the church or her. He considered the fee he had to pay was excessive and upon the threat of him calling the police the Homers returned his money.

Mr. Burrell also briefly mentioned the Redman incident at the trial and the newspapers ran stories about it after the Police Court hearing in Portsmouth. Burrell describes the incident in greater detail in his witness statement. He said that the reading only took around 15 minutes. During this time Mr. Redman had told Burrell that he worked near the docks and that his domestic affairs were not bright and that there was a lady somewhere in the affair and things won't improve until this time next year. He also said he had an Indian guide. After Burrell threatened Mr. & Mrs. Homer with calling the police, he said they assured him that Mr. Redman would give no more readings at the church. Mr. Burrell pointed out that Mr. Redman had returned to the church and taken services there.

What is interesting about this incident is that the information Mr. Redman gave at his clairvoyant reading was very accurate. Mr. Burrell did work in the docks. Mr. Burrell had left his wife and two children and was living with a married woman Mrs. Violet May Lonsdale-Brosman at 77 St. James Road, Portsmouth. She was separated from her husband and Mr. Burrell and her were referred to by some as Mr. & Mrs. Burrell. Mr. Burrell had a small Navy pension and when added to his earnings from the dockyard, he found having to contribute money to his first wife Gertrude and their children and run a new home with Mrs. Lonsdale-Brosman a struggle.

It has been discussed above how Mr. Burrell and Mrs. Lock changed their statements in order to omit all reference to Mr. Burrell's partner Mrs. Violet Lonsdale-Brosman accompanying them to the seances. This omission continued at the trial. Mr. Burrell stated he attended the séance on the 17th with Mr. & Mrs Lock. It was only after the prosecution witnesses had given their evidence that Mrs. Lonsdale-Brosman made a brief appearance as a prosecution witness and stated in passing that she had attended both meetings with Mr. Burrell. Given how the order of appearance of the prosecution witnesses was arranged, the defence probably missed this contradiction in their evidence. This was probably Maude's intention.

There are a number of reasons why the prosecution may have not wanted the defence and the jury to know that Mrs. Lonsdale-Brosman attended the seances with Mr. Burrell. If Mr. Burrell was part of a conspiracy to convict Mrs. Duncan then the knowledge that one person was responsible for bringing almost all the prosecution witnesses to the séance might have placed suspicion on him. It may also have been due to the fact that he was living with a married woman and this was frowned upon in 1944. If Mr. Burrell and Mrs. Lonsdale-Brosman were referred to as Mr. & Mrs. Burrell as Mrs. Lock mentioned, and then it could damage Mr. Burrell's credibility, especially as the original Mrs. Burrell still lived in Portsmouth. His wife Gertrude had refused to give him a divorce. Certainly Mrs. Homer suffered some comment in the Police Court and the press when it emerged that she was not married to Mr. Homer, even though they lived together as man and wife for some 20 years.

The prosecution may have naturally wanted to avoid the same fate to befall a leading prosecution witness. Knowing Mrs. Lonsdale-Brosman attended the same seances as Mr. Burrell may have also led the defence team to question her about what she saw at the seances and what Mr. Burrell's reaction had been at the time. His account was disputed by other witnesses and he had radically changed it from the time of making his witness statement and possibly Mrs. Lonsdale Brosman was unaware of these changes.

Recorder Dodson confuses the matter further by saying that Burrell had said he attended the séance on the 17th with the Lock's and 'all four of these people were there'. Burrell never made this comment so it is difficult to know to what or whom the Recorder is referring. Mr. Burrell never stated that he went with

Mrs. Lock's daughter, Mrs. Harris on the 17th. There is an inconsistency in the evidence about who attended when, in the Burrell-Lock party. Burrell attended the séance of the 17th with Mrs. Lonsdale-Brosman and Mr. & Mrs. Lock but not Mrs. Lock's daughter Ena Harris because her husband was ill.[10] Although Mrs. Lock stated at the trial that she attended on the 17th, 18th and 19th, she also let it slip that she had also attended the séance on the 12th. These inconsistencies seem to point to the fact that Mr. Burrell and the Lock family changed their accounts to suit the prosecution case. They also point to the possibility that Mrs. Lock and Mrs. Harris attended more seances than they admitted to.

The prosecution had presented these people as sincere members of the public who attended on only a few occasions, objected about the high fees charged and reported what they saw. If it was known they attended on more occasions then the question naturally arises why they repeatedly went if the fees were too high and given that they were not wealthy people. Where did they find the money to attend so many seances? Complaining about the high fees does not tally with the picture of ordinary members of public who aren't wealthy going many times to something they weren't very interested in and believed to be fraudulent. This may raise some suspicion that they were motivated for some other reason and did so in order to gather incriminating information about Mrs. Duncan for the case.

It seems likely the prosecution wanted to plan their strategy and they needed to know how their prospective prosecution witnesses would react to what they saw, so they attended on earlier occasions to evaluate their best usage. If Mrs. Lock and Mrs. Harris did attend on more occasions than they declared then the defence would have had an opportunity to cross-examine them on it.

It also allows for the possibility that the incidents they described as occurring at a particular seance in fact may have occurred on another occasion that they had not mentioned. It is likely if the prosecution was planning a case against Mr. Duncan that they would want to use the evidence they had in the strongest way and cover different aspects drawing from evidence gained on different occasions. That way rather than repeating evidence they might want to use the evidence of different witnesses to show the pattern of Mrs. Duncan's fraud over the days in question. In order to achieve this it was best if witnesses said they were present only on the occasions the prosecution wanted to use their selected evidence for. Certainly the prosecution did not want the defence to know that Mrs. Lock had attended earlier seances to the 17th. At the trial Mrs. Harris said she had been before the 19th, even though in her witness statement she claimed she had not. By the time of the trial Mrs. Harris was used only briefly as a prosecution witness and so it may not have mattered which seances she had attended, whereas at the time the witness statements were written her potential role was less sure. Certainly they did not want Mrs. Lonsdale-Brosman mentioned during the time in which testimony was being given on the dates she attended.

Seance of the 17th
Lady With Torch

Burrell was seated in the front row. He testified how a female spirit form appeared. She said she had been downstairs to find a torch that was left in somebody's pocket and a hand appeared from between the centre of the curtains wrapped in kind of muslin. The torch was gripped between the muslin and a hand. A man claimed the lit torch. Burrell said the man recognised it because of its low brilliancy of the bulb or battery. He said it was his torch and the form said she had been down and taken it from his pockets and they handed it over to him and he accepted it in both hands.

Burrell could not discern a face or figure but just a hand or rather a white cloth that was covering the pair of hands. There was no form behind the hands, just a cloth covering a pair of hands. Burrell got himself in a muddle first saying the form held it in one hand that was covered in muslin and then he said two hands held the torch. Before the seance the torches of people in the audience were taken and the others were left in people's coats downstairs because shining a torch could be dangerous for the medium.

In the original witness statement Burrell's story was different. A white cloth came out of the cabinet holding a torch and he saw a hand holding it but 'just sufficient to grip it'. The form held it out and said that it had been through your pockets and a Marine in the audience said the torch was his and that he had left it in his pocket downstairs. Burrell then stated the Marine asked whether it was his mother. The form replied that it was and that she had been through his pockets and here is his torch.

In the police court sworn statement Burrell added some further details. A white shadowy form came between the curtains appearing to hold a lighted torch. The hand holding it was covered in a cloth or misty affair and a Marine claimed it. The form explained that he had been through his pockets and got his touch.

The changes from the witness statement to his trial testimony are interesting. In the witness statement a relationship, although as it turns out the wrong one between the person who claimed the torch and the figure is stated, but in further statements it is not. Consequently in the remaining statements the story is the form or by implication the conspirators have been through all the pockets of the coats left downstairs, they bring a torch to the séance and someone claimed it.

Seeing the incident from the point of view of the person who claimed the torch gives insight into Burrell's approach to his testimony at the trial.

Marine Horace Clayton was seated in the middle of the second row. He described the voice saying there was somebody for a soldier and as he was the only person in the uniform of a soldier in the room he presumed it was for him. The curtains parted and figure of a lady came to centre of room and stood immediately in front of Clayton, about 15" away. He described the face as very beautiful, the form had grey hair and the figure was very much slimmer than Mrs. Duncan. He explained that she stood there and then produced his torch and said that she had been all though his pockets. She produced the torch, flicked it on and off and shone it on her own face so it could be seen clearly. Clayton asked whether she was his grandmother and the form replied that it was. With that the form flicked the torch on and off again, around the room and onto her face. Clayton asked 'Darling will you kiss me before you go'. With that the figure took the fingers of his right hand in her left, raised his hand to her lips and kissed it. The torch was handed back and the grandmother form went towards cabinet and departed into the floor about a foot away from the curtain.

Clayton said the hand was nothing like butter muslin but it was something solid. He said it was a beautiful woman's hand, average size and he could see the fingernails. It felt cold. It was not muslin covering a hand and if it had been he would not have been able to see its features.   It was not anything like butter muslin, but something solid. It was a little cooler than his own hand although the lips seemed slightly warmer.

In support of Clayton's account Mrs. Lock in her witness statement described how the Voice said there was an elderly woman here for someone on Mrs. Brown's left. A white form appeared and a Marine in the back row asked whether it was his mother. The voice said it was, and that she had something to give him and she flashed a torch. The Marine asked how she had got it and the Voice replied explaining that she had been through his pockets and the Marine reached over and took the torch from the form.

Marine Clayton and Mrs. Lock's accounts paint a completely different picture to Burrell's. Burrell's implied that a spirit had been through people's pockets downstairs and produced someone's torch.   Clayton and Mrs. Lock describe a scene where a mother or grandmother of a sitter comes specifically for that person and hands them an object that belongs to them, a torch that they had brought from downstairs. The figure therefore was aware of their relation in another context, was able to take an object and operate it by flashing it.

Burrell's account is also contrary to the format used because figures only appear when a relationship has been acknowledged between the form and a sitter. Burrell's story implies a form appeared without any of the usual request from Albert to the audience and the correct response judged by the voice of the intended sitter. Burrell also claimed the sitter recognised the torch by its low illumination. This is an interesting statement because under Burrell's description of the poor lighting conditions any recognition of features was virtually impossible. He said he was seated in the front within a foot of the figures but he could not see anything. For his account to be consistent Burrell has to introduce a means by which this torch is recognised without any features of the torch been seen. So the sitter recognised his torch by its 'low brilliancy'. There may be many sitters who had low running batteries in their torches. Burrell's change of story from one hand holding the torch to two hands also indicates that he was is making up a story. This type of mistake would be less likely if someone were recounting what had occurred from memory.

Clayton's description of the form shining the torch onto itself to reveal its features, the touching and kissing represent powerful evidence for the defence but both Mrs. Lock's and Burrell's accounts don't refer to it.

Dodson in his summing up of Burrell's evidence said that a white substance appeared and a voice said that the spirit had been downstairs for a torch. It appeared to Burrell to be muslin surrounding a torch and one sitter claimed the torch. The torches had been left downstairs. Dodson makes a mistake when he states Burrell described muslin surrounding a torch. The muslin surrounded the hand that was holding the torch. There is also some ambiguity in Dodson's version as he may be suggesting that the voice that spoke after the form had emerged from the cabinet was Albert's voice, when Burrell had said that the form itself had spoken. This ambiguity is misleading for the jury because they were told on every occasion that Albert introduces all forms but in Burrell's account it makes no mention of Albert introducing the form. Dodson's summing up aligns Burrell's evidence with the consistent pattern of all the other appearances the jury has heard and which he is recounting. Although Burrell's account is flawed in this respect it could have been pointed out to the jury.

In summing up Clayton's evidence Dodson said a lady came out in front of him and she produced a torch and said that she had been in your pockets. Clayton asked whether she was his grandmother and she said 'yes' and shone a torch on his face. She kissed his fingers and he felt contact. It was not anything like butter muslin, but something solid. She gave him back his torch and then disappeared.

It is clear from Dodson's summing up that he misrepresents Clayton's account when he says the form shone the light into Clayton's face. The form shone the light into its own face, which allowed Clayton to see her face very clearly and helped him recognise their features. Dodson misrepresents this important piece of evidence. He also makes no reference to what Clayton saw when he looked at the form's hand.

Press Headline

Ghost Took Torch From Pocket
Daily Herald 29.3.44

Burrell's Guide

The last figure to appear at the séance held on the 17th of January was for Mr. Burrell. It is interesting to see how leading prosecution witnesses such as Worth and Burrell react to forms that wish to appear to them, because if they are part of a conspiracy to convict Mrs. Duncan they would not want anyone they know or who others know, to appear. This might create enormous difficulties for them. If Mr. Burrell were a genuine investigator then the best evidence would be gained by the appearance of people he knew intimately. In this case he should be keen to call out people he knew who had passed over so he could determine to his own satisfaction and knowledge that the spirit forms are genuine.

The time came when Albert said to Mr. Burrell there was someone here for him and he was told to call them out. Burrell explained in his testimony that he had lost his mother and sister who he had loved and he did not feel he could call them out like that, so he said 'Show me a guide'. A white form appeared and salaamed. He said it seemed similar to someone putting a sheet of muslin in front of you and he was not convinced. Given that he had an opportunity to determine the authenticity of Mrs. Duncan's forms, when it came to his opportunity, he asked for someone that he had never seen in person so there was no way it could be verified.

Mrs. Lock also recalled this incident. She said the voice said there was a guide for the gentleman in the front row. Mr. Burrell was the only gentleman in the front row with Mr. Homer. A tall figure emerged and gave three distinct bows to him. Mr. Burrell then said aloud that he didn't see anything to recognise. The voice then said 'Goodnight everybody and God bless you'.

Dodson when summing up this evidence said a figure appeared to Burrell, he was told to call out his mother and sister and it salaamed to him. Dodson's summing up is mistaken, as Burrell was not asked to call out his mother and sister. Burrell had testified about what went on in his mind when he was told there was someone there for him. By his own account it was Burrell that requested a guide to appear and not as Dodson states it appeared without being requested and after he had been asked to call out his mother and sister. Dodson's summing up again makes the séance seem irrational and more confused, by suggesting the voice asked Burrell to call out his relatives when the practice that was followed was one in which the sitter had to make the recognition and establish the relationship. The voice seldom did this beforehand especially with relatives.

Dodson's misrepresentation of Burrell's encounter with his guide is important because he fails to describe what happened or even mention Burrell's request to see his guide. Later Dodson commented adversely on those defence witnesses evidence to whom a purported guide appeared. Mr. Kirkby suffered most from reporting that a purported guide appeared the next day. After outlining some of Mr. Kirkby's evidence once Mr. Kirkby mentions a guide appearing who claimed it belonged to him, Dodson ridiculed him. Dodson announced to the jury that during the course of giving his evidence one may have considered Mr. Kirkby to be a very sober-minded kind of man, but one is a 'little flabbergasted' at the end of discover that he has got a guide. Dodson continued by explaining that according to Mr. Kirkby we all have a guide, and his guide is a Chinaman named Mr. Chang, with a ten-inch moustache and a pigtail complete. Dodson said that had to keep himself from making any comment even though he thought he should because the temptation to do so was almost overwhelming.

Mr. Kirkby described the form that appeared to him on the 18th. He did not request it to appear unlike Mr. Burrell. If Mr. Kirkby's evidence is to be undermined because a guide appeared and certain features were seen, then it is strange that Dodson did not do the same with Mr. Burrell's evidence, who held the same belief and who had actually requested his guide to make an appearance. One cannot escape the conclusion that Dodson, a very capable, experienced and most senior Recorder, deliberately misrepresented Burrell's encounter with his guide. Dodson failed to mention that a guide appeared to Burrell, he did so because he could then use this feature to discredit the evidence of defence witnesses who refer to guides appearing, without his ridicule also undermining Burrell's evidence in the jury's mind.

Freddie and Pinkie

At the trial Mr. Burrell said that he had been very upset at the séances because he had been told that a friend who were a missing airman was safe but later he had found out that the airman was dead.

Mr. Burrell said one or two airman friends appeared. He could not remember which night it was. He said 'We went to find out about an airman who had been reported missing, and one or two airmen friends of mine appeared and he returned to say Fred was saved and we found out later it wasn't him at all because he had not survived. There was some discussion between Mrs. Lock and these airmen. I could not discern any features on the figure but on the second night I did (18th)'. Later on in giving his evidence he went on to say that on the 17th the form had said that Fred had died and on the 18th the form had said Fred had survived.

At the trial, like the evidence she gave at the pre-trial hearing Mrs. Lock told the court of the voice announcing that there was a young boy who passed over in full life at the séance held on the 17th of January. She later said the Voice said that he had a boy that had been shot in the head in wartime conditions here for a lady. A good friend of hers had a son, Fred, who was an airman who had been reported lost and so she asked whether it was Freddie. On getting no answer she asked whether it was a friend of his named Pinkie. She got an affirmative reply and a white form appeared, which she said 'just looked like a white robe'.

Then she asked him to tell her quickly before he went whether Fred had passed over. There was no answer. It just said 'Did you receive that?' She replied 'I could not tell you'. The form then asked her to thank them for being so kind. She said she would. Then he put his left hand up and drew up the white cloth revealing almost black hair and a very red complexion. Mrs. Lock saw this distinctly. The form then drifted towards the ground. Mrs. Lock said the form did not look like Fred or Pinkie. Pinkie was not a friend of Mrs. Lock's but he was a friend of the lost airman. It is clear that Mrs. Lock's testimony directly contradicts Burrell's.

It is interesting to compare this testimony with Mrs. Lock's witness statement made soon after the séance. In it, Albert announced that he had a form that had passed over rather tragically in his health and strength, in a crash. It was for the gentleman again at the door (Mr. Lock). Like other occasions when forms came to her husband, Mrs. Lock did the talking. Mrs Lock then asked whether it was Freddie. There was no answer but a white figure came out from the side of curtains and Mrs. Lock repeated the question. She then asked for the form to touch her. It didn't. Mrs. Lock asked it to speak to her and it said 'Did you get that?' She replied that she really could not tell. The form then thanked her for what she had done for him. The figure then put its right hand to head drew the cloth off and revealed dark hair, red complexion and very full face. Then it disappeared behind the curtain. Mrs. Lock then turned to her husband and said it was definitely not Freddie because he was very fair, but it may have been his pal. She then stated that she has since seen Mrs. Duncan and the face she saw is very similar to hers.

The changes to her account given at the trial are numerous. The initial description of the way the spirit died is different and more sensitive. The spirit wanted to go to her husband not her. No mention is made of the name Pinkie or Fred's pal at the séance. The form did not confirm that it was Pinkie. She asked the form to touch her. She saw the form full face. The form went back into the cabinet and did not drift to the ground. She said the face she saw was similar to Mrs. Duncan's. The only information that matched the trial version was she asked if it was Freddie and the words spoken by the form, asking whether she had received something.

Mr. Burrell made no reference to Freddie or Pinkie appearing at the seances he attended in his witness and sworn Police Court hearing statements, but he did state at the trial that on the 17th he had gone to find out about an airman friend who had had been reported missing and that the forms had talked to Mrs. Lock. Mr. Burrell claimed that the airman had told the audience that Fred had passed over. This is completely different to the account given by Mrs. Lock who Mr. Burrell claimed had spoken to the airman and who was part of the group he brought to the seance.

Mrs. Lock said she asked Mrs. Homer whether she could attend the séance on the following day (the 18th) and a short while later Mr. Homer agreed. Despite attending the next day neither Pinkie or the airman she wanted to appear, did so. Although she described several forms that did appear to her on that occasion, in her sworn police court statement she does not describe an airman doing so. All she expressed was her regret, saying that 'he was supposed to appear again'. Her witness statement confirms that she was keen to get more information about the airman as she mentioned this point as the reason why she wanted a ticket for the 18th. In her initial signed witness statement in which she describes who appeared to her on the 18th she again made no reference to an airman appearing. During her sworn testimony at the Old Bailey Mr. Elam specifically asked her whether anything particular happened for herself during the séance of the 18th and she replied that only her mother came. Again she made no mention of Pinkie coming again on the 18th although she would have obviously keen for him to do so if the reason she gave for attending this seance was true.

Despite Mrs. Lock's statements to the contrary, Mr. Burrell testified at the trial that on the 18th an airman came through saying he had been shot down over France and that his name was Fred, but we could not discern Fred's face. Burrell then said that the form said he knew Fred! He said this form told them that Fred had not passed over but was being cared for by patriots in Holland and we would hear good news of him in time. This 'cheered up' his friend, presumably Mrs. Lock who he said had spoken to the airman.

Certainly Mrs. Lock did not seem cheered up according to her sworn police court statement of the 29th of February, her signed witness statement or her sworn testimony at the trial as she recalled no such conversation taking place or ever receiving good news. Mr. Burrell also stated at the trial that as he had discovered that Freddie had not survived, then Albert had made a mistake regarding Freddie. Nowhere in Burrell's testimony does he state that Albert said Freddie had survived. Burrell stated that the airman who appeared informed him of Freddie's survival.

Mr. Burrell also testified that he told Mrs. Homer that he had more proof from the second séance he attended on the 18th because of the news had had got about the airman, surviving. In his first two statements he made no mention of an airman appearing. He initially told the police he told Mr. and Mrs. Homer that the séance did not impress him at all before he left. He also claimed a different motivation had led him to attend because Mrs. Lonsdale Brosman wanted him to go.

In the papers sent to Counsel for the Old Bailey trial there is an unsigned

Additional Statement in the name of Bessie Lock. In it, it states that Freddie is a son of a friend of hers, Mrs. Nuttal and that he was a navigator and had been reported presumed dead. The statement now asserts that Pinky, the pilot of the plane appeared on the 18th and had said Freddie was not dead but living in France and someone was caring for him. The statement reads that Mrs. Locks thanked him and the form disappeared. It seems that although this page has been added to the file, Mrs. Lock knew nothing about it, as she never mentioned this incident in any of her sworn statements or at the trial and it was unsigned. When Mr. Elam directly asked her who came through to her on the 18th she did not mention it, despite an Additional Statement being presented purporting to show Mrs. Lock said the airman had, and which corroborated Burrell's account.

This Additional Statement was produced between the 14th and 23rd of February. It was not in the batch of Witness Statements sent by Chief Constable West to the DDP on the 14th of February but Det. Insp. Ford mentioned it in a report on the 23rd of February. At the Police Court hearing of the 29th of February Mrs. Lock did not confirm this statement stating only that Pinkie was supposed to appear, meaning he had not. There is a Note to Counsel dated the 9th of March a short time before the trial referring to additional evidence which the DPP wanted to know whether Prosecuting Counsel wanted to use it as it needed to be served.

It is clear that Burrell's testimony regarding an airman coming to the séance on the 17th and saying Freddie was dead is false. It seems equally apparent that the statement he made and supported by the paperwork sent to Counsel by the Additional unsigned Witness statement in the name of Mrs. Lock, is equally untrue. It was done because it extremely damaging evidence to the defence that at a time of war Mrs. Duncan or 'her spirits' were giving false hope and deceiving grieving families. The press were also keen to highlight this most serious aspect of the case.

What is most surprising and frequently overlooked in Lt. Worth's testimony is that reference was made to a son, named Fred, who had been reported missing appearing and talking to his mother in the séance he attended some days before, on the 14th. He said the mother who was seated in the front row seemed under some strain. Worth's witness statement confirms it was the missing airman named Fred who the mother claimed and following a brief conversation the airman disappeared.

Fowler's unsigned witness statement contradicts Burrell's testimony further by also making reference to Freddie appearing on the 14th. It describes how the Voice said that he had a young man who is reported missing. A lady on Fowler's right asked if it was Freddie. The voice confirmed it was and a form appeared at the side of the curtains. The form said he was sorry mother, it had to be this way, you understand. The woman started to cry and Mrs. Homer put her arm around her shoulder and tried to comfort her. This statement goes on to say that what Fowler had seen and heard had made him feel thoroughly disgusted, as he was convinced that none of it was genuine.

So we now have two reports that Freddie had in fact appeared to his mother on the 14th. This might explain the comment that Mrs. Lock apparently could not understand. The form said to her 'Did you receive that' or 'Did you get that'. In her magistrates statement Mrs. Lock states that this reply was in response to her question 'Will you speak to me that I may take a message back to Freddie's parents?' Possibly this message was intended for her friend and the airman's mother, Mrs. Nuttal, or Mrs. Lock herself as she did not appear to have received the news of Freddie's passing. As often occurs in seances the form may have been seeking confirmation that the communication had been received. Certainly there would be no need for Freddie to appear again as he had already spoken to his mother and confirmed the news of his presumed death. Freddie's earlier appearance also meant that the accusation that Mrs. Duncan's séance had given false hope by saying he was safe and being looked after in Holland was unfounded because he had already confirmed his passing to his mother three days earlier.

It seems clear that the intention of the person who wrote Fowler's witness statement was for Fowler to express his disgust at Mrs. Duncan and her co-conspirators for causing such distress to mothers of servicemen. Fowler however refused to sign the witness statement presented to him, as the witness statements sent to counsel in his name show. It seems clear from the statements and sworn testimony of Mrs. Lock and the discrepancy between it and Mr. Burrell's assertions, that someone wanted this powerfully emotive and damaging type of evidence to be presented at the trial. As Fowler had declined to put his name to it, Mr. Burrell was used to present it by amending and extending the story of Mrs. Lock's encounter with the airman. Mrs. Lock seemed unaware of this change because she never once referred to it in her testimony or her sworn Police Court statement and nor did she sign the Additional Statement document. The discrepancies between Burrell's testimony and the Additional Statement also point to this late change. He said Mrs. Lock had been told that Freddie was dead on the 17th when she hadn't, that Freddie appeared when he hadn't and that he was being cared for in Holland when the unsigned additional statement said France.

If Freddie had indeed come to his mother, Mrs. Nuttal then it is inconceivable that Mrs. Lock, who was her very good friend would publicly state that her son's friend had come to say Fred was safe if he had not. If she was sincere it is likely she spoke to Mrs. Nuttal about her experience in the séance and relayed the information she had about her son. Mrs. Nuttal is likely to have done the same. Her good name would have been tarnished beyond repair if she produced yet another story regarding her friend's dead son. Mrs. Lock consistently presented the same information with regard to what she was told by the form in all her statements and none of them match Burrell's.

What is easily missed amongst this deception is the account by Mrs. Lock of the airman taking his hand to reveal his black hair, red complexion and full face for everyone to see and then disappear into the floor. When she told the court this they did not know how to react. A prosecution witness was describing an amazing incident that confirmed Mrs. Duncan's mediumship. It confirmed that the light was good enough for witnesses to see faces in detail from the second row and that it does not correspond at all with the proposal that Mrs. Duncan was covered running around in a white sheet. Certainly at an early stage it was thought that this incident might be useful to denounce Mrs. Duncan when Mrs. Lock openly states the face that was revealed was similar to Mrs. Duncan's. This was subsequently dropped and preference given to all prosecution witnesses saying they could not see any facial features in the seances.

All Dodson said about Pinkie related to Burrell's testimony. 'Mr. Homer asked his opinion about the séance and he said there was more proof about the airman'. Dodson makes no mention that Mrs. Lock's evidence for the 17th and 18th of January did not corroborate Burrell's testimony but flatly contradicted it. Mrs. Lock's evidence showed that Burrell did not have more proof about the airman at all, because the airman did not appear. Mrs. Lock's testimony about the 18th was very damaging to the prosecution and it is interesting to note that Dodson in his summing up said Mrs. Lock was there on the 17th and the 19th. He misled the jury on this point by saying that she was not even present on the 18th, the day her testimony directly contradicted the person she was supposed to have gone with, Mr. Burrell. Such an omission is very serious given that her evidence for that day shows that Mr. Burrell made a false statement and lied on oath. This specific omission by the Recorder seems to point to the fact that the Recorder may have had a role in the conspiracy as he tried to cover it up by making small adjustments to the details of the case. It also suggests that the police who presented the additional statement in the name of Mrs. Lock did so in order to provide supporting documentation to enable Burrell to carry out this deception and further allege that Mrs. Duncan and her co-conspirators exploited the families of missing serviceman. Defence Counsel was certainly deceived because they did not notice the contradiction between Mrs. Lock's and Burrell's evidence.

Press Headlines
MEDIUM TELLS OF FRED THE AIRMAN
"Dead-Alive-Dead
The Star 24.3.44

'Fake seances to cheat war bereaved' charge
Daily Mirror 1.3.44

Mr. Burrell's discussions with Mr. & Mrs. Homer

Mr. Burrell's evidence was initially one of a disgruntled Spiritualist who believed that the Homer's were charging too much for readings by visiting clairvoyants such as Mr. Redman and later Mrs. Duncan the materialisation medium whom he believed was also acting fraudulently.

In his witness statement, sworn Police Court hearing statement and testimony at the trial (and widely reported in the press) Mr. Burrell reported that the following conversation took place with Mrs. Homer after the séance on the 17th. After seeing what she thought was different materialisations Mrs. Homer greeted him saying 'Now Mr. Burrell, after all these years you have been a Spiritualist and you are not convinced'. Burrell replied 'No, I'm not convinced at all. Well there are all these poor people here who don't understand and they are convinced' ('of spirit return'). Burrell said 'Well that's why they are convinced, because they don't understand'. Burrell reports that Mrs. Homer didn't reply but said he might come again the next night (and sit at the back).

Mrs. Lock's witness statement confirms Burrell account of what he told Mrs. Homer that he was not satisfied on the 17th but she did not confirm that any discussion took place in which reference was made to the sitters being convinced because they did not understand.

The next night, the 18th according to Burrell's witness statement he was so dissatisfied that he refused to pay for Mrs. Lonsdale who went with him and stated he did not intend to pay because he realised it was a swindle. Before he left he states that he told Mr. & Mrs. Homer that the séance did not impress him at all. He said he also considered these performances to be very irreverent.

Burrell's account of what he said to Mrs. Homer on the 18th had changed by the time of the trial.   With his new and uncorroborated account of an airman speaking to him his mood had changed completely. He now stated that when Mrs. Homer asked what he thought of the séance he replied 'Well certainly there was more proof of what I was after', concerning Fred whom he and Mrs. Lock were enquiring about. As he had been told Fred had survived and was being looked after by patriots in Holland he thought it was very good. He said Mrs. Homer made no comment, but was rather pleased that it had convinced him a little.

Burrell's accounts are clearly contradictory.   First he states he was so dissatisfied that he refused to pay for his partner, considered it a swindle and that he told Mrs. Homer that he was not impressed at all. At the trial he said that he was cheered at hearing good news about a lost airman and he was more convinced. Clearly both cannot be true.

Under cross-examination Mr. Loseby gave a completely different account of Mr. Burrell's conversations with Mr. & Mrs. Homer. He said that he had a conversation with Mrs. Homer on the 18th in the presence of Marine Waldron in which he said that he had been greatly impressed on the 17th and now following the séance on the 18th he was quite convinced. Burrell denied this was true, that he had said he was not at all impressed but more convinced.

It appears that the first role of Mr. Burrell at the witness statement stage was to be a disgruntled Spiritualist suspicious and angry at the fraud and deception he believed he had witnessed. By the time of the trial when the new story of his encounter with the airman was proposed, his dissatisfaction had changed to good cheer at the pleasing news of the airman's survival. What can we believe given all the evidence points to the fact that he had made up the story about the airman appearing on the 18th? Given the inconsistency of his statements one can only conclude that he made stories up to suit himself and try to secure the conviction of Mrs. Duncan.

Loseby's assertion that he said he was impressed with the séance would certainly match Worth's statements to the Homer's. Encouraging them to believe they were enthusiastic sitters in order to gain their trust and admission so that they could acquire evidence against them. This is the type of work of intelligence officers undertake and it seems Mr. Burrell was used in such a role in support of Worth and WRC Cross. Burrell was an former Naval seaman and a long serving member of the territorial coastal artillery regiment, so being able to play a part in the defence of his country as he saw it, may have appealed to him. His family said that he had the 'gift of the gab' and that he enjoyed making up stories, so this feature of the work may have come naturally to him, as his changing statements indicate.

18th January
The Budgerigar

Like Lt Worth Burrell also had an animal appear at a séance. He initially said it was a small parrot and later agreed it was a budgerigar. He explained that Albert had asked the audience to sing a song very softly and through the curtains he could hear the whistling of a bird. He said some people in the audience said it was a parrot and others that it was a budgerigar but he could not see any bird from the angle he stood. He could only hear a chirruping noise. Albert said he would place the bird on Mrs. Duncan's hands and show it to those in the séance room. He heard people say they saw a bird and one said they recognised it as one that had been lost or died but he couldn't see the bird.

In his witness statement Burrell described how Albert asked Mrs. Duncan to stand up and he put the bird on her hand. One woman said I know whose parrot it is. Burrell said he could not see the bird or Mrs. Duncan's hand.

At the trial Mrs. Lock said a bird came through the curtain on a hand and it seemed to look like the form of a bird or something in the shape of a bird and it had no colour. She also heard twittering. She was more convinced when she gave her first witness statement when she said part of Mrs. Duncan's hand appeared between the curtains and the form on it really did look like a bird and that it was green in colour.

It happened that an expert on budgerigars was at the séance that day. Mr. Kirkby described its colour as scintillating white. He even explained to Counsel the nearest equivalent budgerigar there was to the one he saw on a materialised hand. He said he saw its beak and eyes and that it moved its feathers. The bird moved about with the appropriate actions that budgerigars make and the bird said 'pretty boy, pretty boy' and in the right intonation, but very weak and clear.

Dodson when summing up Mr. Kirkby's evidence stated that he said there was a budgerigar and he did not say it said 'pretty Polly' but 'pretty boy'. Dodson fails to convey that Kirkby gave a detailed account of how the movements, voice and characteristics of the form matched budgerigars in real life and that he took a special interest in them. In summing up Burrell's evidence Dodson said he heard a chirruping bird and someone thought it was a parrot and he did not see anything at all

Mrs. Allen

Many people who regularly attended the Church where the séances took place, knew Mrs. Allen. Her appearance on the 14th, which Lt. Worth attended, is discussed above as well as in the section referring to the lighting conditions.

Mrs. Allen also appeared on the 18th and Burrell referred to her in his testimony. He said he had lost interest in the séance by the time Mrs. Allen appeared. He briefly described how a woman, Mrs. Allen who used to work for the church and had only recently passed over appeared and that the swelling she had had on her arm had not gone down. He said Albert disclosed this information and to prove it he was going to materialise the arm and be shown to those who cared to see it. The arm materialised and it was poked through the curtain. Mrs. Homer stepped up and said 'yes, the swelling is still there'.

Burrell who was in the third row said he could distinctly see the swelling that extended from the biceps to the wrist. He said it looked like a well-defined nice arm, white and flesh-like. He describes the same occurrence in his sworn police court statement. It has already been noted that this observation by Burrell undermines his evidence. In this instance he stated he distinctly saw a nice arm with details referred to from being seated in the third row, yet he claimed he was unable to see details of even larger forms when in the front row because of the poor lighting.

Burrell however gives a very different picture when he gave his two pre-trial statements. The voice explained that someone was here who had passed over in the last fortnight or who quite recently with some trouble with an arm. A white form appeared and Mrs. Homer jumped up. She recognised and greeted Mrs. Allen saying 'Well my dear Mrs. Allen fancy seeing you here' and she asked how she was. Mrs. Allen said her arm has not gone down yet. Mrs. Homer asked about her health and she went over to inspect the arm. In both these statements Burrell also said that he then saw the shape of an arm appear between the curtains, that looked more solid than the flimsy forms that had appeared before.

In his witness statement Burrell said the arm appeared in front of the curtains. Mrs. Homer then held the arm and to her surprise when looking at it she announced that the swelling on the arm had not gone down. According to the witness statement Mrs. Homer blessed her, and then the white form and arm disappeared. Albert then confirmed that the swelling has not gone down. Mrs. Allen's voice then remarked that she was pleased to see her daughters at the previously evening's séance. Mr. Burrell stated that the arm he saw was big and fat from bicep down to wrist and that he had no doubt it was Mrs. Duncan's arm.

It is clear that in Burrell's witness statement and sworn police court statement there are two forms, the white form representing Mrs. Allen who was recognised and greeted and the 'big fat arm' that came through the curtains. The press also reported Burrell's sworn statement of seeing Mrs. Allen with her swollen arm at the pre-trial hearing in front of Portsmouth's magistrates. At the trial Burrell says there is only the arm which is 'poked' through the curtains. He has changed his account yet again and in a way that is most damaging to the defence. His earlier accounts would be good material for the defence to use because if true it shows two forms together at the same time the white form and the fat arm. Naturally it would be quite impossible for Mrs. Duncan to be putting her arm through the curtains at the same time as she is impersonating Mrs. Allen and talking to members of the audience in front of the curtains covered in a white sheet.

Dodson summed up this evidence saying there was reference to Mrs. Allen with a swollen arm and he said the arm was poked through the curtain and Mrs. Allen confirmed that it was still swollen. In fact Mr. Burrell is quoted as saying that it was Albert, and later Mrs. Homer who said to Mrs. Allen, that 'the swelling is still there', not Mrs. Allen. Again Dodson misrepresents what took place on another piece of evidence to the detriment of the defence's case.

Burrell failed to recall two manifestations, Mrs. Coulcher's mother and most significantly Nurse Rust's husband and mother. Accounts of these presentations are provided in the Appendix.

Mr. William Lock's evidence

17th January
Mr. Lock's mother-in-law

At the trial Mr. Lock described Albert saying there was a form here for a man sitting near the door. As Mr. Lock was the gentleman in question he asked whether it was 'Mum'. It said 'Yes' and a form appeared. It never stopped to give a message and it disappeared (this figure was his mother-in-law, who he called 'Mum').

In Mr. Lock's witness statement Albert gave a little more information saying this spirit had passed with chest trouble. Mr. Lock repeated the request for her to come out and touch him but he didn't get a chance as the form disappeared.

Mrs. Lock also described this encounter similarly in her witness statement with the additional observation that it disappeared by going towards the floor.

At the trial Mrs. Lock's account had changed. At the trial she testified that this time Mr. Lock's mother-in-law came out and shook his hand and then went back apparently as though disappearing through the floor. This statement is false and contradicts both of Mr. Lock's statements and her own witness statement.

Dodson in his summing up makes no mention of this discrepancy but falsely asserts that Mrs. Lock corroborates her husband's evidence when clearly on this point she contradicts it.

Mr. Lock's sister Sally

The next form to come forward was Mr. Lock's sister, Sally. The voice said there was somebody else in the cabinet for the same gentleman and Mr. Lock asked whether is was Sally. When the voice said it was, Mr. Lock asked it to come out and shake his hand if it is Sally and then he can believe her. The form then walked out from the side of the curtain and she came up to him. He was about 8' from the curtain. He leaned over the person in front in the front row and shook her hand. He said it felt very fat and clammy and it was more like a human hand. He said the hand looked like a white cloth or substance. It was a white shroud but he could not see any features of anyone on the form but an outside figure of a large person more like Mrs. Duncan than anyone else.

Mr. Lock said the white cloth disappeared through the floor and the figure disappeared towards the curtain. He repeated it did not appear to walk back to the curtain where it came from. Loseby tried to clarify this point. Mr. Lock agreed the figure had come out about 8' and it didn't go back to the curtain. He thought the figure was Mrs. Duncan after taking hold of her hand but he did not think that Mrs. Duncan disappeared through the floor. The Recorder then interrupted and said Mr. Lock had said the cloth seemed to fall to the ground and the figure went back to the curtain. The Recorder was wrong, because Lock had in fact said the figure went towards the curtain, not that it went back to it. When pressed on this point Mr. Lock said he couldn't see where the figure disappeared to but the cloth disappeared downwards.

The muddle Mr. Lock had got himself into by trying to make a distinction between the figure and the cloth is curious. It may have been a honest attempt to elaborate upon a theory his friend Mr. Burrell had presented, that it was a piece of stage craft, an illusion created by the cloth disappearing downwards which must have meant the figure slipped away from the back. Certainly several witnesses said forms disappeared downwards as they were going backwards towards the cabinet. Mr. Lock's witness statement stated the cloth disappeared by quickly lowering itself and suddenly disappearing near the bottom of the curtains. However at the police court hearing he said the white cloth disappeared towards the ground. Mr. Lock's changing statements about how the form disappeared seem to reflect the problems his testimony has for the prosecution. It directly contradicts Worth's and Cross's evidence that they saw the forms return to the cabinet. His changes would seem to reflect a person who believed what he saw and tried to accommodate the other views of people he respected who asserted it was an illusion created by Mrs. Duncan.

Mr. Lock's evidence is significant because he accused Mrs. Duncan of being the form that presented itself to him both by its size and more importantly by the touch and description of the hand that he shook.

Mr. Lock's previous statements offer some interesting details. Both pre-trial statements refer to the hand being very cold which he omitted from his testimony. Naturally human hands aren't normally very cold and very clammy. He claimed it was not his sister's hand and it was not a spirit hand (witness statement) and it seemed to be human flesh (pre-trial hearing). When Sally came close to shake his hand he also said there was a white mist in front of him. He also used the term a misty form in his witness statement. Mr. Lock did not refer to this unusual misty quality of the forms at the trial.

Mrs. Lock also gave evidence at the trial about Sally's appearance. Mrs. Lock was sitting next to her husband in the second row near the door. She confirms that the white form had no face that she could see, even though it came within 2' of her husband and that it disappeared into the floor. Mrs. Lock's witness statement presented a different version. The Voice described the form as someone who passed very quickly and young and then Sally danced out and asked Mr. Lock to shake her hand. They shook hands. Mr. Lock asked if Sally was happy. The figure than went back into the cabinet and disappeared.

Dodson in his summing up said that Mr. Lock had been at the seance on the 17th omitting that he also attended the one on the 18th. This omission also matches his omission of Mrs. Lock on the 18th where her testimony contradicts Burrell's. He said with regard to Sally, a form appeared and he asked if it was Sally and after it was confirmed it was, Mr. Lock requested it to come out and shake hands. It came out of side curtain close to where Mrs. Homer sat and he leaned over and shook the hand and it was very fat and clammy. It was more like a human hand than anything else. That is the evidence of a man who is a sympathetic Spiritualist and himself a medium. He came to the conclusion that the séance on the 17th was not a genuine one.

It is clear that Dodson completely misrepresents Mr. Lock. William Lock was not a sympathetic Spiritualist or a medium at all. To the contrary he was a sceptic and regarded the weekly meetings between Mr. Burrell and his wife and daughter, where Burrell went into trance or gave clairvoyant message as a 'load of rubbish'. Dodson gives the jury a completely misleading impression of Mr. Lock and he gives his evidence greater weight in their minds by claiming he was a Spiritualist. So now thanks to Dodson, the prosecution had two witnesses who are Spiritualists and mediums, who both accuse Mrs. Duncan of being a fraud.

Prosecution Witness Evidence 17th January

Bessie Lock's evidence (standing in/behind 2nd row)
Mrs. Lock's Mother

At the trial Mrs. Lock said her mother came through again on the 17th.

In her witness statement and at the trial she said that the first figure to appear for her husband was referred to as 'mother'. Mr. Lock testified that it was his mother-in-law, Mrs. Lock's mother. At the trial however Mrs. Lock mentioned nothing of her mother appearing to her husband only that a figure appeared who Mr. Lock called 'Mum'. After describing this encounter she goes on to say Sally, Mr. Lock's sister followed and then her own mother came to her.

This may seem a little strange as the same form had come a moment earlier to her husband but had stayed very briefly without talking to her. It is also strange that although Mrs. Lock described in some detail the forms that appeared on the 17th, in her witness statement she made no mention of her mother coming to her after she had already come to her husband. By the time of the police court hearings on the 29th of February her account had changed and she describes her mother coming to her and that she failed to recognise her voice. Mrs. Lock said she went to the séances on three occasions and her mother came to her on each occasion but she also let it slip that she had been to the séance on the 12th.

This admission does not tally with her testimony that she had appeared on the three occasions she described at the trial. In fact Mrs. Lock's statements describe her mother showing herself to her on four occasions, twice on the 17th, and once on the 18th and 19th. Given the inconsistency in her statements it seems likely that she included an incident that occurred at another séance and presented it as if it occurred on the 17th.

At the trial she described this appearance as follows. Albert announced there was an elderly lady who had passed over here who was very weary and it was for the lady at the door. After asking whether is was her mother and a positive reply was heard, Mrs. Lock asked her to speak to her and shake her hand or touch her. The form said she could not do that and that she was too weary and tired and then just drifted to the floor. Mrs. Lock said there was no similarity to her mother's voice. She explained that her mother's voice had been old and very, very weak as she was 93 years old when she died but admitted that the voice she heard was also weak, which seems to be self contradictory.

The first time Mrs. Lock mentions her mother appearing to her on the 17th was at the police court hearing. In her sworn statement she said the voice did not sound like hers, it was not old enough. It is interesting that at the trial she does not refer to the reason she first gave for saying it was not her mothers, that the voice was not old enough given she had admitted that the voice she heard matched her mother's, as it was weak on this occasion.

18th January
Mrs. Lock's Mother

The second occasion Mrs. Lock reported her mother appeared was on the 18th . At the trial she said after her mother had appeared she asked her to touch or kiss her but it never answered and it just went away. She asked if she had met any other members of the family that had passed and she said she had met five of them. She said the voice did not sound like her mother's.

In her witness statement she explained how her mother had appeared for Mr. Lock again and he called her out. He referred to her as Nan on this occasion. Having told the form that her daughter Bessie was present the form entered into conversation with her. The form explained she knew she was Bessie and they could see her. Bessie asked her to touch her but the form said they were too weak and it disappeared through the floor. Mrs. Lock said she was in the front row and seated next to Mr. Homer when this occurred.

A manifestation Mr. Burrell and Mr. & Mrs. Lock failed to recall of Mr. Kirby's Chinese guide can be found in the Appendix.

19th January afternoon
Mrs. Emma Jennings

Mrs. Jennings came on the scene at a late stage. She was recommended by the Portsmouth police just before the trial started as being a potential good witness for the prosecution. Maude admitted that he had not spoken to her before she was called at the Old Bailey.

She worked as the Supervisor of Main Control in the ARP in Portsmouth and she had attended the afternoon séance on the 19th. She claimed her first impression was that Albert's voice sounded like Mrs. Duncan's. As she had had experience as a stage actress she had had some experience of disguising voices. She said in her opinion Albert's voice was definitely that of Mrs. Duncan's.

Loseby in cross-examination pointed out that as different forms appeared with using varying languages and dialects and also if added to appearing like Peggy it would be difficult to do, even for an actress of her experience. Mrs. Jennings said it would difficult to imitate different dialects unless the person was very used to doing so and much more difficult if different languages were spoken, but she did not hear different languages spoken. Loseby pointed out that Mrs. Jennings had formed her opinion from just one sitting.

She said Peggy looked like a figure of no definite shape with a white sheet draped over it with no features. She saw no features on all the forms that appeared. Peggy had danced about 18 inches away from the curtains, but she was over 4' away from it, being seated in the second row. Under cross-examination Mrs. Jennings claimed that Mrs. Duncan could have impersonated Peggy, who looked like a slim young girl and was dancing outside the curtains, under the poor light conditions that existed despite her greater size. She said she had a feeling it was not genuine.

Mrs. Jennings evidence is examined in the 'light' and 'disappearing' sections.

Mrs. Jennings also described the conversation Peggy had with Mrs. Homer's daughter, Christine. Peggy asked her whether she remembered going to a perfume bottle and finding something was missing. Christine and Mrs. Homer agreed. Peggy said she had taken some of the perfume and it was very nice. She said she'd also tried the lipstick but she didn't like it because it was like candle-grease.

Mr. Homer had asked Peggy whether she had taken some of his papers that had gone missing. Peggy replied that she hadn't but she told him where he could find them.

Dodson went through Mrs. Jennings evidence in some detail in his summing up compared to other witnesses even though he said her evidence did not amount to much. Dodson makes the error by misquoting Mrs. Jennings. Mrs. Jennings never said Peggy danced 18 inches in front of her, but that she danced 18 inches from the curtains. The nearest Mrs. Jennings got to a form was four feet and this was closer than she ever got to Peggy. Dodson's error places Mrs. Jennings much closer to the forms than she actually was. She had stated she was seated in the second row 4 to 5 feet from the curtains. In her witness statement she said she was not permitted to sit in the front row because she hadn't been to a meeting before and some phenomena might frighten her.

Although Dodson says it has been said that Mrs. Jennings' evidence does not amount to very much, such a comment was not made at the trial to that effect by anyone. Having said this, it allowed him to go on to assert that it is not for counsel to protest loudly that, "I say this or that", "I say this is genuine" or "I say that is". He tells the jury that it doesn't matter what counsel says which way it is, for they are the judge of what witnesses say. This neatly undermined Loseby's successful cross-examination to put doubt in the jurors minds regarding Mrs. Jennings assertion that not only could a twenty stone Mrs. Duncan dance like a young slim girl but at the same time imitate a range of different dialects. Maude inadvertently assisted Loseby in his re-examination of Mrs. Jennings when she added that all the forms also disappeared into the floor. It is interesting that Dodson did not say it is not for counsel to declaim "I say this is not genuine" which would have presented the point in its most balanced form.

Press Headline
TRIAL STORY OF 'TEMPLE' SEANCE
'Spirit' Called Peggy Liked Lipstick
Daily Sketch 24.3.44

19th January 7.00pm
Mrs. Lock's Mother

At the trial Mrs. Lock said her mother appeared again on the 19th but gave no details of the encounter. She did not mention seeing her mother in her magistrates statement.

In her witness statement she describes a similar encounter occurring on the 19th that she describes at the trial as occurring the previous evening. She said her mother was the first form to appear on the 18th. She said she asked her mother again to touch her but she did not. She asked her if she was happy and the form said she was. Then she asked if she had met any other loved ones from the family and the form said she had met five other members of the family and she then said goodbye and disappeared.

It is interesting that for the 19th in both their witness statements Cross and Worth refer to a person matching Mrs. Lock sitting in the front row to Cross's right near the entrance and at the end of the front row respectively. Cross described a form purporting to be a mother appearing for that lady and after a short conversation it immediately disappeared. Worth goes into more detail saying the woman asked whether the white form had any other relatives with her and the figure replied she had five others with her. Both statements describe a scene where Mrs. Lock is seated in a particular seat in the front row and a conversation takes place. The conversation Worth describes as occurring on the 19th; Mrs. Lock describes as occurring on the 18th, at the trial. Other witnesses appear to agree that the figure for Mrs. Lock was the second to appear on the 19th. Mrs. Lock appears to have got confused about what was actually said and which date it refers to.

Mother with baby

The first figure Worth described coming out on the 19th was a mother. The voice said he had a form of a lady who had passed some time before. A sailor said he had lost his mother when he was a baby. After some prompting by Mrs. Brown the sailor called her out. Worth described a form appearing between the curtains with outstretched arms. Mrs. Brown quickly called out 'look she has a baby in her arms' but Worth saw no baby. He only saw a large white shrouded figure with outstretched arms.   A sailor in the audience said he had lost his mother when he was a baby. The figure said that she didn't take her baby with her (presumably when she went to the spirit world). Mrs. Homer repeated it in a loud voice what she had said. 'She didn't take the baby with her'. Then the form disappeared and the sailor sat down. Worth said the figure spoke in a faint sort of voice.

Worth's witness statement stated the same. He saw a form with outstretched arms come between the curtains and it went back into the cabinet and the curtains closed. Cross's witness statement supports Worth's account, and offers further information that the voice from the cabinet said there was a woman who had passed over with lower part of body affected and called upon someone to claim their relative. At the rear were two sailors. One remarked it might be his mother who died when he was a baby. He could not remember her. The sailor eventually called to his mother and the rest is how Worth described.

It is interesting to observe that other prosecution witnesses contradict the account Worth gave at the trial. Ena Harris in her witness statement described the same incident differently. She said a spirit form first came out of the cabinet but the form disappeared apparently because the audience did not speak up. The voice said that he had a lady here who passed with something wrong with her stomach and she had come for someone sitting at the back. Mrs. Brown asked a sailor to call her out. The sailor said he didn't know his mother because she died when he was a baby. The sailor eventually called out asking whether it was his mother. A white form then appeared between curtains with something, which seemed to be in the position that one would carry a baby in one's arms. The sailor repeated his question 'Is that you mother'? and the voice answered 'Yes'. Somebody called out in surprise that 'She's got a baby with her'. The form replied that she had but that she did not take the baby with her. The form then vanished.

Mrs. Lock in her witness statement also described the incident in the same way. When the first form appeared it was a form holding what looked to be a baby laid in its arms. Mrs. Lock could not see whether it was a baby but it looked like an outline form of a baby. Mrs. Irene Taylor testified that the first form to appear on the 19th was a lady that came through the curtains with her arms as if she were carrying a baby and that she went back into the cabinet. Mr. Bush who was seated next to Worth states that he saw a figure come through the curtains holding something in her arms. He heard the audience simultaneously say that she had a baby in her arms.

Four witnesses, one sitting next to Worth and others sitting or standing to his side or behind him give a different account to his and Cross's. According to them the mother did not come out of the cabinet with outstretched arms, but the mother had a baby laid in her arms. I imagine women witnesses would be particularly sensitive to such a scene given the circumstances described. Worth's and Cross's testimony present a 'ridiculous image' and a far cry from a more intimate encounter where a mother brings a baby to a meeting with a son she had not seen since his birth. Worth's and Cross's statements also unfairly implicate Mrs. Brown and Mr. Homer in contrast to the accounts of the other witnesses who say the audience reacted spontaneously to the scene before them.

Dodson in his summing up describes how Mr. Homer started the séance with a prayer. Dodson reports that a sailor there called his mother. Worth said a white object appeared which seemed to be 'supporting or surrounding something' with what appeared to have both arms held out (demonstrating outstretched arms). Mrs. Brown said 'She has a baby in her arms'. Worth could see no baby and at that moment Cross made dive for figure that disappeared. Dodson is mistaken in asserting that Cross leapt out at this figure. Cross leapt out at the third figure who was a young man. Dodson also asserts that Worth's testified that something lay in the form's outstretched arms, when he made no such statement. This blurs the contrast between Worth's testimony and the other witnesses who report seeing something completely different. Having blurred this contrast, Dodson makes no mention of other witness's evidence contradicting Worth's account on this incident.

How the Forms Disappeared

A consistent feature of the evidence that distinguished Worth from all the other witnesses referred to the way figures disappeared. Worth described figures appearing from between the curtains and then returning back through them. This was consistent with the nature of Mrs. Duncan's purported method of performing her alleged fraud, which involved each figure being covered in a white sheet. In his witness statement Cross described the same method of disappearance for the two figures he observed prior to leaping forward to try and grab Mrs. Duncan. He did not refer to how forms exited at the trial.

All the witnesses with the exception of Worth and Cross however describe seeing a completely different method of exit for the figures that appeared at the seances. This includes four other prosecution witnesses (Mr. Lock, Mrs. Lock, Mrs. Jennings, Mr. Burrell), making 14 people in all. They all describe that all the figures with the exception of the guides Albert and sometimes Peggy seeming to disappear through the floor or sinking to the floor (Mrs. Gill, Mr. Gill, Mrs. Jopling, Mr. Coulcher, Mr. Williams, Mrs. Tremlett, Mr. Homer, Nurse Rust, Marine Clayton, Mr. Lock, Mrs. Lock, Mrs. Jennings, Mr. Burrell and Mr. White).[11] described that the figures seem to collapse as they stand and 'it is just gone' with a large amount of white material on the floor, which also disappeared. Mr. Williams described how the figure of his mother disappeared through the floor practically at his feet. These figures disappeared in a flash or fairly quickly as if they just vanished or simply disappeared. Few witnesses talk of instances where figures returning to the cabinet, except Albert or on rare occasions those figures who returned in order to get something.

The importance of the descriptions of how figures exited can be readily appreciated when considering Cross's (and Worth's) evidence about how he 'red-handedly' caught Mrs. Duncan who he claimed was standing at the front of the curtains with a sheet over her. If Mrs. Duncan was a fraud and she carried out the fraud by covering herself in a sheet then naturally as a large twenty stone woman she needed to return to the cabinet and reappear with the next impersonation. As practically all other witnesses state that figures disappeared on each occasion by sinking towards the floor and this method accords with witnesses accounts that this was the method the figure used on the occasion that Cross leapt out to grab the figure, then it strengthens this account. It also explains the reason why these witnesses did not see Mrs. Duncan being grabbed in front of the curtains by Cross, but that when the curtains were opened by Cross she was seen seated on a chair in the cabinet.

Witnesses used terms such as disappeared, vanished, melted, sinking towards the floor. Even Worth used the terms disappeared and vanished in describing how figures exited in his pre-trial witness statements. Fowler's unsigned witness statement use the same terms. Surely if they simply went back into the cabinet as Worth later testified then why didn't he say so when he first made his statements.

Figures who exited in the way the majority of people describe, did so by the curtains and even well away from the curtains. Witnesses described relatives they identified as doing so and other witnesses with no connection with the figures described the same process.

Even prosecution witnesses described the same method. Mrs. Lock stated her mother disappeared down to the floor when seeing her on the 17th and 18th of January and her friend Pinkie who did so displaying a clear face with a red complexion with hair. He drifted down to the ground. Mrs. Jennings was so stuck by the way figures disappeared she explained in her testimony that she took a special interest and stood to observe the method. She explained at the trial that the head portion went first, then the shoulders down. The last thing she could see was a lot of white on the floor. She explained they all disappeared in the same way. Mr. Lock also described this same method for a figure purporting to be his sister Sally who went across the room to shake hands with him. He described how the white form disappeared towards the ground.

Even Mr. Burrell the medium did not agree with Worth. In his pre-trial statement he states he distinctly saw the white material and it collapsed in front of the curtains. Mr. Burrell asserted that this method was cleverly managed stagecraft and he had seen more convincing performances in London. Whether it was an illusion or not it is still apparent that Worth and Cross did not describe the same 'illusion' as all other witnesses describe. The discrepancies between Burrell and Worth's accounts were minimized at the trial because he never mentioned how the figures exited and Loseby never questioned him on it.

The prosecution however still had Mr. Lock and Mrs. Lock as witnesses that described the same method. Burrell's explanation of the illusion in his February police statement may have had an effect on his friend Mr. Lock, who had attended on the same evening (17th January) and stated in his police court statement that the form claiming to be his sister Sally who had come out from the curtains 'disappeared towards the ground like a white cloth'. In his earlier statement he said the white cloth disappeared, quickly lowered itself and suddenly disappeared near the base of the curtains. At the trial Mr. Lock made a confusing statement with regard to this figure. He said 'It disappeared towards the floor and the figure disappeared towards the curtain, and the white curtain seemed to disappear down to the floor'. He said it didn't appear to walk back to the curtain where it came from. Lock had introduced two features the white material and the figure! Loseby questioned him on this point. Lock confirmed that the cloth appeared to go through the floor but when he asked whether he was saying that Mrs. Duncan went right back to the cabinet, Lock said he couldn't see because of the light.

With the audience seated in an arc around the curtains and figures coming right out to the audience and 'melting' where they stood, then it would have been clearly apparent whether a large twenty stone woman tried to slip out of the back of the white figure. All witnesses report the curtains remaining closed as the figures sank to the floor.

It frankly is not possible for a twenty stone woman outside of the cabinet to return to it, in full view of people within a few feet from her and on either side, without the curtains moving and someone seeing. Chief Constable West made the same point in the BBC Radio 4 programme about the trial in 1979. Mr. and Mrs. Lock sat at an angle to the proceedings for two seances and they never spotted a twenty stone woman slipping out at the back of the sheet. Even Worth in his witness statement stated the bulky figure of Peggy disappeared under the curtain. How can a twenty stone woman disappear under a curtain without it moving?

Moreover, if it did represent an illusion in which Mrs. Duncan slipped from beneath the back of the white cloth to the cabinet without anyone seeing or the curtains moving, how did the white muslin disappear once it lay on the ground in front of everyone? Witnesses report seeing it lay on the floor and disappear. It is not credible. A disappearing twenty stone woman is one thing, endless sheets of disappearing muslin clearly seen a matter of inches away from the sitters is something else.

Those prosecution witnesses, who were unconvinced by the séance but described what they saw, agreed with the other witnesses. Although they could not explain the unusual events they witnessed they were honest enough observers to report what they saw. Worth and Cross, although also unconvinced, denied what they actually saw in order to create some 'logical' consistency to their testimony that corresponded with the scenario of a convincing fraud, so they made up events and simply ignored what everyone else witnessed. The Recorder was well aware of this problem for the prosecution. It had been acknowledged that all the forms disappeared downwards to the floor, by prosecution and defence witnesses alike, with the exception of Worth, who kept to his story that each walked out and returned through the curtains.

In his summing up Dodson misrepresents this position completely. He asserts that the witnesses for the prosecution and other witnesses stated the white substance disappeared downwards towards the floor, which would be the place where it would go if someone was manipulating it. This occurred from the beginning. Dodson fails to point out that the evidence clearly shows that Worth did not describe this method of disappearance at all and so his evidence was completely unsupported by all the other witnesses including other prosecution witnesses.

Dodson wanted it both ways. Mrs. Duncan was described as been seen with a sheet over her head walking out of the curtains by Worth, Cross, Mr. & Mrs. Lock, Mr. Burrell and Mrs. Jennings. Yet only Worth (and Cross) see her walk back apparently to put on another costume. Everyone else including other prosecution witnesses agreed the figures disappeared towards the floor. Either she walked back to the cabinet or she sunk to the floor and slipped through the curtains without them moving. Dodson decides to avoid this uncomfortable position by simply misrepresenting the evidence of Worth by suggesting he said the forms disappeared towards the floor, something he never in fact ever stated during his testimony.

What Loseby and Dodson failed to raise was how the muslin once it had fallen to the floor simply disappeared or presumably found its way back into the cabinet when no one saw it return. Dodson said it was part of an illusion but unlike other aspects of Mrs. Duncan's alleged fraud he kept quiet about how piles of muslin lying in a heap on the floor in front of 20-30 people at different locations in the room as each form exited, managed to do as he acknowledged all the witnesses described, and disappear. How figures sank into the floor and the material disappeared cannot be explained in these circumstances unless an 'unnatural' explanation is applied or that Mrs. Duncan was a great illusionist, which no one seriously believed or proposed.

As it was left the main prosecution witness Worth simply countered everyone else's testimony by asserting his own account and the Recorder misrepresented the evidence. Discrepancies between him and other prosecution witnesses were minimized the best the prosecution counsel could. Loseby never exploited it because he never focused upon this feature, despite it being relevant to the crucial moment in the case, when WRC Cross was supposed to have caught Mrs. Duncan red handed. The options were that Cross actually caught Mrs. Duncan red handed with a sheet over her head or that the figures disappeared as mysteriously as they had always done, towards the floor which everyone present described and that Dodson himself asserted.

It is also interesting to speculate that if Maskelyne, the stage magician, had performed the same illusion as it was asserted that Mrs. Duncan had done, it is likely that everyone would have been in complete agreement about what the illusion was, but uncertain how they might explain it. In Mrs. Duncan's case it was different because while asserting that she was practicing a stage illusion it was also important to assert that it was not doing as the audience described, in case some believed it was genuine.

While Maskelyne accused mediums of being frauds it is worth noting that he never stripped naked, was dressed by three individuals prior to every performance and nor were the audience allowed to inspect every part of his clothes, the apparatus and the stage. This important difference in procedure between Maskelyne and Mrs. Duncan might have served Loseby well in challenging the central thrust of those accusations of stagecraft to account for the events that the audience witnessed in 1944.

Press Headline
'LITTLE LADY VANISHED"
Through Floor, Says Witness
Evening Standard 27.3.44

Where did Mrs. Lock sit on the 19th?

At the point in the trial when Mrs. Lock had completed giving her evidence with regards to the events surrounding Cross leaping forward and grabbing the figure in front of the cabinet, the Recorder presented a seating plan to the jury. Examination of the trial documents show that Worth and Cross made false statements with regard to where prosecution witness Mrs. Bessie Lock was seated on the evening of 19th of January.

Bessie Lock was an important material prosecution witness because she was the only person to confirm Cross's testimony – seeing him hold the white material in his fingers. Cross holding the white material was the only material evidence the prosecution had, as no material was ever found.

Bessie Lock's signed witness statement tells how she turned up at the evening séance without booking a ticket and was told she could attend if she paid half fee and stood at the back. She stated she took her seat 'in the second row by the door'. Mrs. Lock confirmed that she was in this position under oath at the Police Court Hearing on the 29th of February. She swore that 'I was standing in the second row by the door'. She confirmed her position by asserting that 'Mr. Homer was in the row in front'. She then further clarified her position stating 'I was the second or third chair from the end'. Her statements clearly show that Mrs. Lock was by the door seated on the second or third chair from the end of the second row.

Lt. Worth's Police Court statement confirms the principle that determined the seating arrangements on that evening. He explains that his attempt to get a good view in the front row for himself and WRC Cross was denied. Mr. Homer explained that Mrs. Duncan needed experienced sitters in the front row because she drew power from them. Mrs. Lock's placement in the second row confirms this arrangement, as she also had little or no experience of Spiritualism and sitting in seances, notwithstanding that she only paid half price compared to those sitters who paid in full and therefore deserved a better view.

Bessie Lock was the only prosecution witness who supported WRC Cross's account of what took place when he leapt forward to grab the white figure in front of the curtains. Cross said that he grabbed hold of the white material in his left hand when it was upon the ground and felt it in his fingers. Mrs. Lock at the magistrates hearing stated on oath that she saw something white pass through his fingers. In her initial police statement she made no reference to seeing any such incident. At the trial she repeated her later claim.

After Lt. Worth had given his testimony on the first day of the trial Judge Dodson asked Maude to make a copy of the plan of the room for the jury. The next day Elam said Inspector Ford had checked his plan with the defence solicitor and they were in agreement. Elam offered to prove it but the Recorder said he would wait until WRC Cross came to give his evidence. However it was after Bessie Lock's testimony that Recorder Dodson asked the jury whether they would like to see the plan of the room for the evening of 19th January and it was handed to them. The plan was naturally important information for the jury in order to weigh up the testimony of the witnesses. It showed their relative positions at the moment when WRC Cross leapt forward to grab the white figure purportedly being Mrs. Duncan. It also allowed the jury to know the positions of the witnesses with regard to their accounts of this event and the manifestations that occurred that evening. Clearly giving this plan to the jury immediately after Bessie Lock had given her evidence was the optimal moment from the prosecution's point of view, as it showed her seated in the front row with a clear view of the area in which the incident with WRC Cross occurred. Quite unexpectedly a juror questioned the three seats shown on the plan next to the cabinet and Recorder Dodson replied 'pay no attention to the names'. The plan was to be officially 'proved' later when WRC Cross gave his testimony, as he drew up the plan, but it was unclear why jurors should not attend to the names.

The plan was clearly incomplete and full of errors. Inspecting the plan immediately draws one's attentions to a name missing for seat number 12, the second seat from the end of the front row nearest the door. Clearly defence witness Nurse Rust's name is also absent from the plan. The absence of her name in the plan was never mentioned at the trial although her position in the room was obviously important. It was important in weighing up the evidence she gave of what occurred when WRC Cross leapt forward and as she apparently sat next to the seat in which Mrs. Lock had been placed in the plan. During her testimony Nurse Rust strongly suggested she sat in the front row, because she reports only Mr. Cross being in front of her once he had leapt forward, that only he obstructed her view and that on most occasions she sat in the front row. This contrasts with Mrs. Lock who stated that Mr. Homer was seated in the row in front of her.

It also transpired during Mr. Homer's testimony and in discussion between

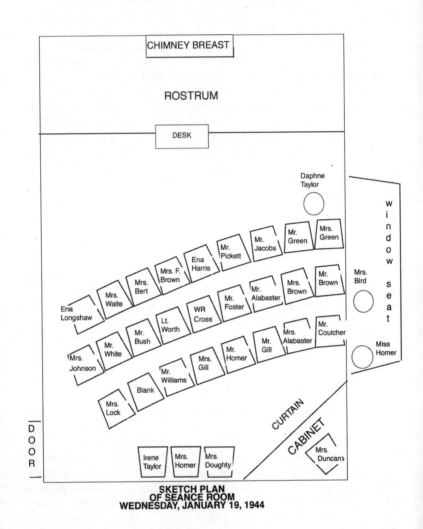

**SKETCH PLAN
OF SEANCE ROOM
WEDNESDAY, JANUARY 19, 1944**

Defence Counsel Mr. Pedler and the Recorder that there were no seats 2, 3 and 4 against the wall to the left of the cabinet. Irene Taylor, shown as being in seat No.4, in her testimony stated she was standing at the back to the left of the rostrum by the red light. It seems probable that the police confused her with Daphne Taylor who is shown on the plan to be standing at the back. In these circumstances it is likely Daphne Taylor was seated at the front, not Irene Taylor. It was established that Mrs. Green, shown as seated in chair 24, was actually seated on the window sill seat. Possibly her husband sat next to her, she moved from her chair to the window seat for a better view, there was another person present at the séance who is unaccounted for or that chair was not there. The third row may only have had 8 chairs not 9 otherwise Irene Taylor would presumably have sat in the remaining chair, unless it was already occupied. It seems likely that a chair existed there because Lt. Worth stated Mrs. Brown was standing directly behind him and Cross, in the third row. The plan shows this is likely to have been the case. Mr. Homer and Defence Counsel Pedler established with the Recorder that Seats 2, 3 and 4 came to the wall but did not have their backs against it. As there were three arced or crescent rows facing the corner of the room these chairs most certainly completed the extension of the first and second rows. Mr. Walter Williams in his testimony stated he was in the fourth seat from the door in the first row, which means there was one more chair in the front row than the plan shows, making 9 chairs not 8. The other two chairs completed the end of the second row, one of which was used by Mrs. Lock.

This leaves three people's positions unaccounted for Mrs. Doughty, Daphne Taylor and Mrs. Homer, assuming Edith Johnson retained her position in the second row when Mrs. Lock is placed next to her on the second chair from the end near the door as she stated. By a process of elimination, it seems reasonable to assert that Mrs. Doughty and Daphne Taylor also sat in the first row. Either one of whom may have occupied the chair that Mrs. Lock was shown as occupying, along with Nurse Rust. Lt Worth testified that Mrs. Homer was seated with her back against the door. Mr. Pedler confirms this position stating that Mrs. Homer sat by the door. This would place Mrs. Homer in the second row next to Mrs. Lock. This accords well with the information given at the trial and in varying statements. It seems to represent the best fit. Mrs. Homer is by the door and Mrs. Lock in the second or third chair from the end in the second row, but standing near the door in the second row.

What is clear from the plan is that Mrs. Lock has been placed in the front row in a seat she never occupied and that the row did not end as it is shown. Witnesses described it was an arc or semi-circle. In Cross's plan Mrs. Lock is seated next to an unnamed chair, which is obviously helpful in order for this deception is work. If the plan had been accurate and complete then the defence's first inspection would be to check that the names corresponded to the correct

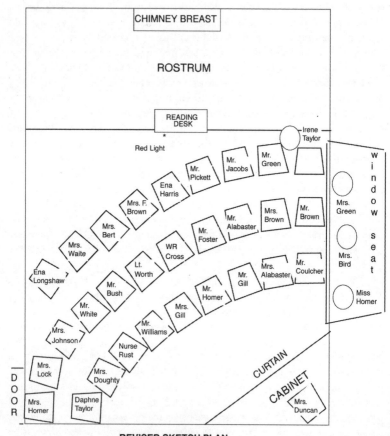

REVISED SKETCH PLAN
SEANCE ROOM
WEDNESDAY, JANUARY 19, 1944

places. The person next to this front row end seat would have been the person most able to contest the fact that Mrs. Lock never sat next to her in that chair, but as the chair was unnamed, making this check would have been more difficult for the defence. As Mrs. Lock sat in the second row and Nurse Rust suggested she sat in the front row the remaining chairs were occupied either by Daphne Taylor or Mrs. Doughty. These witnesses may have had important evidence to give but they were never called. Placing another chair to the end of the first row up against the wall as described also prevents Mrs. Lock from approaching closer to the cabinet from the second row. Instead of a detailed inspection of the plan the unnamed chair and other errors takes the reader's attention and the judge's comment 'Pay no attention to the names' clearly aids this misrepresentation at the time of having heard Mrs. Lock's evidence. Such a comment clearly discourages jurors to raise the question about the missing name, which would have been the first question that comes to mind. If the question had been raised the answer most certainly would have been Nurse Rust as she was the one witness present on that occasion that was not named on the plan, but then this would not have addressed the question of the other placement errors contained in the plan.

The errors and omissions within the plan led to confusion, which aided the police in slipping their one supporting prosecution witness into a false position without detection. When the plan was first produced a juror specifically asked whether there were three chairs next to the cabinet and the judge mistakenly confirmed that there were. Given a likely theory to be considered to explain the manifestations was for the person next to the cabinet to pass items through the side of the curtains then putting the chairs in this position when they were not there is very misleading.

Inspection of WRC Cross's pre-trial signed statement and the testimony he gave at the trial shows that he made a false statement at the trial. WRC Cross in his witness statement described in detail that there were three rows of chairs forming an arc facing the corner of the room. Lt. Worth described this same seating arrangement of three rows of chairs facing the curtains in his sworn statement made at the Police Court hearing and his testimony, stating at the trial that Mrs. Homer as on the previous occasion 'she was sitting near the wall against the door'.

When WRC Cross testified at the trial, he changed this arrangement to falsely state that Mrs. Homer was facing the audience. These discrepancies show that WRC Cross changed his account in order to justify a false seating plan. He was perfectly aware that there were no chairs against the wall next to the curtains and that Mrs. Homer sat against the door near the wall because he said so in his witness statement and Lt. Worth confirmed it. His false statements and plan created confusion and extra work that served to help himself and Lt. Worth and not the jury arrive at the truth.

It is very significant to note that Lt. Worth's signed witness statement confirms this misrepresentation. Lt. Worth seeks to place Mrs. Lock in this seat in the front row by describing the same encounter between her and a shrouded figure taken to be her mother she described in her witness statement that took place a short while before WRC Cross leapt forward. Lt. Worth specifically states the woman in question was seated at the end of the front row. Both Lt. Worth and WRC Cross present this misleading piece of evidence, Lt. Worth and Cross in their witness statement and WRC Cross again in the plan he proved and which was never corrected during the trial. Worth's and Mrs. Lock's account about what was said when her mother came through may have been switched from another time in order to achieve this switch. Whether what was said between the form and Mrs Lock actually occurred on this evening, is not so important. It shows that there was an attempt by Cross and Worth to match testimony in a deceptive way regarding moving a fellow prosecution witness into a better position in the front row than she actually occupied. Consequently there must be serious doubt as to whether their other statements with regard to this incident and others at the trial are truthful or a further concoction aimed to convict Mrs. Duncan.

It is also worth noting that it was at the Police Court Hearing that Mrs. Lock first mentioned seeing WRC Cross hold the white material in his fingers. At this point Mrs. Lock becomes an important material witness and the attempt is made to bring her much closer to the curtains into the front row so her testimony is considerably strengthened, knowing all the other witnesses deny that any such incident took place.

WRC Cross who was facing the cabinet claimed to have grabbed the white material as he bent down to grab with his left hand it as it had fallen to the floor. How would Mrs. Lock be able to see such an act from the second row, some 9 to 10' away and with Cross's body obstructing the view from that angle compared to other witnesses testimony who were very much closer to the incident in the front row? Nurse Rust makes this point in her evidence as she described Cross's body obstructing her view as to what he was doing on his left hand side. As Nurse Rust sat in the chair next to the one Bessie Lock is falsely shown to have sat in, the same obstruction would have obviously applied to her, making it quite impossible for her to see what she claimed to see. By removing Nurse Rust's name from the chair next to Bessie Lock makes it very difficult for the jury to identify this important contrast in the evidence from people seated at the same angle to the events. Bessie Lock's testimony would have been weakened further if she were placed in the same second row where she actually sat. Other witnesses in this row who were better placed than her to see what occurred never managed to see the white material in WRC Cross's left hand as he bent down to the floor.

Another reason for moving Bessie Lock to the front row was because the prosecution had argued that the lighting conditions were so poor at the seance that anyone seated at this distance from the curtains would not be able to see clearly any details of what was occurring. Clearly if she had been placed where she was actually seated this argument could have been used against their own witness.

One can only conclude that this represented a deliberate deception in which the police drew up a misleading plan and combined with Lt. Worth's false statement, sought to move an important prosecution witness, the only other person who supported their account, to a position she never actually occupied. This was done in order to mislead the jury and give her testimony more weight than it had. Had the jury been aware of the nature of this misrepresentation and the method in which it was applied then it may have further undermined the prosecution's case. Had the jury also known about Worth and Cross's close friendship and Worth's close friendship with Chief Constable West and Maude's position as a MI5 officer and the background to Mrs. Duncan leaking Naval information then this deception would have been seen as confirmation of their conspiracy against the defendants. The jury would have been aware that these false statements and false seating plan were being made against Mrs. Duncan in order for their conspiracy to succeed, similar to other evidence presented at the trial.

The question posed is why did the defence not bother to raise some of the issues relating to the plan. A former Judge in India, Adby Collins criticised Loseby after the trial, for not even raising the issue of Nurse Rust's name being absent from the plan. It seems Loseby had made up his mind that he was not going to raise 'technical' points to put the prosecution to proof, in the defence of his clients, preferring to prove Mrs. Duncan can materialise the spirits of deceased people. This lack of interest or attempt to challenge the 'technical' points the prosecution presented led him to overlook the glaring holes in their case. No wonder prosecuting Counsel Henry Elam said "Thank heavens it is over" at the end of the trial.

Rationale for the revised plan [12]

The revised plan accords better with the information provided at the trial than the police diagram. Firstly the number of chairs in the first two rows accords with the testimony of the witnesses with reference to who was sitting or standing where. Measurements were taken of old fashioned wooden chairs, from the edges of the legs, which give an indication of the floor area covered by each one. The distances found were 1'5" along the front, 1' 4.5" along the sides and 1' 1.5" along the back of the chair. The space provided for legroom between chairs was 1' 2". Using these dimensions then natural arcs of the type described by all the witnesses are formed in front of the curtains and the numbers of chairs referred to by the witnesses fit neatly with this presentation. Support for the adoption of these dimensions is indicated by there being no space for further chairs to be fitted in the first and second rows, which reached the walls. The police diagram shows rows of chairs ending short of the walls and not utilising the full scope of the room in order for sitters to get the best view. This feature of the police plan contradicts the evidence presented at the trial, that the ends of the rows of the chairs came to the walls.

The revised plan also fits Mr. Homer's testimony that Cross was seated just behind him and Worth behind him on his right. The three chairs shown as next to the cabinet were not there and their positioning makes it impossible for two of these sitters to see what was taking place in and around the cabinet. Forms were also described, as sometimes emerging from the side of the cabinet which would not be possible if one adopted the police plan, because a chair was placed in the way.

The revised plan is more accurate than the police plan, it represents a better fit in terms of the stated dimensions and it accords with the statements of the witnesses about where they were seated. Most importantly it shows that a deception occurred to place Mrs. Lock in a position she never occupied in order to strengthen her evidence, when from this plan her evidence might be seen as highly questionable. This was in terms of seeing WRC Cross bend down and take hold of the white cloth that Mrs. Duncan was purported to have dropped to the ground when she was grabbed, which all the other witnesses seated closer than her never saw happen.

Cross Leaping on Figure

The importance of the attempt to catch Mrs. Duncan red handed is the crux of the case according to Recorder Dodson. Whatever may have been genuine or not during the rest of the seances if Mrs. Duncan was caught in front of the curtains with a sheet over her head as Worth and Cross claim then she is guilty of fraud.

According to Cross's testimony when the third figure had just appeared he jumped forward and pushed over Mr. Homer's chair in front of him and went forward between him and Mrs. Gill who was on his left. Then Worth switched on his torch and he grabbed Mrs. Duncan by the arms. He said she was standing between the curtains and hurriedly pushing down a white cloth towards the floor when he got to her. The sheet dropped and she stood a little to one side to the right. Cross held her with his right hand and at the same time reached down with his left hand for the sheet and grasped it while it was on the ground (Cross was facing the cabinet and Mrs. Duncan facing the audience). The material felt very flimsy, similar to butter muslin. The material had dropped about 6" to a foot outside the curtains and two feet away from the people in the front row.

At that moment it commenced to move away from him in the direction of the audience, specifically towards the people in the front row. He felt it pulled away towards his left approximately in the direction of Miss Homer who was sitting in the window seat. Although the sheet was pulled it did not stretch out. He then stood up and pulled back the curtains covering the corner of room and the torch showed an empty cabinet. Immediately after Cross had pulled the curtains back the main room light was switched on and he saw Mrs. Duncan bending down to move her shoes with her hand, which she later put her foot into it. Mrs. Duncan remained standing for a full minute then she sat down on a chair someone had pushed forward to her. While she was standing he identified himself as a police officer and arrested her. He didn't see any movement that might have thrown her slippers off. He denied suggesting to Miss Homer that she had got the material. He looked on the window seat and around the back of the room.

Cross's witness statement adds only a few further details. He flung back the curtains with his left hand. His right hand was holding Mrs. Duncan's left arm. As she was bending down to put on her shoes he identified himself as a police officer and told her that she was under arrest. Mrs. Duncan's eyes were open. He said that she seemed quite normal apart from being flustered and she said 'Oh dear, Oh dear'. As she said this she sat down on a chair and then she said that she was feeling ill and asked for a doctor.

He gives the same basic account in his sworn police court hearing statement although Cross said the torch was switched on by Worth when he was about 3' from the cabinet at which point he saw Mrs. Duncan standing between the curtains.

The main additions to Cross's testimony by Worth was that Worth estimated 2-3 yards of flimsy material were thrown to the floor. He saw someone pulling cloth out of Cross's grasp. The cloth was pulled towards window seat. He saw it grabbed up or pulled by someone sitting at the end of the second row by a hand. Mrs. Duncan was standing in her bare feet. Mrs. Duncan stayed standing until she got her shoes on which were behind her and then she sat down.

Worth's account generally corroborated Cross's account at the trial although there was some small ambiguity. Cross always maintained the signal to switch on torch was when he was about to grab the figure. At the trial Worth said Cross grasped the figure and he produced and switched on his torch, suggesting his torch was not switched on until after he had grabbed the figure. Under cross-examination Worth twice clarified the position saying the signal was for him to switch on the torch was immediately Cross leapt forward so as when Cross got to curtains the torch was already on. This was consistent with his witness statement. Obviously there is a difference here. Some Spiritualists viewed this as a serious discrepancy that Loseby failed to pick up on. Worth either switched it on as Cross leapt forward or when he got to the curtains. Worth varies his account on this point.

This inconsistency in his evidence about when the torch was switched on and what he saw also exists in other evidence related to the torch. Worth stated in the witness statement and at the trial that his torch was knocked away at the moment the material had fallen on the floor. At the magistrates hearing he said it was knocked away as Cross was stooping down. In all his statements Worth said it was focused back again when the material was pulled away but only at the trial did he say that at that moment he saw it pulled out of Cross's grasp. In his pre-trial statements Worth never stated that he saw the material in Cross's hand and it was only after some intense cross-examination by Loseby that he said he had seen the material in Cross's hand. If that was the case then it begs the question that once the light was on again, at the moment it was being pulled from Cross's grasp, why did not he see the person who pulled it? There must be some uncertainly as to whether Worth saw the material in Cross' hand or not given his torch was supposed to have been refocused when the material was pulled away.

It is quite possible that no one knocked Worth's torch and this incident is an invention used to account for the fact that no cloth was found. He may well have had his torch focused on the scene, but by saying it was knocked away and the scene was unlit for a moment, this gives an explanation why he did not see the person who took the material. Surely if Worth had good sight and was illuminating the scene that he would have clearly seen a person directly in front of him grab the material, especially as it lay in a heap 6 inches to one foot in front of the cabinet and it did not stretch out when it was supposedly taken. On what basis he can state that a person at the end of the 2nd row grabbed it is very difficult to understand given they would be 6 or 7' away from the cloth. Possibly he meant to say the first row. We cannot know because Loseby never cross-examined him further on this point.

We can be sure that for Cross' account to make any sense someone would have had to gone forward to within a foot of the cabinet, reached out to the side and behind him in order to take a heap of muslin without it stretching out. If Worth saw the cloth in Cross' hand as he said he did at the trial then he would have also seen the person who took it and should have seen where they went and who it was.

The interesting error emerged at those times when these officers had to give their evidence verbally in a court. They only managed to consistently present one a piece of evidence correctly, 50% of the time at hearings. Both Cross (at Police Court hearing) and Worth (at trial) completely forgot to mention Cross pulling the curtains apart. Worth only corrected himself when Loseby pointed it out to him that Cross had pulled the curtains apart. Other witnesses saw Cross open the curtains so this may suggest that it was not part of the account that they wished to emphasise.

Cross's Sequence of Events

Third white form in front of curtains
Cross leaps forward and pushes Mr. Homer's chair and him over
Worth puts torch on
Cross makes a grab for figure standing between the curtains
Mrs. Duncan pushing white material to floor
(Worth shines light)
Cross holds Mrs. Duncan's arm with right hand
Material falls to floor
Worth's torch gets knocked away
Cross bends down to grab white material with left hand
Worth's torch lit scene again
Material pulled away (it doesn't stretch out) into audience in front row/window seat direction
Cross stands up and pulls curtains apart to reveal an empty cabinet
Main white light put on
Mrs. Duncan bending to put shoes on
Cross identifies himself & arrests Mrs. Duncan
Mrs. Duncan either stands for 60 seconds or immediately sits down and appears very ill
Mrs. Duncan complains that she feels ill and asks for a doctor

Mrs. Bessie Lock was an important witness for the prosecution because she was the only other witness apart from Cross and Worth who said that she saw him actually touch the white material. It is interesting to observe how her statements changed. In her witness statement she stated Cross leapt forward and said 'I've got her'. When the torch flashed she saw the cloth go towards the bay window, where Miss Homer was sitting. She heard Cross say 'Who pulled the cloth away from my fingers?' Then she saw Mrs. Duncan in front of the curtains. Mrs. Homer said it is a wonder something dreadful did not happen to Cross through touching the spirits. She said she heard Mrs. Duncan say 'Oh my God what's happened' and ask that a doctor by fetched.

At the police court hearing Mrs. Lock introduces different sightings. She now states she saw Cross leap forward, seize somebody and that she saw something white passed through his fingers that looked like a thin piece of material as it disappeared towards the bay window. After Cross had leapt forward and seized somebody, Mrs. Lock stated that she saw Mrs. Duncan on a chair and a gentleman on the floor, who she believed, was Cross. This statement may be very important in the light of the evidence given by the other people present.

By the time of the trial her description was more elaborate. She stated she saw that a torch was shone at the curtains and she saw someone grab a dark figure. She now saw something white leap down from this figure. 'I saw Cross who had hold of the dark figure and was trying to hold the white material in his left hand and I saw it go through his left hand towards the bay window'. Next she saw Mrs. Duncan sitting in a chair. I heard her say 'Oh my God'. The defence did not cross-examine Mrs. Lock about her account and Dodson only referred to her seeing a white substance come down and her seeing Cross holding it.

It is interesting that in the witness statement Mrs. Lock does not say she saw Cross grab a figure in front of the curtains or that she saw white material in Cross's fingers. She states she only heard Cross say he'd got someone, later asking who pulled the material from his fingers? She did see it go away towards the bay window. Other witnesses agree that Cross called out that he had believed he had grabbed something. She also saw Mrs. Duncan in front of the curtains, but all the witnesses agree that this is where Mrs. Duncan ended up. Mrs. Lock's statement seems consistent with someone seated in such a bad position as she was placed, towards the end of the second row by the door.

By the magistrates hearing Mrs. Lock now claims she saw Cross seize someone and she saw white material pulled through his fingers. As Cross was facing the cabinet and he grasped the cloth in his left hand it is difficult to see how Mrs. Lock could have seen this action, as his body blocked her line of sight. By the time of the trial she supported Cross's account more completely although again she is careful not to directly identify Mrs. Duncan as the person, now it is only a dark figure she presumes is Mrs. Duncan. This is interesting because during the preliminaries of her seances Mrs. Lock had stated that she recognised Mrs. Duncan when she appeared at the curtains but now she sees only a dark figure. No reason is given why she is unable to positively identify Mrs. Duncan when she had recognised her a few minutes earlier, when Cross and Worth state they saw her standing here after being seized or why she saw a dark figure when all the other witnesses saw something white in front of the curtains, prior to Cross leaping forward. In two of her statements Mrs. Lock also states she saw Mrs. Duncan on a chair after Cross made a grab for a figure. This is consistent with the accounts of other witnesses and it also contradicts Cross who claimed

Mrs. Duncan stood in front of the curtains for 60 seconds after he grabbed her, although eventually she did sit down, but by then the lights had been on some good time, according to Cross.

The other witnesses

The descriptions of the other witnesses will be given fully so it is clear what was seen.

Mr. Homer could not see because he was knocked over. The witnesses who made statements about this incident are Miss Homer, Mrs. Alabaster, Mr. Coulcher, Mr. Gill, Mrs. Gill, Walter Williams and Nurse Rust all seated in the front row in a perfect position to see what occurred. There were also Mr. White and Mr. Bush who was seated next to Lt. Worth, Ena Harris a prosecution witness who was in the third row and Mrs. Taylor who was standing at the back.

Mrs. Gill testified that the boy who had materialised and came out of curtains had disappeared. It went towards the floor and she saw a small piece of ectoplasm on floor, the size of a man's handkerchief. Then Cross leapt forward. She thought he was ill and she grabbed his waist with both hands and trying to reassure him said 'it's all right, it's all right. She was pushed forward to the right but she did not come off her chair. She saw that Cross was clawing downwards at the curtains and that his finger was extended. She said 'I jumped up and as I did so he was inside the cabinet. I could see that both his legs were stretched either side of Mrs. Duncan who was in a chair. I put my hands around Cross's waist and said 'oh don't do it', 'don't do it please' and I felt we had all taken a turn as if we were all standing up'.

Mrs. Gill followed Cross into the cabinet. She stepped back holding Cross and described them all seeming to fall. Mrs. Duncan was never standing up. 'Next thing I know I was supporting Mrs. Duncan by my arm'. The light was put on after Mrs. Duncan had fallen on chair. Mrs. Duncan was on an upturned chair and Cross was in front of Mr. Coulcher. Cross was blowing his whistle and had a torch switched on. Cross made a grab for Mr. Coulcher's hands. Cross accused someone of having the sheet. The lights were switched on and Det. Inspector Ford came in the room. Det. Inspector Ford accused Miss Homer.

Mr. Williams sat in the front row next to Mrs. Gill and Nurse Rust. He testified that Cross rushed forward and a torch was switched on. He made a grab for the figure. The sheet sort of melted and disappeared right through the floor very quickly and Cross fell forward into cabinet through the curtains. When the main light went on he saw Mrs. Duncan on an upturned chair. Whistles were blown.

Mr. Gill testified that Cross rushed forward and Mr. Homer was pushed to the floor. A man made a dive towards curtains. He was clawing at the curtains and as he was doing this his wife jumped forward to pull him back. He appeared like a maniac. As he dived the spirit form vanished, seeming to go and vanish through the floor in front of the cabinet. The man fell through the curtains and as he fell a torch was switched on and then I saw Mrs. Duncan in chair with a man staggering across her. He pulled the chair slightly to the right and then he appeared to pull Mrs. Duncan out of chair into the room. At that moment a whistle blew. Mrs. Duncan was on an upturned chair and supported by Mrs. Gill. Mrs. Duncan was very distressed.

Mrs. Alabaster testified that when the third spirit form appeared suddenly there was a shuffle. A figure leapt from his seat and she heard a chair overturn. Mr. Homer was on the floor. A torch went on when Cross was jumping forward and he grabbed the spirit form and called out 'I have got it', 'Have you got it'. Mrs. Alabaster saw the form slowly receding. She heard the curtains being pulled and then saw Mrs. Duncan lounging and immediately after she saw Cross a pace away in front of her. Mrs. Duncan's chair was grabbed and he pulled it away so it was at a slant, which resulted in Mrs. Duncan being on an upturned chair. She was pulled from the armchair and sitting on an upturned chair. Mrs. Alabaster noticed her right shoe had came off in scuffle and she had her left shoe on. She saw her sitting on an upturned armchair and she was calling for a doctor. She saw no sheet pass her. She stated that she was so near that she would have seen it and touched it if it had done so.

Mr. Coulcher testified that a form milky white in colour was in front of the curtains just before the scuffle. It disappeared downwards and there was a large amount of it on the floor. It collapsed as it stood. It is just 'gone' and it vanished in a flash. The form was in the process of moving when Cross went forward. 'I saw a man clawing at the curtains and he pulled them to one side and someone flashed a torch and at same time the lights went out. I turned and saw Mrs. Duncan sprawled on an upturned chair'. Cross then stood in front of him and he said to Det. Inspector Ford that the cloth had been passed around the corner. Ford declared that everyone was under arrest, and asked for everyone to keep quiet.

Miss. Homer testified that when the third spirit materialised a light was shone on the cabinet. Cross made his way to cabinet and pushed over her father. Mrs. Gill grabbed him saying 'Don't do it'. Worth blew a whistle. Cross dived into cabinet and there was a terrific commotion, as if someone had fallen. She heard Mrs. Duncan give a cry of shock. The white figure which was in front of the curtains had disappeared. Cross asked Worth 'Did you see it'. 'No' was the reply. Cross said 'It came round here, somebody has got it' and he immediately pointed his finger at Miss Homer's face. 'It is you'. Miss Homer replied 'Remember that statement friends'. 'He accused me'. She demanded to be searched. She was told 'If you are not careful you will go down'. The room was thoroughly searched. Det. Insp. Ford remarked that he had got what he wanted.

Nurse Rust referred to the third spirit in front of curtains. Mr. Homer was violently thrown aside and Cross jumped over and made grab for at séance curtains and fell forward because he had nothing to hold onto. The white robed figure of a man had disappeared through the floor directly Cross went over. When Nurse Rust first saw Mrs. Duncan she was away from corner. Her chair had been dragged from corner to more in the middle of cabinet facing the audience. She could not see much before that moment because Cross was obstructing her view. Nurse Rust put on Mrs. Duncan's missing shoe for her. Mrs. Duncan was sitting just inside cabinet.

Irene Taylor was standing at the back behind the third row to left of the rostrum. She saw a figure dash forward and she also saw someone standing to the right. She saw the curtains flying around and she could see through to the back wall, but she could not see a definite form. She did not see a white form in front of the curtains when Cross leapt forward. When the lights went on she eventually saw what had happened to Mrs. Duncan, who was sitting on a chair. Cross said he had seen something thrown from the cabinet to a young lady. The young lady responded 'Are you accusing me? You search me' and Mrs. Homer asked for everyone to be searched. Det. Insp. Ford said 'give it up'. Mrs. Taylor didn't see anyone searching the room. She didn't see a spirit form in front of curtains when Cross approached. It was dark. Worth said 'It had disappeared'. She didn't see Cross stooping down. Cross mentioned that the white had gone. Mrs. Duncan said it had to go somewhere it is ectoplasm.

After analysing the different accounts it is interesting that eleven of the twelve witnesses present did not report seeing Mrs. Duncan standing between or in front of the curtains. Even Percival White and Ena Harris did not say they saw Mrs. Duncan standing there. It may be inferred from Mrs. Lock's account because she presumed that the dark figure she saw was Mrs. Duncan, but this statement is not supported by earlier ones and it does not account for the fact that she saw and could positively identify Mrs. Duncan at the curtains a few minutes earlier when the séance started but not when Cross had purportedly grabbed her. Let us consider a sequential breakdown of the sightings.

A Sequential Breakdown

What was seen   **Witnesses**

White form/spirit in front of curtains
        Mr. Gill, Mrs. Alabaster, Mr. Coulcher, Miss Homer, Nurse Rust,
        Mr. Williams, Mrs Harris, Cross, Worth
Cross leapt forward
        Mr. Gill, Mrs. Alabaster, Mr. Coulcher, Miss Homer, Nurse Rust,
        Mr. Williams, Mrs Harris, Mrs. Taylor, Worth, Mrs. Lock,
Mrs. Gill grabbed at Cross
        Mrs. Gill, Mr. Gill, Miss Homer
Cross grabbed at form
        Mr. Williams, Mrs. Alabaster, Worth, Mrs. Lock
Form disappeared downwards quickly as Cross approached or dived at it
        Mr. Gill, Miss. Homer, Nurse Rust, Mr. Williams, Mr. Coulcher
Ectoplasm seen on floor in front of cabinet
        Mrs. Gill, Mr. Coulcher, Mr. Gill
Cross clawed at curtains or opened them before seen with Mrs.Duncan
        Mr. Gill, Mr. Coulcher, Mr. Williams, Mrs. Gill, Mrs. Alabaster,
        Nurse Rust.
Cross dived/fell through the curtains
        Mr. Gill, Mrs. Gill, Miss. Homer, Nurse Rust, Mr. Williams,
Cross seen staggering over Mrs. Duncan
        Mr. Gill, Mrs. Gill
Cross grabbed Mrs. Duncan's chair and pulled it out and round away
        from the wall to the middle of the cabinet
        Mr. Gill, Mrs. Alabaster (Nurse Rust saw chair that had been
        dragged to middle of cabinet)
Main white light on
Mrs. Duncan found sitting on floor/on upturned chair
        Mr. Gill, Mrs Alabaster, Mr. Coulcher, Mr. Williams, Mr. White,
        Mr. Bush, Mrs. Gill
Witnesses who didn't see the ectoplasm come to or pass them
        Mr. Coulcher, Miss Homer, Mrs. Alabaster, Mr. Gill.

There is certainly a marked difference between Worth's and Cross's
testimony and that of many other witnesses. Before we look at this in detail let
us look at the statements of some other prosecution witnesses.

At the police court hearing Mrs. Lock stated that after Cross had leapt
forward and made his grab, she stated that she saw Mrs. Duncan on a chair and
a gentleman on the floor who she believed was Cross. This statement may be

important in the light of the evidence given by the other witnesses because this is what they say they saw Mrs. Duncan on her chair and Cross had fallen on top of her.

Ena Harris, Mrs. Lock's daughter, was another prosecution witness who gives support to the other witnesses. In her witness statement she stated that Worth who was in front of her had jumped up, switched on his torch and at the same time she heard someone say 'I've got her'. After the torch was switched and Cross had said he had grabbed the figure she heard a skirmish on floor. Although the actual moment during which the skirmish took place is unclear from her statement, she, like her mother gave a statement agreeing that a commotion or such like occurred on the floor after Cross believed he had grabbed the figure. Other witnesses testified that as Cross made a grab for the figure he fell or dived forward and there was a skirmish on the floor as he staggered across Mrs. Duncan and pulled her chair out. Miss Homer, Mrs. Gill and Mrs. Alabaster saw and heard the same commotion on the floor in the cabinet.

It is interesting that Mrs. Harris did not see Mrs. Duncan being held by Cross standing in front of the curtains even though she said that she saw the cloth after Cross had declared that he had grabbed a figure. Surely if it had been Mrs. Duncan then she would have seen her standing there, caught red handed by Cross. Her account matches the other witnesses in that she saw the cloth that Cross made a grab for but it disappeared or went away quickly. Cross declared that he had grabbed Mrs. Duncan but like the other witnesses at that precise moment Mrs. Harris did not see her, only that the cloth had gone and that she did not see where, as would be expected from someone standing in the third row.

There is a strange quality to the testimonies and statements of the witnesses about this incident. Their accounts describe the sequence of events consistently until Cross enters the cabinet but then many continue their accounts from the moment the white light went on and they saw Mrs. Duncan on an upturned chair in front of the cabinet. This suggests that there was an interruption or break in the lighting.

Interestingly Mr. Coulcher asserts that as Cross got to the curtains and had opened them while in red light, then someone flashed torch and someone then turned off the red light. Worth also stated in his testimony that his torch was the only light on at the time. This suggests that the plan may have been for Worth to flash his torch and for that to be a signal for the red light to go off, so he is solely in charge of the lighting. Having waited to see whether Cross caught Mrs. Duncan in front of the curtains in the eventuality that Cross hadn't, Worth would flash his torch to signal the lights go out. Worth could say that at this moment someone knocked his torch away. When the main light came on and illuminated the scene Mrs. Duncan had been pulled out of the cabinet. The lights going out and Worth saying his torch had been knocked away allowed

Cross time to try and drag Mrs. Duncan out of the curtains in the darkness, to make it appear Mrs. Duncan had been caught in front of the curtains. If there was a conspiracy Worth and Cross would have needed a plan in case Mrs. Duncan was not standing in front of the curtains and the fact that Cross went straight into the cabinet and dragged her chair round strongly suggests this is what he was instructed to do. Irene Taylor, who was standing at the back, recalls seeing someone standing to her right when Cross leaped forward but that it was dark. This figure might have been Worth or it may have been a person who was to turn the red light off. Until we discover where the red light switch was situated in the room there is no way of knowing who may have had access to it during the séance that evening.

It is interesting that two witnesses stated that there was no red light, although it must be said a number of witnesses do say they saw Cross pull Mrs. Duncan's chair, but they aren't as many as one would expect. This theory requires another accomplice by the red light switch in order to operate the plan. Maybe Loseby thought the red light had gone out but he did not wish to raise it because as it stood he could claim all his witnesses could see perfectly well in the red light. Eventually the main white light came on. Mrs. Brown had taken the bulb out at the start of the séance according to Mrs. Harris, so presumably she put it back during the commotion.

It is also interesting that the person Mrs. Homer immediately thought was responsible for the police raid was Mrs. Harris. Mr. Homer asked Ena Harris if she had anything to do with this. Is it your doing? Do you know anything about it? She said she did not. It must be noted that Mrs. Harris claimed to be a very regular visitor and participant at the church and Worth had also been a very active member since October, yet Worth claimed he did not even know Mrs. Harris when he was asked at the trial. Mrs. Homer obviously suspected something. It is a reasonable assumption given Worth and Mrs. Harris were active participants in the church during this period. Mrs. Homer may have seen them together and given Worth's involvement in the raid she had immediately presumed Mrs. Harris also had something to do with it.

It is interesting to note what witnesses claim they saw when different lights went on. Worth and Cross claim that Mrs. Duncan was bending down trying to put on her shoe when the main light when on. Several defence witnesses say she was seen seated on an upturned chair at that moment. Even witnesses that the prosecution had given notice to give evidence at the police court agreed. Mr. White said he could not see Mrs. Duncan when Worth switched on his torch and at the moment the lights went on Mrs. Duncan was on the floor near the curtains. Mr. Bush who sat next to Worth said after the torch was switched on the first glimpse of Mrs. Duncan he had was when she was half-sitting and half lying between the curtain and the chair immediately behind the curtain. He presumed that she was in this position because of her contact with Cross. Bush's account supports the view that Worth switched his torch back on once Cross had pulled Mrs. Duncan out of the cabinet. Mrs. Lock also supports this version of events. At the trial she stated that after she saw the material pulled away the next thing she saw was a figure presumably Mrs. Duncan sitting outside the cabinet. She made the same observation that she saw Mrs. Duncan on a chair after Cross had leapt forward in her Magistrates Court statement, while in her witness statement she doesn't specify if Mrs. Duncan was sitting or standing in front of the curtains after the material had been pulled away.

Worth and Cross also claim Mrs. Duncan bent down to put on her shoe while Nurse Rust states she was the person who actually put in on her.

There are two completely different sets of accounts here. Two witnesses give the same account against seven who were in the front row and perfectly placed give another account. Even Mrs. Lock and Mrs. Harris's other statements offer support for the defence case along with witnesses who were not called to appear at the pre-trial hearing. The evidence is overwhelming.

Dodson in his summing up went into some detail about this incident. He describes Worth's evidence that Cross dived at the white figure. Worth said Cross grabbed the figure, he flashed a torch and then he saw Mrs. Duncan trying to get rid of a piece of white material which she was trying to get down to the floor. The material was two or three yards long. Dodson announced that this is the crux of the case. He told the jury that if they believe this happened whatever else was genuine about the demonstration, in this respect it is a fraud. Worth said someone knocked his torch, the cloth fell to floor, and someone pulled the cloth into audience to left. Cross said 'Did you get hold of the cloth'.

He summed up Cross's evidence pointing out the matter did not rest with Worth's account alone. Cross seized Mrs. Duncan when the torch was shone and she was trying to work the cloth down from her chest. For a moment or two Cross held it in his left hand. He was handicapped because he was trying to hold onto Mrs. Duncan who is not a small woman. He grasped the sheet and it began to be pulled away. He arrested her and Cross told the jury what it felt like. Mrs. Duncan said 'of course it has gone it had to go somewhere'.

Dodson also quoted Mrs. Lock's vital evidence on this incident, that she saw Cross holding the white substance which went away towards the left.

Dodson clearly directs the jury. The case for the prosecution focuses to this pinpoint in time and place. If the jury is satisfied that Worth and Cross saw and got hold of the material, muslin or whatever kind of material it is then it is quite clear what your decision would have to be with regard to this allegation.

Strictly it is difficult to see why this is the critical evidence, as the material may have been ectoplasm. The critical test surely is whether Cross first grabbed Mrs. Duncan in front of the cabinet or not, not whether Cross managed to touch some disappearing material.

How did Dodson sum up the other evidence on this matter?

Mr. Gill:

Dodson asserts: He does not think Mr. Gill adds anything to this matter except that he did not see any sheet being pulled or passed.

Dodson omits Mr. Gill's testimony which describes the entire incident that completely contradicted Worth's and Cross's testimony. Mr. Gill saw the form disappear to the floor as Cross rushed forward. He saw Cross claw at the curtains when Mrs. Gill grabbed him and then he fell through the curtains. Then he saw Cross staggering across Mrs. Duncan who was seated in her chair. Cross proceeded to pull Mrs. Duncan's chair to the right and then he pulled Mrs. Duncan out of chair into the room.

Mrs. Gill:

Dodson asserts: She saw some ectoplasm on the floor and then Cross broke through she grabbed him and said 'It's all right'. She thought that the séance had upset him.

Dodson omits the evidence that Mrs. Gill saw Cross claw at the curtains and when she grabbed him they fell together through the curtains into the cabinet. She saw Cross with his legs stretched either side of Mrs. Duncan who was still seated in her chair. She stated Mrs. Duncan never stood up. When the light went on she saw Mrs. Duncan on an upturned chair.

Mrs. Alabaster:

Dodson asserts: She saw a flash of the torch when the policeman grabbed the ectoplasm and she said she did not see anything white pass in front of her.

Dodson omits her evidence that she saw the form gradually receding and after she described seeing Cross grabbing the ectoplasm, then she saw Mrs. Duncan lounging on her chair inside the cabinet with Cross in front of her, who then grabbed her chair and swung it round resulting in Mrs. Duncan being on an upturned chair.

Mr. Coulcher:

Dodson asserts: He said he had heard Cross say that the white cloth had passed round his corner. Mr. Coulcher said it never passed him but he heard Cross claim he had seen it and wanted it.

Dodson omits that Mr. Coulcher saw the white form in front of the curtains disappear downwards and vanish very quickly as it lay in a pool on the floor. He saw Cross make a dive for the curtains, claw at them, pull them to one side and Mrs. Duncan was not in front of them. After Cross had clawed at the curtains and the lights went out Mrs. Duncan was seen sprawled on an upturned chair outside the curtains.

Miss Homer:

Dodson asserted: that he did not think we have to deal in detail with her evidence.

Dodson omits that Miss Homer saw Mrs. Gill grab Cross, the spirit form quickly disappear downwards as Cross approached, that she did not see Mrs. Duncan standing in front of the curtains when she saw Cross dive into the cabinet.

Nurse Rust:

Dodson completely ignores her evidence for the 19th.

Dodson omits that Nurse Rust saw the spirit form quickly disappear downwards directly as Cross approached so there was nothing in front of the curtains. She saw Cross make a grab for the séance curtains and dive through them. She saw that Mrs. Duncan's chair had been dragged from the corner to the middle of the cabinet facing the audience. She put Mrs. Duncan's shoe on her foot, which contradicts Worth's evidence that Mrs. Duncan was standing trying to put her own shoe on. Omitting Nurse Rust's evidence in his summing up matches her omission from the police plan and also avoids him having to contrast it with Mrs. Lock's who it was falsely stated was sitting next to her.

Mrs. Taylor:

Dodson asserts: She was present when the disturbance occurred. She said she saw Cross rush forward and the curtains flying about. She remembered Mrs. Duncan saying 'Of course it has gone it had to go somewhere it is ectoplasm'.

Dodson omits that she stated she did not see Cross stoop down, she did not see a white spirit form in front of the curtains when Cross advanced.

Mr. Williams:

Dodson asserts: He said the lights came on and he saw Mrs. Duncan on a chair in a very distressed state. He saw the white substance disappear through the floor.

Dodson omits that Mr. Williams said he saw Cross made a grab for the figure but it melted away and he fell forward into the cabinet and that he saw Mrs. Duncan on an upturned chair.

So in Dodson's summing up he completely and most blatantly misrepresents all these defence witness's accounts. He only selects those parts of their evidence that supports the prosecution case and presents them to the jury in his summing up. He also omits all the most crucial sightings that contradict it. It must represent one of the most biased summing ups in English legal history. He makes no reference at all to the fact that seven witnesses saw something completely different take place when Cross leapt forward. He makes no reference to these witnesses seeing Cross claw at the curtains; dive into the cabinet; fall on top of Mrs. Duncan who was seen still seated in her chair; or that Cross pulled her chair round so that everyone saw Mrs. Duncan on an upturned chair when the house lights were put on. He makes no reference to the fact that none of these witnesses saw Mrs. Duncan standing in front of the cabinet at the time the torch was shone or when Cross made a grab for the figure in front of the curtains or afterwards for a minute as Cross claimed. He makes no reference to the fact that none of these eyewitnesses saw Cross bending down to grab the material.

How can we understand Dodson's conduct? His obituary published in the Times in November 1966[13] characterised his summing ups as clear, even handed and easily understood so that a prisoner could depend on him having concern to carefully put every point that supported him/her to the jury.

The extent and number of times he misrepresents the nature of the evidence in his summing up to the jury and makes false statements himself at this trial contradicts this excellent testimonial. Such conduct by a distinguished and experienced judge can only point to the conclusion that he did so with the deliberate intention to get Mrs. Duncan and the other defendants convicted. Why else did he not did put every point in Mrs. Duncan's favour to the jury as it is stated that he usually did? He must have known the consequences of his actions for the defendants. Some may say that whether Dodson was part of a conspiracy to imprison Mrs. Duncan or not, he did everything a judge could have done to successfully complete the task. This leaves no other option but to conclude that he was central to it.

What was interesting about the press coverage of this crucial aspect of the trial was that not one newspaper presented any evidence from the defence witnesses that contradicted Worth's and Cross's version of what occurred after he rushed to the platform. The Daily Mail and Daily Express make one brief reference when they reported that Maude asked whether Cross practised as a weightlifter. In answering the suggestion that he had swung Mrs. Duncan out of her chair, Cross said he hadn't and as she weighed 20 stone it was quite impossible.

Ian Fleming's expertise with controlling the press for the NID seems to have worked. When seven eyewitnesses' later entered the witness box and gave evidence that contradicted Worth and Cross it was ignored in the same way that the Recorder ignored it. The public was virtually given no information whatsoever to counter the story that the prosecution presented that Mrs. Duncan was grabbed standing in front of the curtains with a sheet over her. It is no wonder that this story has been passed down through the generations and that many people believe that it has been demonstrated that mediums are frauds.

Later when Bechhofer Roberts published a book about the trial titled 'The Trial of Mrs. Duncan' he eulogised the summing up by the Recorder. He regarded it as a 'brilliantly concise epitome of the matters to be tried' and the evidence that both sides called over many days. Loseby considered it to be a scandal and said so in no uncertain terms privately, in the press and this represented an important aspect of his appeal.

Many Spiritualists saw the trial and the appeal as reflecting an attack upon their religion by members of the established church. They pointed out that like Recorder Dodson who was an ardent Christian, the three Judges who heard the appeal also held a strong Christian faith. The Lord Chief Justice (Viscount Caldecote) was a committed Churchman with very strong views and a member of the Ecclesiastical Committee nominated by the Lord Chancellor. Justice Birkett had been a local preacher in his youth and Justice Oliver had represented the Bishop of Norwich.

Loseby was directly asked by the Lord Chief Justice whether he thought Dodson had a crooked motive and that he was improperly biased. Loseby answered 'No', saying instead that he was biased because he had preconceived ideas on the subject of Spiritualism. Knowing now what we do about the security aspects to the case and the attempt by the prosecution to deceive the court, it would most interesting to know what Loseby's answer would be today to this question. Formally in Loseby's view the Recorder's conduct in the case displayed bias but not 'improper bias'.

The conspiratorial aspects of the case also apply to the appeal itself. Spiritualists immediately noted the religious make up of the Appeal Judges and the delay it took for it to be heard. What went unnoticed were the connections between the Appeal Judges and features of the security aspects related to the trial.

Mr. Justice Oliver had carried out an enquiry for the War Cabinet into the security of convoys in May 1941. His report focused exclusively on the problems of leakages of information and the risks they posed to allied trade and war convoys. He made recommendations with the objective of preventing leakages of information about allied convoys and his report identified that steps were needed to counter leakage of information at ports through persons not in government service. During his investigation into the problems of leaks to allied shipping, he worked closely with the Admiralty. He had developed some earlier expertise on this subject because he had been appointed to a high level committee investigating the leak of budget secrets in 1936.

Mr. Justice Birkett had a similar connection to related security issues. When the government brought in Defence Regulation 18B in May 1940 it gave the government the right to imprison people without trial. Birkett was appointed chairman of the Advisory Committee that heard the appeals of detainees, although the Home Secretary made the final decision. Birkett heard case after case where persons were accused of acts prejudicial to the public safety, the defence of the realm or acts where there was reason to exercise control over individuals. He had also heard the case under section 1 of the Treachery Act

1940 of Duncan Scott-Ford a young merchant seaman who had leaked details of allied convoys to German agents in Lisbon. The trial was held in camera and Birkett sentenced Scott-Ford to death. If Birkett regarded Mrs. Duncan as someone leaking information then she was the type of person he could well have recommended continued detention if she had appeared before him under different circumstances.

The final Appeal Judge, Lord High Chancellor Viscount Caldecote had worked for Naval intelligence at the Admiralty throughout World War I. As Thomas Inskip, he became head of the Naval Law Branch and represented the Admiralty on the War Crimes Committee. He had also been Solicitor General and Attorney General for two periods of office, Lord Chancellor from 1939-40 and Minister of Co-ordination of Defence in 1936.

So one of the Appeal Judges had senior links with the branch of the security service purportedly behind the conspiracy that led to the trial, the NID. Another was an experienced investigator on the issue of leakages of information that Chief Constable West declared was the reason for the trial being brought, while the final Judge had ruled on numerous cases raising similar security issues to those surrounding the Helen Duncan case, in recommending continued detention.

Having all three Appeal Judges experienced in aspects of the security situation surrounding the case seems too extraordinary to be a coincidence. Each one had particular reasons to look unfavourably upon someone who had leaked highly sensitive information that put at risk the lives of servicemen and women. These three men were apt to look most sympathetically upon any court that sought to protect the nation at a time of war if this was the only way it could be done.

The Appeal Court did not deal with the case until June 8th and a judgement was not given till June 19th. This delay meant that any purported conspiracy to eliminate the security risk posed by Mrs. Duncan in the run up to D Day had been successful.

With regards to Loseby's complaint that the Recorder did not adequately place the defence to the jury, was rejected by the Appeal Judges. They argued that the Recorder did review and remind the jury of the main points of evidence. They said that the Recorder could not be expected to comment on each piece of evidence and that this was unnecessary when the essential matter to which all the evidence was directed was plainly before the jury from the first moment. That being the case then it was either all a sham or as the defence asserted that everything was genuine.

They repeated Dodson's own argument that as the defence case had been laid out before the jury by the defence counsel it was not necessary for it to be rehearsed again by the Recorder. But had Loseby fully put the defence case to the jury? Loseby was criticised by a former judge in India (and defence witness)

Abdy Collins for not laying out to the jury what had occurred on the 19th when Cross rushed forward and the sheet disappeared. Collins stated that out of a speech covering sixteen pages only half a page was devoted to the events of the 19th as a whole. In fact Loseby mentioned not a word about the discrepancy in the evidence between the prosecution and defence witnesses as to what occurred when Mrs. Duncan was seized. Dodson in contrast either ignored this evidence or misrepresented it. He selected only that information from the defence witnesses that supported the prosecution case. The defendants in fact did not have the evidence relating to what occurred when Cross leapt forward to grab Mrs. Duncan, accurately summed up or addressed at all by Loseby or Dodson and it seems clear that the Appeal Judges overlooked this vital point.

The Appeal Judges judged that Loseby had failed to show the Dodson's misdirection was such that the jury would not have returned their verdict had there been no misdirection. It is a shame that Loseby did not specify the number of omissions and misrepresentations of the defence witnesses' evidence Dodson made in his summing up of the evidence of the 19th. He should also have pointed out that this crucial aspect of the case was not presented to the jury at all by the Recorder in his summing nor himself as defence counsel. No doubt this was an embarrassing admission for him to make.

The Appeal Judges acknowledged that the Recorder had acted appropriately in comprehensively summing up the prosecution witnesses evidence because Maude had not done so. In fairness Dodson's failure to do likewise to Loseby's who had also failed to cover the events that led to the arrest and police raid, then it raises questions as to the reason for this discrepancy and should be weighed in the defendants favour. Certainly the failure by both the defence and the Recorder to present the defence's evidence about what the Recorder regarded as the crux of the case, and his complete distortion of it represents a most serious matter that is completely contrary of most people's idea of justice and everyone's right to have a fair trial.

The issues that occupied the attention at the time focused on the case, the appropriateness of using the Witchcraft Act and whether the prosecution was an attack on Spiritualism. Loseby's conduct in the Appeal hearings was highly praised. He had shown remarkable tenacity and 'performed a difficult task with skill, patience and dexterity'. He needed all his strength because outside the Appeal Court some senior Spiritualists criticised the way he had gone about the prosecution.

Loseby was criticised for not calling Mrs. Duncan, Mrs. Brown and Mrs. Homer as witnesses. He was criticised for not going into more detail about the mechanism of materialisations and explaining the nature of ectoplasm. Critics said Loseby had the witnesses present during the dates specified in the indictment to demonstrate that Mrs. Duncan was a genuine medium, yet he failed to use their evidence effectively. He was also accused of not highlighting the admissions of the prosecution witnesses themselves, which supported the defence case, such as the means by which the forms disappeared.   He was also criticised for not making more of the disappearance of the sheet given the police surrounded the house, a woman police officer was present, many women witnesses volunteered to be searched. The police explanation that a medical officer was required to search for two or three metres of cloth was regarded as ridiculous and it was felt these points were not put strongly forward strongly enough.   Guidelines existed within the police that allowed women police officers and police matrons to search women prisoners. Ford stated that a police matron accompanied him when he entered the séance room, so his excuse that he did not have a doctor present seems without foundation.

Spiritualists naturally examined the nature of the trial in great detail and many tended to focus their criticisms on the failings of one of their own, Mr. Loseby. Spiritualists naturally wanted an effective and vigorous defence and Loseby had failed to successfully defend his clients and had failed in his personal attempt to try and demonstrate the truth of Spiritualism through this court trial. Let us look in greater detail at the nature of the forces that were pitted against him and whether he deserved all the criticism he received given the strategy he adopted after the chapter has been summarised.

Summary

Examination of the prosecution evidence presented in this chapter point to a determined and sophisticated conspiracy to convict Mrs. Duncan.   The evidence presented shows the manner in which this conspiracy was carried out. Prosecution witnesses repeatedly changed their accounts in order to achieve their purpose to convict the defendants, but in doing so they frequently contradicted themselves and each other.

Two prosecution witness statements were shown to be fabricated as well as a police plan. The police plan showed false seating arrangements in order to move a prosecution witness into a position they never occupied and remove a good defence witness from their seating position and from the scene completely. Moving the prosecution witness allowed her to testify to seeing critical events that she could not have possibly seen from her true location. Worth and Cross also gave false statements in order carry out this deception. The prosecution also fabricated a story of Mrs. Duncan exploiting grieving families of servicemen saying that she had declared a serviceman was safe when they were in fact dead. Another fabricated witness statement was presented to the court in an attempt to achieve this deception.

The continuously changing nature of the prosecution witnesses' accounts also provides good evidence of a conspiracy. First Mr. Burrell said he clearly recognised Mrs. Duncan's voice when forms appeared but then he changed this story when Mrs. Jennings came forward to declare the same. Although he stated he could not see clearly from a distance of a foot and no form had features he then declared that he clearly recognised Mrs. Duncan's arm from 9'. Mrs. Lock declared that she recognised Mrs. Duncan's face but then she remained silent about this identification when it emerged that all prosecution witnesses were stating that features were not apparent on the forms.

Contradictions between prosecution witnesses occurred in terms of the evidence they gave relating to the amount of light available and what one could see; whether Mrs. Duncan was seen at the same time as the forms that were produced; whether sound was produced from a location separate from the forms or Mrs. Duncan; how forms disappeared; the events surrounding the missing serviceman; Mrs. Lock's mother touching her husband; whether Peggy was slim or bulky, heavy footed or jigging in a light way and a form appearing holding her baby in her arms.

In instances where strong evidence existed in support of Mrs. Duncan's mediumship, prosecution witnesses asserted contrary evidence, that it simply did not occur or they couldn't remember it occurring. Worth presented evidence that was contradicted by the vast majority of the other witnesses in terms of the forms that were witnessed and his accounts became more incriminating over time.

Contradictions also occurred within the statements made by prosecution witnesses. Repeated contradictory changes occurred in seeking to find a way to present a consistent account to purportedly show that Mrs. Duncan and the forms were never seen together. Burrell said that a form was holding a torch in one hand then it was two. He described how he saw a form appear and an arm poked through a curtain then he asserted only the latter occurred. Mrs. Lock said that she saw a form and Mrs. Duncan at the same time but later testified that she never saw such an event. Mrs. Lonsdale Brosman was removed from the party attending the seances over the statements submitted by Burrell and Mrs. Lock. Worth first stated that some forms disappeared under the curtain but in later statements he said they all walked back through the curtains. He also changed his account about what occurred at the Sunday Service so much so that the defence counsel ended up at the trial arguing the same position as the prosecution counsel had at the pre-trial hearing but contrary to Worth's latest account. Worth admitted that he lied about verifying evidence when he had not done so, while evidence was submitted that Burrell did likewise in terms of stating that he found the evidence convincing when he subsequently said that he had not. Both were presented as examples of the type of deception required in order to gain the trust necessary to achieve a successful conviction.

This evidence coupled with the evidence in Chapter Two, I believe strongly supports the view that the state conspired to imprison Mrs. Duncan and that there was a conspiracy involving the prosecution witnesses so that they gave false evidence in order for the conspiracy to succeed.

The Recorder in his summing up also repeatedly misrepresented the evidence of defence witnesses almost always in favour of the prosecution case. He minimised differences between Worth's testimony and the other witnesses with regards to the disappearance of forms and the purported appearance of a mother and baby. He asserted that witnesses were not present on occasions that they were, when they gave evidence that contradicted other prosecution witnesses or he ignored contradictory testimony. He made interruptions during examination, or requested that witnesses move to another part of the action in the séance when critical evidence was about to covered that might support the defendants. He also repeatedly misrepresented the evidence presented by defence witnesses when Cross attempted to catch Mrs. Duncan red-handed in front of the curtains in favour of the prosecution.

CHAPTER THREE

Impact And Reviews

Loseby's Failed Strategy

Loseby's approach to conducting the defence was criticised by many Spiritualists. It was viewed as a serious mistake not to focus upon the evidence that was presented during the seances covered in the period specified in the indictment, instead of which he called 20 or more further witnesses to speak about other occasions. Many people believed the Defence Counsel damaged his own case. Alternatively it is possible to view this situation as Loseby being allowed to ruin his own case. Loseby's strategy was to summon scores of defence witnesses who repeated the same type of evidence confirming their recognition of materialised forms at Helen Duncan seances and so vouching for the genuine nature of her mediumship. As Dodson pointed out, this became very wearisome and tiring to listen to for the jury and by its continued repetition it defeated itself. It also presented the jury and him with mass of evidence, which smothered everything and which presented a challenge to sort out the relevant detail.

Throughout the trial the Recorder raised the question about the relevance of the testimony that Loseby was calling, outside the dates set out in the indictment. It was acknowledged by the Recorder, in his summing up, that Loseby's strategy to fortify his own case by using numerous Spiritualists to testify that Mrs. Duncan's mediumship was genuine to as far back as 1931 and 1932, meant the rule applied that if one is going to review a person's character or professional character then they can be told the full story. Loseby had brought witnesses who testified to Mrs. Duncan's mediumship as far back as 1931 in order to demonstrate that she is a genuine physical medium. The prosecution argued that in this case the jury was entitled to know that as far back as 1933 a jury thought otherwise and she was convicted of fraud in Edinburgh in 1933. This was fatal to the defence's case. Dodson remarked that if Loseby had kept within the limits of the events set out in the indictment this would not have occurred.

Loseby argued that he had deliberately avoided asking specific questions of his witnesses which directly related to Mrs. Duncan's character or "Is Mrs. Duncan a genuine materialisation medium?" in order that this conviction not be admitted. He said if he had known that the matter would be raised he would have conducted his defence entirely differently. Loseby said he had discussed the matter of Mrs. Duncan's earlier conviction with Maude who had told him that he was not putting it in and this had led Loseby to conduct his case in the way he did. Maude was called to explain this understanding and while he said something of this nature may have passed between them as to the course of the prosecution case, in the light of the way the defence developed its case, no promise or indication was made.

The brief for the prosecution observes that Maude was aware Loseby intended to call in the region of 50 witnesses for the purpose of proving that Mrs. Duncan, on a number of occasions had produced genuine materialisations and that Loseby was hoping to prove there is life after death. Maude considered this was not relevant to the issue that Mrs. Duncan was resorting to trickery. He felt confident in establishing that she was not genuine on the dates cited in the indictment. Consequently they were happy to let Loseby call his witnesses. Loseby, for his part, took the view that the essence of the charge was that Mrs. Duncan was an impostor, so his efforts were aimed at showing she was not, but a materialisation medium. Otherwise, he argued he might as well acquiesce and allow his client to be convicted.

Certainly, it is unlikely Loseby would have undertaken the workload of calling so many witnesses unless he had been given some indication that it would be allowed. The prosecution brief shows that they were ready to raise the 1933 Edinburgh conviction if, Mrs. Duncan gave evidence and her character was put on issue, alleging that she is a genuine medium. This may have been one reason why Loseby declined to call Mrs. Duncan to give evidence. Loseby had discussed the matter of the earlier conviction with Maude, he stated that he had been given an assurance from Maude that he would not raise the earlier conviction and this had led him to present his case in a particular way. Then just as he was concluding it the rug was pulled away from him. One might say Maude the MI5 officer had done his job well. If a trap had been laid (possibly with the help of the Recorder) to disrupt the defence's case then it was sprung most effectively, and any blame was diverted to the victim, Loseby, for being so naïve and creating this problem for himself. While Dodson criticised Loseby's strategy of including testimony outside the limits of the case, it must be remembered that he was responsible for its inclusion. He could easily have restricted the testimony and in this way it would have aided the defendants and the court's search for justice. The Appeal Judges concurred with this view and said the trial was unsatisfactory in this respect. They noted the great latitude given to the defence in conducting the case and that they called evidence outside the period covered in the indictment, which should have been excluded.

Dodson's memoirs may give some insight on this matter. He said that the trial should have been concluded much sooner than it was, but because it was important that it not be perceived as a prosecution against Spiritualists, this had led him to indulge the defence. This is an unusual reason to give, because at the time he repeatedly made the point that the prosecution in no way attacks Spiritualism. At the trial he said 'By no possible exaggeration can this case be magnified into anything more than a commonplace prosecution against fraud, and there is no religious persecution even remotely connected to it'. If Dodson truly wanted to treat the case as commonplace fraud then concentrating on the events during the actual period it was alleged to have taken place would have been its most convincing demonstration. Furthermore, by allowing evidence to be presented beyond the scope of the indictment, by many witnesses who believed in Spiritualism, the prosecution case more directly attacked Spiritualism than if he had not. Dodson's memoirs also raise the intriguing question whether Loseby was informed of the reasons for the latitude he was being given, which he tried to exploit with all his might. As an experienced barrister, Loseby knew the risk he would normally run, many observers criticised him for making such an obvious mistake, but this suggests that he may have been given assurances that led him into making this error.

Whatever viewpoint one prefers to adopt, there is no doubt that the prosecution did do exactly that. It did attack Spiritualism. Spiritualism and physical mediums in particular have still not recovered from the effects of it. This was helped by Loseby's enthusiasm to call some of Spiritualism's most senior and respected advocates. They vouched for Spiritualism's leading medium 'over a long period of years, expressing their belief in her genuineness and informing the jury of the mysteries of the spirit world, the nature of ectoplasm and a variety of matters of that kind'. In his opening speech Loseby explained that each of his defendants were Spiritualists and he confirmed that Spiritualists, as a body welcomed the trial. He wrote later that the not guilty plea involved two propositions, firstly that Helen Duncan was not a fraud and secondly that 'she could demonstrate a spirit world'.

Loseby with the help of the Recorder and the prosecution had effectively put Spiritualism on trial and the verdict went against it. Several observers believed at the time that Loseby, with his strong personal convictions, tried to use the trial to prove life after death. Helen's family felt that the trial had little to do with her but it represented a battle between the State and Spiritualism, in terms of Spiritualist belief and practice. Family members felt very bitter about it. Certainly the way Maude, who represented the Crown went about the case gives support to this view.

Maude organised the prosecution with both the weaknesses of the defence in mind, fraud and the common prejudices against Spiritualism held by a large section of a sceptical public. While claiming the prosecution did not attack Spiritualism, that the prosecution was in no way aimed at the honest beliefs of any man or woman, he then went ahead and attacked it in no uncertain terms and Dodson followed suit. As a senior MI5 officer trying to prevent the spread of rumours during wartime via mediums and seances, no doubt Maude viewed attacking Spiritualism as well as Mrs. Duncan as an important part of his work. Discrediting the source of the rumours, would serve the security of the country. Consequently, it made sense as a Security Service officer to discredit it, as much as the particular medium on trial, so other information coming from mediums were not taken seriously.

He carried out his plan with an eye for the headline. The defence claimed that what took place was part and parcel of a genuine séance, so by implication the foundation of Spiritualist method, mediumship, spirit phenomena, how Spiritualists conducted seances and assess evidence was on trial. If, as the prosecution stated, the activities that were being examined were matters of fraud, undertaken by a calculating team of tricksters, then why should Maude pour scorn on the picture painted by the happenings and the honest belief's held by the sitters. If Mrs. Duncan was a fraud and he did not wish to attack the beliefs of Spiritualists, then surely he would have distanced Mrs. Duncan's fraudulent activities and impersonations from the religious views of Spiritualists. By saying Mrs. Duncan was fraudulent, that the Spiritualists who sat with her were most gullible, then at one stroke he was also claiming that the experiences upon which many Spiritualists base their views were groundless therefore was their religion.

Let us examine some of the ways this attack was mounted. The most obvious way was the evidence that Worth and Burrell gave. We have seen how each part of Worth's testimony has been constructed in a way to not only distort what actually took place but to introduce a quite fictitious scenario. The Navy had established a team of scriptwriters at Worth's Special Branch unit in Portsmouth. It is interesting that Loseby certainly believed, at the time, that the prosecution was involved in spinning a story for the press which was 'clear, simple, blatant and vulgar and lent itself to headlines which were freely given'.

Chief Constable West had said the government had not wanted a 'song and dance' made of the trial and the DPP files show many letters between the Portsmouth police, the DPP and other government departments referring to the press coverage. The press coverage was monitored closely and articles referred to. Loseby suspected someone was involved in manipulating the press. Given that we now know that Naval Intelligence and MI5 had close connections with the press of the day and the Navy had recruited its own team of script and scenario writers (one of whom was a journalist), we know now who they were likely to have been. We have noted how the press failed to present any evidence that countered the prosecutions description of what took place when Cross attempted to catch Mrs. Duncan red-handed. The press also chose not to publicise other strong evidence in favour of Mrs. Duncan's mediumship. For example when seven witnesses described a three year-old granddaughter of a sitter appearing, virtually no mention was made of it in the press.

The New Statesman neatly summarised the destructive nature of the prosecution's case to Spiritualism. 'The evidence for the prosecution was brutal and to the point, 3 at least of the supposed spirits represented non-existent uncles, aunts and sisters; in the light of a 4 watt red lamp at the other end of the room almost anything could and did happen; not only loving relatives but a bearded compere named Albert and a parrot made their appearance; a materialised sailor observed tartly to a Lieutenant in an audience that there were no ranks in the other world; a lady afflicted with bowel trouble when she was deceased 20 years ago earlier was introduced as still suffering from the same complaint; the most embarrassing visitant, perhaps was the 20 year old youth without a face – survival it seemed of a miscarriage; there were bits of nursery rhyme and some Welsh singing, a Chinese "guide" with a pigtail and a moustache eighteen inches long, reassurances about "passing over", voices that said the expected remote thing (though one of them came out with a surprising aside about "bloody twisters") and the curtains of Mrs. Duncan's cabinet kept opening and shutting, animated by one knows not what tireless legerdemain…'

Added to this list were headlines

AMAZING REVELATIONS IN SPIRITUALIST MEDIUM CASE
The Evening News 29.2.44

SPIRIT STORIES AT THE OLD BAILEY
The Star 28.3.44

Dead policeman, cat and parrot were "brought back" in store
temple
Ghost sang 'South of the Border'
Daily Herald 24.3.44

GHOST WANTED TO GIVE EVIDENCE AT WITCHCRAFT TRIAL
MEDIUM WILL PRODUCE HIM
'GREAT OPPORTUNITY FOR SPIRITUALISTS'
Evening News 27.3.44

'WITNESS IS IN A TRANCE
May Call Ghost into Court
Evening News 27.3.44

"MY GRANDPA'S GHOST WAS TALL AND VERY FAT"
WITNESS AT WITCH TRIAL
Evening News 30.3.44

'RED INDIAN' – HER GUIDE
'I Hear Mother Talking Now' – Woman At Trial
Daily Sketch 29.3.44

WOMAN SAYS SHE HEARS SPIRIT OF OLD BAILEY
COURT her Indian Guide.
News Chronicle 29.3.44

'RED INDIAN'-HER GUIDE
'I Hear Mother Talking Now'-Woman At Trial
Daily Sketch 29.3.44

"THE WITCHCRAFT CASE"
A PARALYSED GHOST APPEARS
JUDGE WISHES HE HAD SPIRIT GUIDE
Portsmouth Evening News 31.3.44

MARY, THE HEADLESS SPIRIT Did not get through at   séance
'SHE FADED'
Daily Express 31.3.44

Mary Queen of Scots 'Came to Séance'
Daily Mail 31.3.44

JURY DON'T WANT GHOSTS
Evening News 31.3.44

SPIRITS CAN JOKE, SAYS MRS. DUNCAN'S COUNSEL
Evening Standard 31.3.44

Sweetheart Knew Who She was 300 Years Ago
"SPIRIT WAS LIVE PALPITATING GIRL"
Evening Standard 30.3.44

Women Tell Of Spirit Kisses
Daily Mail 29.3.44

Story of Ghost that did not like lipstick
Daily Express 25.3.44

'FAIRY' FORM AT SÉANCE'   Jigged before Curtain
'Dead-Alive-Dead
Daily Sketch 25.3.44

JURY MAY HEAR VOICE OF SPIRIT
Evening Standard 27.3.44

Albert's Ghost As 'Witness'
No Bogy-bogy
Daily Mail 28.3.44

says dead husband kissed her at séance 'I RECOGNISED HIM BY
KNOBBLY KNUCKLES, WIDOW TELLS COURT'
Felt knobbly Knuckles
Daily Mirror 29.3.44

"MY GRANDPA'S GHOST WAS TALL AND VERY FAT" WITNESS
AT "WITCH" TRIAL
HE MET HIS OLD SWEETHEART, TOO
Evening News 30.3.44

WITCHCRAFT – ALL FOUND GUILTY
SENTENCED MEDIUM CRIES "IT'S ALL LIES"
OH I HAVEN'T DONE IT – SHE MOANED
OH GOD, IS THERE A GOD'? I NEVER DONE IT
Daily Sketch 1.4.33

Mrs. DUNCAN, 'A Humbug' Is Guilty
Disciples in Court Wave Their Farewell to Medium
FORETOLD SINKING
'NO PERSECUTION"
Daily Mail 1.4.44

MRS. DUNCAN SENT TO GAOL
Medium Collapses At Old Bailey
The Star 3.4.44

What is apparent from these headlines is they mostly refer to the claims of
genuine Spiritualists, not the antics of a trickster. This occurred because the
defence counsel asserted that what the sitters experienced was genuine and that
the prosecution counsel was happy to use this prejudice to persuade the jury that
to find Mrs. Duncan innocent is also to support this 'crazy' and 'depressing'
picture of the afterlife. This was in contrast to the more 'spiritual' and familiar
picture painted of the established Christian church that Dodson referred to.

Maude's attack on Spiritualism started by referring to Mrs. Homer's comment to Lt. Worth who asked about bringing his sceptical doctor friend. She said 'I will give him a seat in the front row and scare him stiff'. Maude argued that this was hardly the kind of talk from one who believed in God and ran a church. Similarly he contrasted the use of swear words such as 'bloody' with the prayers said at the start of seances. He went on to describe how, at seances, individuals are asked to call out the spirit by asking 'Is it for me?' 'What I have told you appears to have been the usual practice when poor spirits were called from whatever they were doing or however they were enjoying themselves in another world'.

He questioned how any woman would have felt when being asked to come forward to feel the stump of a mutilated young man. He asked how it came about that providence allows this monstrous shape to come. When a cat appeared in Portsmouth he wondered whether 'it was hunting pink mice in the Elysian fields'. Was the parrot that appeared 'fluttering round from somewhere...from some heavenly forest?' When the policeman appeared he asked whether we were expected to believe that there is a policeman with his helmet marching somewhere amongst the clouds or wherever it is. Can you imagine anything more disappointing than a policeman having passed through life and apparently not having risen to an Inspector, because he still had a helmet? Finding himself in the next world, not in plain clothes, not at ease in a shirt and a pair of plain trousers, but having to look for his helmet... That is all the policeman did. He effected no arrest... I know all this may sound to you absolutely insane but one must remember that persons think it worth while to pay for such demonstrations'.

When he described the activities of Peggy, in moving papers, trying lipstick and using a sitter's perfume, Maude said this is supposed to be spirit who had passed over into something that one hopes is not a 'lunatic asylum'. When it was reported that Peggy remarked 'I'm going down now', Maude did not know whether 'these people live down below'.

Maude's closing statement concentrated as much upon Spiritualism as upon the evidence. He may have done so in the knowledge that Dodson was to do that job for him and put the prosecution case to the jury in his summing up. Maude asked the jurors to imagine an afternoon in the spirit world.

'They are sitting around Mary Queen of Scots, her head is on. St. Sebastian, the pin-cushion saint is there, perfectly normal. There are various persons who have been mutilated, looking perfectly all right. No arm or leg cut off, no eyes out. Then suddenly someone says something that is sad. Off comes the Queen's head – under her arm, I suppose. St. Sebastian begins to bleed, and unmutilated persons become mutilated. It is absolutely fantastic. If this is the sort of thing we are coming to, it is time to begin to pull ourselves together and exercise a little common sense'.

'If a canary had poured out the fullness of its song it would have been remarkable, but a parrot said "Pretty Polly" they might hail it and say "Hail blithe bird spirit thou never wert'.

Like many observers he puzzled why historical figures like Napoleon, Shelley, Keats, Socrates and Shakespeare don't return. He could see no reason why the curtains need to be opened and closed or why medium need to wear black or white clothing. He went on say 'apparently as you got old you kept old in the spirit world'.

He went on 'If there were materialisation mediums it was amazing that some well-disposed scientific association with Mrs. Duncan's co-operation could not finally and conclusively establish the genuiness of her claims'.

'It is an astonishing thing that this woman has not been installed in some special chapel – astonishing if one does not keep one's head and ignore the possibility of fraud'.

Dodson also made his views known. He started by misleadingly saying in his summing up, that a defence witness, Reverend Maurice Elliott, who testified to the importance of Spiritualism for Christianity, although he was not too certain about its value. He continued by saying that he supposed that 'no one doubts that Spiritualism may have some value if a person either has no belief in the Christian faith, or if their faith be so weak that they are unable to accept the Easter story of the Christian belief', in which he thought the 'whole thing was possibly summed up, and seek to prove it by some other means'. He again wondered aloud whether this may be 'the purpose of Spiritualism' and who can say whether its effect is good or bad. It was as if Dodson had transposed himself in place of this 'misguided' witness and summed up accordingly, even though it bore little accuracy to what Rev. Elliott had actually said in the witness box.

Such a comment directly relating to the beliefs of Spiritualists has no relevance to the guilt or innocence of the defendants. It can be only have had the effect of making his own personal views known to the jury and how he viewed the defence witnesses before him, which may have influenced them.

Many of the national newspapers further undermined Spiritualism by referring to the Old Bailey trial under the heading Witchcraft Trial or Witchcraft. The London Evening News, Daily Sketch, Yorkshire Post, Glasgow Herald, The Star and the Evening Standard all used this headline. Maude told the jury, in his closing speech, that Mrs. Duncan had not been charged under the Witchcraft Act to make her look ridiculous, but it is clear that the Witchcraft headline, or reference to it tarnished Spiritualism. Recorder Dodson, during sentencing, further reinforced this connection between Spiritualism and witchcraft when he referred to what took place at Mrs. Duncan's seances as 'dabbling with the occult', which newspapers quoted.

The DPP's prosecuting counsel Edward Robey established this tone at the Police Court hearing at the end of February which received considerable press attention. He referred to the meeting openings with 'some religious preamble, the Lord's Prayer, a well known prayer which the court might think hardly fitting for the matter which they were investigating'. So the lead was set. Even the sincere prayers of Spiritualists or people who attend séances in an attempt to make contact with their loved ones were just 'some religious preamble' and 'hardly fitting' when conducted in a Spiritualist Church prior to a demonstration of physical mediumship. Maude repeated much of Robey's script and continued this theme when he said to the jury 'It is a disagreeable incident of this particular case that Mrs. Duncan started proceedings with a prayer, and all those present joined in the Lord's Prayer'. Loseby regarded Maude's comment as a 'sneer' and 'hardly just'. Maude had taken the view that under the 1735 Witchcraft Act invoking the name of God, such as beginning a séance with the Lord's Prayer and then saying the dead were present in spirit form, then you were guilty of conjuration.

When describing Peggy chanting "Loch Lomond" and the audience joining in, Robey remarked "If that was the best departed spirits could do, it were better for them to stay away."[1] Robey referred to a mutilated form appearing as 'shocking bad taste', and Mrs. Homer's comment after Mrs. Duncan's arrest that "Never mind friends, Jesus suffered like this" as blasphemy. Mrs. Duncan was also referred to as a so-called Spiritualist, with the added reference that she never paid income tax and was convicted of fraud in 1933 in Edinburgh.

Some of the press also took this opportunity to attack Spiritualism and its believers. The New Statesman wrote 'The persons in the witness-box who described the re-encounter with dead husbands and wives – some having even kissed them or touched their hands – were for the most part unquestioning, humdrum and depressed. …Religion surely has never before sunk to more dismal or meaningless depths. For beyond the dubious contact these was simply nothing. No harm done and a little comfort'.[2]

Desmond McCarthy in the The Sunday Times[3] made the point that it is the deep sense of loss experienced by Spiritualists and their desires and expectations that may prevent them from discovering fraud. He strongly asserted that they should be pleased that others seek to defend them against fraud but in his view many are so alarmed at being deprived of their belief in life after death that they consider such a defence as religious persecution.

McCarthy's strong views expressed at this time may have been influenced by his own close ties with Naval Intelligence. He had been recruited to Naval intelligence in the First World War, working in what has become known as Room 40 at the Old Building at the Admiralty. Room 40 was responsible for numerous military intelligence successes during the campaign.

Under the headline 'Spiritualist Frauds' the Yorkshire Post[4] wrote, 'It is not surprising that in the tension and distress of wartime days the fraudulent medium should find greater scope for wicked impositions. There are often easy victims among those who have lost loved ones and have still not adjusted themselves to the loss. Unscrupulous tricksters have long done harm to the cause of psychic investigation, and for this if no other reason all those with a genuine interest in Spiritualistic phenomena should regard with satisfaction with the sentence imposed…. There will nevertheless be misguided people who will still try to discern in this case something akin to religious persecution. They choose to ignore the detachment of the law. Here the law is not concerned with the possibility or otherwise of Spiritualistic manifestations…'

If we examine this picture in the light of the possible involvement of a team of scriptwriters, with a strong theatrical, fiction and documentary film background, coupled with changing and contradictory stories of the prosecution witnesses, we can start to identify those fictional elements. Worth's uncorroborated testimony holds the best examples.

It seems the assembled sceptical scriptwriting team could not resist exploiting the comic potential of the material, in trying to get a conviction. It was funnier if the form appearing for Worth confirmed she was his aunt when he didn't have one. To emphasise the point and complete the joke then an uncle appears who salutes him. But Worth had no uncle that matched the figure and the salute reminded him of a taxi driver's salute. Finally he is presented with a premature sister and he says but I don't have one that was born prematurely. It seems clear that the uncle incident is completely fictitious, along with the confirmation Worth claimed his aunt and uncle gave him. It is most blatant in the case of the uncle because everyone else present claim no form whatsoever emerged from the cabinet and Albert said that there was a sailor for Worth, not his uncle. Take away the fictional adaptation and it removes the heart of Worth's personal testimony that led to the case being brought and so effectively, the case against Mrs. Duncan.

Worth and the prosecution made great play of The Monty Pythonesk animal sequence in which lifeless forms of a parrot and cat are poked through the curtains on a hand and withdrawn in rapid succession. Worth and Burrell could see no animal only a rigid form and the audience reacted saying 'look at the pussy'. It was suggested that this was so ridiculous that fraud was the only reasonable explanation. Such a sequence seems highly theatrical.

A lady emerging from the curtains with outstretched arms surpassed this. It reminds one of the very worst types of horror B movie where zombies walk amongst the gravestones at midnight. It is a powerful and at the same time ridiculous image.

Such scenes were more likely to come from a script writers imagination and indicate a writer's touch rather than Worth whose expertise prior to joining the Navy was as a haulage manager. Add to this the story of a large fat woman with a sheet over her head, thumping around and speaking in a husky voice then we have good material for an Ealing comedy or should we say an Old Bailey trial run by an MI5 officer with good theatrical contacts and a team of script writers.

We had the picture of Mrs. Homer and her grandmother singing a duet either side of the curtain in a language Worth did not understand and moments of ignorance and irrationality. There was an old lady who Albert said was in her 90's when she died but whose relative asserted was in her 70's. Albert replied in answer that he hadn't said she was 95, but in her 90's! Worth failed to remember his lines with regard the mutilated young man who Albert was purported to have claimed had died east of Shanghai in Singapore!

The script also took a change in mood. Jarvis's personal criticisms of Mrs. Duncan, that he didn't think much of the medium, she is 'too fat' and then some swearing and the 'bloody twister' comments were made. It was claimed that this introduced irreverence. The dramatic scenario of Burrell's Pinkie story was most clearly invented because it contradicted the witness statements and testimony of the person most directly involved, Mrs. Lock. This piece of fiction tried to implicate Mrs. Duncan in exploiting the suffering of those who have lost loved ones during the war. The message came for the family that Freddie the airman is alive and safe only for the family to be told he was dead. This story was at the dramatic heart of the prosecution, tricksters exploiting the suffering of grieving families in a major Naval port at a time of war.

First of all Surg. Lt. Elijah Fowler was assigned to play this role but he declined and the part was rewritten for Burrell. Burrell's conversations with the Homer's also seem scripted for the trial with the different drafts apparent in his earlier statements.

Direction was at its height when Mrs. Lock was moved to another seating position along with Worth's and Cross's version of grabbing Mrs. Duncan when no one else saw her standing in front of the curtains. Blocking and lighting effects were necessary for this part of the show, as Mrs. Duncan had to be removed from her chair otherwise the illusion could not work. Viewing the trial in these terms exposes the 'fun' these scriptwriters must have had with the material and that the prosecution themselves were responsible for the conspiracy and the 'illusion', rather than the accused.

Maude, the producer/director had arranged everything perfectly and so to add the authentic quality that a documentary drama needs, he caste Henry Elam, his junior counsel in the major role of examining and cross-examining many of the witnesses, with the assistance of the Recorder. Elam had been chosen because he was a highly competent Counsel who could focus on the matters a prosecution counsel would in such a trial. Being the producer/director and also be expected to perform as the lead actor is too much for any director to manage, so Maude withdrew to allow the authentic documentary quality to unfold with genuine characters. He accounted for his withdrawal by becoming defence counsel, completely without charge, of a murder suspect in a trial that the Chief Constable of Portsmouth police believed that Maude had a good chance of winning. It seems this was a convenient excuse as that trial started five days into the Mrs. Duncan trial.

At the Helen Duncan trial Elam and Dodson would play their parts and Maude would keep an eye on the important strategic aspects of the trial from the wings and possibly coach and rehearse the other prosecution witnesses before they took the stand. The secret of directing any documentary that Max Anderson and Terry Bishop would be well aware as highly talented documentary film makers who a few years later were to receive an Oscar and BAFTA, was as a director you never ask your subjects to do anything they don't do normally. It is interesting that they adopted a similar approach that Anderson had been critically acclaimed for using in a film in 1942 and having adapted it for the trial.

A scripted story was then portrayed in a documentary manner. Viewing the trial in these terms allows one to 'appreciate' the quality of the scenario and the clearly defined characterisation of the leading witnesses and their performances. The adopted style was similar to Anderson and Bishop's later Oscar winning film, 'Daybreak In Udi', where amateurs played the roles in the film. Characters played parts in order to dramatise everyday situations, while in the trial Elam could concentrate on being a barrister, Dodson the judge and Maude the director of the piece could concentrate on his role and intervene at the important moments. One cannot forget that the inspiration, executive producer and backer was also to become one of the nation's leading authors and story tellers, Ian Fleming.

Burrell like Worth was a clearly defined character and he played his role with spirit, unconcerned about possible flaws in his script. Worth was almost word perfect when he came to court. His performance was praised by the Recorder who pointed out to the jury that even the defence had referred to him as a wonderful witness. Loseby conceded that Worth gave his evidence skilfully and that he had a 'good eye to effect' that was aided by a 'flickering smile' that as far as Loseby was concerned, he had full command of. Worth was positive, bold, assertive and convincing. He displayed a humour and seemed to put Loseby on a wrong footing when he picked up on his errors or lack of precision on some of his questioning. Even Dodson adopted a similar style making a joke just as Loseby was starting his serious cross-examination of witnesses or at other points. This no doubt reassured the witness and undermined Loseby. Burrell displayed some of the same qualities. Worth imitated the voices of others during his testimony, gave an impression of Albert, of a cat miaowing and of the parrot saying "Pretty Polly". Burrell was complimented in the Portsmouth papers for the way he gave evidence at the magistrates hearing, by reporting that in contrast with the other witnesses he gave his evidence positively. So both Worth and Burrell were complimented on their performance and received good reviews compared to the other witnesses, while it may have been no accident that they were eventually joined by an experienced actress, Mrs. Jennings.

The policeman with his helmet was heaven sent for the prosecution. He went back to collect his helmet but Worth couldn't see any helmet. Like much documentary footage, editing is necessary and whole scenes ended up on the cutting room floor. Edited out was Shirley the 3 year-old child appearing to her grandmother and singing the rhyme clearly seen and heard by everyone else present. Also edited out were Nurse Rust's Spanish aunt, her husband and mother and the long conversation Mrs. Duncan held in Gibraltarian Spanish. She was edited out herself from the police plan and by the Recorder in his summing up of the dramatic climax of the story when Cross leapt forward in his attempt to catch the medium. The atmosphere and moments of joy and wonder of actually recognising the features of people you know and being reunited were also removed, in order to set the scene for a mystery comedy drama to be played at the Old Bailey in front of packed houses.

Alas the picture Maude and his co-conspirators painted in order to achieve the intended conviction caused real suffering. It dragged the reputation of a mother of six through the mud and led to an attempted 'revival' in Nottingham that led to Helen Duncan's premature death following another police raid, in search of finding that elusive piece of 'material' evidence. Moreover it deepened the prejudice and distorted the understanding of spirit communication in Britain for many decades.

Most physical mediums have been too apprehensive to present their phenomena for public examination ever since, preferring to display it within the narrow confines of a protective Spiritualist community. Much of the press and media continue the successful strategy adopted by the MI5 officer in 1944 of making fun of the subject. Like Harry Price, some psychic researchers still make a name for themselves and appear in the media from time to time to denounce psychic phenomena and mediums in general and to poke fun. Some of the best physical mediums have received personal threats to their safety. Loseby regarded Helen Duncan as a great medium but he was not sure whether it is sufficiently realised how great her contribution was to the cause for which Spiritualists stand. In his mind she demonstrated that the human personality survives the grave. He certainly suspected the motives of those who criticised her and acted against her when he wrote that 'she had to be discredited'.

Those who wrote the police statements were skilled script or scenario writers but Elijah Fowler's refusal to go along with the part assigned to him and Mrs. Lock's and Mrs. Harris's essential naivety and straightforwardness caused a number of inconsistencies that needed to be overcome. Tracing how they tried to do that threw light on the workings of the conspiracy. The prosecution had to maintain their co-operation even though their essential honesty did not easily sit easily with all of the other fictional elements that were created. When the fit was not good, varying the paperwork apparently without their knowledge seemed the best way to get the conviction without bringing attention to itself. Mrs. Harris's role as a trial witness was minimised possibly because she was suspected as the insider who had assisted Worth to bring charges against the couple who ran the church she attended, Mrs. Duncan and her companion Mrs. Brown.

The Question of Credulity

Whatever the religious implications and consequences of the trial, after it a question of true significance remained to be explained, that is to account for the distinct difference in evidence between over 40 defence witnesses and those few prosecution witnesses.

Maude in his closing speech said 'Disraeli said 100 years ago that this was an age of 'craving credulity'. If this is the sort of thing we are coming to it is time we began to pull ourselves together and exercise a little common sense'. He went on to say 'that nobody suggested that the people who went into the witness box did not believe what they were saying'.

Maude explained that in his view, by Mr. & Mrs. Homer and Mrs. Brown working on the feelings of the audience and invoking Almighty God, a state of mind may be produced when people believe such things.

Dodson explained the beliefs of the sitters about what they described as being due to a kind of religious ecstasy. He suggested that the large number of witnesses called for the defence, displayed great enthusiasm which in some cases bordered on a kind of ecstasy. He also referred to a defence witness who said there was an emotional tendency present at seances and the Recorder offered this to the jury to account for a great deal. Referring to the jury as men and women of the world he asked them to exercise their common sense and asked them to consider how people who have got themselves into that condition may be affected.

To emphasise his point he referred to the belief held by a Spiritualist that a child who never touched the earth plane due to a miscarriage can grow up in the spirit world and may be seen in a séance. He described such an assertion as plumbing the depths of credulity. He went on 'You could see that she believed it. It may be a thing that gives infinite comfort, and some people are prepared to pay very high prices for comfort of that kind'.

So the prosecution's case and Recorder Dodson shared the view that although all the defence witnesses told the truth as they saw it, their evidence could not be counted on because they were credulous people. Chief Constable West reinforced this view when stating that Mrs. Duncan 'preyed on the minds of a certain credulous section of the public'.

The problem after the trial was this discrepancy was likely to raise important questions in many people's minds. Was it possible for twenty or so honest people who mostly believe in life after death, seated only feet away from each other, not to hear the sound of a voice speaking in Spanish, see a man dive through a set of curtains and pull a woman seated in a chair, see a form leave the cabinet or not, see a young child walk around in front of them and talk, recognise the features of their close relatives or notice whether a person is standing in front of a cabinet at a particular time or not?

Are we saying when ten or so honest people who describe the same event, see the same facial features and hear the same conversation are mistaken, when compared to one or two people who claim they experienced something different? It seems to go against our common sense. If ten honest people describe something that occurred, then it is most likely to have occurred, or at least it leaves reasonable doubt against something or other occurring. In the case of Spiritualists, the prosecution successfully argued that the evidence of any number of honest Spiritualists or sitters at a séance are worthless compared to a policeman and a Naval Officer who stated that those people around him who gave contrary evidence were 'deluded'.

We can feel sure that if any of these same defence witnesses had described seeing a person similar to Harold Loughans climbing through Rose Robinson's window on the evening of her murder in Portsmouth, then the prosecution would have had no hesitation in calling them to give evidence. They would have also have certainly referred to them as upstanding and reliable witnesses. However, because these same people described seeing and speaking to their husband or some other close relative they were very familiar with, while sitting in a first floor room a few miles away, they are viewed as credulous and unreliable.

Loseby considered that the questions posed to each of his witnesses, 'Are you a Spiritualist?' and later 'Do you know Mr. Homer?' were made to impress the minds of the jury in order to convey that their evidence was less important, cogent and less reliable. Loseby regarded this question as placing each witness on the horns of a dilemma. The Recorder and Maude were using the term Spiritualist so loosely, as to refer to anyone who believed in survival and communication. Loseby argued if a witness answered yes, then he became an interested and credulous person, if he said no, he implied that he was not convinced of the identification of which he had given evidence.

Knowing that the Security Service had good contacts with the press during wartime, the possibility that support for the position of credulity would be reflected in the press after the trial may well be expected.

Immediately after the trial the Sunday Dispatch[5] published an article by Professor Joad who was a colleague of Harry Price. Joad, a Professor of

Psychology, writer and broadcaster was the Chairman of the University of London Council for Psychical Investigation that Price had founded. As we know Harry Price worked with the prosecution in helping present their case. Professor Joad explained that the pressures of our wishes make us extremely receptive to so-called evidence, which if our attitude is dispassionate, we should not consider for a moment. Secondly, he stated that the boring nature of most seances, of sitting in the dark for several hours lead to people being prepared to accept anything. It is interesting that the second reason does not apply to the Helen Duncan case as so-called evidence appeared from the start.

Furthermore, Professor Joad claimed that it had been established that some mediums have secondary stomachs like cows and that they swallow muslin and cheese-cloth and when behind the curtain they can regurgitate from their mouths. Although Professor Joad stated this as fact it was not an accepted fact for no evidence had been found to show mediums had secondary stomachs and Harry Price's regurgitation theory was generally discredited. Hannen Swaffer, a well-known journalist and Spiritualist wrote to Joad at the time pointing this out and Joad immediately recanted. Joad's reputation as a psychic investigator was in tatters after it had been disclosed that supposed incidents described by him were a complete invention and he had claimed to have first hand knowledge of seances that he had never attended. Other newspapers referred to Harry Price's research and stated that the conviction supported the claims of fraud he made against Mrs. Duncan in the early 1930's.

Denys Parsons, an industrial chemist and aspiring film maker was to play a role in the aftermath of the Helen Duncan trial in publishing an article in support of the prosecution case to coincide with the Appeal hearing. Denys Parsons had joined the Society of Psychical Research (SPR) in May 1942 and his wife, Kelty MacLeod joined on the very day of the police raid on the 19th of January 1944. It will be recalled that Brig. Firebrace, the senior Military Intelligence Officer at the War Office who was involved in the prosecution of Mrs. Duncan joined the SPR a short time later at the start of the trial.

From the start Denys Parsons became an active member of the SPR and he attended the trial. Along with Molly Goldney, he ran what was referred to as 'the group' at the SPR during this time. Molly Goldney had thoughts of writing a book about Helen Duncan after the trial, but she was strongly advised against it by some of her colleagues, who were opposed to Mrs. Duncan, did not want her to gain any more importance or publicity and felt it would not assist the development of parapsychology. Molly and Denys Parsons turned their attention to trying to encourage Harry Price to publish a booklet on Helen's mediumship to coincide with the Appeal Hearing, but despite some effort to persuade him Price declined. Price had been unwell. Although a close friend, Molly Goldney was unaware that Price had co-operated with the prosecution, as she asked why he had not given his photographs to them to use in the trial. Price had done so, but he obviously preferred to keep his involvement with the police and the DPP to himself.

Goldney's and Parsons' interest was the phenomena of the 'sitters', who describe such extraordinary events that one does not know what to think. In their view it was this feature that made the trial an 'astounding event'. Denys was keen to speak to Harry Price about this proposal and Molly Goldney did everything she could to arrange the meeting. When Price declined to write a piece about the case, Parsons took up this challenge and wrote an article to coincide with the appeal hearing, in support of the position taken by the prosecution.

Whilst there is no evidence that directly shows that Parson's worked for the intelligence services, or knowingly under Maude's or Naval Intelligence's control in writing this article, the evidence that does exist is highly suggestive. Like the Naval Special Branch officers brought in prior to the raid to Worth's unit, there was family links between him and Maude and he was a friend of one of these officers, Max Anderson the scriptwriter and documentary director.

Like Maude, Phipps, Bishop, Carstairs, Robey and Hyman, Parsons also had senior connections in the world of theatre. Alexander Denys Parsons (known as Denys) was part of a Beerbohm Tree famous theatrical dynasty and his family had close links with Maude's. He was the grandson of Sir Herbert Beerbohm Tree the famous actor/manager who managed the Haymarket Theatre and later Her Majesty's Theatre. His grandmother was the actress Maude Holt known as Lady Tree. His grandfather Herbert Beerbohm had been a friend of Cyril Maude, John Maude's father. They were both council members of the Royal Academy of Dramatic Art that Herbert Beerbohm Tree founded, fellow members of the Boz Club[6] and on several charities together. Deny's mother was Viola Tree the famous actress, his father was Alan Parsons the drama critic and David Tree the actor was his brother. His uncle was Sir Max Beerbohm the famous author, artist and critic whose wife was Florence Kahn the actress. Denys wife of the time was Jean Kelty, the well-known broadcaster famous for her readings of verse and prose on the radio and whose father was in the military, General Kelty MacLeod.

The Beerbohm Tree family also had connections with the Bishop family and George Robey and Nelson Key's as members of the family's appeared together on stage on numerous occasions and at theatres Herbert Beerbohm Tree owned. Like Maude's own sister Margery Maude, Terry Bishop's cousin Marie Lohr had worked with Herbert Beerbohm Tree's Theatre company. Marie Lohr had also appeared with the prosecution counsel's father George Robey and John Paddy Carstairs' father Nelson Keys. She also appeared with Denys Parsons brother David Tree and his mother Viola Tree, and in films produced by Alan Hyman's cousin Michael Balcon 'Oh Daddy' and 'Foreign Affairs' both made in 1935. The family connections between these people involved in the Helen Duncan case were numerous not withstanding the fact that Parsons was a fellow Etonian like Ian Fleming and John Maude.

During the war Parsons was engaged on work to do with camouflage but he had spent sometime involved in film production for the same company that Max Anderson worked for Realist Films. The Realist Film Unit was a small independent production company who made many films for the Ministry of Information and other sponsors. Parsons was interested in developing scientific film section of the British film industry and he later became the librarian of the Scientific Film Association. Both Parsons and Anderson had worked on a film about potatoes during the war (Anderson directed 'Clamping Potatoes' in 1942). Parsons was keen to become a film director and later he achieved his ambition, as he worked as a film director at Realist Films after the war, along with his friend Max Anderson. The question remains how and why this friendship developed for both men to become so closely involved in the Helen Duncan case.

A further contact also cannot be ignored. Denys father Alan Parsons had also been a senior civil servant prior to becoming a theatre critic for the Daily Mail and both he and John Phipps' father had served the Asquith and Lloyd George governments both during and after the first World War, so the social worlds in which they operated were the same.

Denys' article represented the best evidence that could be amassed that supported the prosecution case at the time the Appeal was heard in June 1944. It appeared in Horizon in June 1944. This was an unlikely publication as it was a review for literature and art. Horizon was run by Cyril Connolly who also happened to be a very close friend of Ian Fleming of Naval Intelligence. Connolly like Fleming and Parsons was also an old Etonian. Connolly recalls lunch dates with Fleming and senior military figures such as Generals and Admirals at White's and the Etoile's at which Fleming would push these officers to take out a subscription for Horizon. It seems no coincidence that Parsons' article in support of the Naval Intelligence operation appeared in a journal run by a close friend of the Naval Intelligence officer who was likley to be behind it, Ian Fleming.

Fleming was an expert in managing the press for intelligence operations so articles presenting research findings in support of the prosecution case published at the time of the Appeal represented an important part of the operation. Parsons's relationship with other Special Branch officers serving with Worth and the use of a magazine closely linked with Ian Fleming of the NID, raises the question whether he was working for or had close links with the security service and placed in the SPR in the summer of 1942 to help prepare the research basis for the eventual trial and seek to influence and cover the post trial aspect of the operation. Certainly Molly Goldney and Harry Price had been encouraged by someone to publish on the subject of Helen Duncan's mediumship to coincide with the Appeal, but when they declined it was left to Parsons to do so himself.

His article was titled 'Testimony and Truth' and it focused on the trial. Parsons tackled the central issue. Prosecution witnesses stated only vague outlines of white material were seen compared to twenty five to thirty defence witnesses who testified they recognised their relatives beyond all possible doubt by recognisable features, mannerisms, movement, dialects, distinguishing marks and personal information given and exchanged. Parsons rightly observed both sides cannot be right. He reviewed the available evidence in support of the ignorance and credulity of observers and the trickery undertaken by some supposedly 'self declared' fraudulent mediums. He cited studies that demonstrated that observations and memory can be inaccurate in similar test settings and stated that mistaken identity is common place, so a supernatural explanation is not required.

The research studies he cited were however quite artificial and impersonal and not ones which the subjects believed were actual seances and which had been personally meaningful (not withstanding being interrupted by the police, so that their experiences would be further concentrated upon). The instances he referred to have little or no personal meaning and a large degree of variability in accuracy occurred, compared to the trial in which there was a large degree of consistency in response within the two opposing groups. In the trial it was not a case of mistaken identity but of one group agreeing to the features they saw and the other group seeing no features at all. Where features were seen they were reported with good consistency. Any inconsistency occurred within the prosecution witnesses, not the group that was referred to as 'credulous'. It was members from the prosecution witness group who had given accounts in agreement with the 'credulous' group!

At the trial there were only two areas of comparison where witnesses viewed the same event. These referred to all the witnesses' testimony being in agreement apart from Worth and then Worth and Cross. Parsons placed more value upon a very small number of artificial research studies with limited responses available to subjects than the actual trial itself. In the Helen Duncan case, subjects interacted with the forms, sought and exchanged personal information, the subjects were closely examined, cross-examined on what they experienced and were able to declare what they had not attended to. It is also worth pointing out that in cases of identification of deceased persons the police take the next of kin as the accepted means to establish a legally accepted proof of identity. This situation applied to the séance room for close relatives recognised their deceased relatives. When the identification took place in the morgue the police accepted it however when it took place in the séance room it was rejected.

Parsons later advised Donald West in the preparation of his article on the Helen Duncan Trial where he adopted a similar position when published in 1946. [7]

Parsons article received criticism from Spiritualists for failing to point out that blank incredulity was as bad as stark credulity. Barbanell disputed his claims regarding the conclusions of other investigators he cited in support of his hypothesis and generally thought Parsons wrote from second hand knowledge as he had never sat with Helen Duncan, as other writers on the subject had.

Parsons's article however, presented the best case possible in support of Maude's proposal, while not considering for one moment the obvious counter position that Lt. Worth and WRC Cross might have been deliberately untruthful or the 'defective' observers. Certainly he would have been aware of the argument that Worth was a stooge put up by the Admiralty to convict Mrs. Duncan. Molly Goldney who had worked with Parsons and who had approved the article, had declared this proposition as the defence view of the case. Parsons focused the public's and scientists attention exclusively on the issue of credulity rather than conspiracy.

On hindsight, and given the evidence presented here, the next time there is a discrepancy between a number of honest people and a policeman, naval officer or even a psychic investigator then the same rigour and investigation into the more obvious likelihood of deception by the latter should be applied. The 'common sense' that Maude asked the jury to apply, should be applied. Simply put, when a large number of honest people say that a certain event occurred, then it is most likely that it did occur. That should be the starting point not the reverse. The same rigour should apply in both directions in cases of psychic investigation. There was reason to believe that there was a conspiracy to convict Mrs. Duncan yet psychic investigators ignored this possibility. They preferred to explain the extreme position that honest people cannot see what is directly in front of them, hear what is being said out loud and to which they contribute or discern the content of information that is being conveyed verbally, even when it related to an 'ordinary' event such as a person leaping forward from a chair in an audience and what they did next.

Parsons pointed out that some that sat with Mrs. Duncan say when you have seen the phenomena with your own eyes it is futile to refer to test conditions and stomach examinations. He asked whether you can really trust the evidence of our own eyes. Ironically Parsons was later criticised by some psychic researchers some short time later when he did just that, and believed his own eyes when witnessing a transfiguration medium Edith Balmer in 1948. So the person who was led to support the view, adopted by Maude in his conspiracy, eventually believed his own eyes when he saw Queen Victoria appear while studying a medium and then other sceptical investigators never believed him!

Parson's experience highlights the trap investigators are perpetually caught in. If a sceptic like Molly Goldney, who considered all possible explanations, finally believed her eyes and proclaimed the genuineness of physical phenomena then another sceptic would take her place and dispute her claim. And so it goes on. Year after year, decade after decade and little is resolved. If a scientist does not believe it is possible that people survive their death then they find it difficult to accept the testimony of those who are sure they have witnessed instances that demonstrate it. What is the point of going round in circles when in fact we are all waiting for the time when we can film the phenomena appropriately? Until decisive studies are undertaken, sceptics will dispute the explanations of those who are personally satisfied they have witnessed spirit phenomena. And those who are personally satisfied cannot demonstrate their experience to others. Under these circumstances we don't have the evidence to determine the question one way or the other. The effort must be to move the field on and do the necessary research. Until that time comes these types of arguments reflect the failure of the research community to put resources into critical research.

A few months later in October 1945 Harry Price did write on the subject of the trial. He anonymously reviewed Bechhofer Roberts' new book 'The Trial of Mrs. Duncan' in The Listener.[8] He answered the question how intelligent sitters recognised their relatives when Mrs. Duncan was purported to use only a length of cheesecloth, by declaring in dim red light 'faces' can be seen in the irregular creases of crumpled cheesecloth and enhanced by the shadows that are created if they are close together and of a similar size. He declared 'imagination plus a certain subconscious elaboration of details plus expectation do the rest'. This description is interesting because Bechhofer Roberts never addressed the means by which witnesses recognised their relatives and friends using a piece of cloth. He had simply asserted that Mrs. Duncan was a fraud, who was passed the cloth by a confederate when she entered the cabinet and at the end, the same person recovered it at the close of the seance.

Privately Bechhofer Roberts shared the jury's view writing to Donald West that Worth told the 'truth in all essential matters', while the two most impressive defence witnesses Mackay (sic) and Rust 'rhapsodised'. He adopted Parsons's position, stating he believed all the defence witnesses tried to tell the truth but were incapable of doing so. They were 'unintentional liars' because their evidence was conditioned by their mentality. Unfortunately he failed to apply his argument to himself.

Desmond McCarthy, apart from being a former Naval intelligence officer also happened to be a friend of the Parsons family. When reviewing Bechhofer Roberts' book in the Sunday Times[9], not unsurprisingly some will say, he supported Parsons' conclusion. He acknowledged that the witnesses were completely honest and reliable but in his view they were uncritical and not trained researchers.   They were too readily prepared to accept as the only explanation that could account for the phenomena that they remembered or thought they remembered, as being supernatural.

George Stonier, a fellow literary editor, at the New Statesman in September 1945 judged in his review of Bechhofer Roberts book that as witnesses filed into the witness box the division grew wider between the sheep and goats, the faithful and the sceptical.   A reader of the book may be left wondering whether there is any limit to human credulity...   'Defence witnesses were for most part unquestioning, humdrum and depressed.   There was no question of their truthfulness: such squalid intimacies, one felt, required the dim red light in which they originated'.

Professor Donald West a young psychic investigator at the time published the only article that questioned Worth's testimony, which in places was totally unconfirmed, and when considered from a psychical research point of view it has nothing in it to prove fraud.   He analysed several of the discrepancies within the evidence between prosecution and defence witnesses and concluded the evidence for both was 'entirely governed by previous bias'.

Carl Bechhofer Roberts played a significant role in the aftermath of the Helen Duncan trial writing the foreword to a book that fiercely supported the prosecution case.   Carl Bechhofer Roberts' was a prolific author, playwright, journalist, former private secretary of the Lord Chancellor, the Earl of Birkenhead, military and government interpreter and barrister, being called to the bar in 1941.   He had also written a book that was critical of Spiritualism titled 'The Truth About Spiritualism' in 1932.

The publication of his book in 1945 titled 'The Trial of Mrs. Duncan' in the Old Bailey Trial Series was eagerly awaited at the time.   It contained a narrative and transcript of the trial, but it excluded Maude's closing speech and made no reference to it or the reason for its omission.   When it was published it brought a stinging reaction from Loseby who saw Bechhofer Roberts as going out of his way to condemn Mrs. Duncan anew, so leading some sections of the London press to make 'further contemptuous assaults upon her, and make allusions to myself which are wholly inaccurate'.

He regarded Roberts as cynical and that the 'narrative did everything possible to prop the prosecution and to justify the Trial as being in accordance with sound conceptions of justice'.   Like Dodson's summing up, Loseby regarded Bechhofer Robert's book as making no attempt whatsoever to put the case for the defence.

He called Roberts' narrative a prolonged sneer at the defence witnesses and accused his summary as being neither accurate nor reliable.   Despite this Roberts went on with 'complete recklessness' to label them all as 'Spiritualists' and 'made clear his nonsensical view, that "Spiritualists" as a class, were credulous, irresponsibles, whose word on oath might be treated lightly by men of the world'.   Loseby picked out Roberts' statement that the evidence of defence witnesses should be read 'by everyone who wishes to understand' the temperament of Spiritualists. They were gullible people who were disposed to believe 'they saw what they were told to see'. Loseby response was 'Greater rubbish could hardly be imagined'.

Roberts labelled Lord Dowding and Loseby himself as Spiritualists, with Loseby being called 'an ardent Spiritualist'.   Loseby pointed out that neither Dowding nor himself were in fact Spiritualists.

While Roberts eulogised Dodson's summing up, Loseby was damning about it.   He said that 'no point that might help the prosecution was unstressed. No matter of prejudice was omitted'. Loseby didn't believe the case for the defence had been put at all and he was unable to find five lines in Dodson's summing up that satisfied him.   He said each defence witness was mauled in turn.

Loseby certainly must have suspected Roberts motives because he noted that not only did his errors and inaccuracies always point in one direction but that 'hardly a word can be found that is generous or even just or fair'.   Loseby accused him of only picking out words which lent themselves to his 'rather ponderous humour and ridiculed them', making no effort to set out the points that really mattered and explain the implications drawn from them.   Loseby goes further to claim Roberts did so knowing that the press, who treated him as a writer of some weight, would rely on him for his accuracy.

In the light of the recent knowledge that Maude was a MI5 officer, then some influence direct or otherwise cannot be ruled out in Roberts publication which clearly misrepresents several important aspects of the trial and seeks to support the status of the Recorder.   It is worth pointing out that Bechhofer Roberts was appointed to the position of editor of the Old Bailey Trial series in 1944 and in this capacity he would have been known to Maude, but he also had other links.

As a playwright Bechhofer Roberts also had close links with the world of theatre and like many others involved in the trial with Maude's family in particular.   He had co-written a play "Nurse Cavell' that John Maude's aunt, the actress Nancy Price had starred.   The play went from the Q Theatre to the Vaudeville Theatre in the West End in the 1930's and was unexpectedly revived with her still as the lead in August 1942 after the sinking of the Barham.

Like Parsons, after preparing a publication supporting the prosecution case, Bechhofer Roberts too had the good fortune to make a move into the film industry, having a novel he published becoming the basis for a feature film in 1945, titled 'Don Chicago', a crime comedy.   We can only guess as to whether the realisation of these films projects and ambitions represented another co-incidence or a reward or incentive.

Bechhofer Roberts' background is also of interest.   After joining the 9th Lancers, Roberts like Firebrace trained as a military interpreter and went to

Russia. He also spoke German. He was a member of the Russian Government Committee set up by the Board of Trade between 1917 and 1919 and like Firebrace he was attached to the British Military Mission in Russian. He worked as a journalist and as a correspondent for British, American and Swiss papers in Russia, the Middle and Far East and America. He mixed in the highest political and social circles as Private Secretary to the first Earl of Birkenhead, who was a former Attorney General and Lord Chancellor and a close friend of Churchill. He also worked for the Daily Express and gained a reputation as a debunker, writing books focusing on Dickens, the biblical story of Joseph, and Spiritualism. He also wrote biographies of literary and political figures including Churchill and the Earl of Birkenhead, writing under the pseudonym 'Ephesian'. He became a barrister being called to the bar in 1941 and in 1944 he was appointed the editor for the Old Bailey series that eventually published a book of the Helen Duncan trial in support of the prosecution a year later.

It is worth noting that the society columns of broadsheets show that John Maude's MI5 assistant John Phipps, had good relations with the social set who Bechhofer Roberts had been part of, as private secretary and biographer to the first Earl of Birkenhead. Phipps was regarded so highly that he was part of an intimate house party of the then Earl of Birkenhead at the Goodwood races in the summer of 1938. It is also worth noting that the fathers of both these men had served the government many years earlier during the First World War, Lord Birkenhead as Attorney General and Sir Edmund Phipps as General Secretary in the Ministry of Munitions. Their service continued after the war, one becoming Lord Chancellor and the other returning to the Board of Education as Deputy Secretary. Phipps' relative Waldorff Aster (husband of Nancy Aster) had also been Lloyd George's Parliamentary Private Secretary during the first World War, who would have brought him close to Lord Birkenhead, a close ally of Lloyd George. It is important to note that Denys Parsons' father Alan was also a senior civil servant in the same governments.

Denys Parsons's family were extremely close to the Asquith family and his grandfather Herbert Beerbohm Tree had also been good friends with the Earl of Birkenhead, being a member of 'The Other Club' that the Earl and Churchill founded. By the same token they were frequently invited to the parties held by Herbert Beerbohm Tree at his theatre, that were known as 'Beerbohm Tree At Dome'. His wife Maude Tree was a particularly close friend of the Asquith's and she had directly asked Herbert Asquith to give her husband Herbert Beerbohm Tree a knighthood, which he duly did. Parsons' mother Viola was also a very close friend of Asquith.

Like Phipps, Denys's Parsons father Alan also served the Asquith (and Lloyd George) government as private secretary to Asquith himself, McKenna the Home Secretary, the Chancellor of the Exchequer and later to Edwin Montagu for six years. First when Montagu was Financial Secretary at the Treasury, then from 1917 when in was Secretary of State for India, while at the same time he was part of the War Cabinet as Private Secretary to the Chancellor of the Exchequer. There were few government departments he did not serve between 1914 and 1923. When Montagu retired from political life Denys' father moved to the Home Office where he had started, to be an Assistant Principal.

The Parsons', Asquiths' and Montagus' formed a coterie whose headquarters was the Montagu's home in Queens Gate, although they were familiar with Churchill and the Fleming family in Oxford, as Asquith was Earl of Oxford and Fleming's father Valentine, the High Sheriff and MP. After Montagu died Parsons also helped his wife Venetia edit his Indian Diary in 1928.

These close friendships also had a clear naval intelligence link. Edwin Montegu's nephew Ewen worked as a high ranking Naval intelligence officer at the Admiralty with Ian Fleming. He was a barrister and like Fleming his most senior status give him complete access to the sources of the nation's secrets and he was given a relatively free hand within the department by Admiral Godfrey. He was Admiral Godfrey's DNI representative on the top-secret Inter-Services Twenty Committee, he wrote the daily 'Orange Summaries' and he ran NID 17M, handling counter-espionage. Montagu was famous for running the operation known as 'the man who never was', which Fleming had contributed to in the planning. If Naval intelligence needed to find someone to aid the operation Ewen Montagu may have well suggested a trusted family friend Denys Parsons, especially as Parsons, like Bechhofer Roberts, had shown an interest in psychic research prior to the sinking of the Barham in 1941.[10]

MI5 also had good connections, with Maude and Phipps, who are likely to have known Bechhofer Roberts and Parsons via theatrical, legal, and their family and social connections related to those serving the Asquith and Lloyd George governments.[11]

It is interesting to observe that many of the men involved in the Helen Duncan post trial events had close social, work or family connections with senior Ministers of State (and their private secretaries) in Asquith's (and Lloyd George's) first World War government. Desmond McCarthy another old Etonian, had worked for Naval intelligence during the same period but he was also a trusted friend of this circle, a friend of Denys Parsons's parents, a confidante of the Asquiths having published Herbert Asquith's letters to Hilda Harrison in 1932. McCarthy was also a member of Churchill's and Lord Birkenhead's 'Other Club'.

These contacts brings us into the domain of the private secretary and the world of the close and trusted friendships that develop between those in the highest offices of state and their families during this period. It is understandable at a time of war that these types of trusted relationships were used in selecting individuals for sensitive security service work on behalf of the state. If Naval intelligence and MI5 did orchestrate the operation to get Mrs. Duncan out of the way as Chief Constable West has suggested, then these links seem the obvious and accepted ways in which people playing important post-trial roles were identified and eventually selected for the task.

Roberts' extraordinary praise of Dodson's summing up might be seen by some as an admission that the Recorder had exceeded his position, had gone 'overboard' in trying to serve his country as he saw it and get Mrs. Duncan convicted. Dodson was a man with a deeply patriotic, romantic view of sailors and protecting the nation. His opera and writings demonstrate this side to his character and the shocking degree of bias in his summation is clear. In the light of this situation one must ask why Roberts publicly applauded it. Possibly it was viewed that in his own attempt to serve the nation Dodson had placed himself in some risk from criticism. Apart from Loseby, few observers, even Spiritualist writers openly criticised the summing up. Loseby was not so inhibited, calling it a scandal. He had an unexpected ally in Molly Goldney a SPR member, sceptic and friend of Harry Price's. She privately commented on Dodson's summing up in a letter to Harry Price during the trial, that 'he did not comment; he merely recapitulated, telling the Jury with every word that she was a fraud'. She called Dodson's summing up 'very feeble' and 'futile'.

Publicly few criticisms of the summing up came from those psychic investigators reviewing the trial. Just as many psychic investigators find it hard to publicly affirm that they are satisfied that they had seen genuine spirit phenomena without coming under criticism from their colleagues, criticising the nation's most senior and respected Recorder also raises inhibitions in the minds of many. The truth and all its associated contradictions is an uncertain place in which to reside. Certainly Loseby felt some discomfort and the urge to leave the English law courts and seek work in Hong Kong at the age of 64, following the trial, in 1945.

Loseby's accusation of bias in Bechhofer Robert's narrative seem justified, given Roberts also claimed that Surg. Lt. Fowler's testimony corroborated Worth's account of the séance of the 14th. Many observers, even the Recorder himself acknowledge that this was not the case as Fowler was not cross-examined on it and he barely referred to Worth's evidence. It is difficult to fathom out why Roberts would take such an extreme position that flies in the face of the findings, unless it was an attempt to support and add to the already biased account of the trial published in the media in support of the judicial process and the prosecution. The question remains as to whether the publications that appeared after the trial represented part of a co-ordinated operation to support the prosecution position. My view is that the evidence suggests that they were and that this endeavour may have continued for sometime after.

The case of the missing cheese-cloth

Denys Parsons was also to become involved in another aspect of the Helen Duncan trial in 1946. This time it involved the mystery of the missing cheesecloth that WRC Cross was supposed to have touched and as the prosecution had claimed that someone had grabbed back into the audience.

Parsons informed the SPR that in 1945 he had been told a story by his friend Max Anderson that a sailor named Jacobs had grabbed the cheesecloth at the séance when Lt. Worth had shone the torch, and that he had stuffed it into his coat. This sailor then took it back to barracks and used it as a hammock.

This rumour had circulated at the time of the trial and it sought to provide an explanation for the major weakness in the prosecution case, that no material evidence was found. Bearing in mind Maude was responsible for rumours and the armed services used rumour as part of its own war time activity, the source of this rumour may well have come from Maude and his fellow conspirators. It should also be remembered that Ian Fleming who was Anderson's senior Special Branch officer at the Admiralty wrote papers and advocated using 'rumour as a weapon' and urged that much wider media coverage had to be given to rumours to counter the enemy, so an effective 'rumour gun' can be created. Now Max Anderson, one of Fleming's former Special Branch officers was here continuing to spread one with his friend Denys Parsons to the SPR.

The protocols at the SPR demanded that the rumour be checked out thoroughly before it could be published. Max Anderson went on to explain that a friend of his James Robinson, who was also stationed at Portsmouth, told him the story. Like Anderson and Parsons at that time, James Robinson also worked in the film industry, in animation. James Robinson put his story in writing to Denys Parsons confirming Max's account and this in turn was passed on to the SPR.

Robinson said when two of his friends who were fellow instructors returned from Mrs. Duncan's séance they produced cheese-cloth about eight foot square in size. He said he was told that Jacobs had made a grab at the ghost and contacted a full fist of cheesecloth when there was a disturbance and after stuffing it into his greatcoat they both made a hasty exit and returned to barracks. Later Robinson remembered that the name of the other man was Pickett. It is interesting that Robinson's description corresponds with details of the evidence presented by the prosecution that emerged at the trial. He explained that the reason, the cheesecloth was not seen being grabbed away by other witnesses, was a fist of cheesecloth was grabbed, so it did not stretch out as one would expect. This is precisely what Cross had stated and that the defence had challenged.

Both Pickett and Jacobs were present at the séance of the 19th. Robinson said he did not think his friends would make up such a story. Robinson gave two misleading contacts for Jacobs and the wrong Christian name when attempts were made to contact him. Donald West had got also involved in the matter being the SPR Research Officer at the time. Eventually a breakthrough was made when the correct Jacobs was found following assistance from Henry Elam. At a meeting in Parsons' flat, he and Donald West interviewed Woolf Bentley Jacobs who denied the story and said it was "fantastic". He explained he had sat at the back of the séance room with Peter Pickett, who had since died. He said that he was in no position to seize the 'ectoplasm' and that he would have handed it to the police if he had. It was proposed that the documents relating to the investigation of the rumour be published in the SPR journal. The decision to decline publication was made in April 1948.

Parsons described this research work in a chapter titled: 'Detective Work in Parapsychology' in 'A Skeptic's Handbook of Parapsychology'. [12] He claimed to have solved the mystery of the rumour but it begs the question of what was solved. It is clear that another mystery remains. Max Anderson and James Robinson were involved in spreading an unfounded rumour. Given that Max Anderson served with Lt. Worth and the prosecution case would have been greatly strengthened if the cheesecloth had been found then it is inconceivable that the police would not have called Jacobs and Pickett as witnesses and retrieved the cloth, if it ever existed. It is also almost certain that Anderson knew the cheesecloth had not been used as a hammock because he was a Special Branch colleague of the leading prosecution witness Worth.

It cannot be discounted that Parsons account was as much an attempt to plant a rumour than the detective work to quash it. Parsons quoted the story as an example of the detailed detective work often required in parapsychology but he never followed it completely through. Did James Robinson ever serve at Portsmouth? Why didn't Parsons apparently ever meet Robinson? He worked in the film industry at the time along with Anderson and Robinson, so one might have thought it most likely he would have swiftly interviewed him about his claims, rather than base his inquiries on a letter. Parsons also never publicised details about his friend Anderson and his contact with Worth although it is most likely that he was fully aware of his involvement and such information would raise serious suspicions.

When placed within the context of Maude being a MI5 officer in charge of rumours, Anderson being brought to Worth's unit with other script writers and directors prior to the police raid and Parsons publishing an article in support of the prosecution case through a close contact of Fleming of NID, then the rumour of what happened to the missing cheesecloth raises an important question. Did Parsons take the stance he did because he was aware of the true source of the rumour and it was an elaborate attempt to spread a rumour or did he innocently investigate it?

What is clear is that he did not carry through the investigation as rigorously as he could have done in terms of being a 'detective' with regard to his friend Max Anderson, and James Robinson, who it was shown had lied about the incident. Certainly if it was an attempt by intelligence officers to plant and publicise a rumour through the SPR then it shows that the perceived threat from mediums continued after the war and attempts were still being made to influence the perception of the case. Given that the account did not come from its reported source Woolfe Jacobs, its nature suggests it was a deliberate attempt to plant further misinformation in the same dismissive and ridiculing style adopted by the prosecution at the trial. This possibility is supported if one considers a particular detail included in the story. It is significant that the rumour refers to a surprising feature raised by the prosecution at the trial that the cloth did not stretch out but was grabbed in a clump by someone. The two sitters in question, Pickett and Jacobs sat in the third row in a position where they could not have seen the incident and it is unlikely they would have had access to such precise details of the prosecution evidence on their return.

This strongly suggests that whoever created this rumour for Robinson to distribute was very familiar with the fine details of the prosecution case which they sought to include in the story as part of the immediate telling by the sailors on their return to barracks.

The SPR decided not to publish the story but in doing so Mrs. Salter noted that it was a good example about how a rumour can get into circulation. This seems to be a reasonable conclusion to come to and most importantly it castes the focus back on those who were involved in spreading the rumour in the first place.

Another rumour has also been circulated to account for the major weakness in the prosecution case. This rumour had the cloth being hidden in a large sling being worn by a woman sitting in the front row near the cabinet. In a Channel 4 television documentary interview, Worth said that he and the police believed that this was where it had gone. This statement must also be classed as a rumour because there was not a woman at the séance on the night of the police raid who was wearing a sling and Worth at the time testified that the cloth had gone into the second row. The only woman in the front row who was wearing a bandage on that evening was Mrs. Alabaster who had one on her finger.

There has been much criticism of the police for failing to thoroughly make a search and find any material evidence of fraud once Cross had leapt on Mrs. Duncan, who was accused of wearing a cloth over her head. Chief Constable West in his own defence asserted 'believe you me it was combed inside and out, in every conceivable corner and no one was allowed to leave that building that night'. He stated he didn't know how they got rid of it. So we have two rumours, one about a sailor removing it to make a hammock and a woman secreting it in a large sling, while the Chief Constable states everywhere was searched thoroughly and no one was allowed to leave until the police were satisfied.

Denys Parsons and Donald West's articles represented some of the last writings of members of the Society of Psychical Research on the trial to appear for many years. They both arrived at the same conclusion as intelligent investigators. They said such matters as the truthfulness of the claims of mediums as Helen Duncan will only be resolved when such seances are filmed by infra red cameras or some other light sensitive means. They made these comments 60 years ago and they are still as relevant today as they were then. This is precisely where I came in and where my story began. Although we approached the subject differently our conclusions are the same.

What happened to the characters?

Researching the lives of the men such as John Maude, Max Anderson, Terry Bishop, James Drever, Alan Hyman, Denys Parsons, Roy Firebrace and others show that they are intelligent, respectable, talented men who made a contribution to their nation in many ways, in the arts, academia, music, trade unions, and the law.

Max Anderson and Terry Bishop won an Oscar and BAFTA in 1949 for a documentary film 'Daybreak At Udi'. Max continued as a documentary film director but branched out into fiction film as a scriptwriter and director of children's films. He became very involved in film union activities and became Vice President of the Association of Cinematograph and Television Technicians. He died aged 45 in July 1959 leaving a wife and two young daughters.

Terry Bishop went on to have a successful career as a feature and television director and writer. He directed popular TV series such as the 'Adventures of Robin Hood', 'The Buccaneers', The Adventures of Sir Lancelot', 'The Adventures of Sir Francis Drake', 'The Adventures of William Tell', 'The Sword of Freedom' and 'Danger Man'. Even though he was very ill himself with cancer, he continued to make films for the Cancer Fund for Children. He died of cancer in 1981 leaving a wife and a son.

Like many film makers of the time Alan Hyman moved to the field of Public Relations working for Shell for many years. He continued his interest in radio broadcasting and wrote a number of books on the theatre 'The Gaiety Years', 'Sullivan and His Satellites' and 'The Rise and Fall of Horatio Bottomley'. He was also script consultant on the Thames Television production 'God Knows Where and Port Talbot' in 1985. He died in 1999 leaving a daughter and two sons.

Elijah Fowler married, had two daughters and became a GP in Stockport and died in 1997.

James Drever helped push forward the field of psychology and academic life in Scotland.   After becoming the Professor of Psychology at Edinburgh University he became the Principle and Vice Chancellor of Dundee University. He died in 1991 leaving a son and a daughter.

Shortly after the trial Gerald Dodson started to lose his eyesight due to a serious affliction of the eyes and started to learn Braille.   The cause of the disability responded to treatment and he continued his work.   He continued as the Recorder of London to 1959 and became the longest holder of that office. After his retirement he continued to sit at the Old Bailey as a Commissioner to help with the heavy list of trials.   He retired with a reputation of being 'the greatest of all Recorders at the Central Criminal Court'.   He died in November 1966.

John Maude became the MP for Exeter from 1945 to 1951.   He was the Chancellor of the Diocese of Bristol from 1948-50 and Governor of the Royal Victoria Hall Foundation in 1953.   He continued his interest in the theatre becoming a Director of the Old Vic Trust 1951-54 and the Chairman of the British Drama League 1952-54.   After losing his parliamentary seat he became a member of the Bar Council and similar to Dodson he became an additional judge at the Mayor's and City of London Court.   He remarried in his 50's in 1955.   His second wife was Maureen Dufferin, the daughter of Arthur Guinness. In 1964 he became an additional judge at the Central Criminal Court.   He died in August 1986 leaving a daughter.

In September 1944 Henry Elam was the prosecuting counsel in another case at the Old Bailey brought against a Spiritualist medium under the Witchcraft Act, with Recorder Dodson again presiding.   72 year old Mrs. Jane Yorke of Forest Gate, London who went into trance and had a Zulu guide, was charged under seven counts and found guilty.   Dodson bound her over for the sum of £5 to be on good behaviour for 3 years after giving an undertaking not to pursue any similar practices during that period.   In 1946 Elam moved from being the Recorder at Poole to Exeter where he stayed until 1953.   Elam went on to become a circuit judge and from 1953 to 1976 he was Deputy Chairman of the Court of Quarterly Sessions in inner London.

Rupert Cross emigrated to New Zealand in the 1980's along with Worth and settled in Auckland.   He became a company director and he died in March 1996 aged 86 of cancer.   Stanley Worth still lives in New Zealand maintaining the same story that he told in 1944 and some might consider that he is continuing to carry out his duty as a Naval intelligence officer.

Charles Burrell continued to live with Violet Lonsdale-Brosman in Portsmouth and work as a labourer in the dockyards.   He died aged 59 years from a brain tumour, 5 years after the trial.

Bessie and William Lock lived to a ripe old age around the corner from The

Master's Temple, in Stubbington Avenue, Portsmouth, while their once 'tearaway' son, Launcelot, remarried and worked in the city as a respectable butcher. He died in 1980 aged 70 after suffering from hypertension.

Emma Jennings, became a widow in 1936 at the age of 29 years after only 2 years of marriage and remarried when in her 50's. She worked as the supervisor of the short hand typists for Portsmouth Authority Planning Department and died in 1987 aged 79 of cancer.

Arthur West OBE KMP became the first Chief Constable of the British Transport Police in 1958 and served for five years. He was also the Hon. Secretary of the Association for Chief Police Officers. He was always referred to in press releases as the policeman responsible for imprisoning Helen Duncan using the Witchcraft Act. It was his claim to notoriety, similar to if he had captured Bonny and Clyde!

Percy Worth MBE, Stanley's uncle, set up what he called the 'Ghost Squad' at Scotland Yard in May 1945.[13] It was a special undercover team intended to get amongst the criminals and gather information that will be handed to local divisions and the Flying squad who will make the arrests. Worth said none of the squad will give evidence in court. He told John Capstick whom he asked to head the squad, that as far as the criminal underworld was concerned the squad will have 'no more material existence than ghosts'. Setting up such a squad only months after the Helen Duncan trial raises the intriguing question where he may have got the idea. Worth left the Metropolitan Police in 1948 after 36 years service. He had become the Chief Constable for CID at Scotland Yard. He became the Chief of Greyhound Race Track Security Police. He died in December 1963 following a car accident.

Charles Loseby moved to Hong Kong in 1945 at the age of 64 and took silk. In later years he resettled in Guernsey and died aged 88 in 1970 leaving a daughter.

Denys Parsons went on to work as a film director and producer for Realist Films along with Max Anderson. He directed, produced or was technical consultant on a number of scientific films made between 1945 to the early 1950's. He then entered public relations becoming Information Manager of the National Research Development Corporation and later the Head of Press and Public Relations at the British Library. Throughout his career he wrote numerous humorous books, some of which included humorous extracts from newspapers and magazines. He also wrote 'What's Where In London' and guides of London. He continued his interest in psychic phenomena and became an active member of the SPR and a member of its Council, a year after the trial in 1945 until 1966. He was joint Honorary Secretary from 1948 for ten years. He was interested in radionics, ESP, PK and dowsing and he was a member of the British Branch of the Committee for the Scientific Investigation of Claims of the

Paranormal. He was a good friend of James Randi and securely resided within the sceptic's camp. He was also a flutist and pianist and became well known for devising a system for people without any musical ability to identify a tune that may be teasing their minds. His system identified the up, down or repeat sequence of notes in the melody up to the 16th note (or less) and it appeared in 'The Directory of Musical Tunes and Themes', which distinguished over 10,000 classical, popular and anthem themes. In 1980 during retirement he became a self-employed piano tuner. He died in July 1995 leaving a wife and a son. Since his death he has been described as an 'eclectic genius'.

Carl Bechhofer Roberts had one of his many books turned into the film 'Don Chicago' in 1945. He continued his writing but was killed in a car accident in the early hours of Thursday the 15th of December 1949 in which his estranged wife Peggy was injured. He was 55 years old. The car he was driving crashed into a street refuge near Euston Station. He left a married daughter.

Harry Price died in March 1948 of heart failure whilst sitting in his chair smoking his after-lunch pipe. Many psychic investigators and Spiritualists have continued to criticise much of his research, many accusing him of acting fraudulently.

John Paddy Carstairs became a screenwriter, film and stage director, painter and author of humorous novels. He worked in British commercial cinema for 30 years. He is well known for directing many Norman Wisdom comedies. He also successfully directed films for Frankie Howerd, Charlie Drake, Tommy Steele, Jimmy Edwards, Ronald Shiner and Bob Monkhouse. He directed an Ealing comedy with George Formby in 'Spare A Copper' and a series of thrillers. Later in life he concentrated on his painting and writing and died aged 60 in December 1970 after a period of ill health.

Brigadier Roy Firebrace CBE served in the armed forces for 37 years. He made a major contribution to the field of astrology and co-founded the Astrological Association and a quarterly review titled SPICA, which he published and edited from 1961 to 1974. He joined the SPR during the Helen Duncan trial and continued his interest in psychic phenomena including radionics and physical mediumship and published books on healing. He resigned his membership of the SPR in 1951 in response to Mollie Goldney's obituary of Adby Collins, which many people found objectionable. Firebrace found when he wanted to leave the country he had to use an alien's passport because being born in Canada he had no claim for British citizenship. He wrote to the Times about it. He had been an author, diplomat, soldier, interpreter, editor, statistician and astrologer. He died in November 1974 leaving a wife, son and daughter. His wife Esme died 2 months later.

These men and women were loving fathers, mothers, husbands and wives and loyal friends. The importance of the role Harry Price played in influencing the decision to prosecute and the actions of the officers involved in it, cannot be underestimated. Many of these men and women would have uncritically accepted Price's claims and the 'evidence' he presented purporting to show that Mrs. Duncan was a fraud. It was on the basis of his research that many officials probably based a sincere belief that Mrs. Duncan was a fraudster and who needed to be harshly dealt with. If Harry Price had acted reputably in the first place then it is questionable whether the events would have taken the course they did.

If life continues as Helen Duncan always asserted, then they must live with their actions and the mistakes made in this life, as we must all. I don't believe it is my position to judge them. There is always an opportunity to make up for the past. I am sure if they are in the spirit world they are best able to judge for themselves and to weigh up the consequences of their actions and accept their responsibility. Whatever someone's conduct and the reasons for it, most people agree that the truth needs to be told so we can move forward and the wrongs righted. That's part of the responsibilities we hold to each other. Let's hope if the messages I have received are correct and a film project is developed, that one day I might interview some of them and they can tell us exactly what occurred in 1944 and see what has happened to them in the meantime. As a film director endeavouring to 'film the spirits' via physical mediumship then I also need to establish a trusting relationship with potential participants, even if they may be currently residing in another dimension! I trust the reader will understand my responsibilities and position. Given the experience of many sitters and indeed those who attended Mrs. Duncan's séances and gave evidence at her trial, then this consideration may not seem as farfetched as one might think.

I needed to take stock of where this adventure was taking me. It has been discovered that an MI5 and intelligence officer attached to the War and Cabinet Office engaged in the specific area of concern related to Mrs. Duncan leaking secrets acted as prosecuting counsel. We have the major prosecution witness whose uncle was one of the most senior Scotland Yard officers and who is also a good friend of the Chief Constable who undertook the investigation and the policeman who undertook the raid with him, despite denying it at the time. The Chief Constable, the Head of Scottish Military Intelligence, a Judge who was junior prosecuting counsel and a former Judge in India Abdy Collins and a senior member of the Ministry of Home Security admit that Mrs. Duncan was prosecuted because she was a security risk and that the Navy instigated it. We have the stamp on this affair of a most senior Naval Intelligence Officer who was renowned for being involved with and devising many spectacular Naval Intelligence operations, Ian Fleming. The operation has many of his characteristic qualities and accords with his experience of covering a Stalin show trial in the 1930's. We have another leading prosecuting witness who is an ex Naval serviceman and who was responsible for bringing along most of the other prosecution witnesses to testify against Mrs. Duncan. The son of two of these prosecution witnesses, a petty criminal placed a bet two weeks before the raid describing what was going to occur and naming the Naval officer who initiated the prosecution. The Navy bring in three scriptwriters two of whom have social and family connections with the MI5 officer who joins the leading prosecution witness' Naval unit while the other is acclaimed for portraying stories in a realistic documentary way and who also has connections with other Special Branch officers in the same industry and the MOI. The Naval prosecution witness and his friend the policeman who accompanies him to the raid give testimony that is unsupported by any other person present and they place one of the prosecution witnesses who claimed to support their story, in a position she never occupied at the scene. Prosecution witnesses change their accounts, contradict themselves and each other in their witness, magistrates court statements and trial testimony. Witnesses' statements are fabricated for two leading prosecution witnesses whose statements have identical passages in several sections and a fabricated plan of the seating arrangements is submitted to the court. The DPP against all rules request the particular judge they wanted who also happened to be an ex Naval officer. The judge then systematically misrepresents the summing up of the defence witnesses and allows evidence outside the terms of the indictment to be admitted so that an earlier conviction can be admitted. Both the summing up and allowing the earlier conviction to be known ensures the jury convict the prisoners. Then the Appeal is heard by three Judges, one of who carried out an enquiry into leakages of information, another worked for Naval intelligence and the other who was familiar with the security issues associated with the case. Then another man who also has close family connections with the MI5 officer and who is a friend of the one of the Naval Special Branch officers brought in by the Navy publishes an article that supports the prosecution to coincide with the date of the appeal. This article is published in a journal belonging to a close friend of the person in NID most likely to have planned the operation. Then a fellow barrister, a former private secretary of an Attorney General and play write who also has theatrical links to Maude's family, brings out a book in which he misrepresents some important aspects of the trial in support of the prosecution.

In these circumstances most people would say that there is a case to answer and certainly Helen Duncan might not have been found guilty of conspiracy under the Witchcraft Act if the jury had been aware of these facts and the people involved brought to court for cross-examination. It seems to me that in these circumstances the Spiritualist claim that there was a government conspiracy against Helen Duncan has very strong support. Each necessary condition required to exercise a conspiracy has features consistent with one occurring.

Some campaigners raise more sinister possibilities noting the timing of the deaths of three policemen. The Portsmouth headlines next to those about the police raid on Mrs. Duncan reported the deaths of three senior retired

Portsmouth police officers. Ex Det. Insp. George Ford died on the day prior to the raid, Ex Deputy Chief Constable Charles Stanley died suddenly on the day of the raid and Ex. Supt. James Paice died the next day. There is no evidence to suggest any connection between the security operation in arresting Mrs. Duncan and the death's of any of these men, but such is the degree of suspicion surrounding this case that some supporters of Helen Duncan have raised the issue of this uncanny co-incidence.

By its very nature, the evidence presented relating to the way the conspiracy was carried out is suggestive rather than conclusive and by their very nature security services do not tend to publicise their work and when they do we are rightly suspicious about their reasons for doing so! The Security Services are necessary departments of state so we expect secrecy from them. The flaws in the prosecution case and links between many of the people involved on their side have been discovered and presented so it allows the reader to make up their own mind. It may be possible to investigate these matters further and seek clarification if others eventually wish to come forward or we can speak to Helen Duncan!

Throughout this whole affair the authorities had tended to ridicule and dismiss the claims of Spiritualist mediums and those who believed in their powers, yet their actions and response seem quite out of proportion to a case accusing someone of common fraud. They involved MI5, the judiciary, the police, the military, justices talk of special and grave circumstances, the DPP misrepresent the reasons for the trial being transferred to the Old Bailey to the Home Secretary who in turn passes on this flawed account to the Prime Minister. The members of the production involved in the eventual court room drama included a senior MI5 officer attached to the Cabinet Office and legend at the bar John Maude, one of England's most senior and respected judges, Sir Gerald Dodson, two future Oscar winners and documentary directors Max Anderson and Terry Bishop, an established writer who had had recent success with a mystery feature film Alan Hyman, with an executive producer and sponsor Ian Fleming, the Personal Assistant to the Head of Naval Intelligence, who was to become one of the nation's leading and successful authors and story teller.

Bringing all these talented men together, many of who have family connections and involving the highest offices of State strongly suggests that the intelligence services did not regard Helen Duncan as a common fraud. The actions that took place seem more consistent with a security service who took the 'source' of the information coming from this medium very seriously indeed, and so much so that in order to deal with it effectively, they had to discredit it. This was a tactic frequently considered by Military intelligence when dealing with enemy sources who were giving out information and who posed a threat to Allied plans and their deception programme. Discrediting Helen Duncan as the source may be equally viewed as good evidence that they took it seriously and that they may well have considered it to be authentic. An accurate perception may have been given by Brig. Firebrace, a senior officer in Military Intelligence in the War Office, who described that the intelligence services viewed her mediumship as 'splendid but dangerous'. The events fit such a description. If they had truly believed it had been done by a fraudulent means, as they assert, surely it would not have produced such a reaction from the major departments of state.

There was great concern over the amount of rumours and leakages of information occurring around the country. Soon after Maude had been given responsibility to set up a MI5 section to tackle rumours and leaks of information late in 1939, by February 1940 a major 'anti-gossip' campaign was announced after high level discussions in government. The campaign took many forms, such as the BBC broadcasting special programmes, there were public meetings and talks to servicemen, posters were put up, photographic exhibitions held, films made for cinema, slogans put on pottery. One of the biggest problems centred on places where the public gathered. Breweries were specially instructed to get their staff to implement measures in public houses to discourage gossip. Part of this campaign was also to ask established writers to publish articles pointing out the serious dangers posed by going to public gathering where careless talk might take place.

During 1940 the Daily Sketch published a series of articles referring to the dangers of information being leaked at seances. They ran the headlines 'That Spies Are Hearing Our Secrets'.. And This Is How. 'Ghost World Tapped by Nazis'. The story asserted that Nazi spies were going to seances attended by airman and sailors. At the seances these servicemen received information from dead colleagues and so ran the risk of unwittingly giving valuable information away to the enemy about our bases. The article stated that Naval and Military authorities were so concerned they were giving warnings to their men about the danger of 'careless talk' at seances and counter espionage services had proof that German spies had tried to gain admission and had obtained information. It went on to explain that the police had had to take action to deal with this problem. Certainly we know that the Magic Circle were working with the police around the country, tracking mediums and aiding them to bring about successful prosecutions.

The Psychic News newspaper ran story after story, week after week of identified servicemen communicating through to their relatives and friends eager to demonstrate their survival. Often after the seances the families of the men contacted the military authorities to inform them of the information and sought confirmation of the details of their death they had received. As Maude was in charge of this counter espionage section dealing with leaks, reference to it attracting the interest of the security services brings it to his desk. The interesting feature of this story was that they did not question the authenticity of the spirit communications. The evidence publicised by the Psychic Press and the stories of many recipients of such messages that were eventually shown to be accurate made it difficult to counter. Doing so would have given rise to protest and possibly numerous stories of such messages, appearing in the press, which was obviously not helpful.

The Daily Sketch followed this story with an article by Beverley Nichols the writer and a regular columnist, who claimed that spirit guides who came through Spiritualists were effectively working for Goebbels, and presumably with their mediums, by spreading propaganda. He asserted that some mediums in our midst were working for the Germans and they also gained valuable information from the relatives of fallen servicemen. It is interesting to note that during this period the film director John Paddy Carstairs stationed at HMS Excellent was making three films for the Ministry of Information about the dangers of 'careless talk' with Alan Hyman's cousin, the producer Michael Balcon. It is also an interesting co-incidence that Carstairs and Beverley Nichols had co-written a feature film together in 1932 titled 'Nine Till Six' and Nichols had worked in the War Office for a short time himself some years earlier.

Nichols's article[14] alerted readers to the dangers of servicemen going to seances and it was followed up by other similar stories. The Daily Sketch reported in May 1940 that the Nazi's had sent fake mediums to neutral countries such as Yugoslavia in order to 'manifest spirit guides' who predict catastrophe for the allies and all the countries that associate with them. It reported that arrests had been made in Yugoslavia, Greece and Holland. At the same time the Roman Catholic publication the Tablet also claimed that it had been discovered that the Nazi's were using mediums and Spiritualist Associations.

The message was clear. The authorities and presumably Maude in his 'B19' section, were worried about the dangers of the leakage of sensitive information occurring in seances across the country either emanating from the purported 'spirit world' or the serviceman who attended. Presumably fraudulent mediums had no secrets to disclose. An attempt to discredit the mediums and discourage people from attending was the aim of the message asserting that the mediums may well be German spies or their 'spirit guides' working for the Nazis, as Nichols argued.[15] It seems these rumours served their purpose because the Lock family recall that they were conscious in 1944 of the rumour that Helen Duncan was a German spy, prior to William, Bessie and their daughter Ena appearing as prosecution witnesses. The newspaper articles that appeared have also to be placed in the context of the serious concern of the authorities about 'careless talk' at the venues servicemen frequent, such a pubs, hotels, clubs and even when attending seances and Spiritualist churches.

The published reply from Estelle Roberts, one of Britain's leading mediums in the Daily Sketch cannot have eased Maude's problems and only confirmed his view that something needed to be done. Whilst pointing out the dead servicemen who communicated always sought to aid the nation and resist the Nazis, Estelle Roberts then attested to the accurate security information that had been communicated through her own guide named Red Cloud. She said on the 6th of April 1940 that Red Cloud had warned that Holland, Belgium, Luxembourg and France would be invaded by mid May. On the 29th of May he had also foretold that the majority of the British Expeditionary Force from Dunkirk would be brought back safely, over 24 hours before the news was received. In both cases her message had been correct. Estelle Roberts explained that Goebbels was not responsible for these facts being broadcast in advance and that indeed mediums and Spiritualism was banned in Germany. It is interesting that Brig. Firebrace of Military Intelligence knew Estelle Roberts and regarded her mediumship very highly.

What is easily overlooked in all the many messages coming from the prosecution, police and press that criticised Helen Duncan and that accused her of fraud, is that she provided accurate information that the nation's most secretive organisations were unaware. Britain and Germany both had intelligence departments with their nations most talented intelligent men and women, they sent highly trained spies and agents to acquire such information, yet a working class woman in trance disclosed top secret information that no one else knew at the time. In the case of the sinking of HMS Barham she disclosed information that was so sensitive that only a handful of the most senior security personnel knew and it was essential that the German's did get to hear of. Although HMS Hood and HMS Barham have been cited as the reasons for the trial, Helen Duncan throughout the war, like other mediums, brought through dead servicemen at each séance who gave details of their passing to grieving relatives. We can recall at the Portsmouth seances she brought back Freddie Nuttal the RAF pilot, reported missing over France, Wing Commander Mackie's nephew blown up in Singapore and other servicemen were referred to by other witnesses. On many occasions relatives immediately went and informed the military authorities. No wonder it was a problem the military could do without. It must be considered that if one were a security service who took seriously the possibility that physical mediums were indeed genuine, then their reaction would precisely match the one that took place in 1944.

Geraldine Cummins the distinguished automatic writing medium recalls that shortly after Helen Duncan's arrest, a letter she sent on the 29th of January 1944 to her researcher, Miss Gibbes detailing the death of a missing airman Flying Officer Ian MacLean was held up at the Censor's Office by London CID. It reached her researcher over two weeks late on the 23rd of February. The airman's death was not reported to his family until February 26th. A short time later her researcher, Miss Gibbes, received a visit from a woman claiming to be

Miss Cummins' Canadian cousin, who then proceeded to ask her an assortment of questions. It turned out that Miss Cummins had no such cousin. It may be no accident that the police were particularly sensitive to communications about missing officers being reported by distinguished mediums at a time that they were prosecuting Helen Duncan for doing precisely the same. Miss Cummins believed that the police may have done so because they were unsure about the source, knowing that she lived in Ireland they may have believed she got it from the German Dublin Legation. No further action was taken no doubt because unknown to the London police she was working as an agent for British Intelligence at the time. During the war she gave details of the deaths of several officers before the news had reached relatives. In one case her, information was communicated four months before the news was known.

One must also note that Brig. Firebrace the Deputy Director of Liaison for Military Intelligence and Lord Dowding were highly decorated and most respected men, given senior positions and they firmly believed that such communications were genuine. Might it be that the authorities were also fully aware that mediumship might be genuine and they were desperate not allow such a source of information to be exploited against them or used in a way that might scupper their plans. Certainly this possibility cannot be ruled out, as there were many highly distinguished scientists and military personnel whose judgement was trusted and who were at the heart of the state, and who believed such mediumship was a genuine faculty. What is interesting to observe is while the authorities were busy seeking to 'get Helen Duncan out of the way' for giving out accurate security information, Estelle Roberts and Geraldine Cummins had done the same. Moreover Geraldine Cummins, the automatic medium was thought of so highly by British Intelligence that she was working secretly with the security services during the war.

In April 1939 Geraldine Cummins produced a series of automatic writing scripts purportedly from a former German stockbroker, called the 'Financier' from the spirit world detailing Hilter's and Mussolini's thinking and plans and also details of the actual discussions that had taken place when Chamberlain visited Mussolini. It is inconceivable that these most startling and sensitive spirit communications about Hilter's plans did not reach British Intelligence. It is unknown if they 'officially' worked with Miss Cummins using this approach but this is suggested as it has been reported that between 1940-4 that she performed investigative psychic work 'undertaken for patriotic purposes'.[16] We also know that they recruited her and by the latter part of 1940 Miss Cummins had been trusted enough to be working as a fully blown agent for British Intelligence from her home in Ireland. It was probably essential that British Intelligence recruited her as having someone capable of revealing such secrets posed a security threat if at large, like Helen Duncan. Miss Cummins worked for the secret service for three and a half years under the code-name Kate, with this work ceasing around the time of D Day.

Michael Howard in his book 'The Occult Conspiracy' states that the Security Service used a medium codenamed 'Anne' to gain information about the enemy. After first being set a number of tasks to psychically investigate the actions of colleagues, which she passed to the astonishment of some sceptical Intelligence officers, she was used in a trance state to project her mind to Nazi High command's headquarters in Berlin. She then reported back the contents of top secret documents.

The evidence that exists gives support to the suggestion that the authorities did take the view that the information conveyed through many mediums was accurate and therefore possibly genuine communications, but they needed to deny it publicly. After the war Geraldine Cummins's friend Air Marshall Sir Victor Goddard a firm believer in mediumship and Spiritualism disclosed that even despite his unconventional beliefs he had been the Deputy Director of Intelligence at the Air Ministry. He claimed that his own psychic abilities had impressed those working with him, as did Miss Cummins'. It seems British Intelligence were not against entrusting their most senior positions to those who believe in mediumship or who practised it during and after the war.

This begs the question why they did not fully investigate the source of the leaks in the same way they would have done under normal circumstances. This would mean interviewing Mrs. Duncan and Albert, her guide about the leaks. If it was discovered that a creditable source of information could be accessed, as with Geraldine Cummins and agent 'Anne', then the question arises as to why they did not suggest some form of collaboration to assist the security services. It is likely that if the question was ever considered, Mrs. Duncan's reputation was such that she was not seen as a suitable person to be trusted with such a secret work on behalf of the nation.[17] Moreover the alternative option to reduce the threat she posed was more attractive. It was probably thought as less risky and simpler to 'get her out of the way' for a critical few months by charging her with fraud. This method also had the advantage of allowing the security services to deal with this risk posed on a wider and more longer term basis by discrediting the source and those who believed in it, while at the same time leaving them free to use it for their own purposes if they wanted.

Many an intelligent observer has noted that when a person's character gets discredited in public by the authorities, similar to the way Helen Duncan's was, it may be a good indication that this person is becoming a threat. Discrediting a person's character in this way is relatively rare and when it occurs it is because they are getting very near to the truth and giving out information that the authorities wish to conceal. Otherwise the authorities just don't go to all this trouble. Loseby made this observation about his client at the time.

When observing the worries the authorities had about leaks of sensitive information occurring in seances across the country in 1940 and top secret information being leaked a year later by Helen Duncan then one should not ignore that it was quite remarkable feat in itself. In these instances it was spectacularly demonstrated that Helen Duncan's mediumship was highly accurate. Brig Firebrace and the mother of the sailor who appeared from HMS Barham were certainly not regarded as credulous sitters and her message came to the attention of the most senior people in government. No one has seriously suggested that a group of fraudulent individuals posing as mediums and their accomplices operated to leak top-secret information, that even MI5 and Military Intelligence is unaware. Where would they get it? Frauds by definition do not like attracting attention to themselves and especially from investigating services like MI5 or the police.

Looking at the pattern of security service and police activity against mediums during the war may give us a clue as to the reason why Helen Duncan was convicted. In 1940 the security services were concerned about the risk of leakages of information occurring at seances and Spiritualist meetings. In 1941 two serious leaks of security information occur from seances after the sinking of two Naval war ships. It would seem highly probable that the security services implemented measures after the sinking of the Hood in 1941, and decided on a concerted plan by early 1942 to deal with this serious security risk.

We know that the Magic Circle had organised themselves into local groups to track mediums, in association with Scotland Yard, and they managed to get convictions in Cardiff and Liverpool. In the context of the expressed concern of the authorities it may not be accidental that the convictions occurred at important ports, where the Navy was particularly sensitive, the security was tight and fear of foreign agents high.

The risk posed by foreign agents at ports was dramatically demonstrated in Southsea, Portsmouth in 1940. Two members of the British Union of Fascists William Swift and Archibald Watts were approaching servicemen and trying to recruit sympathisers into local defence volunteers groups so they could participate if a German invasion took place. They were working for a German national Mrs. Marie Ingram who was an ardent Nazi, married to a RAF officer. She also worked for a high ranking Naval officer. After a three day hearing Watts was acquitted, Swift was jailed for 14 years and Mrs. Ingram for 10 years for acts calculated to assist an enemy. One can understand the fears expressed by the security services if an agent such as Mrs. Ingram had heard the local news about HMS Barham coming from seances operating from the local Spiritualist church and she had decided to investigate. Against this type of security risk, Portsmouth was a most important Naval port and it was to become one of the most security sensitive areas of Britain in the run up to D Day.

The events leading to Helen's arrest seem to match the developments that were taking place with regard to Operation Overlord and may account for the timing of the action against her. In August 1943 the combined Chiefs of Staff approved the general tactical plan for the invasion of Northwest Europe by allied forces. From March 1940 the Inter-Services Security Board, based at the War Office oversaw all major security issues. Senior figures in the nation's armed forces, security services and government departments met regularly, including MI5 and MI6 officials. They co-ordinated all special measures for preventing leakage's of information. Rumours and leakages of information that had been reported around the country were regularly submitted to each meeting and action taken or referred to the relevant security sections to be dealt with. Inspection of the minutes of meetings shows that they were very concerned with preventing leaks. They were also not adverse to using rumour as a weapon, spreading their own rumours and using 'cover stories' to mask the true purpose of their security activities. The whole gamut of cloak and dagger activity was used to make the nation's operations as secure as possible, as one would expect.

Immediately, approval for the tactical plan for the invasion was given the Inter-Services Security Board (ISSB) set up a subcommittee. This included representatives from all the major security organisations of state charged with co-ordinating the security measures necessary in the run up to D Day on June the 5th (it later changed to the 6th). The job of Major Boddington of MI5 and attached to the War Office and a senior member on the ISSB was to set up and oversee Coastal Belt Security Committees. He would be the representative from the ISSB on these Committees.

The south coast was split into different regions and Portsmouth was part of the Central Region. MI5 officers Major Boddington and Major Phipps the RSLO for Region 6 were on the committee along with Naval Security Officers, Paymaster N. E. Summers RN representing the Commander in Chief of Portsmouth, Captain L. A Brook Security Control Office, Portsmouth as well as other senior officials and the Chief Constables of Portsmouth Arthur West, Hampshire Lt. Col. Lemon based at Winchester, and the Chief Constable of Southampton. All the most powerful and senior security officials of the civil and military authorities in this region were brought together to consider all manner of security issues that might put Operation Overlord at risk. It will be recalled that Major John Phipps was Maude's close friend and fellow barrister, having also been his assistant in section 'B19' when it was set up. He is now the Security Service Liaison Officer responsible for the region in which Portsmouth is located, and a member of the committee deciding upon the security measures to be put in place prior to the run up to D Day. It is interesting to observe that soon after this Coastal Security Belt Committee was set up in early November 1943, Lt. Worth went to 'work' at Mr. & Mrs. Homer's Spiritualist Temple at 301 Copnor Road, in preparation for the arrest of Helen Duncan.

Under Operation Overlord, Portsmouth was to become one of the most security sensitive parts of the country. Portsmouth was to be a major embarkation point for troops leaving for the Normandy beaches. Thousands of allied troops were about to be brought to the surrounding area to be housed in specially secluded camps in preparation for D Day, and their presence needed to be kept secret from the Germans. Restrictive areas were designated and there were concerns about the interaction of local residents and military personnel. No doubt the Security Committee considered the security problems posed by seances and the visit of leading Spiritualist mediums. It was almost certainly felt that they could not risk sensitive news being leaked out and spreading to Portsmouth families and incoming troops who were preparing for D Day or adverse developments communicated that might lead to a repetition of the problems of the HMS Barham sinking. The security services would also have been aware that these types of problems were likely. Even Estelle Roberts' guide had broadcast news of developments when the evacuation took place at Dunkirk, prior to the news becoming known and released publicly.

The concern of the security services towards mediums working in highly sensitive military areas seems to have been confirmed by the action of the police in Redhill, Surrey a short while later. In May 1945 at a meeting of Chief Constables, Major Geoffrey Nicholson, the Chief Constable of Surrey referred to the difficulties he had experienced in a recent attempt to prosecute a fraudulent medium. Malcolm Gaskell in his book 'Hellish Nell' mistakenly identifies Major Nicholson as an MI5 officer. Gaskell misquotes the document referring to the meeting when Major Nicholson called for greater co-ordination between the DPP and the police, due to the 'difficulties he had experienced in the recent prosecution in this area' (sic). Gaskill mistakenly claimed that Major Nicholson was referring to the Helen Duncan case but Major Nicholson is actually reported as saying 'in his area'.

He was the Chief Constable of Surrey and his Superintendent in Redhill, Superintendent Beecher had investigated a complaint made against Mrs. Emily Johnson who ran the Redhill Christian Spiritualist Church. Two officers had gone to Mrs. Johnson's home and warned her that she was at risk of being prosecuted under the Witchcraft Act for personally carrying out trance and clairvoyance in the church and bringing other mediums to the church. They threatened to close down the church. Frightened, Mrs. Johnson agreed that she would discontinue mediumship demonstrations at the church and she put this undertaking in writing, because the officer said that if she refused she would be prosecuted.

Like Portsmouth, Redhill represented a highly important military area. Redhill housed the Headquarters of No. 2 Tactical Air Force Group and the Canadian and Polish squadrons and prior to D Day over 200 fighter aircraft were based there to support the invasion forces. Many hundreds of airmen of different nationalities had come from around the country to Redhill, as it became one of the principal aerodromes used by the RAF in the fight against the Germans in 1944 and 1945. RAF Groups No. 2, No. 83, No. 84 and No. 85 flew from there and there work was most secret.

No doubt Emily Johnson's messages and those of her guest mediums to the pilots and the local population that visited created some cause for concern over security issues, if only on the morale of the pilots who came to find out about the fate of their friends. It is understandable that the authorities did not want to risk a repeat of what had occurred in Portsmouth, if information needed to be tightly controlled about the course of the air campaign. Getting Mrs. Johnson to agree to stop giving out messages and close down her Spiritualist church effectively dealt with this problem.

The Spiritualists, unaware of the possible security issues involved in demonstrations of mediumship in an area of such military importance, made loud protestations against this police action, through the Spiritualist National Union (SNU). It was also personally embarrassing for Chief Constable Major Geoffrey Nicholson because his wife also happened to be a trance medium with a spirit guide called Torchbearer. He and his wife had happily socialised with Spiritualists a short time before this police action took place. As part of their attack on the police action the SNU publicly called for Major Nicholson to prosecute himself and his wife for contravening the Witchcraft Act at home! Like the Helen Duncan case the SNU pointed out that the police action had also contravened the Home Secretary's earlier assurance.

The SNU arranged a defiant protest meeting in Redhill and invited the press and the police. Mediums also took part, in order to openly defy the police. Hannen Swaffer and Dr. Sidney Peters, MP for Huntingdon took part and the police kept away. No doubt Major Nicholson's plea for future police actions against Spiritualist mediums to be centrally dealt with by the DPP would avoid future embarrassment for himself and his force. Instead of seeing the affair as a matter of wanting to persecute Spiritualists, he may have well taken the view of his Special Branch officers that an uncontrolled stream of information that often proved to be correct in a highly sensitive military area needed to be controlled.

Major Nicholson had top class military and police credentials and he would have liased closely with the military authorities in his area. Incidentally he also had good contacts in Hampshire having being the Deputy Chief Constable of Hampshire from 1922 to 1930 before taking the position at Surrey. He may have known Arthur West as West had joined the Hampshire force just before Major Nicholson became Chief Constable. He was also married to the daughter of Major Andrew Warde the former Chief Constable of Hampshire. He had been a Major in the Hampshire Regiment in the Great War. He had contacts in the Navy having been educated on HMS Conway and at the Imperial Service College and RMC Sandhurst. Major Nicholson was also a devout Roman

Catholic. The actions in Redhill occurred at a time when he became a serving brother of the Sovereign Military and Hospitaller Roman Catholic Order of St. John of Jerusalem of Rhodes and Malta. The Crusaders had founded the order in the 11th Century.

The action that drove the Admiralty to insist that Helen be convicted in 1944, may have been influenced by some further considerations. The leakage of the news of HMS Barham in November 1941 had damaged the relationship between the people of Portsmouth and the Navy. Portsmouth was a historic major Naval port with large Naval dockyards yet many families of the sailors who lost their lives on HMS Barham believed that the Naval authorities misled them regarding the news of the sinking. The news coming from Helen Duncan's seance had proved to be true, despite the Navy's denials at the time. This had created embarrassment and no doubt some resentment in Naval circles. The conviction of Helen Duncan after her seances in Portsmouth in 1944 allowed the Navy to re-establish their relationship and their trust with the families of their servicemen. One can understand that it was helpful for the Navy to discredit the source that had led to such discontent in the town. They had demonstrated Mrs. Duncan to be a fraud, and 'shown' that she was responsible for exploiting the grieving relatives of deceased servicemen. One would have thought that if the security services had wanted to get Mrs. Duncan quietly out of the way then Chief Constable West would not have mentioned her leaking the news of the sinking of a Naval ship at the trial. West's public announcement about this security matter probably sought to justify a heavy sentence but it was also a message to the people back in Portsmouth. The source of the information that had caused so much distrust and concern in 1941 had come from a convicted fraud, humbug and pest, who was now publicly humiliated and discredited.

It is evident that the three most senior men in Portsmouth at the time had a role in her conviction. Chief Constable West as outlined above and ex Marine and Lord Mayor Sir Denis Daley a staunch Roman Catholic was the chairman of the Justices at both pre-trial hearings that led to her case being transferred to the Old Bailey. Town Clerk Sir Frederick Sparks prepared the initial legal action against her. He was also the controller of the ARP in Portsmouth, for whom Kitty Jennings, who came forward at a late stage as a prosecution witness, had been promoted to Supervisor of his ARP control room.

What occurred in 1944 was brutal and an abuse of our legal system but it was at a time of war and those actively involved probably acted in the way they did in order to protect their nation and the lives of allied servicemen and women. If a wrong occurred then that it should be righted especially as the war was fought for the ideals of justice not persecution and repression. We are now over 60 years after the event and the circumstances that led to it no longer prevail unless it represented an attempt to suppress Spiritualism and Spiritualist mediums. The damage needs to be repaired.

Having researched the subject there may be support for the views of some campaigners who suspect that the spin Loseby identified around the time of the trial may be still operating. Several writers refer to using particular sources and archives in the course of their research. Having used the same sources I am surprised that in places they have omitted what I consider to be relevant evidence and presented a picture that apparently obscures the historical reality. Let us take the example of the case of William Lock's son Launcelot, referred to in at the time as John Lock, placing a bet with Mr. Spencer while they worked together at Morris Motors in Cowley on the 3rd of January 1944. You will recall that Lock described the forthcoming police action against Mrs. Duncan and actually named Worth as the person working at the Spiritualist church to bring it about.

Malcolm Gaskell in his book 'Hellish Nell' used the SPR Archive at Cambridge University and when describing the above event questioned whether it had ever actually occurred. He presents it as an 'astonishing claim' made by the Wilson's (Percy, Richard and Geoffrey Wilson), but asserts that its truth was impossible to establish.

What is ignored is that Loseby, the defence counsel himself stated the same in his notes housed at the archive and he gave the personal details and addresses of those involved with the bet. Loseby also referred to this bet being made on the 3rd of January at the trial itself. This gives the account much greater creditability as defence counsel himself refers to it. Also in the archive is a letter written to Donald West shortly after the trial by Richard Wilson, a member of the defence team, outlining the affair in which he states that he actually met Mr. Spencer and took a signed statement from him confirming these details.

Confusion is added and this potentially important piece of evidence is undermined further when Gaskill adds that in November 1958 Percy Wilson repeated this account at the College of Psychic Science conference in Brighton but now stated that Spencer was Worth's nephew! The reader is informed that in the SPR archive is a document with notes taken by Mollie Goldney MBE of Percy Wilson's paper given at the conference, but these notes show that Percy Wilson said no such thing.

Goldney's note 2) states that Wilson asserted that the young man, who placed the bet with Mr. Spencer, was the nephew of the principal prosecution witness, not Mr. Spencer. Furthermore as Percy Wilson did not give the name of the prosecution witness, it was doubly confusing and erroneous to state that the relative in question was known to be Worth.

Given the circumstances it is reasonable to suggest that Wilson believed the young man who made the bet, Launcelot Lock referred to as John Lock, was the nephew of a principal prosecution witness. Percy Wilson had probably failed to discover any son of William Lock named John or he had forgotten his name and assumed he must be a nephew. But young Lock was the son of prosecution witness William Lock and not a nephew, as Percy's son Richard's letter to Donald West outlining his research undertaken for the defence team and Loseby, at the trial, specifically referred to their father-son relationship.

As Percy Wilson did not refer to the young man's name in his speech theoretically his relative may have been Lock, Worth, Burrell or Cross or he may have made a simple slip during his speech over their relationship or Mollie Goldney made a note taking error. As the prosecution witness's name isn't given it could be any of the leading male prosecution witnesses. Indeed just to confuse matters further, Launcelot Lock had a brother named Spencer Lock!

Contrary to Gaskill's assertion there was never any suggestion in Mollie Goldney's notes that Percy Wilson said Mr. Spencer was Worth's nephew. The failure to refer accurately to the evidence contained in these documents gives a distorted account of this important event. It also serves to ridicule and undermine those that sought to defend Mrs. Duncan and the source of this evidence, that if true provides strong evidence in support of the suggestion that there was a government conspiracy to convict her as Chief Constable West later suggested in 1979. It also allows another unfounded rumour, common in this case, to circulate, which justifiably fuels campaigners fears that spin may still be operating.

Changes to this account do not end here. Richard Wilson stated at the time in his letter to Donald West that the event took place as he described at the Cowley motor factory two weeks before the arrest and which Loseby and his father Percy Wilson confirmed. He has more recently stated that this all occurred in a pub in Portsmouth six months before the arrest, in the summer of 1943. He stated in a Channel 4 documentary that two men made a bet and one man was named Spencer.

This account varies considerably from the one he gave at the time and like Gaskill's it diverts the attention away from the Oxford evidence that strongly points to a leak occurring about the conspiracy. Ironically Gaskill castes grave doubt on the Wilson's claim about Oxford, and then Richard Wilson claim's it was Portsmouth! It seems unusual for the person who lived in Oxford at the time and who acting for the defence team took a detailed statement from Mr. Spencer in Oxford should later say the event took place in Portsmouth six months earlier. One may have thought that given the degree of personal involvement by Richard and his brother Geoffrey, that the circumstances may have been more accurately recalled.

Other inconsistencies worthy of comment are not only found for those using archive material but also with archives themselves. There are a set of 13 photographs produced by Esson Maule in 1933 that are housed in the Harry Price Collection at London University and catalogued under the title 'Exposing Helen Duncan'. Esson Maule instigated the Edinburgh prosecution against Mrs. Duncan in January 1933 and the photographs depict items and the reconstruction of scenes relating to the conviction for fraud. One will recall that when this conviction came to light in the 1944 Old Bailey trial, Mrs. Duncan's fate was sealed.

One photograph in the set shows the undervest that Mrs. Duncan wore that she was accused of using to masquerade as the spirit of Peggy. This photograph is frequently published in books and articles about Mrs. Duncan purporting to show the way she fraudulently produced her forms.

I asked to use two other photographs from the same set for this book. One showed the same 'undervest' next to a chair, to illustrate the actual size of the garment and the other a photo recreating the appearance of an adult form seen by Miss Maule and produced by Mrs. Duncan at the seance. The latter photograph was considered important because it showed a tall figure wrapped in many feet of white material. This photograph contradicts the evidence given by Miss Maule and the other prosecution witnesses. They had stated that the only white material Mrs. Duncan possessed that evening was a short 10" long undervest that she was wearing. This small undervest could not possibly have produced the effect shown in Miss Maule's reconstruction. When my request was made I pointed out that the collection had allowed Malcolm Gaskill the use of a photograph from the same set of photos in his book. The Archivist replied that he was not allowed to copy photographs where the photographer was unknown or if the photographer was someone other than Harry Price himself. He said that he did not wish to use Dr. Gaskill's book as a precedent as the copyright law had changed since his book was published.

I asked him to reconsider his decision when I had found further instances where the collection had allowed additional photographs of the undervest and seals from the same set to be published more recently on the internet. Naturally if Esson Maule's photographs were not going to be allowed to be published (or indeed any other photo taken by an unknown photographer) this applied equally to the frequently published 'undervest' photograph and other photos in this set.

After receiving a reply a month later that refused use of the reconstruction photograph I discovered from a revised catalogue that the photographs relating only to the 'undervest' were identified as being separate from those showing Miss Maule's reconstructions, dating them as being taken in May 1933 and not January as Miss Maule's other photographs. This allowed publication of the undervest photos and similar ones but not Miss Maule's reconstructions. The archivist asserted that these particular photos were taken at a different time and it was believed that Harry Price held copyright. This position allowed the collection to continue to allow publication of the evidence that supported the view that Mrs. Duncan had been 'exposed' as acting fraudulently for a further twelve years, whilst denying publication of the evidence that counters that view for the same length of time. The description in the catalogue misrepresented the origin of the photos and contradicts the evidence that the photographs themselves show.

Each photograph in the set has a description of it in Miss Maule's own handwriting in pencil on the back. In some instances she has even signed it with her initials. Furthermore a photograph of the familiar 'undervest' pinned against a velt background has a black carved wooden chair next to it that is also shown in other reconstruction photos. These facts show that these photos were taken at Miss Maule's home in Edinburgh on the same occasion in January 1933 as she prepared her case and that the undervest was pinned up by her and not by Harry Price at some later occasion to be photographed. The date given by the archive of May 11th 1933 for these photos refers only to the date of the decision of the court rather the date these photos were taken, which would have been much earlier. Esson Maule's own handwriting on each photo seems to seal the point.

When we get to a position where an archive at a leading University erroneously classifies important photographs that may throw light upon the authenticity of Mrs. Duncan's mediumship and the soundness of a criminal conviction, we can understand that something unusual surrounds this subject. Harry Price and Esson Maule had repeatedly publicly accused Mrs. Duncan of being a fraud yet all the while they held evidence that if it were produced at the time in 1933, it would have caste grave doubt about Miss Maule's testimony and the prosecution case against Mrs. Duncan. I pointed out the importance of the photo in terms of the case and was firmly informed that the photo I wanted would not be permitted to be copied because 'the photographer was unknown' and this would be illegal and nor would copies be allowed for use in fair dealing for even non-commercial research or private study.

I then checked the legal position and found that not knowing the photographer doesn't prevent publication at all. Indeed such a circumstance is one of the few exceptions to copyright infringement. Copyright of such a photograph extends for 70 years from the date it was taken. As it was taken in 1933 and the photographer was unknown, the photographs in question were all out of copyright and could be used. The accepted practice adopted by archives and libraries across the country of allowing photographs to be copied in these circumstances had not been applied here.

These types of mistakes can only serve to discourage researchers from entering the field and damage the development of this research area. It also puts researchers on notice that caution is required when entering this field, especially if one finds oneself looking at the evidence of those who gained a reputation by 'exposing' others. When the origin of evidence is presented in such a way that it is used to favour the research and promotion of a particular viewpoint compared to another then we can understand why many consider that the attitudes of the past still influence this research area in an unhelpful way. No doubt this is due to the lack of new research being conducted. Eventually permission was gained to use the photograph but only after some considerable delay and effort.

Some errors found in the literature point the reader in the wrong direction. Gaskill describes Roy Firebrace as a Brigadier in Royal Artillery and that later in the war he became Military Attaché to Riga and Moscow.   Firebrace in fact became a Brigadier while serving in Military Intelligence and after the leaking by Mrs. Duncan of the sinking of HMS Hood and HMS Barham he was posted to London to eventually become Deputy Director of Liaison and Munitions in Military Intelligence at the War Office, where Maude was also attached. This was one of the most senior positions in the Military Intelligence and so his admission that he was involved with the police in seeking ways to curtail Mrs. Duncan's activities may have some real significance. Contrary to Gaskill's claim that Firebrace was Military Attaché to Riga and Moscow later in the war, in fact he remained in Military Intelligence throughout the war and he had served as a Military Attaché in Riga between 1931 and 1935 and in Moscow at the beginning of the war in 1939. The Major Nicholson episode has been referred to.

These may be examples of the type of error that is made in the course of historical research but a distinguished historian made them who believed Helen Duncan was a fraud and they give a misleading impression. I'm not a historian but it is worthy of note when evidence is not presented accurately. It may well be a case of views 'being governed by previous bias' as Donald West concluded about the trial, but such errors may have historical significance when one is addressing the work of the security service who by their own admission will use every means to deceive and misinform in order to protect their secrets.

It is unrealistic to assume that we will ever get to the bottom of or reveal the full nature of any conspiracy by the security services using conventional research or unless the security services release their files. The conclusion also cannot be avoided that the fascination the case has in the public imagination is greatly enhanced by elements of the fictional story that was written using the talents of leading authors and scriptwriters engaged by Naval Intelligence and intertwined with the real life events occurring at the Old Bailey. In this way the story has all the elements of a thrilling mystery drama better suited for the cinema or stage play. These writers 'dramatic' success ironically works against the wishes of the security services, because the case just won't lie down and be forgotten. People seem to want an encore or a revival!

Having researched the subject in the same way I would have done a documentary film and despite my efforts to explore the central question of whether there was a conspiracy, I have repeatedly found myself asking the deeper question. What does it matter if there was a conspiracy and we discover its nature? A posthumous pardon or successful appeal may be awarded which will be important for Helen's Duncan's family, friends and many Spiritualists, but if the current situation remains as it is, then nothing has really been achieved, because physical mediums haven't adequately addressed and built on the legacy left by her. Her legacy is the courage of her repeated attempts to openly and publicly demonstrate through her mediumship that there was no death and that those we love still exist and wish to help us. Her mediumship tried to make this spiritual life part of our reality that was open to be questioned and tested rather than remain a belief or an act of blind faith. For this she was persecuted and discredited. Even if a posthumous pardon or a successful appeal of the conviction is achieved it will still leave the current unsatisfactory situation. Donald West wrote in 1946 that physical phenomena is in an 'atmosphere of perpetual darkness and emotional stress' and the same is true today almost 60 years later.

A true memorial to Helen Duncan would be for other physical mediums to develop and follow her example, address the spiritual challenge that faces them and go the extra mile and demonstrate the truth to the public as she attempted to do throughout her life. Technology has developed greatly and we are a lot wiser than when she made her attempts and hopefully we are able to learn the lessons of her struggle. It seems to me that if my personal experiences of adopting a working method of seeking to communicate with the 'spirits' involved in this project were genuine then the purported 'spirit world' certainly want it done on their terms. Is it any wonder given the shambles of what occurred when they allowed Harry Price and the London Spiritualist Alliance to conduct the investigations? It is possible now for mediums and trusted professionals to set the parameters and define the nature of the inquiry.

It should be recognised that we are unlikely to ever know the full extent of any conspiracy against Helen Duncan and Spiritualism unless mediums do it themselves. Discovering the extent of any conspiracy isn't the real point of the challenge or the story, if Helen is alive today. The current situation only reflects and repeats the same problems of the past hundred years for mediums and genuine investigators and it is stultifying and destructive. If there was a conspiracy against Helen then the conspirators have been successful.

Before Helen's conviction newspaper headlines regularly referred to the experiences of seances because it was considered important and in the public interest. After her conviction experiences of the séance room were no longer considered newsworthy. Although Spiritualists concentrated their attention on attaining their religious freedom by campaigning to get the Witchcraft Act and section 4 of the Vagrancy Act repealed and replaced by the Fraudulent Mediums Act in June 1951, a significant change had occurred. The decline of Spiritualism cannot be accounted for by Helen's fate at the trial but it was a critical turning point. The State had challenged one of Spiritualism's most outstanding mediums and it had won. Spiritualist organisations have gradually stopped trying to engage in a public debate in the way they once did. Physical mediums from the time of Mrs. Duncan's conviction have become rightly weary and many continue to feel intimidated to publicly demonstrate the authenticity of their phenomena. It was and is a minefield out there for the naive. Just as 60 years ago all we have to rely on are the accounts of witnesses with all the problems of accuracy, reliability and bias attached to them. This no doubt will be seen to apply to this book as any other on this subject.

Those who publicly ridicule and belittle mediums still undermine and set the agenda. They create a climate of mistrust. Possibly this is their intention. Just like documentary directors who show up their subjects in their films, it makes it extremely difficult for serious investigators to work in the field and gain the trust necessary to undertake important and necessary research.   Such conduct reflects more upon these professionals and how they used their position than the subjects who trusted them. Donald West recognised in 1946 that if physical mediumship is vindicated then those doubting 'Thomas's will gain a reputation akin to that of the Spanish Inquisitors'. At the moment the inquisitors are still in town and they effectively control the agenda. They have exercised their power most effectively because they have successfully created an inhibition in the minds of the mediums, so the mediums inhibit themselves and they mistakenly feel relatively powerless.

The ball however is in the medium's court and the power is with them because they can move the situation on and completely transform it. Only they can demonstrate the truth of physical phenomena and silence the doubters and so truly vindicate Helen Duncan and the many other mediums who suffered like her in the past and surely will do in the future unless they do something. Whether they do so is up to the individual medium.   The possibility of demonstrating the reality of spirit phenomena to mankind is literally in their hands and in doing so it opens up the whole new field of inquiry. That is their power and potential, which they can freely exercise. If done thoughtfully and carefully it should be an enriching adventure and achieve a great deal of good. If the invitation comes then the medium will have to decide for him or herself whether they accept it. I adopted an unconventional working method for investigating spirit phenomena as a film director and scientist, that I assume most mediums already adopt, so I presume they are more likely to receive such a communication.

If Helen Duncan was a genuine medium then it must be recognised that the damage done by the conspirators relates to a greater truth that was denied during that trial that overrides all others. It is the truth about ourselves as human beings and our spiritual lives. Unknown to those involved in the conspiracy at the time, their actions may have acted to deny opportunities for many millions of people in the spirit world, who are separated from their loved ones and so it cannot go unrectified. If this is the case then it is reasonable to assume that these men and women will now be aware of the spiritual consequences of their actions and may wish to help the project, especially as they must now be in a spiritual form.

Most people would agree that the security services have no place in interfering with providence. They have no place in trying to interfere with man's attempt to develop their link with a loving God, be it through exploring spirit phenomena or by other methods. Certainly unjustly attacking anyone on a genuine spiritual quest or a genuine medium is by implication also effectively attacking the spiritual realms who wish to use them. It should be remembered that a purported 'spirit' offered me this 'commission', so this research was instigated from those realms or the medium's imagination. Subsequent events appear to indicate that it may have been from the former.

It should be remembered that Helen Duncan always stated that she worked in the name of God and asked for prayers to be said before each demonstration. It is for these reasons that I am intrigued to know if James McQuarrie's mediumship was accurate when those who have identified themselves as the White Brotherhood presented this film project and asked me to undertake it. The discovery of the truth in this instance is a scientific, spiritual and philosophical adventure that I have always been personally keen to take, so I offer to openly share the journey with those who are interested to see where it takes us. The truth is what everyone is interested in.

I am confident that if Helen Duncan is alive today then she and the purported spirit world she sought to prove will wish to demonstrate the truth. Given the opportunity that has arisen from this dark episode that victimised and humiliated her and cut short her life, then let's hope the truth brings us understanding and knowledge and that it may heal the past. We all await the opportunity so let us together use our critical but open minds to see where the truth takes us. I for one want to know what happened to Helen Duncan and what has been planned as part of this project. I also have many other more questions that naturally arise, if and when spirits of people present themselves through physical mediumship and who have had experiences that possibly await us all in time. There is so much to discover.

I can only personally conclude from all the communications and experiences I have had, that one needs to take seriously the possibility that the so called 'spirit world' want to move the existing situation on and work with mediums under their guidance, in order that a body of evidence be presented. It seems however that the process by which it is carried out is just as important. A new agenda and working method can be established and from the experiences of Helen Duncan and other mediums it seems clear it is best done in collaboration between those asked to participate but necessarily under the authority of those whose project it ultimately must be. In the past their mediums failed to heed their advice and warnings and some scientists have not conducted themselves appropriately, to the detriment of science and this field. In an endeavour to achieve some degree of success I am happy to continue my working method to see where it takes us. As a filmmaker I am freer to adopt such an approach, unlike many scientists who have their positions to consider, but it should be remembered that the value of my approach will be judged by results, so we will have to wait and see.

It seems clear to me that any research project of this nature needs to consider the spiritual dimension of the work. If it is truly commissioned for the highest purpose, then it needs to be carried out for genuine spiritual reasons. I believe this represents a positive vision for the future and one that will necessarily involve others invited to undertake the research and spiritual challenge involved. Hopefully we will soon be able to hear what Helen herself has to say about her experiences of the trial and what her plans are when she can reliably communicate independently from any influence from the mind of the chosen medium. I look forward to presenting further evidence so the reader can judge for themselves the validity of this approach and the recordings I hope to make. I await the time, when the medium Helen invited to participate in this project is fully prepared for this to take place or if other mediums are asked to help, to collaborate with them. Hopefully the mediums who accept this challenge will receive the support needed, so this will start an important process of investigation and discovery that has been needed for many years. Hopefully we will see what the people involved in the trial have to say for themselves when an opportunity exists for them to do so, so we can all move forward and find out exactly what is involved when forms appear, as a genuine physical medium gets to work.

My exploration of the Helen Duncan case took another unexpected twist when I tried to track down the identity of the man in the psychic portrait that had been drawn by Tony Katz. You will recall that the accompanying message I received referred to 'Portsmouth' and 'Albert'. I wondered long and hard about who it might be and considered whether it represented part of my methodological connection with the purported 'spirit world'. If it did, I suspected the portrait might be of Rupert Cross, the policeman who jumped on the figure appearing in front of the cabinet and gave evidence against Mrs. Duncan 1944.

In order to test my hunch I took the portrait to Portsmouth and showed it to those surviving members of Mr. Cross's freemason's lodge. After spending some considerable time talking to each of these elderly gentlemen what I found surprising was that not one lodge member denied it was him, but by the same token not one confirmed it was. Surely I thought they would know whether this portrait looked like Mr. Cross or not. They looked at it hard, said nothing and passed me on to a colleague. Being freemasons I knew they had a code of secrecy, so it seemed to me that their noncommittal might be viewed positively. As I travelled from one to another I thought that if it had not been Mr. Cross then surely they would have said so, as this would not breach their code and there was no further purpose for me to bother them. Instead, each one sent me off across Portsmouth to see yet another member of the Masonic Lodge who knew Rupert. I spent a day being sent backwards and forwards across Portsmouth introducing myself and showing the portrait to a stream of elderly gentlemen, with each one in turn declining to neither confirm nor deny whether it was he.

They did inform me that Mr. Cross had emigrated to New Zealand and that he was dead. On my return to London I checked old New Zealand telephone directories and found his former address in Auckland. Later I applied for his death certificate and learned that he had died about 9 months before Tony Katz had produced the psychic portrait for me. I needed to contact people in New Zealand who knew him so that the portrait might be independently verified. If it was truly Rupert Cross then this seemed good evidence that some of those involved in the conspiracy truly wanted to assist me from the other side of life!

Knowing that Mr. Cross had resettled in New Zealand and having tracked down his last address, my friend Peter Grant, a successful New Zealand photographer working in London put me in contact with an old friend back home who worked in the media. I faxed through a copy of the psychic portrait to Alastair Gaudin, a researcher who is based in Auckland. Alastair went to Mr. Cross's last address and met his neighbour Muriel Osborne and someone who had known him for a good time Lois Pearce. Muriel had been his long time neighbour and Mr. Cross had often visited her at the end of each day. Lois Pearce, a care worker who had also known Mr. Cross for many years and had assisted him in his later years.

When they were shown the portrait both women confirmed that it was a fair likeness of Rupert Cross as he would have been some years before. Both women were told that the portrait was part of a documentary film that was being made and that it needed to determine whether the portrait was of Rupert Cross. They were comfortable with doing so and in making their assessment. On receiving the news I could not escape the possibility that this surprising verification supported my methodology and suggested that Rupert Cross, the policeman involved in the trial, may have wanted to make himself known to me and give me some encouragement. This evidence seemed consistent with other messages I had noted at that time about going to Portsmouth prior to receiving the invitation to make the film. This raised lots of questions in my mind. The portrait certainly seemed to represent good evidence that the supposed 'spirit world' wanted me to undertake this project as had been confirmed from other sources and it seemed that those who had a role to play in Mrs. Duncan's difficulties, wanted to contribute in some way to the project's success, as Helen Dunne the medium had told me.

The next phase of this story to be covered in the next book begins with my preparation to drive up the M1 to the north of England to meet the group that responded to my advert in the Psychic News asking whether Helen Duncan was communicating. It seemed clear to me that if she was not a fraud then she must still be alive somewhere in the spirit world. As I had been invited to make a film about her, then it was clear that it was best if I try to speak to her about it.

To my complete surprise I received a phone call saying she had been coming through Sandy Sinclair's circle for a couple of months, and that she was saying that there was a special project and that she had invited the group to take part. She had also said to the circle that she would bring a man to them. They were as interested as I was to discover whether I was that man.

I trust everyone will give Sandy all the support and help she requires to complete her undertaking, and assume her intended role as the physical medium, so the next part of Helen Duncan's story can be told and the project proposed by the purported 'spirit world' be completed!

Chronology

25th November 1898 Victoria Helen McFarlane born at Callander in Perthshire, Scotland.

Late October 1930 London Spiritualist Alliance (LSA) starts a series of tests of Helen Duncan's mediumship (Helen had been psychically warned that a disaster loomed in London).

28th February 1930 Report published in 'Light'.

11th March 1931 Harry Price has had scientific analysis made of ectoplasm (teleplasm) and confirms Professor Schrenk-Notzing's chemical, physical and microsopical analysis of ectoplasm made in 1914 (letter from Dr. Gerela Walther to Harry Price)

4th May 1931 Harry Price poaches Mrs. Duncan and starts sittings without LSA's knowledge. He describes amazing phenomena with Mrs. Duncan after he had examined her in the nude with streams of teleplasm trailing around the room and sometimes enveloped her in good light. (letter 7th May 1931 Harry Price to Prof. Flugel)

16th May 1931 Report published in 'Light', LSA committee asserts Helen Duncan's mediumship is genuine.

12th June 1931 London Spiritualist Alliance research sittings with Mrs. Duncan end after 50 sittings had taken place. LSA discovers that Mrs. Duncan has broken her contract with them and is sitting for Harry Price's National Laboratory for Psychical Research

17th July 1931 LSA published a Report in 'Light' dismissing Helen Duncan's mediumship and attributes it to regurgitation

Mrs. Henry Sidgwick the President of the Society of Psychical Research denounces Harry Price and the SPR Council refuses to deal with him.

October 1931 Harry Price publishes a bulletin outlining his sittings with Mrs. Duncan titled 'Regurgitation and the Duncan Mediumship'. He claims to have 'proved' that Helen Duncan is an out-and-out fraud and a regurgitator of no mean ability.

6th November 1931 In Empire News, Harry Price confirms that he produced photographs using a model similar to Mrs. Duncan and butter muslin and that her husband, Mr. Duncan, could not discern the forgery.

22nd February 1932 Mary McGinlay, a former maid of Helen Duncan issues a statement under oath claiming that she was sent out to buy butter-muslin and had to wash it after seances. She also claims to have recognised rubber gloves and picture cut-outs used in Price's research.

December 1932 Esson Maule contacts Harry Price

5th January 1933 Police called to Helen Duncan séance in Edinburgh organised by Miss Esson Maule, who was advised by Harry Price.

16th January 1933 Esson Maule and five of the sitters appear before a magistrate testifying that Helen Duncan had been detected of fraud.

3rd May 1933 Proceedings start at Sheriff Summary Court, Edinburgh. Helen is charged with fraud. Harry Price observes the trial.

4th May 1933 Sheriff decides to reserve judgement for a week.

11th May 1933 Sheriff found the charge of fraud proved and Helen Duncan is fined £10.

1939 John Maude appointed Recorder at Devizes

December 1939 Maude put in charge of MI5 section dealing with rumour and leakages of information

April 1940 MI5 section called B19. Maude is assisted by John Phipps his junior.

27th May 1941 HMS Hood sunk.

Helen Duncan's purported spirit guide Albert tells audience at a séance in Edinburgh attended by Colonel Firebrace, Head of Military Intelligence in Scotland that a great British battleship had just been sunk.

Colonel Firebrace immediately after the séance he makes enquiries about whether a battleship had been sunk. Later that day he receives confirmation that HMS Hood had been sunk

25th November 1941 4.30pm HMS Barham sunk in Mediterranean. The War Office kept information secret from the public and relatives of the crew. Soon after

At The Master's Temple in Copnor Road, Portsmouth Helen Duncan materialises a sailor who had recently been drowned to his mother in the audience. The sailor had been serving on HMS Barham.

The news spread like wild fire around Portsmouth that HMS Barham had been sunk, which the Navy denied.

4th December 1941 Lt. Stanley Worth joins Naval Special Branch as a Sub Lieutenant

18th December 1941 Lt. James Sheffield Jones a Navy Special Branch Officer writes to Harry Price requesting his assistance in getting the police 'called in' about Mrs. Duncan, who he declares as a fraud. He enclosed a letter he had received from Mrs. Marion Gray calling for this to occur.   Lt. Jones also requested any reports or documents, and any information in connection with his investigations of Mrs. Duncan.

19th December 1941 Announcement made that Henry Elam has been appointed the Recorder of Poole.

26th December 1941 Guy Liddell, Director of MI5's counter espionage 'B' Division notes in his diary that Edward Hinchley-Cooke and Edward Cusson of MI5 S.L.B. section were investigating the leak (with a view to bringing criminal proceedings).

1st January 1942 Percy Worth of Scotland Yard awarded an M.B.E.

28th January 1942 The Government makes the news of the sinking of HMS Barham public, over 2 months after the sinking

4th February 1942 Home Office Police Report states criticism had occurred over the long delay in reporting the loss of HMS Barham

10th February 1942 Maurice Barbanell replies to letter from Mrs. Gray. Letter is forwarded to Harry Price

Navy view Helen Duncan as a security risk and dangerous

Scotland Yard contact Col. Firebrace to ask how they can stop Helen Duncan leaking information

10th March 1942 Percy Worth receives the M.B.E. from the Queen at Buckingham Palace.

April 1942 Helen Duncan gives seances at Portsmouth

Between January and April 1942 2nd Lt. Donovan Pedelty leaves the Royal

Fusiliers, City of London Regiment. He had been attached to the HQ of the 177th Infantry Brigade, and permission to leave was given by Brigadier M. S. Ekins.

27th May 1942 Denys Parsons joins the Society of Psychical Research

June 1942   John Maude returns to Britain from working for MI5 in Washington.
He becomes acting Major under Special Employment in Military Intelligence the War Office and is attached to the War Cabinet.

1st January 1943 Portsmouth Town Clerk and Controller of ARP Sir Frederick Sparks awarded a Knighthood

May 1943 Helen Duncan gives seances in Portsmouth at 301 Copnor Road

14th June 1943 John Cyril Maude appointed Kings Council.

July - September 1943 Henry Elam Sq. Leader in the Legal Department of the RAF leaves the service.

September 1943   Helen Duncan gives seances in Portsmouth, at 301 Copnor Road.

19th November 1943 Coastal Belt Security Committee for the Central South Coast Region set up to co-ordinate security measures as part of Operation Overlord in the run up to D Day

November 1943 Worth gets involved with activities at The Master's Temple Spiritualist Church at 301 Copnor Road, Portsmouth. He joins development circle at the Church and attends services and events.

Max Anderson leaves the Realist Film Unit in London

2nd December 1943 First meeting of the Coastal Belt Security Committee for the Central South Region held. Chief Constable West present along with Major Boddington of MI5 and War Office and other civilian and military security officials, including Major Phipps of MI5.

1st January 1944 Chief Constable of Portsmouth Arthur West Awarded 'The Kings Medal for Police and Fire Services Medal' for distinguished services.

3rd January 1944 Launcelot Lock, known as Jack Lock, son of prosecution witnesses William and Bessie Lock places bet in Oxford at the Morris Motors works at Cowley with a Spiritualist William Spencer. The bet witnessed by Reginald White and Mr. Surman and states that within two weeks a summons would be issued against Mrs. Duncan and a man named Worth will be involved.

10th Helen Duncan arrives in Portsmouth and stays with Mrs. Bettison in Milton Road.

11th January Alan Hyman journalist and script writer of mystery crime films serving with the Naval Film Section, Max Anderson and Terence Bishop documentary directors and script writers making films for the Ministry of Information are made Acting Special Branch Sub. Lt.s and join Worth's Special Branch unit on HMS Excellent

12th January (Wednesday) Helen Duncan starts her first séance at The Master's Temple in Portsmouth.
At 8.30pm Worth arrives and goes upstairs at The Master's Temple to speak to some sitters immediately following Helen Duncan's séance. Mrs. Lock attends this séance. He paid Mr. Homer 12s/6d for one of two tickets he had booked for the séance on the 14th, that being for himself and Surg. Lt. Fowler.

13th séance (Thursday) held

14th January (Friday) 1944 3pm Lt. Worth and Surg. Lt. Elijah Fowler attend Mrs. Duncan séance in The Master's Temple, Copner Road, Portsmouth

15th January (Saturday) 1944 Morning Lt. Worth complains to the police

16th January (Sunday) 1944 3pm Lt. Worth attends a Mrs. Duncan trance meeting with a sermon and Mrs. Brown giving clairvoyance

17th January (Monday) 1944 During the day Worth reports to the police Det. Insp. Ford about the Sunday meeting. A plan is conceived to raid the séance.
7pm Lt. Charles Burrell takes Mr. & Mrs. Lock to the séance with his partner Mrs. Violet May Lonsdale-Brosman.

18th January (Tuesday) 1944 7pm Charles Burrell attends séance again along with Mr. & Mrs. Lock and Mrs. Violet Lonsdale Brosman. Séance also held in afternoon.

19th January (Wednesday) 1944 Worth and Fowler make statements to Det. Insp. Ford, who then makes an application to Magistrates for an arrest warrant.
Afternoon 3pm: Mrs. Emma Kitty Jennings and Mrs. Ena Harris attend Mrs. Duncan séance
Evening 7pm: Lt. Worth with War Reserve Constable Rupert Cross attend séance along with Mrs. Lock and her daughter Mrs. Ena Harris. Lt. Worth and WRC Cross halt séance and instigate a police raid and Mrs. Duncan, her companion Frances Brown and Mr. & Mrs. Homer who arranged the séance are arrested.
Mrs. Duncan taken to Kingston Cross Police Station and charged under Section

4 of the Vagrancy Act. Nurse Rust accompanies her along with Esther Clarke of the Women's Auxiliary Police Corps.

Lt. (Sp. Br.) Alfred Attfield is appointed to Worth's Naval Special Branch Unit.

Mrs. Denys Parsons, wife of Denys Parsons and daughter of General MacLeod joins the SPR.

20th January 1944 Helen Duncan and defendants appear before Portsmouth Court of Summary Jurisdiction and application made for her to be remanded in custody until January 25th.

Surg. Lt. Fowler is transferred from HMS Excellent to HMS Tartar

25th January 1944 Appearance before Portsmouth Magistrates and granted bail of £100 and adjourned until 8th of February. Loseby makes statement that police have breached an undertaking made by the Home Secretary not to use the pre-trial machinery of the Vagrancy Act against Spiritualist mediums

27th January 1944 Thursday Chief Constable West meets Assistant Director of Public Prosecutions in London to discuss the case.

Douglas Craggs of Magic Circle recommends Harry Price to Chief Constable of Portsmouth Police as an expert witness in the forthcoming Helen Duncan case (telegram Douglas Craggs to Harry Price)

30th January 1944 Douglas Craggs confirms Magic Circle been in touch with Scotland Yard and they have been asked to assist them. He confirms Magic Circle members have been trailing one or two mediums with the knowledge of the police and succeeded in getting conviction in Cardiff with Hatcher and Little.

2nd February Sir Grimwood Mears (Chairman of the local Magistrate's bench) writes to Home Secretary complaining about Loseby's comment at Magistrates hearing on 25th January that Home Secretary gave assurance he would not use the Vagrancy Act against Spiritualist mediums, when the procedure has not been repealed.

3rd February Chief Constable West sends a report about the case to the DPP

4th February Friday Det. Insp. Ford interviewed by Arthur Sefton Cohen Assistant Director of Public Prosecutions in London

7th February Monday DPP write to Chief Constable West requesting he asks for an adjournment on the 8th and asks for the defendants to be charged with conspiracy to cheat and defraud, a more serious charge.

Edward Robey (DPP Prosecuting Counsel) and Chief Constable West have a conversation about the case

8th February 1944 Tuesday Helen Duncan and defendants charged with conspiracy at 10.50am and they appeared before Magistrates. DPP asks Chief Constable West to make personal application to the magistrates for case to be adjourned until Tuesday 29th February.

9th February 1944 Chief Constable of Portsmouth Police confirms Harry Price had sent his book about Mrs. Duncan to the Portsmouth police which has been received and he has sent to Mr. Robey of the DPP who will conduct the case in the Magistrates hearing on the 29th of February. West informs Robey that former maid Mary McGinlay is willing to testify against Mrs. Duncan.

10th February Harry Price sends Chief Constable West a letter.

Home Office write to Chief Constable West outlining a letter they had received from Sir Grimwood Mears Chair of the local Judiciary. They ask for facts about the case, his observations and refer to public interest in the case and the letters Grimwood Mears informs the Home Office he had received from the public.

14th February 1944 Chief Constable West sends Frances Graham Harrison of Home Office full report on Helen Duncan case.

Chief Constable West confirms Harry Price had sent an 'interesting letter' and he seeks further help from him

15th February West sends Robey details of Edinburgh conviction and states he has a plan of the séance room of the 19th of January.

17th February 4.45pm Robey phones Portsmouth Police requesting that a meeting takes place with Chief Constable West on the 28th and asks Portsmouth police to book two single rooms.

25th February Chief Constable West sends articles about the London Spiritualist Alliance sittings with Mrs. Duncan, copy of Psychic News and further details of the Edinburgh conviction to DPP.

Home Office reply to Sir Grimwood Mears.

28th February 1944 Monday Meeting takes place between Robey, Chief Constable West and another unknown person at the Queen's Hotel in Southsea.

29th February 1944 Tuesday Magistrates Hearing. Defendants committed from Portsmouth Magistrates Court to Central Criminal Court in London. Prosecution witnesses make signed statements under oath. Chair of Magistrates is ex Royal Marine and staunch Roman Catholic Lord Mayor of Portsmouth Sir Denis Daley.

1st March 1944 DDP send Nomination Form to Attorney General requesting Maude and Elam as Prosecuting Counsel.

Edinburgh Police send report on Helen Duncan to Chief Constable West

2nd March Attorney General approves nomination of Maude and Elam.

3rd March DPP write to Under Secretary of State informing them that Loseby did not repeat inaccurate statement about the Vagrancy Act at the Magistrates Hearing of the 29th of February

4th March Signed statement taken from Dorothy Evans about the faulty communication she received from Llewellyn Rosser a medium stating her husband was alive when he was dead, whilst attending a Master's Temple meeting in November 1943. Det. Insp. Ford includes statement in a report that claims Rosser had a criminal record and that he was sentenced to 2 years imprisonment for gross indecency a short time later in December 1943. He also stated that the Mr. & Mrs. Homer were friends with another medium Reginald Scott-Horscroft who had a conviction for larceny. Report sent to DPP.

Chief Constable West sends more newspaper and Psychic News articles to Robey at DPP.

Chief Constable West receives a letter of complaint against Mrs. Duncan from Mrs. Varina Taylor of Southport (written 1st March). She is the wife of a policeman.

6th March 1944 WRC Policeman Rupert Cross confirms Harry Price had sent him letter and information and a meeting is arranged between them

Frances Graham Harrison of Home Office writes to Chief Constable West that the defendants will be committed to trial at the Old Bailey for conspiracy and that the charge under the Vagrancy Act is adjourned.

8th March DPP receive a letter of complaint about Mrs. Duncan from Harold Bealey of Paddington, a retired opera singer (letter written on 7th).

14th Det. Insp. Ford sends copies of Mrs. Brown's photographs to DPP

Chief Constable West meets Lt. Col. Combe and other members of the Inter-Services Security Board along with the Chief Constable of Brighton. The meeting relates to police and military co-operation.

15th March Tindal Atkinson, the Director of Public Prosecutions writes to

Recorder Dodson asking him to hear the Helen Duncan case.

16th March 1944   Additional evidence sent by DPP to Mr. Elkin defence solicitor. DPP write to Chief Constable Arthur West explaining that Harry Price does not wish to be called as a witness although he is willing to give prosecution every assistance. DPP ask West to bring the plan of the séance room to court. Maude wants Mary McGinlay, Mrs. Duncan's former maid to be present during trial and she may be called.

Arthur Sefton Cohen writes to clerk of Central Criminal Court informing him Maude and Elam have been nominated and he has asked them to settlement the indictment.

18th March 1944 Harry Price sends photographic prints and communications to the DPP and to Chief Constable of the Portsmouth Police

21st March 1944 Letter from Arthur West to Harry Price, confirms receipt of Price's letter of 18th March, a copy of A. Miles letter received by Price on 6th Sept. 1939 and 3 prints of Mrs. Duncan and communication addressed to DPP.

Harry Price's photographs & negatives of Mrs. Duncan ready for collection by the police from University of London library.

23rd March (Thursday) 1944 trial starts at Old Bailey in Court No. 4.

24th March (Friday) Brig. Firebrace of Military Intelligence at War Office joins the SPR

27th March (Monday) Opening speech for the Defence

28th March (Tuesday) Maude also starts murder trial as Defence Counsel in Court No. 1.

30th March (Thursday) 1944 Dr. Geoffrey Wilson who undertook errands for the defence Counsel (whose father Percy Wilson was a senior figure within Spiritualist movement) reports holding a séance with Mrs. Duncan in the evening and a pronouncement was made 'Two will be convicted and two will go free' (letter to Alan Crossly dated 11th April 1997).

31st March (Friday) 1944 Closing speeches for the Prosecution and Defence and Summing Up

Mrs. Duncan, Mrs. Brown and Mr. & Mrs Homer found guilty

3rd April 1944   Helen Duncan sentenced to 9 months imprisonment. Frances Brown sentenced to 4 months imprisonment. Mr. & Mrs. Homer were bound over to be on good behaviour for two years for £5.

Prime Minister, Winston Churchill asks why the Witchcraft Act was used. What was the cost of bringing the trial to London?

6th April 1944 Chief Constable Arthur West writes to Harry Price expressing thanks for all the assistance and help he gave with the case before the magistrates hearing and Old Bailey trial.

Chief Constable West sends report of prosecution to DPP and expresses warmest thanks.

Theo Mathew of Home Office writes to Sir Edward Tindal Atkinson D of PP refers to press coverage of using Witchcraft Act and Spiritualist criticisms of using it.   He asks for information, what were the charges that the defendants were committal for trial by the Portsmouth justices, why was Witchcraft Act added and were they convicted on any charges apart from the Witchcraft Act?

Herbert Morrison replies to Prime Minister.

Minutes of Document reports from Chief Constable West that Robey told him charges under the Witchcraft Act added to the indictment without consulting the DPP.

10th April 1944 Maude appointed Recorder of Plymouth

11th April E. H. Tindall Atkinson D of PP replies to Theo Matthew (Home Office) saying that Maude and Elam decided to use the Witchcraft Act. He said he'd have preferred using conspiracy to cheat and defraud.

13th April Theo Matthew thanks E. H. Tindall Atkinson DPP for letter and informs him that with Robey about to send him the Recorder's Summing Up, that is all he needs.

24th April Molly Goldney writes urging Harry Price to publish a booklet about Helen Duncan to coincide with the appeal hearing. She requests that he meet 'the group' headed by Deny Parsons and herself to discuss this proposal.

2nd May Molly Goldney writes to Harry Price trying to arrange an urgent meeting between Denys Parsons and 'the group' with him.

6th May Denys Parsons writes to Harry Price asking for permission to use his photographs in the forthcoming Horizon article, which is due to be published. He includes a part of the draft of the article.

27th May Harry Price meets 'the group' with Denys Parsons and Molly Goldney.

Early June 1944 Denys Parson's published article about Helen Duncan trial in 'Horizon'

6th June D Day

8th June 1944 Court of Appeal heard case

19th June 1944 Appeal judgement given. It was dismissed on all counts.

5th September E. H. Tindal Atkinson Director of Public Prosecutions writes to Mr. Reed of the Law Office Dept. of Royal Courts of Justice outlining advantages of using the Witchcraft Act over ordinary law of misdemeanour. States he waited until after appeal before proceeding with Witchcraft Act prosecution against another medium Mrs. York.

22nd September 1944 (Friday) Mrs. Duncan released from Holloway prison.

28th October 1944 Detective Inspector Ford speaking at Police Conference about Mrs. Duncan case in a few months' time and Chief Constable seeks to retain Harry Price's book.

15th February 1945 Assistant Chief Constable returns Harry Price's book, after Detective Inspector Ford had given a series of lectures.

October 1945 Carl Bechhofer Roberts publishes 'The Trial of Helen Duncan', part of the Old Bailey Trial Series.

Carl Bechhofer Roberts gets a feature film made based on his book 'Don Chicago', a crime comedy.

1948 Harry Price dies of heart failure

1949 Prosecution witness Charles Burrell dies of cancer

28th October 1956 Helen Duncan séance raided by Police in Nottingham, as four policemen jump up during a séance and two policewomen grab her. Helen is injured and becomes very ill.

Early November 1956 Helen Duncan admitted to Hospital in Edinburgh

6th December 1956 Helen Duncan dies at home in Edinburgh.

APPENDIX

Manifestation Lt. Worth recalled under cross-examination

Mrs. Allen

Worth acknowledged under cross-examination that a form recognised as Mrs. Allen who was known to a number of people present appeared, although he gave no details about it. This maybe because another prosecution witness, Mr. Burrell was to give evidence about Mrs. Allen appearing in a later séance in which he was present.

Mr. Homer explained that on the 14th the figure of Mrs. Allen came from the cabinet to Mrs. Cole who was sitting in the window seat. Mrs. Allen had died only weeks before, she had been a regular visitor to the church. She had died of cancer and had a swollen arm due to her condition. Mr. Homer and Mrs. Cole recognised her. She was 5' 2-3" tall. When Mrs. Allen came out she showed her arm and said that she was in no pain now. She just came to show the condition of passing as she went to the spirit world. Mrs. Cole testified that she recognised Mrs. Allen's voice and face. She presented herself with her head held sideways which was a characteristic of hers. Mrs. Allen referred to the orchids that her family had put on the wreath they sent to her funeral. Mrs. Cole only found out later that her son had gone around Portsmouth looking for the orchids and had put them in a wreath at her burial. The figure came very close to Mrs. Cole so that she was almost on top of her. Mrs. Cole had to stand back because the unpleasant smell of the ectoplasm was overpowering. Mrs. Cole noticed that the arm was still swollen and Mrs. Allen raised her arm up for the audience to see. It was very fat and swollen as it had been she had passed. Mrs. Cole asked Mrs. Allen whether she would like to talk with Mrs. Homer and at this point the form disappeared and the next moment Mrs. Allen was around the other side of the cabinet talking to Mrs. Homer. Mrs. Homer had given her healing at the church for her condition. Mrs. Homer asked about her health and her arm. She said the arm was still swollen. The form then disappeared. It did not walk back to the cabinet. Under cross-examination Mrs. Homer said that she had asked about her health and her arm. She said that the arm was still swollen. Mrs. Cole was completely sure this was not Mrs. Duncan and she recognised Mrs. Allen's voice only it was a little quieter than normal.

The fact that evidence was given about the placing of orchids by her son at the funeral is good evidence because there is no way Mrs. Duncan could have gained this fact by telepathy or talking to Mrs. Cole, as she did not know this information.

Press Headline
Witchcraft Trial.
Ghost said: Thanks for the Orchids
Evening Standard 28.3.44

Manifestations Lt. Worth failed to recall

Commander Mackie's mother

Worth remembered Wing Commander Mackie talking to his mother. When Loseby asked him about a service friend appearing to Mackie he could not remember. Mackie stated that his mother came and he had no doubt that it was her. The form said they wouldn't have come if it hadn't been for Muriel his daughter. Wing Commander Mackie confirmed that he had a daughter named Muriel who lived in the north but he said he didn't know whether Mrs. Duncan was aware of this.

Mrs. Sullivan's mother

Worth said he cannot remember
Mrs. Sullivan's testified that her mother appeared at the centre of the curtain and that she recognised her by her voice and the shape of chin and her eyes. She could not see shape of face because her eyesight was not good.

Manifestations Mr. Burrell failed to recall

Nurse Rust's husband and mother

Burrell did not recall any such encounter.
Nurse Rust reported that her husband materialised and she immediately got up and bent over and kissed him. She had no doubt it was he. She recognised his voice and he appeared to her as he was a year or two before he died. They

held hands and she said although it was cold it was his hand, because the knuckles were knobbly due to the rheumatism he suffered from. She was quite sure it was not Mrs. Duncan because the figure she regarded as her husband was not quite so big and that she had felt Mrs. Duncan's hand and it was not like her husband's. He said he had her mother with him and soon after a form she recognised as her mother emerged from the cabinet and stood to the side. She said to her 'you are not coming back this time without kissing me'. Nurse Rust was asked by her mother to come over and she made her stand facing her and as she was doing so the form turned to the audience, patted her daughters shoulder and eventually put her arm around her, introducing her as 'my loving daughter'. They kissed. Nurse Rust recognised her mother's voice and distinctive facial features such as a mole in the hollow of her chin and another over the left eyebrow. Her mother was a little woman.

A little later her aunt Mary appeared and they spoke together in Spanish, in the type of Spanish spoken in Gibraltar. She recognised her aunt because she looked very similar to her mother.

It is interesting to note that the defence did not mention in defence of their client that the prosecution was suggesting that Mrs. Duncan happily kissed women sitters in her pretence of deceased husbands and fathers around the country and that these women could not tell the difference. Whether such a point would have been helpful is uncertain, but if she was a fraud as the prosecution asserted then this aspect of the pretence could have focused the jury upon a weakness of the case. The prosecution was asserting that not only was Helen Duncan so morally bereft as to kiss other women but also a wife doesn't know the features or kiss of their husband. Naturally the same point applied to husbands.

Press Headlines

says dead husband kissed her at séance
'I RECOGNISED HIM BY KNOBBLY KNUCKLES,
WIDOW TELLS COURT
Daily Mirror 29.3.44

Widow Says She Kissed Spirit Of Her Husband
The Star 28.3.44

WOMEN TELL OF SPIRIT KISSES
Daily Mail 29.3.44

Mrs. Coulcher's Mother

Burrell did not recall

Mrs. Coulcher recognised her mother by her facial features and her figure, which was smaller and stouter than she was. They had a conversation about familiar family affairs.

Manifestation Mr. Burrell and Mr. & Mrs. Lock failed to recall

Mr. Kirkby

Mr. Kirkby described a Chinaman named Chang appearing. He had a long moustache eighteen inches long and his pigtails swung round. Mr. Kirkby claimed to have recognised this form as his spirit guide, as he had seen him many times. He claimed this form was clearly visible to the other sitters, including Mr. Burrell and Mrs. Lock who were present. As it is unclear whether Anne Potter and Mr. Williams attended the afternoon or evening séance on the 18th their descriptions have not been included.

Press Headline

SPIRIT HAD 20-INCH MOUSTACHE
Old Bailey Story Of Chinese Guide At Séance
The Star 29.3.44

Notes

General

A number of books have been written about Helen Duncan. 'The Two Worlds of Helen Duncan' by Gena Brearly 1985, Maurice Barbanell's 'The Case of Helen Duncan' 1945, 'The Story of Helen Duncan Materialization Medium' by Alan Crossley 1975, 'Medium On Trial: The Story of Helen Duncan and the Witchcraft Act' by Manfred Cassirer 1996, 'Hellish Nell' Malcolm Gaskill 2001, 'Helen Duncan: My Living Has Not been In Vain' Mary Armour 2000, 'The Strange Case of Hellish Nell' Nina Shandler 2006, 'The Trial of Mrs. Duncan' by C. E. Bechhofer Roberts (Editor) 1945, Gerald Fitzgerald's biography of Mrs. Duncan published in the Sunday Mail January 1957. I was also lucky enough to be sent the manuscript of Gena Brealey's book.

The other main sources were the British Newspaper Library at Colindale, London and the Harry Price Library of Magical Literature at Senate House, London University Library, Malet Street, London.

Introduction

A description of the White Brotherhood came from 'The Wellspring' by Fenella Rundell 1993, 'The Truth from the White Brotherhood' by Robert Goodwin 1998, 'Sun Men of the Americas' by Grace Cook 1975, 'Illumination' by White Eagle 1937

1 See 'Phenomena of Materialisation' by Baron von Schrenck Notzing 1920

2 Information about Helen Duncan's relationship with Harry Price and Esson Maule can be found in the Harry Price Collection at London University Library at Senate House, London

3 Although the photograph shows while material coming down to the model's knees, Esson Maule's statement about the séance does not mention seeing Mrs. Duncan's feet below the adult forms. Possibly she ran out of white sheeting when creating the photograph.

4 'The Vindication of Helen Duncan' by Charles Loseby (parts of an unpublished manuscript)

5 The newspaper extracts are sourced as follows in order of appearance:

1 Daily Herald 24/3/44, 2 Daily Sketch 24/3/44, 3 Evening Times 23/3/44, 4 News of the World 5/3/44, 5 Daily Express 25/3/44, 6 Daily Herald 29/3/44, 7 Daily Herald 28/3/44, 8 Daily Mail 29/3/44, 9 Daily Sketch 29/3/44, 10

Daily Express 28/3/44, 11 Daily Express 29/3/44, 12 Leicester Mercury 28/3/44, 13 Evening Standard 29/3/44, 14 Daily Express 30/3/44, 15 Leicester Mercury 30/3/44, 16 Daily Express 31/3/44, 17 News of the World 2/4/44, 18 Daily Express 1/4/44, 19 Evening Times 4/4/44

6 When Loughans heard the not guilty verdict he ran down the steps of the dock at the Old Bailey shaking hands with himself. His joy was short-lived, because he was immediately rearrested when he left the Old Bailey and accused of robbery with violence. He appeared the next day at St. Albans Magistrates Court. There he told the magistrates that he had just been acquitted of murder on a framed murder charge. He denied the charges against him and explained that he had spent the last 15 weeks in custody, but even so he was placed once again into custody.

Chapter One Pre-production & Casting

The main sources for this chapter can be found at the National Archives at Kew (HO144/22172, DPP2/1204, CRIM1/1581, DPP2/1234, CRIM4/1707, CRIM2/256) and the Army and the Navy Lists.

Information about Ian Fleming and Security Service matters were obtained from 'The Life of Ian Fleming' John G. Pearson 2003, 'The Silent War' Richard Deacon 1988, 'British Intelligence in the Second World War' Francis Hinsley 1990, 'The Security Service 1905-1945' John Court Curry 1999, 'Ian Fleming' Andrew Lycett 1995, 'You Only Life Once: Memories of Ian Fleming' Ivar Bryce 1984, '17F The Life Of Ian Fleming' Donald McCormick 1993, 'MI5' Nigel West 1983, 'The Guy Liddell Diaries' (Edited) Nigel West 2005, 'The Man Who Was M: the Life of Maxwell Knight' Anthony Masters 1984, 'The Occult Conspiracy, Secret Societies' Michael Howard 1989, 'Very Special Admiral' Patrick Beesly 1980, 'Fascism, the Security Service and the Curious Careers of Maxwell Knight and James McGuick Hughes' John Hope, Lobster No. 22 November 1991.

Information about the filmmakers came from the British Film Institute Library, The National Film Archive, IMBD website, BECTU, The East Anglian Film Archive and the BBC Written Archives at Caversham. Information about theatre contacts came from Westminster Library (theatre section) and the Theatre Museum London.

1 Radio 4 Programme broadcast on 3rd October 1979.

2 The Guardian edition 31st January 1998

3 Letter dated 15th March 1944

4 'Consider Your Verdict' Gerald Dodson 1967

5 Maxwell Knight who once was the Director of Intelligence for the British Fascists prior to being recruited to MI5, had successfully infiltrated British fascist organisations. Maude regularly defended fascists in court in the 1930's, which may suggest that he combined a security service role with this work as a barrister.

6 See Knight's account at the National Archives PRO KV4/227

7 Marion Gray's letter dated November 15th 1941

8 Hampshire Telegraph January 28th 1944

9 Sir Grimwood Mears letter sent Home Secretary dated 2nd February 1944.

10 Rt. Hon. Osbert Peake's letter to Miss Rathbone MP dated 2nd March 1944

11 Interview with Stanley Worth's sister Madeleine Pierson

12 Interview with Stanley Worth's cousin Kathleen Newton

13 Harry Price's letter to Professor Flugel dated 7th May 1931

14 Max Anderson may have met James Drever's father, Professor James Drever Snr. when making his two films about blindness in 1940 and 1942. Professor Drever was the Chairman of the Royal Blind Asylum & School' and National Institute for Blinded Soldiers and very active in the field.

15 See 'Cine-Technician' Nov-Dec. 1943

16 in 'Documentary Newsletter' May 1942

17 in 'Hadn't We The Gaiety?' by John Paddy Carstairs 1945

18 See 'Joyce Grenfell Requests The Pleasure' by Joyce Grenfell 1976

19 Harry Price was also involved in the film world being the Chairman of the National Film Library Committee from 1935 – 40 and he was a generous benefactor. He later referred to himself as the first Chairman of the BFI although he never was. He was actively involved in the formation of the National Film Library and he was also a founding member of the Shakespeare Film Society.

20 Transit January 2005

Chapter Two Staging and Performance

The sources used for this chapter are the trial transcripts and exhibits shown in Bechhofer Roberts's book 'The Trial of Mrs. Duncan' and housed at the National Archives (see above). Loseby's papers and trial documents housed at the SPR Archive at Cambridge University and at the Islands Archive in St. Peter Port, Guernsey were also consulted for this chapter and the following one.

1 Although Mr. Homer didn't say so in examination he later said he did see them together when under cross-examination.

2 The actual trial transcript refers to 'left', but as the letters are the same and all other statements refer to 'felt' I presume this is a typing error.

3 Ada St. George's witness statement

4 Ada St. George was down to be called for the prosecution at the Police Court Hearing.

5 Except when a young child spoke

6 Mr. Burrell's witness statment

7 Worth's magistrate's statement

8 Worth's witness statement was identical to Fowler's unsigned statement on

this point

9 Photographs of an ectoplasmic Voice Box can be found in 'The Mediumship of Jack Webber' Harry Edwards 1940, 'The Mediumship of Arnold Clare' Harry Edwards 1942, 'Spirits & Spirit Worlds' Roy Stemman 1976. Other detailed accounts of their structure has been made by investigators studying Margery Crandon (USA SPR 1926-7).

10 Mrs. Lock's witness statement

11 Mr. White's witness statement

12 The revised plan shown represents the reported dimensions of the séance room, computer reduced to 60% of an original plan that was drawn to a scale of 1cm : 1 foot. The police plan has also been similarly reduced to 60% of the original drawing.

13 Obituary published in The Times on 3rd of November 1966

Chapter Three Impact and Reviews

1 Portsmouth Evening News 29/2/44

2 New Statesman 2/9/45

3 Sunday Times 2/9/45

4 Yorkshire Post 4/4/44

5 Sunday Dispatch 2/4/44

6 Boz Club was a club founded by those who had personally known Charles Dickens

7 'The Trial of Mrs. Helen Duncan' Proceeding of the SPR 47 (1942-5) Donald West

8 The Listener 4/10/45

9 Sunday Times 2/9/45

10 Denys Parsons had written to Harry Price in 1941 about Stella C. His interest may have been encouraged because Sir Oliver Lodge believed he received an authentic communication from his grandfather, Sir Herbert Beerbohm Tree, after his death. Lodge asked Lady Tree for her support to publish the communication but she declined. The report of the communication had been mislaid and as good evidence Lodge reported where Sir Herbert told his wife it could be found, specifying the actual drawer in a desk in a particular room. Despite the detail of the communication Lady Tree adamantly refused to believe her husband was communicating as a spirit and I believe the matter was dropped.

11 They also had an Etonian connection with Parsons. Herbert Asquith's son Anthony Asquith also knew the Parsons and Phipps' families and he had become a leading British film director. He was a good friend of Deny's mother Viola. He had also caste her and his brother David Tree in his successful film 'Pygmalion' in 1938. He directed David again in 'French Without Tears' in 1940. Asquith had become President of the Association of Cine-Technicians,

the film trade union in 1937 and he would have served with Max Anderson, himself an active ACT trade unionist for many years and fellow General Council member. Asquith had also caste the actor John Slater on a number of films in the early 1940's, Anderson's closest friend. Asquith would have known of Anderson's great skills as a documentary film-maker and his qualities as a man. Anderson and Asquith's friendship was a ready link if required for Max to assist and work with his friend Denys Parsons. This is especially so as there were clear affinities with Parsons being a scientist and Max known as a 'scientific humanist'. As a leading director and President of the ACT trade union, Asquith's links were obviously far ranging within the film industry while at the same time being part of the same social world that several of those involved in the Helen Duncan case came from. It is also interesting to note that Anthony Asquith also worked at Gainsborough Studios in the early 1930's at the same time Alan Hyman worked there and had worked with his cousin the producer, Michael Balcon. He had also caste Marie Lohr, Terry Bishop's cousin, as Mrs. Higgins in Pygmalion. Asquith also directed a number of wartime documentaries for the MOI like Bishop and Anderson.

12 'A Skeptics Handbook in Parapsychology' Paul Kurtz (Editor) 1985

13 'Scotland Yard Files' Paul Begg & Keith Skinner 1992

14 Later Beverley Nichols was to become a firm believer in survival after death and he frequently appeared in columns of the Psychic News and spoke on Spiritualist platforms. In 1955 he was pleading with the Ministry of Health to investigate spirit healing. He also wrote the book on the subject titled: 'Powers That Be' in 1966.

15.   It is interesting that this warning should be given as part of a government campaign, because Max Knight of MI5 had adopted the same method of using an agent, who claimed to have psychic powers, in order to get close to, obtain information and influence the German spy Anna Wolkoff. He may have feared that the enemy might wish to adopt a similar method of using fake psychics against ourselves.

16 From Macolm Gaskill's book 'Hellish Nell' 2001

17 While they were prosecuting Helen Duncan, British Intelligence were using the skills of Jasper Maskelyne the famous stage illusionist and 'Anti-Spiritualist'. He was recruited to 'A' Force who manufactured and deployed dummy units, tanks, camps and men to deceive the enemy. Maskelyne became a leading figure during the war in the art of visual deception, so much so that Hilter put a bounty on his head. He established 'Station M' in Canada where he created top-secret illusions that were used around the world. The 'M' stood for Magic. The 'A' Force created a bogus 7th Division and 74th Armoured Brigade as part of their 'visual deception' operation which had a significant effect on the war ('British Intelligence in the Second World War' Vol 5 Michael Howard 1990, 'The War Magician' David Fisher 1985).

Index